SPO   KD CONCEPTS

SPORTS COACHING CONCEPTS

A FRAMEWORK FOR COACHES' BEHAVIOUR

John Lyle

Routledge
Taylor & Francis Group

LONDON AND NEW YORK

First published 2002 by Routledge
11 New Fetter Lane, London EC4P 4EE

Simultaneously published in the USA and Canada
by Routledge
29 West 35th Street, New York, NY 10001

Reprinted 2003, 2004

Routledge is an imprint of the Taylor & Francis Group

Typeset in Bell Gothic by Keystroke, Jacaranda Lodge, Wolverhampton
Printed and bound in Great Britain by TJ International Ltd, Padstow, Cornwall

Some of the concepts in this book were originally explored by the author in
The Coaching Process. This resource supported the National Coaching Foundation's
(NCF) BSc (Hons) course in Applied Sports Coaching, validated by De Montfort
University. sports coach UK (formerly NCF) offers a wide range of services –
for further details visit www.sportscoachuk.org.

British Library Cataloguing in Publication Data
A catalogue record for this book is available from the British Library

Library of Congress Cataloging in Publication Data
A catalog record has been requested

ISBN 0–415–26158–9 (pbk)
0–415–26157–0 (hbk)

▼ CONTENTS

List of figures	x
Preface	xii
Acknowledgements	xv

PART 1 WHAT IS COACHING ABOUT? — 1

Chapter One
Historical and Developmental Context — 3
Introduction — 3
Historical Roots — 5
Physical Education — 8
Higher Education and Academic Development — 11
Overseas Influences — 12
Recent Developments — 13
Concluding Comments — 16
Summary — 18
Projects and Reading — 18

Chapter Two
Developing a Conceptual Framework — 20
Introduction — 20
Contemporary Sport and Conceptual Questions — 22
Building a Conceptual Framework — 24
Coaching and Theory Development — 28
The Contribution of Literature on Sports Coaching — 31
Sport as a Concept — 33
Summary — 34
Projects and Reading — 34

Chapter Three
The Coaching Process — 35
Introduction — 35
A Definition of Coaching — 38

Definitions   40
Coaching as a Process   43
Boundary Markers   46
Process Skills   50
Participation and Performance Coaching   52
Summary   57
Projects and Reading   58

Chapter Four

The Role of the Coach   **59**
Introduction   59
Role Concepts   61
Purpose and Function   63
Role Complementarity between Coaches and Support Personnel   67
Organisational Impact on the Coach's Role   70
The Uniqueness of the Coaching Role   72
Summary   75
Projects and Reading   76

PART 2 HOW DO COACHES BEHAVE?   **77**

Chapter Five

Modelling the Coaching Process   **79**
Introduction   79
What is Meant by a Model?   80
Problems in Model Building   84
An Evaluation of Existing Models   85
Models: Application, Constraints, Implementation   91
Summary   94
Projects and Reading   94

Chapter Six

A Proposed Model for Coaching   **96**
Introduction   96
Prior Assumptions for the Proposed Model   97
Identifying the Building Blocks   99
The Model   106
Operationalising the Model   107
Summary   115
Projects and Reading   115

Chapter Seven

Coaching Practice   **116**
Introduction   116
Systematic Coaching Behaviours   119

The Picture from Research   125
Planning the Process   125
Implementation Behaviour: Explaining Coaches' Expertise   131
Coaching Practice: A Condensed Description   142
Sport Specificity in Coaching Practice   144
Summary   146
Projects and Reading   147

PART 3 COACHING AS AN INTERPERSONAL RELATIONSHIP   **149**

Chapter Eight
A Question of Style and Philosophy   **151**
Introduction   151
Coaching and Interpersonal Relationships   153
Coaching Styles   156
Philosophies of Coaching   165
Summary   172
Projects and Reading   173

Chapter Nine
A Humanistic Approach to Coaching   **174**
Introduction   174
Basic Assumptions   176
Humanistic Coaching Practice   178
Discussion of Issues   183
Summary   186
Projects and Reading   186

PART 4 COACHING IN ITS SOCIAL CONTEXT   **189**

Chapter Ten
Coaching and Social Context   **191**
Introduction   191
Sports Coaching and Social Enquiry   193
Social Issues   195
Status and Professionalisation   198
Commentary   206
Summary   207
Projects and Reading   207

Chapter Eleven
Motivations and Recruitment in Sports Coaching   **209**
Introduction   209
Review of Evidence   212
Conceptual Issues   216

Summary   219
Projects and Reading   219

Chapter Twelve
Where are All the Women Coaches?   **221**
Introduction   221
Women's Participation in Sport   223
Review of Evidence   224
Possible Explanations   226
Conceptual Issues   229
Commentary   232
Summary   232
Projects and Reading   233

Chapter Thirteen
Coaching and Ethical Practice   **234**
Introduction   234
Ethical Issues   235
Problem Areas   239
Conceptual Framework Issues   241
Codes of Ethics and Codes of Conduct   242
The Legal Dimension   244
Professional Sport: A Suitable Case for Treatment   245
Summary   247
Projects and Reading   247

**PART 5 A BASIS FOR PROFESSIONALISATION –
THE WAY FORWARD**   **249**

Chapter Fourteen
Effective Coaching and the Effective Coach   **251**
Introduction   251
What is Meant by Effectiveness?   253
Coaching Effectiveness Literature   260
Further Conceptual Issues   262
Alternative Approaches to Effectiveness   263
Commentary   270
Summary   272
Projects and Reading   272

Chapter Fifteen
Coach Education and Coaching Practice   **274**
Introduction   274
Education and Training   275
Historical Development   277

Conceptual Lessons   279
Coach Learning and Coaching Practice   281
Principles of Coach Education and Training   282
Delivery Issues   285
Reflective Practice   288
Summary   289
Projects and Reading   290

Chapter Sixteen
Setting a Research Agenda   **291**
Introduction   291
The Research Process   292
The Coaching Process and Research Issues   294
An Expert System   298
Suggestions for a Research Agenda   299
Implications for the Researcher in Coaching Studies   302
Summary   304

Chapter Seventeen
Springboard to the Future:
A Short Essay on Developments in Sports Coaching   **305**

Appendix 1 Study Questions   312
Appendix 2 Useful Websites   318
References   320
Index   333

▼ LIST OF FIGURES

1.1	Percentage of coaches trained as teachers, by country	9
2.1	Elements of a conceptual framework for sports coaching	25
2.2	The relationship between conceptual framework elements and application issues	27
2.3	Factors arising from the complexity of interaction of athlete, coach and performance	28
3.1	Process characteristics and coaching practice	45
3.2	Boundary markers for the coaching process in sport	47
3.3	A typology of sport leadership roles and organisational contexts	49
3.4	Coaching process skills	50
3.5	The relationship between forms of coaching and boundary criteria	53
3.6	A diagrammatic representation of the balance of performance and participation coaching roles	57
4.1	The functional roles of the coach	64
4.2	The support and replacement roles of the coaching role-set	68
4.3	Support team roles and role function	68
4.4	Organisational role determinants	71
5.1	Common types of models	82
5.2	Process components and coaching issues	85
5.3	Coaching process model (adapted from Franks *et al.* 1986)	86
5.4	Coaching process model (Fairs 1987)	88
5.5	Coaching process model (Cote *et al.* 1995a)	89
5.6	The future of model building in sports coaching	93
6.1	The building blocks of the coaching process	99
6.2	The coaching process	109
6.3	The control box of the coaching process	110
6.4	Threshold responses by coaches in three sports	111
6.5	Coaches' responses to performance deficit	112
6.6	Principal model phases	112
6.7	Generalised competition phase	113
6.8	Upgraded model of the competition phase	114
7.1	Factors influencing the likelihood of systematic practice	119
7.2	Quality control stages	121
7.3	Potential barriers to systematic practice	122
7.4	Coaches' responses to systematic coaching criteria	123

7.5	Selected research studies on coaching practice	126
7.6	Training theory principles	128
7.7	Planning issues related to competition cycle	129
7.8	Potential models of non-deliberative decision making	135
7.9	Results of the allocation of decision making incidents to potential models	135
7.10	Coaches' mental models	141
7.11	Sport-specific factors in coaching practice	145
8.1	The relationship between the coaching framework and interpersonal characteristics	155
8.2	Factors impinging on interpersonal relationships	156
8.3	The distinctions between autocratic and democratic coaching practice	158
8.4	Coaching styles	160
8.5	Factors influencing leadership practice	162
8.6	Potential linkages between values	165
8.7	Criteria for evaluating coaching values	168
8.8	Evaluation criteria for coaching philosophies	170
8.9	Identification of values by Meaning Unit	171
8.10	Steps towards constructing a coaching philosophy	172
9.1	Simplified model of humanistic practice in sports coaching	179
9.2	Illustration of a shift in coaching paradigms	181
10.1	An evaluation of sports coaching in relation to criteria of professionalisation	205
11.1	Factors involved in the recruitment and maintenance of performance coaches	210
11.2	Motivations for UK coaches in the four-country study	213
11.3	Motivations for UK coaches in the ESC 1993 survey	213
11.4	Coaches' responses to selected recruitment motives	214
11.5	Motives expressed by coaches in the TOYA study	214
12.1	Male and female participation in sport by participation category	223
12.2	Percentage of women coaches by level of coaching award	224
12.3	Type of NGB award by gender	225
12.4	Percentages of female coaches in the UK Summer Olympic squads	225
12.5	Low expectation model of preparation for coaching	226
12.6	Factors influencing the engagement of women coaches	230
13.1	Examples of ethical issues	236
13.2	Four elements of the coach's practice and associated ethical concerns	241
13.3	Coaching style and ethical practice	243
14.1	Factors involved in the 'effective equals goal-achievement' approach	258
14.2	Potential coaching process competences	264
14.3	Simplistic representation of the evaluation of value added	268
15.1	Summary of findings of Coaching Review Panel (1991) on coach education	278
16.1	A research typology related to the coaching process	293
16.2	Simplified model of the coaching process as an expert system	298
16.3	Simplified coaching process, competition phase	300
16.4	Refined model of the competition phase	301

▼ PREFACE

The academic treatment of sports coaching in the UK has focused largely on the science of performance, with much more limited attention given to coaching behaviour and practice. The consequence of this has been a lack of conceptual and theoretical development, resulting in a poor research framework and an incomplete appreciation of the role and effectiveness of the coach. This is somewhat surprising, given two particular trends. The first is the much increased attention to the contribution of the performance coach now that National Lottery funding in the UK has greatly improved the resourcing of high-performance sport. The second concerns the expansion of coaching-related courses in higher and further education. There are more and more courses and routes in sports coaching, coaching sciences and coaching studies at all levels, including Master's degrees. These are complemented by much more substantive governing body awards than was previously the case.

The resourcing of courses at all levels is problematical, because there are few non-sport-specific textbooks available to support teaching. Even more so, there are few attempts to deal in detail with the conceptual issues that underpin coaching practice and that should form the basis of education, training, evaluation and research. This book is intended to provide such a resource.

There is a central theme, which informs the core of the text. Sports coaching is a process when it is implemented in a systematic, constraint-supportive context. That is, it is an integrated, interdependent and serial accumulation of purposeful activities that are designed to achieve a set of objectives centred on improved competition performance. This has to be understood in the context of the normally much less intensive participation coaching, which is focused on the single coaching episode and is to be found with young persons, in education contexts, in recreation and development stages, and also (and at high levels of performance) in the 'instructor' mode. The distinctions between these forms of coaching determine the relative significance of skills and knowledge, appropriate measures of effectiveness, professional development, and education and training. Most importantly, however, this conceptual understanding of the coaching process is necessary to analyse coaching practice and coaching behaviours. In particular, it provides a basis for understanding the relationships between performer and coach, and increasing professionalisation and career structures.

This book is not simply a distillation of the existing literature, although this is drawn upon as necessary. It is the outcome of a considerable period of writing, researching, experiencing and reflecting on the coaching process. The author has fulfilled coaching roles at all levels from school teams to international sport, and has experienced these as a performer. He was instrumental in driving forward the UK's first higher education Diploma in Sports Coaching, and the first Master's degree in Coaching Studies. He has extensive experience of working with undergraduate and postgraduate students. In addition, the author has contributed extensively to the National Coaching Foundation's education and development work, and directed the National Coaching Centre in Edinburgh. The outcome of this considerable involvement in coaching and coach education was a questioning, critical approach and dissatisfaction with the existing analyses of coaching practice. The ideas that developed over that period of time form the basis of this text.

The book presents a coherent attempt to construct a framework with which to delimit, describe and analyse the coaching process, coaching behaviour and coaching practice. It is designed for students of sports coaching at all stages but will have particular value for undergraduate students and as a resource for postgraduate students in generating research ideas and clarifying research assumptions. Insofar as this is a resource text, one of the objectives has been to bring some order to the material available and to the ideas that have stimulated its writing. Nevertheless, the book is written from a critical and questioning perspective and often acknowledges that it is setting an agenda and fostering debate and further academic study rather than providing all of the answers.

Each chapter identifies critical concepts and further questions as the text progresses. At the conclusion of each chapter, there is a short summary, a selection of potential projects and a guide to suggested reading. The 'question boxes' are designed as an aid to students and tutors, and can be used to stimulate critical enquiry. For easy reference, the questions have been collated in Appendix 1.

The contents are divided into five parts. The chapters in Part 1 provide an historical perspective, make the case for a conceptual framework and deal with the issue of how coaching is defined and bounded, and the ways in which the coaching role differs from other sports leadership roles. Part 2 examines coaching practice: what do coaches do and how can this be modelled? A conceptual framework for the coaching process is proposed as an aid to analysis and an integrated picture of the coaching process is created from the available evidence. Part 3 focuses on the extremely important relationship between the performer and the coach, the factors that influence this and the challenges of implementing a more humanistic approach to coaching. The relevant chapters adopt a critical approach to the literature. The chapters in the fourth Part deal with the implications for the coach and the coaching profession of the social context within which coaches operate. This is built around key themes – motives, recruitment, gender and ethics. Part 5 asks how we evaluate coaching and coaches, and focuses on coaching effectiveness and coach education. This Part attempts a future perspective on sports coaching and includes a chapter on setting a research agenda.

The book is written with the strongly held belief that the quality of sports coaching is the most important environmental factor in determining performance improvement and success. It is also a contribution to debunking the belief that sports coaching is a mystical process that is dependent on the vagaries of the coach's personality and is an intuitive artistic process capable of neither inspection nor introspection. Sports coaching continues

to strive towards professionalisation, and this process is dependent on the profession's capacity to identify a body of knowledge and skills, to educate its initiates, to promote its distinctive values and to defend its boundaries. In this context, coaching practice and behaviour must be subject to purposeful analysis and explanation. This text is a modest contribution to this end.

▼ ACKNOWLEDGEMENTS

Some of the concepts in this book were originally explored by the author in The Coaching Process. This resource supported the National Coaching Foundation's (NCF) BSc (Hons) in Applied Sports Coaching, validated by De Montfort University. SportsCoach UK (formerly the NCF) offers a wide range of services. For further details telephone 0113-274-4802 or visit <www.sportscoachuk.org>.

PART 1
WHAT IS COACHING ABOUT?

CHAPTER ONE

▼ HISTORICAL AND DEVELOPMENTAL CONTEXT

- Introduction   3
- Historical Roots   5
- Physical Education   8
- Higher Education and Academic Development   11
- Overseas Influences   12
- Recent Developments   13
- Concluding Comments   16
- Summary   18
- Projects and Reading   18

INTRODUCTION

The central purpose of this book is to devise and elaborate upon a conceptual framework for sports coaching. The historical and developmental context and frame of reference within which this conceptual treatment emerges clearly impacts on the substance of the chapters. The historical development of the role, the place of coaching studies in higher education, the status and professionalisation of the role and the level of academic support available on which to base the framework will all combine, with other factors, to situate this conceptualisation in a particular time and place. Although it may be tempting to launch immediately into the substance of the conceptual framework, it is important to describe some of this historical background. What this chapter does not attempt, however, is a fully fledged treatise on the historical development of sports coaching, although it is worth noting in passing that this is long overdue. The purpose of the chapter is merely to give sufficient historical context to provide an explanation of the need for the book and the factors that have shaped the practice of sports coaching on which the book is based. There is a dearth of material to illuminate each of the themes within the chapter. To some extent, therefore, there is a focus on the immediate past to which I am able to bring a personal perspective.

The distinction between participation coaching and performance coaching receives considerable emphasis in the chapters that follow. The precise distinctions between these roles will be dealt with at length but, for the moment, it is sufficient to characterise the former as sports leadership, sports teaching and other less intensive engagements in sport. In these, the immediate satisfaction of participation outweighs the demand for extensive preparation and a focus on regular and organised competition. On the other hand, performance sports coaching is characterised by the opposite of this: participation in sport in which there is extensive preparation, intensive commitment and a focus on competition goals. Although this latter form of coaching would be expected for those developing or pursuing excellence in sport, in practice the features of performance coaching are to be found in a wide range of athlete/team-coach relationships and supporting a range of developed athlete abilities. Two points are important. First, no value judgement is made about different forms of coaching. All forms of sport leadership are needed in a comprehensive sport development programme. Second, the best exemplars of the coaching process will be found in those situations conducive to the most efficient and effective coaching practice. This is performance sports coaching, in which athlete commitment, resources and expertise combine to best effect. There is an assumption, therefore, that this book and its contents are based on a concept of coaching, and a practice of sport development, participation coaching and performance coaching, that is in evidence at the beginning of the twenty-first century.

Later in the book, there is a section on the social significance of sports coaching and the relationship between coaching practice and social values and responsibilities. Although not possible in this brief introduction and not the focus of this book, there is a need to provide a critical appreciation of sports coaching in its social context, the agencies involved, the key individuals involved, and its role in the development of sport. This is hinted at in the 'figurational' treatment of sports coaching summarised by Cusdin (1996), in which she charts the 'coachification' of modern sports. Just as with any social phenomenon, sports coaching practice will have been shaped by social structures, power relationships and social trends and will, in turn, have contributed to those emerging social patterns. This will be evident in the impact of provision and practice on gender and ethnicity issues in sport and education, in power relationships within coaching agencies – National Governing Bodies (NGB) of sport, National Coaching Foundation (NCF), Sports Councils, the British Olympic Association, and in the values promulgated by prominent practitioners in coaching. Sport is today characterised by globalisation, commercialisation and capitalisation, media-reliance, emphasis on triumphalism, spectacle and personality. At the same time, this is balanced by a recognition of sport's place in addressing social exclusion, regenerating urban blight, contributing to the economy and improving the quality of life. Active recreation is a vital part of combating health and well-being issues in an increasingly sedentary and obese nation. What part has sports coaching played in these social trends? Is sports coaching helping or hindering the implementation of socially inclusive sport policy? We could also ask if these trends are helping or hindering the development of the profession of sports coaching!

The first question to ask is, how did sports coaching come to be the concept and practice described in this book? For the answer to that, it is necessary to examine its historical roots.

HISTORICAL ROOTS

The inception, growth and institutionalisation of modern sport that began with the industrialisation and urbanisation of the eighteenth and nineteenth centuries in Great Britain spawned a pattern of sports participation and provision that greatly influenced the development of sports coaching. Cusdin (1996: 7) suggests that this development can best be understood 'as an unplanned process or unintended consequence of the wider processes affecting the development and modernisation of sport'. Three main periods emerge that help to illustrate this relationship: the period to the end of the nineteenth century; the early decades of the twentieth century; and the post-war period from the late 1940s.

Early diffusion

McNab (1990) describes how coaching developed, albeit slowly, from the sporadic preparation of working-class boxers and runners in the early 1800s, through to the early coaches of largely team sports in the public schools – ex-university athletes who had moved into teaching. Coaching became the prerogative of enthusiastic young teachers who had been introduced to the game at university, although cricket and rowing tended to be coached by artisan professionals (Rennick 2000). These were often former professional athletes using their wealth of experiential knowledge (and often co-opted into competition). Coaches to the gentlemen amateurs were working-class individuals and acknowledged to be of lower status.

The 'coaching' by the teachers may be thought of as an exercise in the diffusion of sport. The professionals were athletic trainers using esoteric and idiosyncratic forms of knowledge. In the racket sports they were often ball carriers and feeders.

This issue of the tension between the gentleman amateur and the professional was one that persisted as sport spread into clubs and as NGBs reinforced their amateur ethic. For example, the use of professional coaches was banned at Henley Royal Regatta from 1902. Mason (1989) provides an excellent account of the early development of coaching in a social history context. The amateur/professional and volunteer/professional tensions became evidenced later in the shamateurism of the Olympic Games and in power struggles within Governing Bodies of Sport (Midwinter 1986; McNab 1990).

It is important to recognise that, although sport was evolving its competitive structures and professional spectator sport began to emerge in this period, there were two distinct forms of participation. Sport for some was a recreation or pastime – even if competition was involved. Ability and improvement were considered to be matters of natural endowment, and systematic attention to preparation was 'ungentlemanly'. For professional sportsmen – for example, the cyclists, pedestrians and soccer players – athletic trainers were engaged. There was no education system for these 'coaches', who learned through an apprenticeship system and whose training methods owed much to diet and exercise (McNab 1990).

The abiding legacy for sports coaching from this period was the Victorian amateur ethic and the values associated with a 'non-professional' approach to sports coaching and development. Perhaps just as crucial was the emergence of a 'closed-shop' system within professional sports, with trainers/coaches relying on practitioner experience.

Stagnation

The period to 1945 was one that has been described as static in terms of coaching development (Coaching Review Panel 1991). Coaches continued to be either professional instructors or athletic trainers, but were not incorporated into the emerging club structures, which had a recreational ethos. There remained an amateur ethic in which preparation was less important than breeding and natural ability. Once again Mason (1989) provides a very useful account of the machinations within sports as they improved their structures and administration.

Geoff Dyson, who became the first National Coach appointment in Britain in 1947, compared developments in Britain in the 1930s to other countries overseas that had recognised the value of a more systematic development of performance sport. He suggested that Great Britain was 'one of the last of the great sporting countries to turn to coaching' (Dyson 1980: 20).

Although some sports (notably athletics, soccer and swimming) had begun to hold courses and conferences for teachers, it was not until the 1950s that coach education on a national basis began to emerge.

Beginnings of coach development

A concern that Britain should not be slipping behind other countries had persuaded the Ministry of Education to provide financial support for the salaries of 'national coaches' (Holt and Mangan 2000). Sutcliffe (1995) records the early national coach appointments as athletics 1947, tennis 1948, soccer 1949, rugby league 1955 and swimming 1956. Women's hockey, weightlifting and fencing also had national coaches. These coaches, many with an educationist background, created coach education programmes that developed and expanded through the 1950s and 1960s. However, this was still a difficult period for development. The coaches' ideas of diffusion and development of their sports and concepts of preparation and progress were foreign to the more *laissez-faire* attitudes of the sports administrators. *Coaching Matters* (Coaching Review Panel 1991: 11) provides the following commentary:

- Coaches were not perceived to be part of a systematic process for improving performance. Coaching was something for the recreative performer. The 'training' ethos remained in foot-racing and soccer.
- The 1950s is described as a period when individual national coaches had some influence but NGBs did not have developmental policies for the support of coaching or coaches.
- National coaches often became organisers and administrators (even income generators) and became distant from performance coaching.
- Coaching schemes emerged, very often directed to teachers. An example was the provision of rugby courses for teachers from the mid-1950s but not for club coaches until 1969 (Williams 1989).

In response to concerns about standards of performance, the MCC began a 'coaching scheme' in 1952 (Holt and Mangan 2000: 26). Polley (1998) makes assumptions about the links between 'training and coaching' and the success of the English soccer team in the 1950s and 1960s. He also acknowledges the influence of overseas practice, and the recognition of coaching as a mark of the growing professionalisation of sport.

There is no doubt that the creation of national coaches made a significant impact on the development of coaching. However, these coaches were appointed to a difficult environment in the 1950s. McNab (1990) records that NGBs and national coaches did not always see eye to eye. He also acknowledges the dilution of impact on performance sport because of their coach educator role. However, he mentions individuals such as Geoff Dyson and Wilf Paish (athletics), Bert Kinnear and Hamilton Smith (swimming), Alan Wade and Walter Winterbottom (soccer), John Atkinson (gymnastics) and Ray Williams (rugby union) for making particular contributions. Much of the developmental momentum and direction in coaching within NGBs came from the appointment of these Directors of Coaching. For the most part, these (mostly male) directors organised the coach education programmes, contributed to the general organisation of the sport, led the appointment of national team and squad coaches and were very influential within their sports. It would also be true to say that many served for a long period of time, that there was no career structure within NGBs and that the emphasis became orientated to participation rather than performance coaching.

Overall, coaches existed to train those who competed or exercised for their own reasons – rarely as part of a national (or even club) structure. Coaches were instructors (some technical advice plus 'feeding'). The vacuum in 'coaching' was filled by teachers. Although courses were being held, the education and training had all of the hallmarks of later critiques: minimalist, technique-based, limited (if any) practical experience, and modest (if any) underpinning knowledge. In practice, these were teaching awards and the purpose was spreading the word about the sport and acting as a recruitment mechanism. Coaches and teachers were volunteers and likely to be deployed within participation sport.

Coaching was acknowledged in plans around 1959 by both the Labour and Conservative parties. In the Wolfenden Report (1960) the value of coaching in sport development and for revitalising Britain's place in world sport was acknowledged (a familiar theme!) and recommendations were made on coach education, deployment and elements of professional development. Nevertheless, there was slow progress as NGBs, dependent on Government/Sports Council funding, struggled to balance competing priorities. Professional sports failed to progress largely because of restrictive recruitment practices and a failure to adopt an outward-looking perspective. Overseas influence was slow to penetrate coaching practice.

Following the appointment of national coaches in a range of sports, an organisation was formed in 1965 to support their interests: the British Association of National Coaches (BANC). Geoff Gleeson was the moving force behind this organisation for many years. BANC organised national conferences and the membership was expanded by the inclusion of associate members. Coghlan (1990) gives a detailed account of the politics and power plays evident in the administration of British sport from 1960, including relationships between the Sports Council and coaching agencies such as BANC and the soon-to-be established National Coaching Foundation (NCF).

It is difficult to summarise developments in coaching as sport moved from the 1960s into the 1970s and 1980s. Sport became an element of social policy and provision in schools and local authorities expanded, often through facility provision. Funding for sport, particularly performance sport, remained problematical. Sport development became an emerging occupational grouping and development schemes encouraged participation sport. Coach education became the prerogative of the National Governing Bodies of sport. In one or two cases these became quite sophisticated schemes but overall they exhibited characteristics of technical orientation, minimalism in scale, teaching focus, limited discipline knowledge, limited education of the trainers, divorced from practice and, for the most part, did not deal adequately with the coach education of coaches of higher-level athletes. The more significant point is that the coach education of the NGBs reflected their autonomy and was often isolated from the influence of other sports, academics and examples of good practice. Schemes grew (or did not) in isolation, and the major NGBs – soccer, rugby union and cricket – had schemes that made little if any impact on the sport. Other major sports, such as athletics and swimming, showed more willingness to change and incorporated ideas from the sport overseas. However, there would be significant changes to NGB programmes in the late 1980s and 1990s.

Question Box

To what extent can the failure to develop coaching at a national level be explained by the autonomy of NGBs?

To what extent has the amateur ethic constrained the professionalisation of sport?

Before looking at more recent developments in coaching, it would be valuable to examine some of the trends and relationships that help to provide an understanding of how coaching has developed.

PHYSICAL EDUCATION

The development and diffusion of sport through the public-school system in the 1800s is well documented (McIntosh 1968). However, it is with the emergence of a trained Physical Education (PE) profession from the 1930s and 1940s that a strong relationship between PE and sports coaching evolved, with its profound influence on the development of coaching.

The less well-documented impact occurs in the period to the 1960s. Many NGB coach education courses could better have been described as teaching awards, designed as they were for the introduction and basic development of the sport for young people. Very often the course participants were teachers (and not just PE teachers). By the 1960s a stable development pattern had emerged. Sport for young people in the UK was introduced through school physical education and school sport (with the exception of 'early development' sports such as swimming and gymnastics). Young persons then moved into clubs as their affiliation to a sport or sports developed. The school system also acted as a talent identification mechanism.

Coaching courses have been part of most formal or informal curricula for PE training. However, Whitehead and Hendry (1976) also note in their review of Physical Education in the 1970s a view that 'colleges' physical education courses should be regarded as qualifying the students for responsibilities such as coaching and refereeing' (1976: 59), and 'there often appears to be a conflict among those whose interests lie in sports coaching, those whose interests lie in research and those to whom the teaching of children is of paramount importance' (1976: 133). The confusion between the roles of teacher and coach is also demonstrated in the early review by Hendry (1972) (although there is no better up-to-date analysis of the psychological characteristics of coaches). The relationship between teaching and coaching was one that Anthony (1980) championed for the strategic development of the coaching profession. The assumption that 'coaching courses' are a necessary mechanism for extending subject knowledge has become even more important in recent times as the period of time spent in initial teacher training has been reduced (Capel 1997).

It is understandable that many PE teachers should be predisposed to sports coaching, since sport is an integral (albeit continually re-evaluated) element of PE (Murdoch 1990). The continuing impact of teachers in reviews of coaches' characteristics is notable. A Sports Council report (English Sports Council 1997) found that 13 per cent of the sample had come into coaching from teaching. However, Figure 1.1 presents selected data from a four-country survey of coaches in which the relationship was more obvious (Tamura *et al*. 1993).

	Teachers in sample %	Trained as teacher %
Australia	20	22
Canada	30	40
Britain	14	21
Japan	26	27

Source: Adapted from Tamura *et al*. 1993

Figure 1.1 *Percentage of coaches trained as teachers, by country*

In Britain, it is certainly the case that the relationship to the teaching profession will depend on the sports selected for a sample population. Lyle *et al*. (1997) found that there was an inverse relationship between teacher status and parental route into coaching in school-based team sports such as basketball and volleyball and individual sports such as swimming and athletics. Attempts to reinforce the relationship between teaching and coaching have not diminished (Cooke 1996). It is also necessary to remember, of course, that there are commercial and ideological reasons for reinforcing the similarities of provision and delivery in participation sport.

Overall, the impact on coaching has been mixed. PE teachers have attended very many 'coaching courses' and acquired many certificates. These have mostly been early-level certificates and based on teaching the sport rather than coaching. In many cases, teachers have considered that their PE training was at least as good as that offered by the governing body and relied on that training. A situation has developed over time in which PE teaching and coaching were regarded as synonymous. The great majority of PE teachers were 'coaching' after-school clubs and very often in sports clubs in which they themselves were members. The PE teacher was likely to be a talented performer and (naturally!) gravitated to coaching positions. PE undoubtedly made, and makes, an enormous contribution to the teaching of sports to young people, and the PE profession as a whole has clearly made a very significant contribution to the make-up of the coaching (mostly voluntary) workforce. There was a clear perception that a successful engagement in extra-curricular school sport was a necessary part of the ambitious teacher's programme and promotion was influenced by non-curricular involvement (Evans 1990: 151).

 Critical Concept

A situation has developed over time in which PE teaching and coaching are regarded as synonymous. PE undoubtedly made, and makes, an enormous contribution to the teaching of sports to young people, and the PE profession as a whole has clearly made a very significant contribution to the make-up of the coaching (mostly voluntary) workforce.

Teachers had training in delivery methods, organisation and control, lesson planning, and elements of child development. The teacher was often contrasted therefore with the non-PE coach who had had traditionally much less training in these areas but was recognised to have (often) superior subject knowledge. One of the consequences was a sense of protectionism as teachers 'distanced' themselves from performance coaches, who were considered to be over-concerned with competition, and protected their educational territory. Much more integrated sport development schemes involving young people, and often centred on the school, have brought schools and other agencies closer together and diminished many of the barriers that previously existed (Thorpe 1996).

On the other hand, it can also be argued that the closeness between PE and coaching and the confusion of roles has not helped the coaching 'profession'. A sense that 'any generalist' could be a coach was heightened by the assumption that PE teachers could 'turn their hand' to many different sports. The truth was that they could, because this was about sports participation coaching which is not dissimilar at all from sports teaching. The impact on performance coaching has been less penetrative but nevertheless significant,

 Question Box

Has the low status of sports coaches been influenced significantly by the 'generalist' sports teaching contribution of the PE teacher?

relying more on the coincidence of interest between talented sportspersons attracted to PE and a developed capacity for leadership.

Overall, the coincidence of interests between a predisposition to sport, desire to continue in sport, links with young people and sport organisations, perceptions of career advancement, the taking of 'coaching' certificates, and the influence of PE colleges/lecturers on coach education in particular sports make it seem hardly surprising that there has been a symbiosis between PE teaching and coaching. It is likely that this has lessened a little in recent times as the boundaries of the respective roles have become more clearly recognised and reinforced; such a proposition deserves more research. Factors such as extended coach education programmes, the reduced extent of PE training, extension of the coach recruitment base, some movement of young people's sport away from schools to clubs and development schemes, and a more specific, more rewarded performance-coaching structure may well have reduced the dependence on PE teachers as a recruitment source.

HIGHER EDUCATION AND ACADEMIC DEVELOPMENT

Of particular interest to a book the purpose of which is to contribute to the academic development of coaching is the extent to which the study of sports coaching has penetrated higher education. In 2001, there were 26 institutions in the UK offering courses at degree and higher national diploma levels with sports coaching in the title. However, this has been a recent phenomenon and, historically, there has been very limited penetration of higher education by sports coaching. Dunfermline College of Physical Education, Edinburgh, offered the first Higher Education Diploma in 1979. This became a Diploma in Professional Studies (Sport Coaching), and as the institution evolved into Moray House Institute of Education, the award developed into a Master's degree in Coaching Studies.

The awards proved to be very successful in accelerating many of the experienced student coaches into positions of considerable influence in sport. In 1990, the National Coaching Foundation (NCF), based in Leeds, offered a similar diploma on a distance-learning basis, intended to attract experienced coaches of high-level athletes from around the UK to a flexible style of study and delivery. This award evolved into an undergraduate distance learning degree (supplemented by a series of workshops), validated through De Montfort University, and delivered via a network of co-operating institutions.

The latter part of the twentieth century witnessed an explosion of undergraduate provision in sport and leisure studies, and part of this was the gradual emergence of sports coaching and coaching science routes and courses. These were populated largely by young undergraduates with limited coaching experience, although the courses were often complemented by some form of practical experience. The 1990s also saw the emergence of a number of Master's degrees, normally with an emphasis on coaching studies or coaching science. A similar expansion in sports-related courses occurred in further education in the UK. This provision also became characterised by courses (at Higher National and BTEC level) with a coaching emphasis – often with sports development or exercise studies. The focus of these courses was on participation coaching and delivery, and was often integrated with the NCF's certificate and diploma awards and a National Standards NVQ-led curricular design.

The national awards have not attracted the intended number of high-profile coaches and impact and insinuation into professional sport has been limited. The dependency evident in the link in the USA between coaching practice and educational qualifications has not yet been established. The rise in the number of undergraduates with exposure to coaching studies has not yet had sufficient time to demonstrate any impact. It seems likely that this will, initially at least, be felt in participation rather than performance coaching.

One of the most significant consequences of the failure to establish coaching studies within higher education has been the dearth of both research and teaching materials. Attention in universities has been focused on performance research, with very little support for research into coaching practice and behaviour. The NCF has made a very considerable impact on provision of support materials for coaching, but those publications dealing with 'conceptual/principle/theoretical' issues have been targeted at a less challenging audience (Crisfield *et al*. 1996). Nevertheless, the need to develop teaching and study materials to deliver the distance learning NCF/de Montfort degree was an opportunity for academics throughout the UK to turn their attention to coaching-specific output.

OVERSEAS INFLUENCES

One of the questions to ask in identifying trends within coaching development is this: which overseas countries have significantly influenced the development of sports coaching in the UK. The USA might have been expected to exert considerable influence, given the prominence of the role of coach in American culture (Coakley and Dunning 2000), the shared language and common media coverage. This, however, has been less than might have been anticipated. Part of the answer lies in the different educational/sports agency structures and in the nature of the major sports in the two countries. First, the career coach to be found in US high schools, colleges and universities (within a structured and hierarchical competition programme) is not matched in the UK and differs in almost all respects from the traditional voluntary club/NGB structure of the UK. The effect in the USA has been to produce an entire infrastructure of job opportunities, career pathways, educational requirements, and associated literature and research. It is also true to say that the coaching practices of top-level collegiate sports mirror those of the professional sports for which they are a direct recruitment pathway. Second, the sports with the highest profiles in North America (football, basketball, baseball, and ice hockey) are all 'coach-dominated' sports, with a prominent competition role for the coach. This has given the coach a high status in the USA and contributed much to the stereotype of the coach.

 Critical Concept

Coaching practice in North America has provided images and role exemplars for coaching in the UK but the 'system' differences have prevented any significant borrowing of practice.

A second source of coaching images has been derived from what was called 'Eastern European sport'. The post-war success of the USSR, East Germany and other Soviet satellite countries focused attention onto their system for producing successful athletes. Subsequent revelations have disclosed widespread use of performance-enhancing drugs and less humane treatment of individuals (Houlihan 1999). Nevertheless, the apparently systematic approach to talent identification, development, training and preparation was regarded in the West with a mixture of envy, cynicism and wonder (Hoberman 1992). The enormous state support inherent in the system meant that this approach could not be copied in the UK. However, the attempt at 'systematic' or 'scientific' coaching did influence practice, particularly in individual power sports, in which 'training theory' principles were derived largely from Eastern European practice (Schmolinsky 1978; Dick 1997b; Bompa 1999).

In the late 1970s and throughout the 1980s, the UK had realised that there was a need to modernise its approach to coach education. Coach education was characterised by traditional practice, autonomy and specificity of governing body practice, emphasis on technical and tactical content, and a minimum (in most cases) of supporting discipline knowledge. Similar catalysts had been at work in Canada as part of a more widespread new approach to sport following disappointing Olympic performance (Gowan and Thomson 1986; Sutcliffe 1995). Australia followed the same approach (Pyke and Woodman 1986; Sutcliffe 1995). Each of these countries developed coach education programmes in which a national system of accredited levels of coaching awards was supplemented by the availability of non-sport-specific material on topics such as prevention of injury, coaching children and analysing technique. These systems became the model for the pattern of coach education provision to be developed in the UK.

RECENT DEVELOPMENTS

A growing realisation and acknowledgement in the early 1980s of the need for the expansion of coaching services led to a review of provision and the setting up of the NCF in 1983 (Coghlan 1990; Pickup 1996). The NCF has had a very significant impact on the development of coaching in the UK, particularly in participation coaching and NGB award schemes. Sue Campbell, its energetic director for most of its existence, was a strong advocate for the interests of coaching. The NCF was established as the 'coaching arm' of the Sports Councils and in recognition of the growing awareness of the importance of sports coaching at all levels of sport. Pickup (1996) describes the gradual increases in investment in the NCF and the working relationship with the Sports Council in the early 1990s. The organisation became immediately very active in promoting coach education. It developed rapidly and increased its range of interests; facilitating a national system of accredited coach education materials and awards, training coach educators, publishing materials to support education, establishing a network of National Coaching Centres, hosting workshops and conferences, liaising with NGBs and other agencies, and also taking on a promotion and advocacy role. The Champion Coaching programme, begun in 1990–91, was a notable success.

In the late 1980s and the 1990s the NCF embraced the NVQs/National Occupational Standards approach to education and training, producing materials, training and accrediting mentors and tutors, and promoting the incorporation of National Standards into NCF/NGB curricula. National Standards were developed to provide an 'industry-wide profile of what coaches at different levels of training and practice should be able to do' (Miles 2001: 15). The NCF has played a significant role in the Sport Recreation Industry Training Organisation (SPRITO), the industry lead body for education and training in sport and allied professions. The organisation also developed a distance learning diploma for experienced sports coaches, which later developed into an undergraduate degree programme. More successful have been the certificate and diploma courses that have been incorporated into many further and higher education awards. It has also been active in European organisations – notably, the European Network of Sport Sciences in Higher Education – co-operating in a programme to harmonise and standardise levels of award across Europe, based on a five-level coach education framework similar to that intended to emerge in the UK (Campbell 1993).

Overall, the NCF has had a successful advocacy role. The impact of NCF programmes at lower levels of coach education, the recognition of the need for licensing, mentoring, supervised experience, inputs from expert coaches, the NVQ/National Standards and the gradual emphasis on performance coaching have transformed coach education. Later chapters will question the influence of coach education on performance coaching, on which it has had less impact. In 2001, the NCF became sportscoaching UK (SCUK), reflecting changes to the structure of UK sport. The multiple interests and scope of SCUK, the British Olympic Association (BOA), the United Kingdom Sports Institute, the universities and the NGBs have yet to be co-ordinated fully in terms of performance coaching direction and leadership for the future.

British Association of National Coaches (BANC) had become established in the mid-1960s to further the interests of directors of coaching and national coaches, and to speak for coaching interests more generally. However, there was a need to expand the association and its scope and purposes. BANC became the British Institute of Sport Coaches in 1989 and a membership drive began. This had limited success, although its range of membership categories, services and advocacy role was expanded. In 1993, this organisation was absorbed by the National Coaching Foundation as its 'membership arm', becoming the National Association of Sports Coaches. One of the successes of the successive organisations was the Coach of the Year Awards. It is remarkable, and for advocates of coaching disappointing, but perhaps a mark of the failure of the 'profession of sports coaching' to develop, that the UK does not yet have an independent professional association for sports coaches.

 Question Box

What impact has the absence of a strong professional body had on the profile and professionalisation of sports coaching?

Despite changes in coach education, these had a limited effect on performance sport. Individual governing bodies of sport continued to network and to learn from the practice of others, but it was perceived that the lack of career opportunities, investment in achieving competition success, and the absence of a national approach to performance sport with its attendant support systems was constraining coaching (which was always rated as very important by top-level athletes). The advent of the National Lottery and the increase in funding, both revenue and capital, for sport provided the opportunity for the UK to devise a national system of sport development in general and performance-sport development and support in particular. A protracted period of planning and politicking (Theodoraki 1999) was originally focused on a Sports Institute modelled on the Australian Institute of Sport in Canberra. This was gradually amended, and as the funding and power battles between sport agencies settled down, became a more restricted hub-and-spokes network model.

However, this was complemented by a programme of development culminating in the World Class Performance, Potential and Start programmes, and sport-specific provision. The availability of National Lottery revenue funding to individual performers and a sport science infrastructure have been situated within long-term performance plans. Most importantly, the funding has meant that performance coaches have been appointed to targeted sports, with very focused remits. These developments have changed for the better the climate within which performance coaching is situated. Coach education is also changing, with advanced workshop programmes, mentoring programmes and needs analysis of and assistance to the needs of individual coaches.

There have also been advances in participation coaching. Development officers with a participation coaching remit were gradually introduced into local authority provision, during the facilities expansion of the 1970s and 1980s. Also, coaching courses/training of volunteers became evident in sports development schemes such as Action Sport (Coghlan 1990). Sports development initiatives of the 1980s and 1990s – Champion Coaching, the TOPS Programme and, more recently, the Active programme are good examples – have gradually become sport specific, and with increased funding from the National Lottery there has been more significant expansion. These development officers often have a coach development role and a participation coaching remit. The 1990s have also been marked by an increase in the number of sport-specific development officers.

It has already been remarked that professional sports in the UK should have been the cradle of good practice and a potential career pathway for coaches. However, a protectionist system of recruitment and appointment has not yet been overcome by advances in licensing and training. In most professional sports (such as soccer, rugby union, rugby league, cricket and basketball) the influx of overseas coaches has been very marked. This is also a trend in performance-coach appointments to British representative teams. This influx in professional sport has largely been a result of increased commercialisation and it is not immediately clear that the development of native coaches has always been factored into current developments.

Education provision by SCUK/NCF reflects the increased attention given to performance sport and the recognition of the significance of the coach's role at this level. The diet of courses includes performance-coach workshops, and the High Performance Coaching

Programme provides educational, developmental and information services to support coaches. The more structured approach to developing elite sport has been stimulated by the inception of the United Kingdom Sports Institute (UKSI) and increased co-operation in coaching provision between the UKSI, the BOA and the NCF (NCF 1998).

Following an extensive consultation exercise, a strategy document – *The UK Vision for Coaching: A Strategy into the Twenty-first Century* – was published by UK Sport (2001). The document is aspirational in nature and does not identify plans, priorities or resources. It acknowledges that implementation plans have to be devised by the many agencies contributing to coaching provision. Objectives have been identified in five key areas: ethical practice (including widening the recruitment base), a structured qualification framework based on benchmarked national standards of competence, regulation and professional development of coaching as an occupation, employment practices, and continuous professional development. This new strategy document complements and expands the Government's strategy and planning document – 'A Sporting Future for All: The Government's Plan for Sport' (Department of Culture, Media and Sport/DfEE 2001). The strategy itself says little about coaching, being focused on social inclusion and school sport. However, the planning section identifies the following objectives: more full-time posts, enhanced recruitment, a licensing system, a more centralised education system, increased financial support, and the development of a coaches' association. Interestingly the document acknowledges that 'research into the development of coaches and coaching is required to inform policy and support programmes' (2001: 17).

CONCLUDING COMMENTS

There is no doubt that future historical analyses of sports coaching will demonstrate that, despite the collective efforts of key individuals and groups of individuals, the practice of coaching and the worth attached to it have often been marginalised by more general sport policies and social attitudes. It is difficult to escape a sense that, until recently, sports coaching did not receive the attention necessary to give it recognition and a priority within sport that its proponents and initiates felt that it deserved. There are a number of potential explanations: a throwback to the amateur ethic; a failure in the UK to take performance sport seriously; volunteer versus professional issues in governing bodies of sport; minimalist education and training; protectionism and lack of vision in professional sports; the 'generalist' influence from physical education; and an absence of academics with a desire to stimulate study and research. There were also inter-agency issues, ranging from protecting the sport specificity of coaching to questions of territoriality between NGBs, the Sports Councils and the British Olympic Association. This was exacerbated by the lack of influence of coaching organisations, despite their earnest attempts at advocacy.

These factors were exacerbated by a public policy emphasis, particularly in local government, on sport for all and a facility-led approach to recreational provision. The UK tradition, in the voluntary sector, of relatively small clubs failed to generate resources to support full-time coaching appointments. Until the advent of National Lottery finance, successive governments had adopted a mostly benevolent but hands-off and resource-constrained approach to sport. Many of the traditionally 'amateur' sports had examples of good coaching practice, but the restricted scale of provision and the limited rewards for athletes and coaches prevented significant progress until National Lottery funding arrived. It is worth pointing to swimming as a sport in which the numbers involved in the teaching programmes, in clubs, and because of public sector support for externalities such as safety and health created an environment in which there was a career structure, albeit somewhat limited in scale.

 Critical Concept

The aggregated outcome of these factors was an absence of a career pathway for sports coaches, which in turn failed to stimulate education and training demand for coaches. The overall effect of this was the rather haphazard and tentative growth of the occupation or profession.

The aggregated outcome of these factors was an absence of a career pathway for sport coaches, which in turn failed to stimulate education and training demand for coaches. The overall effect of this was the rather haphazard and tentative growth of the occupation or profession.

While this may seem rather negative, it is important to understand that there were some implications for the development of academic knowledge in sports coaching. In the period up to the 1990s, there were very many distinguished coaches, a vast army of dedicated volunteer coaches, some NGBs with well-organised and progressive education programmes, innovation and the introduction of sport science, and a small, almost esoteric, collective representing the world of coaching. Nevertheless, the failure to establish more than a toe-hold in higher education and the absence of depth in coach education had militated against the production of non-sport-specific academic material.

There are grounds for optimism from developments in the 1990s. The inception of the National Coaching Foundation (now Sports Coach UK) in 1983 and its continued expansion through the 1990s stimulated demand for the production of materials for its coach education courses, up to degree level. The advent of National Lottery funding has stimulated and enabled the appointment of performance coaches and support personnel, and focused attention on an instrumental approach to success in sport. Performance planning has brought with it recognition of the essential elements necessary for improving and maintaining sports performance. There is evidence that good practice is more wide-spread in professional sport. Financial support for all levels of sport development has enabled Sport England and other agencies to adopt a more all-embracing and systematic approach to sport development. This in turn has stimulated participation coaching and development posts. The expansion of sport education in higher education has continued into the twenty-first century, with sports coaching benefiting from the increased scale and a facilitative environment for academic application.

This book is partly a product of the increased attention paid to coach education and also a response to the demand for more sophisticated tools with which to analyse coaching practice and underpin coach education. Much of coaching practice has been taken for granted as the emphasis has fallen on the athlete's performance. The nascent demand for improved understanding of sports coaching, of analysis of coaching practice, of research into coaching and performance, and for study materials have been inhibited by the absence of a conceptual understanding of the sports coaching process. This book addresses that vacuum.

SUMMARY

This chapter will have familiarised you with the following:

- the gradual emergence of athletic trainers and the relationship between professional coaching and the amateur–professional divide;
- the appointment and impact of national coaches and the development of NGB award schemes;
- the relationship between the development of sports coaching and the teaching profession;
- the influence of the penetration of sports coaching into higher education in the UK and the production of coach education products;
- the influence of overseas developments on the pattern of sports-coaching provision in the UK;
- the inception of the NCF and its impact on coach education and provision, including support for NVQs/National Occupational Standards;
- the direct and indirect impact of National Lottery funding on the professionalisation of coaching and increased attention to elite sport;
- the agenda for the development of coaching as set out in recent official documents.

PROJECTS

- Use magazines and historical material from within your sport to chart the development of coaching, identifying key figures and evidence of growth. Compare findings to trends within sport more generally.
- Undertake a public policy analysis of coaching provision by examining Sports Council, NGB and BOA/CCPR (Central Council for Physical Recreation) documentation. Compare rhetoric and practice.
- Quantify the influx and diffusion of overseas coaches into UK sports. Carry out a qualitative enquiry into the impact on coach recruitment at elite levels.
- Using evidence gathered from one particular sport, chart the changes in coach education provision over the past fifteen years. Appraise this critically in the light of developments at national level.

Reading

There are no very detailed and authoritative accounts of the history of sports coaching. However, McNab (1990) and *Coaching Matters* (Coaching Review Panel 1991) are very useful introductions. Coghlan (1990) and Pickup (1996) are valuable sources for recent developments in sports administration and policy as they affected sports coaching. It is important to be familiar with the UK Strategy document (UK Sport 2001).

CHAPTER TWO

▼ **DEVELOPING A CONCEPTUAL FRAMEWORK**

- Introduction   20
- Contemporary Sport and Conceptual Questions   22
- Building a Conceptual Framework   24
- Coaching and Theory Development   28
- The Contribution of Literature on Sports Coaching   31
- Sport as a Concept   33
- Summary   34
- Projects and Reading   34

INTRODUCTION

Images of sport permeate our culture. Few individuals escape contact with sport, whether in an active or passive sense, forming as it does a significant part of our leisure, educational, economic and social experiences. Those who have taken part in school sport, those who watch sport on television, and those who constitute the vast numbers of performers and officials in active sports participation will be familiar with the sports coach. This familiarity may be expressed in coaching stereotypes, opinions on respected characteristics, or views on the excesses of unethical behaviour at all levels in sport. On the other hand, coaches may have been persuasive role models or a positive personal influence for a very large number of individuals. For many, these popular images are sufficient and there is no need to delve beyond the familiar. There is no need to treat the breadth and diversity of coaching roles or any lack of clarity in skills and knowledge as problematic issues. However, the very pervasiveness of the coach and coaching militates against precision in the kind of knowledge and understanding required in academic study.

This chapter explores the need for a clear set of conceptual principles about sports coaching and what this entails. It also provides an insight into what might be termed 'coaching theory', and examines the available literature, and the research on which it is based, for the extent to which it provides such a conceptual underpinning.

Conceptual precision and clarity have become more necessary for a number of reasons. Coach education has improved in scope and quality. Along with the more established professions, the coach's expertise and accountability in the public domain have come under closer scrutiny. At the same time, there has been a significant increase in the level of academic interest in all aspects of the coaching process. For each of these reasons, and also simply for the enquiring mind, the popular image has to be replaced by an analytical framework that will permit the level of analysis and academic enquiry necessary to sustain developments in coaching education and practice. It may be understandable that the popular image is sufficient for the spectator. However, for those with responsibility for improving perfor-mance, whether as practitioners, researchers or educators, it is unforgivable that the business of coaching should ever be treated as taken-for-granted rather than disputatious and critical in impact. The non-problematic approach has to be replaced by a knowledge and appreciation of the part played by the coach in improving performance or achieving other goals.

This book is intended as a resource text for those engaged in the study of sports coaching. The primary purpose is to provide the coherent conceptual framework for all aspects of sports coaching that will permit the required analysis of practice. This theme of identifying key concepts and exploring their relationships is applied to all facets of coaching. There are many texts dealing with scientific sub-disciplines applied in the coaching context and there are emerging bodies of knowledge and principles in coach education, social context, interpersonal behaviour and coaching practice in specific sports. However, the central message, which is reinforced throughout, is that an explicit and comprehensive set of concepts about sports coaching is a first step, a prerequisite, for subsequent analysis and application. Understanding and improving coaching practice is a necessary stage in professional development and an appropriate aim for everyone involved. It is important that an emphasis on athlete performance or the immediacy of coach behaviour does not detract from the need to focus on these conceptual insights.

 Critical Concept

An explicit and comprehensive set of concepts about sports coaching is a first step, a prerequisite, for subsequent analysis and application.

The term 'conceptual appreciation' suggests a set of analytical tools with which to understand better the coach and the coach's practice. This understanding will be achieved by addressing a range of questions:

- What language and terminology is best suited to describing unequivocally both the coaching process and coaching practice?
- What is the purpose of sports coaching and how does it differ in this respect from other sports leadership roles?
- Which are the constituent, pivotal and essential elements of the coaching process?
- How can the coaching process be best represented for the purposes of analysis, modelling and prediction?
- What is the most appropriate set of concepts to describe the range and variability in coaching behaviour and practice?

- How can a balance be achieved between generic coaching concepts and the 'real-time' application of these in specific sports?
- Which criteria are most usefully applied to issues of evaluation, accountability, impact and effectiveness?
- How can sports coaching be conceptualised in order to appreciate the impact of environmental factors – organisational, ethical, social and cultural?

 Question Box

Does this set of conceptual 'posers' adequately represent the full range of questions necessary for a complete analysis of coaching practice? If not, what would be added?

Providing answers to these questions has guided the structure and content of the book. The motive for the book was a perception that these important questions had not been addressed adequately thus far.

CONTEMPORARY SPORT AND CONCEPTUAL QUESTIONS

The suggestion that there are unanswered questions about sports coaching may seem a little theoretical and removed from practice. However, it is possible to illustrate the fact that everyday practice in sports provision and delivery raises problematical conceptual issues. Consider the following issues and associated questions:

The advent of National Lottery support for elite sport in the UK and the provision of national and regional structures and systems to complement this have been accompanied by the targeting of efforts towards specific goals (for example, the Olympic Games). The continued deployment of Lottery funding has been linked quite specifically to quantifiable performance outputs. The appointment of performance coaches is recognition of the central place of coaching in achieving these goals. However, to what extent can the coach be held responsible for performance outputs? Is it sufficient to be 'successful by association with successful performers'? How much 'value added' is acceptable? How is it measured? Are these questions important if the athletes are successful!

Government policy in the UK has promoted an integrated framework of accredited learning at all levels, including vocational and work-based experience. Agencies have been established to regulate and accredit qualifications and to set standards for practice within a common framework. Sports coaching has become incorporated into these structures and initiatives to promote and incorporate National Vocational Qualifications/National Occupational Standards into National Governing Bodies of sport qualifications was a feature of coach education in the 1990s. National Standards have been identified with which to assess coaching competence. However, this process raises issues about the compatibility of the framework assumptions and the concept of the coaching role. Is it appropriate to conceive of the qualification levels as embracing a concept of coaching that is differentiated only by the standard of the athlete? Is the higher-level coach characterised by managerial responsibility or by other measures of expertise? How is capacity rather than performance to be measured? Are there any coaching competencies that are more important than others?

Traditionally, school sport has been a significant part of the process through which young persons were introduced to sport and made progress on a developmental pathway. This area was largely the prerogative of the physical education teacher with other volunteer colleagues. However, a number of professional and policy changes have resulted in a different pattern of provision. National Governing Bodies of sport have paid more attention to their own developmental ladders of opportunity, and agencies such as Sport England and the Youth Sport Trust have attempted to embrace school-age activity within a much broader youth sport policy. Initiatives such as Champion Coaching, the National Junior Sport Programme and, more recently, Active Schools are complemented by specialist sport colleges, Sportsmark accreditation schemes and the introduction of School Sport Co-ordinators and other development officers. Which forms of sport leadership are most appropriate in these contexts? Can this activity be usefully conceptualised as sports coaching? Are there any coach characteristics that might be most appropriate in these situations? Is there any distinction between sports teaching and sports coaching?

The continuing commercialisation of top-level sport, increases in public and private funding and increased rewards for performers have resulted in greater levels of commitment to preparation for sport and more full-time athletes and coaches. The professionalisation of rugby union in the UK in the 1990s and the rise in the number of National Lottery-funded athletes and coaches are examples of this. This occupational development has brought with it a number of issues. What are the recruitment mechanisms for coaches into professional and elite-level sport? What are the implications of being a player-coach? How appropriate is coach education for the demands of elite sport? What is the role of the coach in relation to other support staff?

Sports scientists have developed increasing levels of expertise, technology and support practice to enhance performance both in preparation and in competition. This is accompanied by more sophisticated medical, personal and career management practices. What is the nature of the coach's role in relation to these other experts? How do the coach's integrative, co-ordinating and sports-specific skills and knowledge relate to these complementary bodies of knowledge?

A number of high-profile cases of misconduct relating to sexual harassment, abuse of young persons, and performance-enhancing drugs abuse have focused attention onto coaches' ethical behaviour. In addition, the well-documented paucity of female coaches in top-level sport points to the mirroring in coaching of more general social and cultural patterns. Is professional development being accompanied by adequate coach education? How is coaching practice influenced by environmental factors? Have issues of ethical standards, codes of conduct and licensing of coaches been related sufficiently well to an understanding of the coach's role and employment practice?

Question Box

A large number of questions have been raised in the preceding paragraphs. Aggregate these questions and attempt to answer them for one sport. Are some of the questions more important than others for understanding coaching practice?

The questions raised in this short and selective review of contemporary practice and provision form a significant agenda on their own. The intention was to demonstrate that answering most, if not all, of these questions satisfactorily requires a precise identification of the issues, an adequate interpretation and analysis of the issues and an overarching appreciation of how they interrelate. This is not possible in the absence of a comprehensive conceptualisation of sports coaching. Enquiry into issues about role, education, expertise, accountability and behaviour are dependent on a capacity to describe, analyse and explain coaching practice. This leads to understanding and application.

BUILDING A CONCEPTUAL FRAMEWORK

Earlier in the chapter a number of questions were raised, which constituted the beginnings of a conceptual schema. In other words, what would a conceptualisation of sports coaching involve? Figure 2.1 incorporates these questions into a simple but helpful framework.

The worth of this approach has been noted elsewhere:

> it is a necessary part of the development of a profession to have a (conceptual) model with which to demystify practice, to provide a common vocabulary, to form a basis for research and enquiry, to create a template for education and from which ideological approaches and individual value frameworks can fashion their contextual significance. There are many empirical questions that cannot be adequately framed as a consequence of the absence of such a [conceptual] model.
>
> (Lyle 1996: 16)

Although there is a strong emphasis here on a consensual and coherent set of principles with which to analyse and make sense of sports coaching, these should not be viewed as resulting in a narrow or restrictive perspective on coaching. Individual differences are not negated by a common framework, and there will be enormous variety when it comes to implementation strategies, styles, value frameworks and sport-specific approaches. What is important is that the means exist to describe, debate, compare and disseminate such differences. It is also important to affirm at this early stage that an emphasis on conceptualising sports coaching should not understate or undervalue the human element. There is no doubt that sports coaching is an interpersonal phenomenon and that there cannot be a complete appreciation of coaching without a recognition of the aspirations, qualities, motives, emotions, abilities and values of both athlete and coach, and of the dynamics of the interaction between them.

Concept	Purpose	Typical questions
Language and terminology	Communication; professional development	What precisely do we mean by 'training', 'preparation', 'performance', the 'coaching process', 'intervention', 'decision-making', etc.? Is there a consensus in interpretation and meaning?
Purpose and nature	Defining boundaries; clarifying accountability and responsibility	What is the difference between sports coaching, teaching and instruction? To what extent can coaches be held responsible for athlete performance?
Essential elements	Coach education; analysis of coaching performance	Which are the most important parts of the coaching process? What is the effect of failing to implement a comprehensive programme?
Modelling	Description, analysis and prediction	How can the coaching process be portrayed in such a way as to facilitate analysis of practice and inform research design?
Specificity versus genericism	Description of individual behaviour; application	Are coaching 'styles' useful behavioural categories for analysis? How can the variety in specific sport practice be usefully comprehended?
Expertise	Coach education; professional development; identifying knowledge and skills	In which ways do expert coaches differ from novices? Which functions are specific to coaches?
Role	Boundary responsibilities; professional development; inter- and intra-role conflict	How is the coaching role influenced by organisational demands? Which factors influence the role at different levels; e.g. representative group/team coaches?
Values	Understanding behaviour; recruitment and selection; professional development	Is there a relationship between context and value framework? How do personal values interact with organisational ones? How is the human element built into the coaching process?
Evaluation	Professional development; accountability/effectiveness	Are there any useful measures of coaching effectiveness? Is there any distinction between effective, competent or successful coaches?

Figure 2.1 *Elements of a conceptual framework for sports coaching*

Critical Concept

Individual differences are not negated by a common framework, and there will be enormous variety when it comes to implementation strategies, styles, value frameworks and sport-specific approaches. What is important is that the means exist to describe, debate, compare and disseminate such differences.

The conceptual framework, which will be developed as we progress through the chapters of the book, provides a bridge between coaching activity and our capacity to make sense of it and is not, therefore, a sterile exercise. The understanding derived from the framework informs a number of practical and important issues. These can be divided into implementation issues and more general developmental issues.

Coaching practice

This is a catch-all term for the totality of the coach's professional and personal activity and experience. It embraces observable and cognitive behaviour, and acknowledges the environmental context within which the coach operates. There is a need to have a very clear distinction between direct intervention and other coach activities because of their role-specific character and differentiated skills and knowledge.

Coach education

Coach educators are in an impossible situation unless they are operating within an appropriate framework of knowledge and skills. Issues of progression, staging, role specificity, balancing of components, knowledge structures and priority skills depend on a comprehensive conceptual overview of the needs of coaches. The means of achieving higher levels of expertise, rather than simply identifying those needs, is very much underdeveloped.

Professional development

Since in the UK coaching is characterised by uncrystallised occupational development, it is important to have a very clear understanding of the interplay between embryonic professional standards, organisational demands, and social and cultural expectations. This is facilitated by a framework that recognises the consonance between coaching behaviour, coach education, athlete aspirations and professional status.

Coaching effectiveness

There are very difficult issues to be overcome in dealing with effectiveness measures, and sports coaching is a prime example of this. Professional accountability and individual concerns over esteem, selection, advancement and reward will maintain the spotlight on how coaches and coaching can be evaluated. A very thorough appreciation of the concepts in coaching is required to approach this issue.

Research

Attention will be paid to the notion that research into coaching matters is very variable in rigour, scope and impact. To some extent the absence of a consensual conceptual framework has prevented the meta-theorising necessary to generate key research questions.

Figure 2.2 summarises these relationships in a simple diagram.

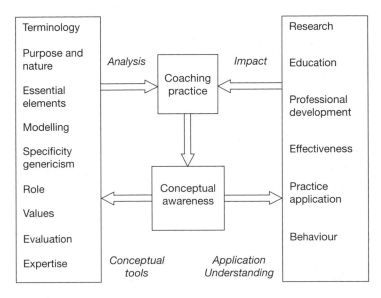

Figure 2.2 *The relationship between conceptual framework elements and application issues*

The final point to be made in closing this section is that the conceptual framework and its attendant issues are made more complex by the three-way relationship between athlete, coach and performance. This is evident in the dearth of literature and research linking the coach and performance outcomes, despite the fact that the coach's effectiveness or success is often judged by those performance outcomes. At the risk of assuming some of the argument to be presented later, Figure 2.3 illustrates how each of the relationships generates a specific range of issues. Of course, the sets of issues are not completely divorced from each other but they demonstrate the number of opportunities on the conceptual map at which the relationships can break down. They also generate questions about the factors that are in the control of the athlete, the coach or both. (It is worth mentioning at this stage that the coach–athlete dyad is used as a shorthand assumption. In practice, of course, the coach(es) may be working with teams or groups of individuals, with consequent implications for the complexity of practice.)

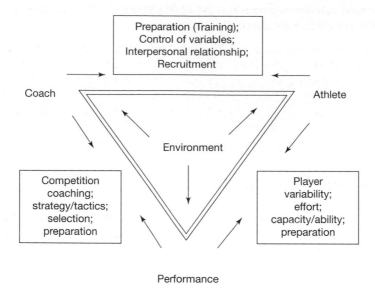

Figure 2.3 *Factors arising from the complexity of interaction of athlete, coach and performance*

COACHING AND THEORY DEVELOPMENT

The term 'coaching theory' is used quite extensively, and it would be useful, therefore, to review what is meant by a 'theory' before moving to an examination of the status of theory development in sports coaching. A theory gathers a set of claims about causally linked relationships between concepts. These concepts are organised in such a way as to 'attempt to provide persuasively an explanation of phenomena' (Morrow 1994: 43). Theories can be guides to policy and practice, but are most useful in identifying the crucial questions for researchers. These 'empirical' theories are complemented by 'normative' theories, which are more akin to social criticism, and 'meta-theory', which is not susceptible to direct verification from sensorily derived data and is more 'theory about theory'. Generally, theories are held to be provisional unless there have been substantial and unsuccessful attempts to refute them.

The characteristics of 'good' theories are that they integrate existing ideas and evidence, and claims and counter-claims, into a coherent set of propositions that 'make sense' and display an inherent logic and consistency. The theory should provide clear propositions that are open to disconfirmation through observation or experiment. Although simplicity is preferred, attempts to achieve generality of application may result in increased complexity. One convincing ideology is that theories are not verified or proved but that they are 'not refuted' through repeated and rigorous attempts (Dooley 1995; Crotty 1998).

It would be wrong to say that there are no theories about coaches and coaching. There are many examples of theory development in specific coaching behaviours, leadership, motives or gender issues. However, these most commonly involve the application of existing theories from other disciplines to coaches in context (rather than the coaching process) or fairly simple relationships between characteristics (male/female, expert/novice), and so on. It is more appropriate to say that:

- there have been few attempts to theorise the more complex coaching-specific factors, with or without existing theories – performance effect, expectation modelling, decision making, contingency planning or emotion-related cognitive behaviour;
- there are no overarching theories or unifying theories about sports coaching, which is not entirely surprising – the field has been conceived of as too diffuse in purpose and practice to encourage this.

 Critical Concept

There are no overarching theories or unifying theories about sports coaching. This is not entirely surprising: the field has been conceived of as too diffuse in purpose and practice to encourage this.

It would perhaps be more accurate to ask if there should be a family of theories, which, if taken together, would inform education and greatly increase our understanding of coaching. The focus in this book, on the underpinning concepts involved in coaching practice, is designed to encourage the development of coaching-related theory. To date, this has not happened. Despite the reference above to research on coaches' leadership styles, or behavioural elements, there have been few attempts to draw together the findings from such work (see Abraham and Collins 1998; Kuklinski 1990) and the literature generally bemoans the absence of appropriate conceptual development (Lyle 1984a, 1986, 1996; Sherman *et al.* 1997; Abraham and Collins 1998; Potrac *et al.* 2000).

The lack of emphasis on theory or conceptual development is surprising in the context of sports coaching's emergence as a legitimate area for academic study. There are, however, a number of plausible speculations as to why this might be so.

- Despite sporadic interest from academic departments in universities – for example, in sociology or psychology – sports coaching has suffered from sport's generally lowly status in the academic world. This has been exacerbated by the performance science bias in academic studies.
- There have been a number of characteristics of coaching that have made it less attractive to academics: a leisure time activity for many; a voluntary activity for many; the slow rate of professionalisation; the scale of provision; and the absence of a systematic career/management ladder.
- Although there are high-profile coaches in a number of sports, many coaches have woven an aura of mystique about coaching. A claim to esoteric knowledge, method and experience has created a protective occupational shell. This is perhaps most evident in situations in which recruitment is irregular, is not based on coach education and qualifications, and may not be open to scrutiny. This is also evident in the assertion that coaching is, at least in part, an 'art' (Woodman 1993). This may really be a

reflection of an inability (or unwillingness) to describe the skills, knowledge and processes (particularly the cognitive ones) involved.

■ The 'amateur ethic' in early sport development detracted from the role of the coach in some sports. Unlike the team sports in North America (ice hockey, basketball, football, baseball), the role of the coach in soccer, rugby and cricket in the UK has traditionally been less powerful and may have exacerbated the absence of academic attention.

■ The eclectic range of disciplines contributing to the study of sports coaching and the complex interrelationship of variables have tended to funnel academics into quite specific and narrow channels.

■ Traditionally, coach education content has emphasised sports-specific technical content and personal sports-specific skills, particularly in beginner awards. This has been supplemented in more recent years by what has been termed 'common theory'. Nevertheless, the rudimentary nature of this information has not encouraged academic exploration.

■ In addition, it is not evident that coaches have valued or incorporated 'theory' that is not sport specific. This is an implied criticism of coach educators but it also illustrates a reluctance to seek out and translate more generalised research into coaching practice.

■ Sports science research has been concerned with achieving incremental improvements in performance and with obviating distracting influences before and during performance. A considerable proportion of the research funds available has been expended on these goals (for example, Sports Council/NCF 1993). However, much less attention has been paid to the coach's application of this research. Such applied research is, of course, more 'untidy', but it is difficult to escape the conclusion that those who control research funds may limit the value of existing research by ignoring its application and implementation.

 Question Box

Is it unreasonable to expect meta-theory development in a field so diverse as coaching? Compare to a theory of teaching! However, this should not preclude the conceptual clarity necessary to analyse practice.

There is an element of speculation in this catalogue of contributory factors and a more extensive examination would certainly be welcome. They will not apply to all sports and to all individuals. Nevertheless, and for whatever reasons, there is undoubtedly less of an emphasis on coaching 'theory'. The outcome of this is that there is no extant or extensive body of knowledge with which to support academic study. In addition, the failure to aggregate this corpus of knowledge, the modest scale of specialist coaching studies and the absence of agreed conceptual principles have lessened the value of much of the literature.

THE CONTRIBUTION OF LITERATURE ON SPORTS COACHING

The following analysis of the literature is a personal commentary rather than a detailed review. The intention at this stage is to comment briefly on the value of the literature for the purpose of creating the necessary body of knowledge.

It is rare for authors to state their assumptions about the inferences to be drawn by the reader about the coaching process, based on the sample population of coaches used in their studies. It is common to use opportunistic samples or samples based on occupational or organisational settings. This produces considerable problems for comparative studies or even for thematic analyses of the literature, since the assumptions about the coaching process have not been made clear or controlled.

Much the greatest proportion of the North American literature has a focus on institutional career coaches in high schools and in the intercollegiate system. One of the outcomes of this is that career or occupational issues predominate. The considerable literature on opportunities for women coaches and coach 'burn-out' are examples of this. There is no doubt about the value of these studies but they do not deal with the nature of the process itself. An emphasis on the coach's characteristics or qualities much outweighs that available on effectiveness, planning or decision making, particularly in the context of performance outcomes.

Another focus within the literature has been on an 'episodic' interpretation of the coaching task. Focusing on the 'session' and on direct intervention between the coach and athletes has advantages for controlling variables, devising coaching interventions and employing systematic observation instruments. Nevertheless, the outcome has been to highlight observable behaviour and focus attention away from longer-term process variables. There remains much about coaching practice that is unknown. There are few examples of rigorously examined good practice in managing competition, managing the elite athlete's programme, crisis management, problem solving, and many more 'regulatory' procedures.

A subsidiary effect of the episodic approach is that there has been some considerable confusion between teaching sport and the direct instruction element of coaching (Lyle 1998a). Much of the literature is focused on relatively simple tasks with 'beginner' athletes.

There are many descriptive accounts of coaching practice, but these need to be analysed and interpreted in order to highlight the key principles that might be applicable to all coaches. Understandably, it is those coaches with marketing potential who find their way into print. Academics should take the opportunity to provide a greater number of descriptive accounts, chosen for their expertise and employing agreed conceptual principles to facilitate comparison and generalisability. Most accounts of practice are, of course, sport specific.

The words 'coach' or 'coaching' appear in the titles of many books, the purpose of which is to describe for the reader mainly sports-specific technical and tactical content. Few of these texts deal with coaching practice, although the more comprehensive ones may have sections on the role of the coach, organising training sessions, planning or conditioning.

These resources are most often prescriptive accounts and add little to the body of knowledge on coaching practice.

There have been a number of 'textbooks' dealing with coaching but the emphasis within these is largely twofold: occupational issues (although this includes recruitment) and episodic practice (for example, Fuoss and Troppmann 1981). In the absence of textbooks dealing with the theory of coaching, texts dealing with 'training theory' have substituted in academic study (Dick 1997a; Bompa 1999).

Some texts (Pyke 1980; Crisfield *et al.* 1996; Martens 1997), normally accompanying coach education programmes, have focused on the generic aspects of coaching. However, this material is rarely critical or targeted beyond the participation coach. The content tends to be derivative and simplistically presented and, therefore, makes little contribution to the development of knowledge or theory.

The following questions may prove useful in directing a critique of coaching-related literature:

- Did the author define the terms 'coach' or 'coaching' and were assumptions stated about these terms?
- Was the role of the sample population of coaches expanded at any length and the assumed tasks and functions of the coaches identified? Was there any evidence or supporting literature to complement this?
- Was there an 'episodic' emphasis or was coaching treated as a longer-term process?
- Did the research focus on the coach's personal characteristics, an element of athlete–coach interpersonal interaction, an occupational issue or a specified intervention programme?
- Was the research based on naturalistic (meaning undisturbed *in situ*) practice, and, if so, how was this recorded?
- Was there any attempt to relate the findings to specific organisational goals or to specific athlete aspirations?
- Was the intervention/activity related to preparation for an identified competition for which goals were specified?
- Was there any attempt to suggest a relationship between the focus of the research and identified performance outcomes?

Inevitably, this review of the coaching literature may seem unduly negative.

 Critical Concept

The literature is characterised by an absence of critical insight and with few challenges to the unproblematic approach to coaching described earlier. Less than challenging coaching contexts have been used for research, with a participation sport, episodic emphasis, often on observable behaviours. Crucially, the literature available has neither used conceptual principles nor contributed purposefully to their development.

Research in sports coaching

A number of criticisms and shortcomings have been identified in research and the resultant literature. These include lack of impact on coach education and coaching practice, and a failure to progress adequately a substantive body of knowledge on coaching practice. Some of these shortcomings can be attributed to the complexity of the coaching process and the interdependent athlete–coach–performance relationship. However, it has also been argued that the lack of attention to the conceptual framework supporting the research has reduced its usefulness and accumulative impact.

It would be inappropriate, however, not to attempt a more positive interpretation of the potential of coaching research. A much more comprehensive treatment of sports coaching research is given in Chapter 16, which delineates a research agenda for sports coaching.

SPORT AS A CONCEPT

As the chapter draws to a close, it would be inappropriate to imply criticism of those who do not treat the concept of coaching as problematic, but not to deal with the issue of 'sport' as the context for coaching studies.

There can be no doubt that the emphasis in this book is on sport. There are other contexts in which the term 'coaching' is used: music, drama and management, for example. However, it will also become obvious that, although there is a very strong argument that the process is a generic one, the context in which it is elaborated is clearly sport. The salient question is not 'what is sport?' but which forms of sport most appropriately provide the context within which the purpose and scope of sports coaching is required. It should be acknowledged, however, that participation/recreation and performance are two forms of sport from within the same family but which require different forms of coaching.

Sports coaching, as defined in this conceptual framework, is most often found in what is often described as a narrow definition of sport. That is, coaching's purpose and rationale are most fully utilised in sport contexts that require significant preparation, significant athlete commitment, physical training, extensive planning, competition strategy and tactics, and an extrinsic reward system. This will occur most often in culturally accepted and acknowledged sport activities with an extensive infrastructure of competition and provision. A subsequent chapter will deal with the distinction between participation and performance coaching. Participation coaching is a truncated form of the coaching process. There is no implication that this is of lesser 'worth' – it is simply different because the demand on the coaching process is different.

Performance sports coaching is not associated directly with only the higher standards of sports performance, although these are likely to be found in circumstances demanding the fullest implementation of the coaching process. Performance sports coaching will be found in situations in which there is a demand and a need for organised and effective management and preparation of the production and maintenance of improving sports performance.

SUMMARY

This chapter will have familiarised you with the following:

■ the questions that need to be answered to provide a conceptual appreciation of sports coaching;

■ examples of contemporary practice in sport that generate issues about sports coaching;

■ the central elements of a conceptual framework and how these can contribute to understanding coaching practice;

■ the important issue of the three-way relationship between athlete, performance and coach;

■ what is meant by theory and what sort of theory development can be expected in sports coaching;

■ the factors contributing to the lack of academic development in coaching theory and practice;

■ a commentary on the shortcomings of the literature on sports coaching in relation to the use of a conceptual framework or a contribution to its evolution;

■ a reminder that sport is a multifaceted practice and that sports coaching will find its fullest expression in performance sport contexts.

PROJECTS

■ Take five research articles dealing with sports coaching. Use the questions identified in the chapter to create a critical analysis of the concept of coaching employed or assumed by the authors.

■ Choose one element of the coaching conceptual framework (for example, expertise, role or effectiveness). Explore the literature to compare the depth of understanding about this element with that in another profession.

■ Identify a contemporary sports development initiative. Examine the assumptions made about the contribution of sports coaching to the initiative and highlight any problematic issues.

Reading

There is no substantive reading in this area – remember that it was the dearth of attention to conceptual development in sports coaching that was the catalyst for the book. Some useful background reading can be found in Lyle (1996,1999a), Sherman *et al.* (1997), Abraham and Collins (1998) and Potrac *et al.* (2000).

CHAPTER THREE

▼   THE COACHING PROCESS

- Introduction   35
- A Definition of Coaching   38
- Definitions   40
- Coaching as a Process   43
- Boundary Markers   46
- Process Skills   50
- Participation and Performance Coaching   52
- Summary   57
- Projects and Reading   58

INTRODUCTION

This chapter deals with the question of what coaching is about and what makes it distinctive from other roles. This may appear to be a rather unnecessary deliberation over what might turn out to be quite small differences in role or purpose. However, there have been significant inter-role and intra-role confusions. The ambiguity between teaching and coaching roles is a good example, as is the interpretation in some sports of the coach's sole purpose as technique and tactics specialist. The question of boundary markers is a key part of the conceptual framework for which arguments were presented in the previous chapter. In fact, the rationale for clarifying the precise nature of coaching is very similar to that outlined in Chapter 2.

The following statements point to the need to define very precisely what is meant by sports coaching:

- There is a tremendous range of sport leadership roles. The terms 'coaching', 'instructing', 'leading', 'teaching' and 'training' have been used somewhat indiscriminately. In fact, these roles are largely defined by the participants' intentions and, therefore, the demands of the situation, rather than the capacity and competence of the individual leader. This distinction between the person and the role is one that will be explored in greater depth.

- Although there is a generic concept called the 'coaching process', common sense tells us that this process will not be equally applicable in all circumstances. A key question, therefore, is, when are the circumstances appropriate to the coaching process? This is not an issue of status or mere terminology. The boundary balance between expectations, accountability, skills, knowledge and planning, and the demands and potential of the context is an important one.
- The matching of individuals' capacities to the needs of the situation has a number of practical implications. Employment, recruitment and selection should be determined by the correspondence between the coach's abilities and qualities, and those required by the 'job'. The boundary markers indicate the likely demands of the job and the education, training, and perhaps value system, required to fulfil that role.
- The role of academic enquiry should not be overlooked here. All professions have a healthy regard for the substance and scope of their business and it is legitimate to seek clarity of purpose and to chart developments in the field. The setting of boundary markers is part of the professionalisation of the coaching enterprise.

The following questions illustrate some of the developmental issues that the emerging profession of coaching would wish to clarify:

1   If it is accepted that there are different sport leadership roles, is there transferability between roles and is there a progression from one to another? Should we be trying first to recruit coaches into 'participation' coaching, or is the pathway into 'performance' coaching a quite specific one?
2   Is there sufficient commonality of purpose among all who are currently termed coaches to justify one form of membership of a professional body or should there be several categories (or several professional bodies)?
3   Professions are served by a range of products and services, including the expertise of other specialists as required. Much of this involves technical services, but would also include continuing professional development, training aids, software products, insurance services, current awareness services and so on. Is there currently a complementarity between the specific needs of each group of professionals and these services?

There is a final point to be made about identifying and clarifying the nature of the coaching role and the coaching process. A simple definition will not be sufficient to provide the operational clarity required. There is a need to explore in some depth the concept and meaning of sports coaching in order to interpret and evaluate practice and to guide further development. Conceptual clarity leads to operational clarity.

All human endeavour is imbued with meaning: sets of values are shared or disputed. These values are related to questions of 'should' or 'ought'. In other words, there will be many ways of operationalising the coaching process and many standards by which to make judgements about them. Two separate questions arise, therefore. First, what is coaching about and how do you know that it is sports coaching? The second question is, how are we to make sense of the varieties of practice? For example, are there any guidelines with which to understand how coaching practice is related to particular sets of contexts, purposes, ethical standards and personal idiosyncrasies? How generic is the process and to what extent is this process influenced by the sport to which it is applied?

Question Box

The search for commonality and genericism takes place in the context of considerable sport-specific differences and the unusual situation of coaches competing with one another. Is there sufficient commonality in the role to justify the search?

The answers to these questions have shaped the content of the chapters that follow. However, before exploring the boundaries of coaching in more depth, a short rationale for attending to teaching–coaching differences is presented. This acts as an exemplar of inter-role confusion and justifies the need for the conceptual clarification that follows.

Coaching–Teaching Similarities

The failure to distinguish satisfactorily between teaching and coaching can be demonstrated in three ways: (1) the extensive reliance in the literature on dual role teacher-coaches in North America (see Laughlin and Laughlin 1994); (2) the emphasis on episodic/sessional interpretations of the coaching role; and (3) the use of 'teaching' tasks in coaching research (Lyle 1998a).

The impact of this conflation and an emphasis on the teaching 'model' has been pervasive in coach education and in stereotyping the coaching role. Process characteristics and the management of performance have been undervalued in favour of a skills teaching model of coaching (see Sherman *et al.* 1997).

There has been a steady stream of papers on the theme of teacher–coach differences (Figone 1994; Chelladurai and Kuga 1996; Donovan 1997; Schempp 1997; Hardin 1999; Drewe 2000a). Chelladurai and Kuga (1996) note that schoolteachers are likely to have more attitudinal and attentional problems. Jones *et al.* (1997) were not surprised to find similarities between teaching and coaching behaviours since they both 'taught fundamental motor skills to small groups of relatively young and inexperienced children in laboratory settings' (1997: 456). This, of course, is an entirely inadequate interpretation of the coaching role and reinforces the above comments about research design.

The most important trend to emerge in research has been the adoption and adaptation of teaching observation instruments for coaching research (Abraham and Collins 1998), which has again reinforced the behavioural episode interpretation of coaching. The majority of papers have pointed to the motor skills commonality, although many have suggested a difference in value frameworks between the roles (Drewe 2000a).

A DEFINITION OF COACHING

Having recognised that a short, pithy, catch-all statement will not suffice, it will be valuable to reflect on the characteristics of a 'definitional framework'. This framework should offer:

Discrimination: This is the primary purpose of the definitional framework. It must delineate the boundary markers in sufficient detail to demonstrate how coaching differs from other roles.

Criticality: The framework will identify the features that must be present in the process or circumstances to fulfil the definition. Criteria will be identified.

Substance: This is where the detail of the definition provides some operational guidance. The vocabulary used is a map for the key elements of coaching.

Expertise: The definitional framework should be obviously applicable to the practice of expert coaches.

Applicability: The usefulness of the framework is that it can be translated into criteria that are precise and obvious in practice. On the other hand, there needs to be sufficient flexibility to permit a measure of interpretation, while retaining discrimination.

This is a demanding set of requirements. However, with any phenomenon, we might begin to 'flesh out' the framework by answering a few key questions: what is the central purpose, which are the essential features, who would it apply to, and where would it be found?

Rationale

Sports coaching centres on the improvement of an individual's or team's sporting ability, both as a general capacity and as specific performances. The improvement is purposeful and stable, and not reflective solely of chance or maturation. The stability of improvement and the specificity of the preparation reduce the unpredictability of performance.

Method

Performance objectives are achieved by influencing, either directly or indirectly, the factors that affect performance. These performance variables are manipulated and co-ordinated within an intervention programme characterised by competition and preparation units.

Role

The role of the coach is to direct and manage the process that leads to the achievement of identified (and normally agreed) goals. This involves the integration of the performer's aspirations and abilities, the goals identified, the external environment and the necessary intervention programme. 'Co-ordination' and 'integration' are key words.

Constituent parts

These are defined by the rationale and method. Therefore, the substance of the coaching process will embrace the performer, the coach, the form, nature and extent of the relationship between them, the intervention programme, the sporting performance, and the context. Each of these elements is interdependent and has many sub-elements.

Frame of reference

In the context of this conceptual analysis, sport is assumed to be essentially competitive in nature and is to be found in the organised and institutionally recognised structures and agencies that have been developed within particular sports. Improved performance becomes evident by achievement within recognised forms of competition, but the scope of coaching involves all training and preparation contexts, and is not restricted solely to the highest levels of performance.

Terminology

There are a number of terms that need to be clarified in order to provide a consistent vocabulary and interpretation with which to analyse and understand sports coaching. The most obvious starting point is to distinguish between coaching and the coach. This may seem rather obvious or even unnecessary but coaching research has often treated the coach as unproblematic and research into coaches has often failed to contextualise the sample population.

The general position adopted here is that it is much less useful to focus on the individual than on the role characteristics adopted by that individual. The terminology should not concern us unduly – it is not what individuals are called but what role they fulfil that is important. Of course, this in no way disparages appropriate research on coaches, for example, describing and analysing occupational circumstances or personal characteristics. However, in these cases, the coaching role must be clearly specified. To say that someone is a coach describes *either* an occupational grouping or professional position (including voluntary roles) *or* an assumed capacity.

The occupational category is not helpful unless accompanied by a more specific role descriptor. (Compare this to describing someone as an engineer, a technician or a scientist. Only the broadest of expectations can be attributed to the category and it does not generate the operational clarity specified earlier.) However, the 'assumed capacity' may be helpful if it describes a minimum set of attributes or skills, although this assumption can only be made if there is an agreed accreditation and licensing system on which to rely.

DEFINITIONS

The coaching process

The use of the term 'the coaching process' implies both the contract or understanding which is entered into by the athlete(s) and coach, and the operationalisation of that agreement.

1   The arrangement will be different and distinctive in all cases and is determined by the organisational setting, the performer's aspirations and commitment, and the coach's contractual obligations. It becomes manifest in the role responsibilities, expectations and accountabilities of both the athlete and the coach.

2   The operationalisation consists of the purposeful, direct and indirect, formal and informal series of activities and interventions designed to improve competition performance. The most evident part of the process is normally a planned, co-ordinated and integrated programme of preparation and competition. This is devised by the coach and the athlete(s), although the balance of responsibilities will be determined by the nature of the agreement between them. The overall implementation of the process is the responsibility of the coach, although this may involve a significant group of other specialists.

 Critical Concept

The coaching process is the contract/agreement between athlete and coach and the operationalisation consists of the purposeful, direct and indirect, formal and informal series of activities and interventions designed to improve competition performance. The most evident part of the process is normally a planned, co-ordinated and integrated programme of preparation and competition.

A sports coach

A sports coach fulfils a leadership role within sport, which is characterised by goals based on improved sports performance. There are many coaching roles but the most useful distinction is between the *participation sports coach* and the *performance sports coach*. The appropriateness of the term 'coach' is measured by the scope and scale of the coaching process.

Coaching practice

Coaching practice refers to the full range of behaviours, activities, interactions, processes, individuals and organisational functions that result from the operationalisation of the coaching role and the coaching process.

These are the most important definitions. However, some clarification is required on the use of other, related terminology. These terms are less central to the definitional framework but reflect common usage.

Coaching (used as a noun:
'The basketball team needs some extra coaching.')

It is not helpful to use the term in this way because it implies an isolated 'session' or 'episode'. Common usage of the noun would suggest a specialist or expert input normally based on previously identified technique, tactical or physical training. A more precise description of the input would be helpful for identifying the appropriate expectations from such a session. Remember, of course, that the phrase 'I will be coaching at the track tonight' merely describes the 'act of being a coach' and is too general to assist the definitional framework.

To coach (used as a verb:
'I have been asked to coach the local hockey team' or
'May I have permission to video you when you are coaching?')

The first of these is simply a shorthand way of describing the contract or agreement between the coach and the hockey team. However, the second is more problematical. 'To coach' is to carry out the role of a coach and not simply the delivery aspect of the role. Nevertheless, in common usage the phrase has become synonymous with the physical act of directing a training session or managing a competition episode. This has been very unfortunate because it has reinforced the assumption that coaching is a practical act and has highlighted a particular set of delivery skills. In turn, this has undervalued the less public (but perhaps more important) cognitive, planning and personal interactions that characterise the coaching process.

Having attempted to describe an appropriate terminology to assist the conceptual framework, it is now necessary to explore in more detail what is meant by the coaching process and what the boundary markers might be. Before doing so, there is a short case example that examines the lessons to be learned from the concept of coaching as it is used in other spheres (derived from Lyle 1997a).

It is not unusual to hear actors speaking about their 'voice coach'. Similarly, the term 'coach' is common in drama, poetry and music. The use of the coach to prepare artistes for performances suggests the potential for a generic coaching process and, therefore, for some transfer of principles and practice. The coaching of individuals has a traditional place in industrial training and is current in management practice.

Assisting novices or beginners to improve their craft skills has always been a feature of industrial practice. This is the basis of situated learning (Lave and Wenger 1991) or the apprenticeship process. As the practice of training in industry has become rather more of a structured process and has been given a higher priority, so the coaching role has been recognised. In an earlier text, Jinks (1979) identified the role as that of 'training a subordinate to improve performance' and portrayed the role of the coach as a directive one. More recently, Torrington and Weightman (1994) differentiated between the trainer, as an individual engaged with someone who is learning a new skill, and the coach, concerned to improve the performance of a worker who is already competent. At this stage these roles seem fairly narrow and restricted to manufacturing and craft-based skills. However, the development of a management ethos that was more humanistic or person-orientated began to encourage the incorporation of an element of counselling into the coaching role. This was directed towards the realisation of an individual's developmental potential and brought new purpose to the 'training' function.

The emphasis on realising human potential and empowering individuals complemented and characterised the expansion of coaching as a management tool. Mumford suggests that coaching was already recognised in the 1970s as the 'up and coming management tool' (1993: 152). In the literature of the 1980s and 1990s coaching skills become part of a range of techniques used to improve performance in the workplace: Philpott and Sheppard even describe them as 'core skills for performance management' (1992: 100). Although coaching remained linked to skill improvements, the philosophy of empowerment, participation and feedback reflected a more participative management approach. Mumford (1993) contrasted coaching, which he characterises as short-term, targeted, competence based and related to performance goals, to mentoring. His list of coaching skills – active listening, reflective listening, goal setting, recognising feelings, giving feedback, matching coaching style to the demands of the situation, and adapting to the needs of the learner – are all reflective of an approach to interpersonal relationships that will be demonstrated later to be common in writings about sports coaching.

Coaching has now also become established as a technique for training managers. The literature of the 1990s is characterised by references to the 'coaching' approach of top managers (such as Barry 1994; Bartlett and Ghoshal 1995; Tichy and Charan 1995). There is no doubt that this underlying approach is one that stresses individual training, self-determination, devolution of power and the setting of agreed performance targets. The skills training approach has given way to a more generic management style that recognises the value of one-to-one inspired learning. Nevertheless, a desire for commercial success has emphasised the value of effective strategies for managing human resources (Beech and Brockbank 1999).

What of mentoring? This can be defined as work-based training under the guidance of an experienced and expert practitioner. Such a definition demonstrates a very close affinity with coaching. Pegg (1999) identifies coaching as one of seven mentoring roles. On the other hand, Veenman *et al.* (1998) suggest that mentoring is a forerunner to a more advanced role – that of coaching. The issues raised in the mentoring literature will be familiar to students of coaching: empowerment (Conway 1998; Brockbank and Beech 1999), moving from novice to expert (Maynard and Furlong 1995), two-way communication (Jones *et al.* 1997a), the commitment of the mentor (Reid and Jones 1997), and the need for a bond between mentor and trainee (Mawer 1996). The key distinction between mentoring and sports coaching is that the mentor is a practitioner expert in the role being learned. The sports coach is often a former sportsperson but, although this may be advantageous, it is not essential and the coaching role is less craft based. Nevertheless, the mentoring role becomes important in coach education where learning from more experienced and expert coaches is a valuable process.

Question Box

Does the ambiguity between the roles of mentor and coach raise the possibility that the term 'a sport mentor' is a better term for the holistic role of the coach, perhaps leaving the coaching role to performance enhancement?

Although there are obvious parallels in the way that coaching in industry, business and management is related to performance improvement, we should not try to make too much of the comparison. Whereas coaching as a management tool is a means to an end and is one of a number of roles exercised by a manager, sports coaching is rather more centrally concerned with the performance itself and, indeed, the coach is most often part of the execution of the performance. Despite this, the effect of a person-centred approach, a recognition of the potential variation in coaching methods or style (developmental, mentoring, educational, confrontational and so on), and the acknowledgement of coaching as a process rather than an event are useful comparisons.

The final part of this brief exploration of the relationship between management and coaching reports on some research into the use by management training products of the sports coaching analogy. Lyle (1997a) carried out a content analysis of six management training products – two in-house management training manuals, two textbooks, one video series, and one management training seminar. All were selected because they explicitly used the sports coaching analogy as a promotional or delivery device. The findings demonstrated that (1) there were a number of points of similarity between the coaching roles in management and sport in terms of overall objectives and principal functions, (2) there was little evidence of 'borrowing' from sports coaching, other than by recourse to sweeping generalisations, and (3) there is a very clear 'human relations' model employed throughout the products. The sport analogy was used to contextualise the training product and to establish a point of contact for the trainee.

COACHING AS A PROCESS

The literature has come to accept that coaching should be treated as a co-ordinated and integrated process (Woodman 1993; Lyle 1996; Abraham and Collins 1998; Cross and Lyle 1999a) rather than as an unsystematic aggregation of isolated training episodes. There are significant implications from treating coaching as a process, the most important of which are that the relative priorities of skills and function areas become process-driven. There has been relatively little research emphasis on the process elements of sports coaching (see Lyle 1996) but this perhaps reflects the absence of a suitable conceptual framework rather than any serious dispute over the serial nature of coaching. Comment has also been made about a reliance on the observable behaviour of coaches and this has served to emphasise the episodic rather than an extended and integrated time-line nature of coaching.

The first stage is to match the generic aspects of a process with the characteristics of sports coaching that have previously been identified. Figure 3.1 demonstrates the relationship between process characteristics and coaching practice.

The inference to be drawn from Figure 3.1 is that there can be some confidence in describing sports coaching as a process. This confirms the previous assertion that the term 'the coaching process' is the most appropriate one to use when describing the purposeful engagement of the athlete and the coach for the purpose of improving performance. Note, however, that conceptual clarity appears to strip the process of its human, social and emotional character. Identifying the essential elements of the coaching process is important for the development of the conceptual framework, but it should be remembered that the actual engagement of the athlete(s) and the coaches is an extended period of social activity, commitment, success and failure, emotional highs and lows, interaction within organisations, personal ambition and status, personal cost and achievement, and a mix of short-, medium- and long-term satisfaction and enjoyment. This human element in recognised and explored in subsequent chapters.

 Critical Concept

Conceptual clarity need not deny the human, social and emotional character of the coaching process. Identifying the essential elements of the coaching process is important for the development of the conceptual framework, but it should be remembered that the actual engagement of the athlete(s) and the coache(s) is an extended period of social activity, commitment, success and failure, emotional highs and lows, interaction within organisations, personal ambition and status, personal cost and achievement, and a mix of short-, medium- and long-term satisfaction and enjoyment.

Insofar as the intentions and circumstances of the athlete(s) and coach(es) satisfy the criteria of the purpose and rationale of coaching, they become engaged in a co-ordinated, integrated and serial process, which is focused on the achievement of sport performance goals. This recognition of coaching as a process is important because it highlights two key issues: the boundaries of the process, and the skills that are particular to that process.

 Question Box

The failure to acknowledge sport as a process is perhaps the most limiting aspect of coaching research. However, is the purposeful aggregation of a series of coaching interventions sometimes challenged by practice in team sports?

Process characteristic	Coaching element	Coaching practice
Multivariable; Interdependence	Performance	Sport performance is a complex display of physical, technical, tactical, psychological, and emotional elements. Performance is influenced by genetic disposition, learned behaviour, and environmental factors, including the opponents.
Multivariable; Interdependence	Intervention programme	The intervention programme reflects the interdependence of performance. Technical, tactical, physical and psychological components of training affect each other.
Multivariable; Interdependence	Athlete Coach	Sports coaching is a human endeavour with significant element of interpersonal behaviour. The vagaries of human emotional behaviour add to the multivariable nature of the process. This is made more complex by the coach and athlete's social circumstances.
Incremental	Improvement profile	The limitations of the human organism and the difficulty of simultaneous and stable improvements in contributory components of performance result in incremental progress. Training principles and sub-discipline knowledge confirm that an extended serial process is required to bring about stable performance improvements.
Principled ordering	Training schedules	Sport sciences, training theory principles and common practice demonstrate that there is a necessary ordering of preparation and competition units to achieve effective improvement. This is evident in the training unit and over an extended planning period.
Specified objectives	Competition achievement	The planning process, the specificity of goal setting and the sport competition programme ensure that each process has targeted, albeit multifaceted objectives.
Instrumentality	Competition achievement	The coaching process is not (normally) an end in itself. The coaching process is a means to an end (individual or organisational aspirations).
Planned	Planning	The interdependence of variables, the cyclical nature of the competition programme, and the aggregative effect of component improvements make planning a necessity. This is compounded by the need to react contingently to the changing environment.
Regulation	Monitoring	The process nature of sports coaching emphasises planning, monitoring and regulating. Coaching practice is characterised by data gathering, testing, profiling and target setting.

Figure 3.1 *Process characteristics and coaching practice*

BOUNDARY MARKERS

The arguments presented thus far imply that an understanding of coaching practice, expectations and accountability are dependent on whether or not the minimum requirements for a coaching process are being fulfilled. Figure 3.2 identifies a set of criteria for making such a judgement.

1   These criteria are dictated by an interplay of performance improvement principles and the sporting context.
2   They have to be interpolated from the assumptions about the coaching process already identified.
3   They presume a sufficiency of rational effort to bring about effective and efficient performance improvements.
4   To some extent, these criteria are 'setting an agenda' for research and debate.

Figure 3.2 demonstrates that the criteria that set the limits to the coaching process will be determined by quite basic features of (any) process, for example, the extended timeline, an intervention to bring about change, and identifiable inputs and outputs. However, the specificity of the process is the requirement to bring about a stable change in sport performance capacity and it is this purpose that requires these particular boundary criteria.

Having set out this list of boundary markers, it is reasonable to ask whether, in implementation, this demanding list of criteria need to be satisfied fully, and what the implications would be of a coaching contract that did not match these rather strict criteria. The following series of statements expands on the implications of implementing the criteria.

■   Building a conceptual framework can result in a rather idealised set of concepts, and these criteria of the coaching process describe a quite specific and demanding type of engagement between athlete(s) and coach. The coaching practice of many coaches will not meet these criteria, but it would be too simplistic to judge them as 'therefore, not coaching'.
■   A more helpful position is to acknowledge the criteria as very useful for analysis purposes, but to recognise that the idealised context may not always be possible or appropriate. The picture painted here is of full-time athletes operating with a full-time coach and in constraint-free circumstances. It seems likely that many coaching processes will certainly be based on these principles but may not match them in practice.
■   The critical factor is to match output expectations from the coaching process to the degree to which they satisfy these criteria. Reduced expectations will result from a truncated coaching process. It may be worth stressing at this point that the value

 Critical Concept

Output expectations from the coaching process should be matched to the degree to which they satisfy boundary criteria. Reduced expectations will result from a truncated coaching process.

Boundary marker	Boundary criterion	Rationale
Obligation	Stability of personnel	The long-term and serial nature of the process, the intensity requirements of training principles, the establishing of interpersonal relationships and stability of goals depend on a stable group of actors.
Obligation	Continuity of engagement	The objective of improvements in stability of performance requires maintenance of engagement in the process. This is exacerbated in team sports where lack of continuity would be likely to impact on social and tactical cohesion.
Scale	Extended time period	Performance goals, competition programmes and performance improvement increments are dependent on cyclical planning that is medium- to long-term in nature.
Scale	Frequency and duration of engagement	The improvement of performance components require an intensity of engagement that is reflected in the total time-span to which the actors are committed.
Purpose	Commitment to a goal-orientated instrumental relationship	(Notwithstanding any immediacy of satisfactions/ enjoyment) the actors are committed to a process in which the delayed gratification of overall goal achievement is dependent on an accumulation of constituent parts.
Purpose; Nature	(Attempted) control of variables	The multivariable nature of both performance and the intervention programme means that optimum improvement is dependent on controlling all of the variables that impact of performance. This is manifest in life-style management and the scale of the process. Limited control implies more limited achievement.
Intervention	Planned progression	The improvement objective requires progression in workloads. This is not simply a matter of scale but implies record keeping, testing and monitoring.
Specificity	Individualisation	Performance improvements are constrained by the abilities and capacities of the individual athlete. The component parts of the coaching process should be tailored to individual needs for optimum effect. This may be more complicated in team sports.

Figure 3.2 *Boundary markers for the coaching process in sport*

of this exercise is that analysis and understanding of coaching practice is greatly enhanced: it is not an exercise to evaluate coaches.

■ There will be some common reasons for a truncated process:

1 The reward environment available to athletes may not be sufficient to justify an intensive commitment to training and preparation time. Thus, athletes who are able to train two or three times per week will make less progress to performance goals.

2   Team sport personnel may change quite significantly during competition programmes and a continuous progression in workloads may not be appropriate with league sports.

3   Athletes who are in employment will have less flexibility in scheduling training sessions and the demands of employment or studying will impinge on life-style control factors.

4   Resource limitations may influence total training time durations, access to sport science assistance and the desired competition programme.

5   Continuity of engagement will be broken by regular occurrences such as long-term illness or injury.

■   Particular attention should be given to team sports (implying those involved in protracted competitions). The coaching process in these circumstances often appears to be 'untidy'. Short- and long-term injury disruption is common, changes in personnel may also occur, performance targets are often aspirational rather than specific, maintenance rather than improvement is a common target, individualisation may be difficult, and performance outputs and outcomes are not easily measured because of their relative, not absolute, values. This is discussed later, in the section on systematic coaching practice, but it does point the way to differentiating between these sports and sports based on individual technique or power output.

■   Most of these criteria are easily measured but the threshold values are not a simple matter of quantification. What is an extended time period or sufficiently frequent preparation? Even more difficult is the qualitative judgement about control of variables or commitment to a competition goal. Although sport science may be able to provide some of the answers to the thresholds for physical conditioning, many of the criteria may be relative to a particular set of circumstances and need to be understood in that context. There is a clear role for research here. There needs to be a body of knowledge that links the parameters of the coaching process to the outcomes achieved. These principles may never be translated into statistical guidelines but analysis and understanding of coaching practice will be incomplete without an acknowledgement of the relationship between the scope and scale of the coaching process and the resultant outputs.

 Question Box

There is no doubt that the boundary criteria are important. Are they more important as concepts or is quantification necessary?

■   To facilitate understanding, it is possible to create a simple typology of coaching contexts (see Figure 3.3), in which the application of the boundary markers will be varied by the circumstances of the coaching contract. The most striking of the differences is that between the participation sports coach and the performance sports coach. This is given much more attention later in the chapter.

WHAT IS COACHING ABOUT?

Category	Participant profile	Competition profile	Deployment characteristics	Boundary notes
Sport teacher	No long-term commitment; no permanent relationship with the coach; irregular attendance	No competition external to the programme	Sport development schemes; sports centre classes; physical education; play schemes	The teacher attempts to improve performance but with short-term goals. The scale of the process is limited.
Participation coach	Involvement irregular; formal organisation but loose membership; some improvement objectives but participation emphasised over practice	Competition involvement, but unlikely to be at a high level	Leadership/ organisational roles; recreation sport context	Little formal progression in a very limited preparation programme. Short-term goals. Intensity low even if long-term involvement. Not all performance components given attention.
Performance coach	Increasing commitment; stable relationship with coach; specific competition objectives; commitment to preparation	Formal competition structures	Club/squad coaches; contractual arrangements and full-time posts more likely; administrative and other non-intervention duties increase	Full to partial implementation of the coaching process. Most boundary marker thresholds reached.
Representative team/group coach	High level of commitment; performance objectives are more public; less permanent relationship between coach and athletes	Formal competition, likely to be at a high standard	National team/squad coaches; area/regional coaches	Not necessarily operating at a higher level than the club coach. Truncated coaching process: emphasis on some performance components, with often more limited preparation programme.

Figure 3.3 *A typology of sport leadership roles and organisational contexts*

PROCESS SKILLS

Identifying the skills required by the coach is a key feature of coach education, recruitment and personal development. It is also necessary for modelling the coaching process and analysing practice. Coaching skills are highlighted at this point because an acknowledgement of coaching as a process has implications for the identification of these key skills. On a number of occasions reference has been made to craft skills, sport-specific skills and process skills. It is now necessary to integrate these into the developing conceptual framework. The key linkage is the existence of a process, which is a justification for the constituent functions and their associated skills. The coaching process was characterised as being planned, serial, progressive, multivariable and integrated. It follows from this that the skills necessary to plan, implement and sustain the process will be crucial. These are identified in Figure 3.4.

Figure 3.4 is not intended to model the coaching process itself but merely to illustrate the coaching skills involved. The coaching process is characterised by three sets of skills: planning, delivery and management. The delivery element refers to the direct intervention programme between athlete and coach. Delivery can usefully be subdivided

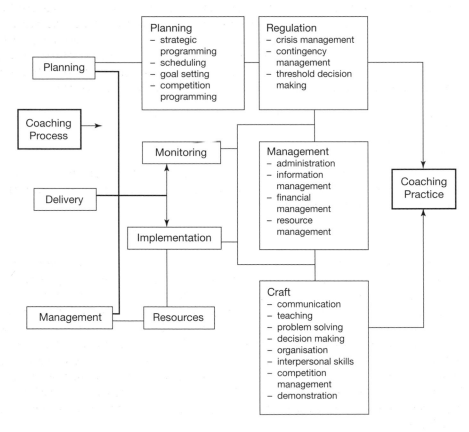

Figure 3.4 *Coaching process skills*

into implementation, monitoring and regulation. Implementation consists of a series of craft-based skills. Craft and regulation skills are facilitated by management skills. The regulation element is important because it feeds into both the planning element and the ongoing delivery. Accompanying the delivery is a management function that deals with the resources available – both human and material.

There are a number of significant issues for analysis, education and professional development that arise from this consideration of coaching process skills:

- Delivery skills are only one group of essential skills, albeit very important.
- Indirect skills (those not involving the delivery of performance-based workloads) are very important – planning, monitoring and regulating the process.
- Management skills will be necessary to maintain the process – financial, personnel and resource. The scale of the management function will differ with the scale and scope of the process.
- The skills identified are required to engage in the coaching process. However, this does not imply that each of these functions and skills must be implemented by the coach. At a later stage, the coach's role in co-ordinating the contributions of assistant coaches, support personnel and managers will be considered. It does seem likely, however, that the coach being required to co-ordinate, deliver and manage the complete process may well be a limiting factor to effective and efficient delivery.
- Sport specificity and a partially applied coaching process will influence the priorities in coaching skills. Coaches in situations in which the episodic nature of the process is emphasised will rely more on delivery and contingency planning skills. In some sports the impact of competition management skills will be quite marked.

Question Box

The diversity of skills required by the coach is considerable. This suggests that coach education should be 'skills based'. Are some skills more important than others at each stage of professional development?

One of the emerging features of the conceptual framework is that the comparison between the rather more idealised, conceptual representation of the coaching process and coaching practice will become increasingly contingent on a range of context-related factors. This is to be expected. The focus on the nature and purpose of coaching is complemented in subsequent chapters by an emphasis on practice-driven behaviour and the social context. Remember that the purpose of developing the conceptual framework is that it provides the means for an analysis that goes beyond mere description and the immediacy of the context. The capacity to base judgements of accountability and performance (including job security) on a judicious blend of individual contribution, principle and context should be the hallmark of professional behaviour and evaluations of effectiveness.

To end this section it is important to reinforce an earlier comment that the coaching process is different from other sport leadership roles and not simply a sophisticated or advanced form. Put another way, a truncated or partially applied coaching process is just that and does not become an instructional, recreational or teaching process. Having said that, any sport leadership process that has performance improvement as a goal can be usefully evaluated for its effectiveness on the basis of its application of the boundary criteria of the coaching process. This will become clearer with an exploration of the distinctions between participation and performance coaching.

 Critical Concept

The coaching process is different from other sport leadership roles and not simply a sophisticated or advanced form. Put another way, a truncated or partially applied coaching process is just that and does not become an instructional, recreational or teaching process.

PARTICIPATION AND PERFORMANCE COACHING

In an earlier diagram, a distinction was drawn between general groups of coaching roles in order to demonstrate that the coaching process was likely to be partially and differentially applied. The conceptual framework of sports coaching concepts becomes very much clearer if two distinct forms of coaching are recognised: sports participation coaching and sports performance coaching.

Reference has already been made to the assertion that participation and performance coaching are two distinct forms of coaching and not two points on a continuum. This has implications for recruitment and education and training.

Common sense suggests that the demands of performance coaching, since they are based on the 'fullest' application of the coaching process (fulfilling the greater number of boundary criteria), will be the most complex and could be regarded as the epitome of sports coaching. Nevertheless, the conceptual framework should display comprehensiveness in addition to precision, and for that reason it is important that the framework offers an explanation for all forms of coaching behaviour and coaching roles.

The terms 'coach' and 'coaching' are used in a wide variety of circumstances. For example, it would not be unusual for the terms to be applied in the following circumstances:

- schoolteachers working with school sports teams;
- soccer academy coaches working with players for one session per week and during school holidays;
- those directing instructional classes in local sports centres;
- instructors in ski schools;
- coaches operating with young beginner groups in gymnastics or athletics clubs;
- teaching professionals in golf clubs;

- representative team coaches in age-group rugby or soccer;
- local authority swimming programme teachers;
- those who select and organise teams, in circumstances in which there is minimal or no specific preparation for competition;
- coaches delivering TOPS or Champion Coaching programmes.

These examples have been chosen because they have several characteristics in common: there is an intention to improve sports performance, and there is an element of sports teaching. However, there is also a more limited intensity of involvement and often there is no specific competition preparation. It is also important to remember that, in some circumstances, a partial application of the coaching process would be anticipated. Those who are representative team coaches and whose players normally operate on a day-to-day basis with their club sides will have a truncated coaching process.

Despite the enormous variety of circumstances for which the term 'coaching' might be used, the relationship between the criteria can be expressed in a simple diagram (see Figure 3.5) that brings together the nature of the contract, the performer's aspirations, involvement in recognised competition structures and the performer's development stages.

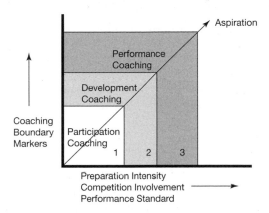

1 *Participation Coaching*: This is largely to do with initiation into sport and with basic skills teaching. Some individuals, usually young people with greater levels of potential, will move quite quickly through this stage. Others will become more recreational or casual participants, often as they move into adulthood.
2 *Developmental Coaching*: This is characterised by rapid skills learning and a developing engagement with a sport-specific competition programme. This is a key stage for talent identification. This stage is almost exclusively for younger persons in age-group sport who are accelerating their way though the performance standards. (Later it will be argued that 'instructors of adult sportspersons' who wish to improve but who do not satisfy the boundary criteria – golf instruction comes to mind – should be included in this category.)
3 *Performance Coaching*: Performers and circumstances come together to fulfil the majority of the coaching process boundary markers. It is characterised by relatively intensive preparation and involvement in competition sport. Can apply to all ages and levels of developed ability. There may be some special cases, such as representative team/group coaches.

Figure 3.5 *The relationship between forms of coaching and boundary criteria*

Although the conceptual framework is made more complicated to apply by the presence of a developmental middle ground, the most useful categorisation of coaching categories is into participation and performance coaching. For the moment, developmental coaching can be considered a subset of performance coaching, but with a number of the characteristics of participation coaching.

Participation sport coaching is distinctive because:

■ competition performance is not emphasised;
■ participants are less intensively engaged with the sport;
■ sport performance components are rarely given individual attention (e.g., physical condition, psychological training);
■ objectives are characterised by short-term horizons and immediate satisfactions;
■ there is more focus on individual sessions (episodic) than on an integrated, progressive process;
■ key skills are delivery based rather than planning based;
■ the 'coaching contract' is less distinctive;
■ in the context of these distinctive features, relatively few boundary thresholds of the coaching process are triggered.

Participation sports coaching is to be found in circumstances in which 'sports teaching' seems a more appropriate description. This implies that either there is no specific preparation for competition, or, alternatively, that participation in competition is not supported by an extensive preparation programme. Likely contexts involve teaching basic techniques to large groups of youngsters within a club, initiating beginners who are not yet committed to a sport, or organising recreational forms of activity. The most important conceptual issue is that there is almost no attempt to influence or control the variables that affect performance – either because of choice (performer commitment is limited) or appropriateness (developmental stage).

Question Box

Participation and performance coaching are not on a coaching process continuum – they are distinctive processes. On the other hand, the performers can generally be placed on a performance continuum. Is level of sport performance a better conceptualisation for coaching forms?

On the other hand, *performance sport coaching* is distinctive because:

■ there is a more intensive commitment to a preparation programme;
■ there is a more obvious attempt to influence/ control performance variables;
■ individual performance components are identified separately in the programme;
■ objectives are both long- and short-term, and specific competition goals are identified;
■ the intervention of the coach is integrated into an integrated and progressive process;
■ performers operate within recognised competition structures in their sport;

- although delivery skills are important, there is more emphasis on decision making and data management – recording, monitoring, planning and analysis;
- there is a more extensive interpersonal contact between coach and performer(s).

These characteristics mirror very closely a more idealised interpretation of the coaching process. Although it is understandable that this profile would match the coaching practice of those coaches who work with elite performers, this is not exclusively the case. There will be a broad spectrum of performers who share a commitment to the sport and who participate regularly, and with a training programme, in competition. Although the circumstances of their participation (like duration or frequency) may not always suggest that the benefits of a coaching process will be fully realised, this is undoubtedly performance sports coaching. Similarly, the fact that the relative performance standards of 'age-group' performers may be modest does not prevent a performance coaching process from being appropriate with young performers. (Nevertheless, it may be appropriate to think of a 'development' stage in which the intensity of the programme is not overemphasised and control of variables is ameliorated somewhat.)

Figure 3.5 illustrated the deceptive ease with which a continuum between the forms of coaching can be interpreted. It is undoubtedly the case that, in general, the standard of performance will improve as the performers' aspirations and capacities allow them to move through competition structures and levels. It is also the case that even the best performers will have spent some (usually accelerated) time going through beginner and developmental stages. Nevertheless, the form of coaching is very different in each set of circumstances and this raises a number of issues of matching individual coaches to needs:

- An individual may be able to operate within more than one form of coaching. It seems more likely that this will be feasible for the performance coach who wishes to operate in developmental or participation contexts.
- Given that the skills and knowledge demands differ within these forms of coaching, the individual coach may not have the necessary abilities to work with performers as their performance standard improves. There is a danger that a coach may wish to be associated with a developing athlete beyond the stage for which the available skills and knowledge are suitable. Deployment of coaches within a sport is, therefore, an important issue. Some coaches, particularly at the developmental stage, may be appropriately termed and deployed as 'transition coaches'.
- It may also be the case that those coaches with the skills, knowledge and experience to work with the most able performers (that is, those who match capacity to process requirements) should work with 'developmental' performers to ensure that those athletes with potential are not always operating with 'learner performance coaches'.
- Many individual coaches will wish to have the opportunity to progress as coaches and to achieve expert status. Further research is required on how performance coaches enter coaching roles and how they progress. One interesting feature of this will be whether performance coaches have started out as participation coaches or have made a transition from being performers themselves. There are obvious implications for coach recruitment and education.
- The most salient ramification of a participation coaching process or a partially applied performance coaching process is that the expectations of performance improvement

and competition success have to be modified to fit the scale and sophistication of the process. There are a number of instances in which there is a deliberate narrowing of the performance expectations from the process, and these need to be dealt with separately.

■ *The sports instructor*: this is a commonly accepted role in many, mostly individual sports. Golf, tennis and skiing instructors, for example, offer what might be more appropriately termed 'technique instruction'. The use of the term 'lesson' is quite illuminating here. This is not to denigrate what may, in fact, be a very sophisticated process, but it is clear that the full range and scope of the coaching process is not the intention. Improvement may be targeted at basic skills for the beginner or at skill refinement for the more advanced, and often elite, performer.

■ This specialised 'coaching' can also been seen in the specialised roles of coaches within the support structure of team sports. For example, individuals may be specialists in defence, goalkeeping or speed development. This is dealt with later in the 'role of the coach'.

■ Finally, to reiterate what has already been pointed out, representative team and group coaches may deal with high-level performers but the responsibility for the greater part of the coaching process may lie with club coaches. Given that there is a 'co-operative team approach' to this, the benefits of an integrated process will still be attainable. However, the accountability of the representative coach should be mitigated in such circumstances and the more common features of the process (such as tactical and psychological preparation) recognised.

To finish this section, here are a few key statements about these coaching categories:

1 Participation coaching is generally more episodic in orientation.
2 Life-style management (reflecting an intended control of variables) is characteristic of performance coaching with 'fast-track' performers and those already pursuing excellence.
3 Not only skills and knowledge will be specific to forms of coaching but also particular experience may be very significant.
4 It is not the individual coach who is key, but the nature of the coaching process required.

Despite what has been said, it is evident that these are broad categories and are useful for analysis purposes rather than precise or quantifiable definition. Figure 3.6 demonstrates how a chart might determine the balance of criteria between participation and performance coaching, when each is rated on a simple ten-point continuum.

WHAT IS COACHING ABOUT?

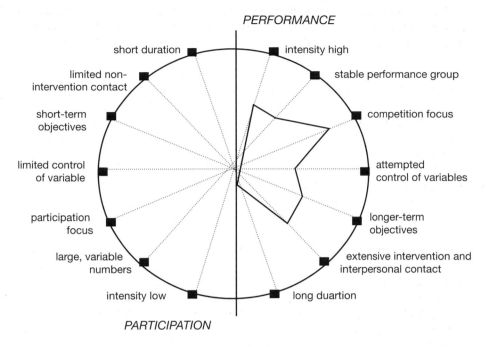

PERFORMANCE

intensity high
stable performance group
competition focus
attempted control of variables
longer-term objectives
extensive intervention and interpersonal contact
long duartion

PARTICIPATION

short duration
limited non-intervention contact
short-term objectives
limited control of variable
participation focus
large, variable numbers
intensity low

Note: The exemplar footprint shows a clear performance profile on a scale drawn between the pairs of criteria.

Figure 3.6 *A diagrammatic representation of the balance of performance and participation coaching roles*

SUMMARY

This chapter will have familiarised you with the following:

- the reasons for establishing conceptual clarity and some key questions about the coaching process;
- the nature of a definitional framework and elaboration on the essential features of sports coaching;
- definitions of the most important terms;
- an example of the coaching process in industry and management;
- a conceptualisation of sports coaching as a process and examples of the process elements applied to sports coaching;
- the boundary markers and criteria that delineate the sports coaching process, and the likely contexts and the implications of a partially applied coaching process;
- sports leadership roles with attendant process characteristics;
- the skills necessary for the coach as a result of implementing a process – planning, delivery and management;

the characteristics of, and differences between, participation, development and performance coaching. Some examples of practice associated with these distinctive roles.

PROJECTS

- Interview two coaches who work in both participation and performance contexts. Focus on perceived differences in coaching practice and then relate these to the coaching process.
- Devise a simple conceptual framework for coaching that conceives of the role as that of a performance mentor. What insights might this achieve?
- Use Figure 3.3 to prompt an investigation into organisational context; interview individuals in each category and compare the details of the typology to the findings.
- Interview six coaches to establish boundary markers. Attempt a qualitative and quantitative analysis, and add or subtract from the proposed criteria.
- Use and adapt Figure 3.6. Is this a useful method for profiling coaches?

Reading

This chapter moves well beyond the detail available in other sources. Lyle (1999a) provided a summary of the process approach and the content had begun to be explored in Lyle (1998c). For more in-depth summaries of specialised themes, read Lyle (1997a) on coaching and management and Lyle (1998a) on coaching and teaching.

CHAPTER FOUR

▼ **THE ROLE OF THE COACH**

- Introduction   59
- Role Concepts   61
- Purpose and Function   63
- Role Complementarity between Coaches and Support Personnel   67
- Organisational Impact on the Coach's Role   70
- The Uniqueness of the Coaching Role   72
- Summary   75
- Projects and Reading   76

INTRODUCTION

The development of the conceptual framework continues with an examination of the relationship between the individual (the coach) and the coaching process. This is termed 'the role of the coach' and can be expressed both as a matter of interpretation and as a matter of implementation. The nature of the coach's role can be divined from the basic purpose of sports coaching and from a consideration of what is necessary to put that role into practice. Insofar as this stage of conceptual development begins to take into account the context within which the athlete and coach are operating, an issue arises about the extent to which the role of the coach is context-specific. Certainly there has been relatively little sound academic work on the role of the coach. Partly, this is a result of an uncritical acceptance of the role of the coach within North American educational establishments, but also, to return to the theme of the book, an absence of a conceptual framework within which to express such an analysis. This lack of attention is a little surprising, since there has been an increase in the number of support staff operating within performance sport and the more sustained interest in performance standards and achievement has highlighted the issue of accountability. Each of these issues points to the role of the coach as a matter for fruitful investigation.

The use of simplistic role descriptors is a common approach in the early stages of coach education (Crisfield *et al*. 1996; Martens 1997). Aspirant coaches are informed that the coach should be a counsellor, scientist, motivator, friend, teacher and so forth. Although this points to the range of potential roles and highlights the complex nature of the coach's task, it does little to emphasise the intra-role and inter-role conflict and confusions that may arise. Even the inference that the individual coach should be able to move from role to role is one that deserves far more detailed attention.

'Role' will be conceptualised as the typical and expected range of behaviours and practice that results from the coach's interpretation of the part to be played by the coach in achieving the improved or sustained performance that is the purpose of sports coaching. This allows for an individual interpretation of role, but raises the question of whether there is a generic role that all coaches should, or do, fulfil. Therefore, to take a simple starting point, role needs to be considered in the context of (1) an 'essential' element, (2) the organisational dimension, and (3) the contributions of other relevant individuals. It is immediately obvious that the discussions of the previous chapter are very important. Boundary markers may play a considerable part in defining or delimiting the role, and the distinction between sports performance coaching and sports participation coaching is likely to impact on role behaviours.

 Critical Concept

'Role' will be conceptualised as the typical and expected range of behaviours and practice that results from the coach's interpretation of the part to be played by the coach in achieving the improved or sustained performance that is the purpose of sports coaching.

From this consideration of the issues involved, a number of questions can be identified that give shape to the remainder of the chapter:

1   In what way might the role of the coach be most usefully portrayed, so as to inform an analysis of practice?
2   What degree of freedom is available in the individual's interpretation and implementation of the role?
3   Which conceptual and practical issues arise from the relationship between the coaching role and that of others involved in contributing to the coaching process?
4   Is there a correlation between organisational structure and purpose and the role of the coach?

The argument to be developed in the chapter is that the role of the coach is the direction and control of the coaching process and all that that implies. This does not imply that the coach would or should implement all that is needed – but it does suggest that the primary function of the coach is to co-ordinate and integrate all of the inputs to the coaching process. The club coach, even in performance sport, may well find it necessary to perform most of the duties and responsibilities necessary. With more elite sport and larger-scale support teams, the coach may have a more specialised set of 'delivery responsibilities' (perhaps technique and tactical development, in addition to overall strategy). Nevertheless, the role of the coach is to provide the direction (perhaps the term 'management' would be appropriate) necessary for the strategic overview of the design and implementation of the coaching process.

 Critical Concept

The primary function of the coach is to co-ordinate and integrate all of the inputs to the coaching process.

To define the role of the coach in this way has implications for the role of the performer and the performer's contribution to the operationalisation of the coach's role. It is also obvious that it raises questions about relationships with performance directors, managers, sport scientists and others. There may not be agreement about the role of the coach, but what is essential is to be able to explain deviation from the role model and to be able to identify what this might mean for achieving optimum progress towards performance goals.

ROLE CONCEPTS

There is a set of commonly used concepts and terminology that is employed as a framework for most discussions about role. It would be valuable to review these before moving to their application to sports coaching.

Expectations accompany the execution of a particular role – expectations that are independent of the individual performing the role. This is the basis of a definition of role as *a pattern of behaviours or tasks individuals are expected to perform because of a particular position they hold*. The role of coach is an occupational role (even if conducted in a voluntary capacity) but one that is not constrained at the present time by a very rigid set of expectations.

An *assigned or ascribed role* generally refers to the pattern of behaviours associated with a set of relationships or hierarchical position within a formal organisation. The expectations of the assigned role are the *core expectations* circumscribed by the contract or shared assumptions attached to the role. In practice, the lack of clarity about boundary markers and the purpose of coaching has not provided sufficient guidance to devise a set of shared assumptions. A working hypothesis might be that inter-sport differences and situational factors have masked a common set of assigned role expectations.

The *achieved role* refers to the element of embellishment or additionality that the individual can bring to a role, beyond that of the core expectations. This will be a personal interpretation of the role but within the limits of the assigned role. In sports coaching the achieved role will be dependent on a mix of personal and situational factors. The range of specific sport behaviour patterns, the lack of agreement on the assigned role, and the formality (or informality) and scale of the organisational context have combined to place greater emphasis on the achieved role.

A role exists only in relation to other roles and helps to define the other roles. A *role-set* describes the family of roles that act together in a particular context or organisation. *Complementarity of roles* is achieved if there is a shared set of expectations within the role-set. The key role – other than for the coach – is the athlete (strange that few chapters are entitled 'The role of the athlete'!). This relationship is one that will be given very detailed attention throughout the book. Role conflict will be prevented if there is an agreement about the complementarity of the roles of athlete, manager, coach, parent, doctor, sport scientist, agent and so on. This also deserves further attention.

Role conflict takes a number of forms: (1) lack of complementarity in the role-set; (2) inter-role conflict resulting from the individual fulfilling two or more roles that have competing expectations; and (3) intra-role conflict, in which the demands within the role are incompatible. A potential lack of complementarity has already been identified in the athlete's support team. Inter-role conflict may arise if a coach attempts to fulfil responsibilities of a club coach and national team coach. The broad range of responsibilities within the coaching role means that intra-role conflict is common. Compare, for example, the incompatibility of acting as a counsellor and a selector, or of fulfilling an expectation to win with a demand to develop younger players.

Role ambiguity is the result of individuals not being aware of the demands or expectations of the role. One important issue here is how new professionals learn about (become socialised into) their roles. It would be wrong to overplay the 'uncertainty' element of the coaching role. Despite an apparent lack of commonality, individual coaches appear to have a firm grasp of anticipated patterns of behaviour within their sports. Perhaps the more important question is how they learned this. What part in their learning was played by coach education, by mentors, by copying traditional practice, or by their own experience as performers?

 Question Box

This role-related terminology can be applied to all complex occupational activities. Nevertheless, the role of the coach is problematical. Is it a matter of historical development, lack of occupational development or simply the vast array of situations within which athletes wish to improve their performances that causes the confusion?

These concepts will now be woven into a more detailed examination of the coaching role. This will be achieved by investigating the lessons to be learned about the coach's role from an examination of the purpose and function of sports coaching. The role of the coach in relation to other support team roles is considered, along with the effect of organisational constraints. The final section attempts to identify the uniqueness of the coaching role.

PURPOSE AND FUNCTION

One common approach is to focus on what is perceived as the most important aspect of the role. These are often short, pithy statements and are designed to convey an ideological position rather than a precise description or analysis of behaviour or practice. This is more about the purpose of sports coaching and less about particular behaviours. It is difficult to judge whether this is more relevant to the additionality of the achieved role or says something fundamental about the assigned role. Nevertheless, each statement will imply that one interpretation of what coaches are trying to achieve is the most important. For example, the following statements represent common approaches:

■ *The role of the coach is to become redundant.* This implies a developing sense of self-reliance and self-direction in the athlete and suggests an emphasis on a certain combination of coaching styles, leadership and interpersonal relationships.

■ *The coach's role is to mediate between the performer's goals and their achievement.* This suggests an emphasis on an 'objectives model' of planning, but also stresses the centrality of the athlete and the importance of goal setting.

■ *The role of the coach is to reduce the unpredictability of performance.* The message here is that the coach wishes to emphasise the part played by well-structured and informed preparation, by careful control of variables and by specific competition preparation.

The important point is not whether there is any consensus about such statements (this is unlikely) but whether or not these 'role statements' are a valuable part of the developing conceptual framework. Insofar as they represent more of an ideological position and a statement of values, it is necessary that they can be located in the section on the coach's values and their implications. However, they do not say enough about the coach's practice (even if we agree with them), and there is a need to construct a more detailed examination of the coaching role in order to provide an analytical tool.

Another approach is to attempt to subdivide the coach's role in relation to the implementation of the process. The general statement that role is about the relationship between the coach and the coaching process gives no clear guidelines about what this means in practice. For this, it is necessary to construct a conceptual diagram of the coach's functions. The general statement that the coach is responsible for the direction and co-ordination of the coaching process will be better understood if the role is divided into a number of subsidiary roles: direct intervention, intervention support, constraints management and strategic co-ordination. This is illustrated in Figure 4.1.

Direct intervention embraces the purposeful activities that are focused on performance enhancement. Obviously, the athlete is always involved in this and the coach will normally be present or involved. This activity is expressed as training sessions (including recovery), competitions, schedules, remedial activity and so on. The range of activities will vary from sport to sport but is extensive. The coach's behaviours will match the delivery aspect of the sub-role: including technical instruction, feedback, demonstration, rallying, observation, organisation and recording.

Intervention support refers to those coaching activities that support or prepare for the direct intervention. These are mostly carried out by the coach, although the athlete will

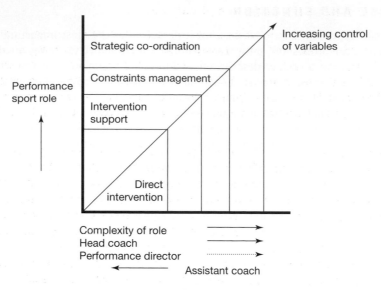

Figure 4.1 *The functional roles of the coach*

be involved to the extent that their agreement empowers. The most common activities are planning, administration, data management and counselling.

Constraints management is the coach's attempt to manage the situational factors to the best advantage of the athlete and the coaching process. This is done in two ways. First, the coach will incorporate the situational factors (such as training access, support services, competition schedules, funding, and availability of personnel and equipment) into the ongoing intervention programme – a form of contingency management. Second, the coach will attempt to influence positively the contextual features of the sport organisation and system that impact on the coaching process. This may involve recruitment issues, athlete support services, governing bodies, development plans, financial support, sponsorship matters and so on. The influence of the individual coach will be limited in some of these matters.

Strategic co-ordination is a specific function, which ensures a continuous overview of the progress of the coaching process in relation to the stated objectives. This involves a degree of strategic planning based on a process of monitoring and regulation, and judgements about inputs, progress and likely outcomes. This is the stage at which the interrelationship of variables identified in the coaching process needs to be recognised but gives the coach a particularly difficult job of evaluating and predicting the combined effects.

Subdividing the coach's role in this way provides an additional and very powerful analytical tool for understanding coaching practice. The relationship between the functions also furthers an understanding of coaching practice and the role(s) of the coach.

Using functional roles as an analytical tool

The degree of control exercised by the coach over the multitude of variables that influence performance development will be increased as the 'levels' of role are implemented. Thus the participation coach will emphasise only the direct intervention role, and this reflects the more limited attempt of the participation coach to control variables outside the contact activity. The variables are subjected to increased management as the coaching roles of intervention support, constraint management and strategic co-ordination are put into practice.

It is always necessary to return to the role of the performer in the process. Depending on the nature of the formal and informal contract between coach and athlete, the athlete's contribution to the coaching process may be quite extensive or fairly minimal. Later chapters will demonstrate how some coaching value structures place great emphasis on empowering athletes to become involved in the process, although empirical evidence on their preferences is somewhat ambivalent. One extreme version of this would be the athlete who is 'self-coached'. This implies that the athlete performs many if not all of the functions that would be exercised by the coach. What is interesting here is that, while the strategic and management roles can be fulfilled by knowledgeable, experienced and mature athletes, the prevalence of 'self-coached' athletes will be greater in those sports in which the direct intervention role is not complex (individual power/repetition-technique sports). However, greater use of support personnel and video observation may extend this possibility.

The relative balance of emphasis between the functional roles is a potentially very useful tool for cataloguing and analysing coaches' behaviour. It also gives a potential for comparative studies. With such a tool, it would be possible to address untapped (but seemingly obvious) research questions:

- Is there a greater emphasis on intervention support with elite athletes?
- Is the balance of functional roles different for team sports and individual sports?
- Is the balance of functional roles different between club coaches and international squad/team coaches?
- Does the extent and balance of responsibilities and functions vary with the intensity and scale of the coaching process?

Although these are simple questions, there is currently no empirical evidence to answer them.

Coaching behaviour across cultures may also be compared by using these categories. Correlations between quantifiable measures of direct intervention and intervention support and output measures of coaching effectiveness may yield some useful findings for coach education.

The link between participation coaching and a preponderance of direct intervention behaviours (albeit of a reduced intensity and complexity) has already been noted. This also explains the assertion argued earlier in the book that participation-coaching skills are different in emphasis from those of performance coaches. Performance coaching skills and knowledge will be centred on the planning and regulation function of intervention

support and the management and co-ordination functions that give direction to the intervention programme. The participation coach does not need strategic and co-ordinating skills because the thresholds of the requisite boundary markers of the coaching process are not reached.

The strategic function will be made more complicated, both intellectually and practically, if there is a large team of support personnel and other parties involved in the process.

Common sense will point to the fact that few coaches will operate in completely constraint-free circumstances. It is also evident that coaching is a contested activity and coaches will operate with different resources, but at the same time try to optimise their access to such resources. Resources are exemplified by the most able performers, the best equipment, access to the best facilities, optimum financial support, personal development opportunities and so on. The constraint management function is therefore particularly important to those coaches who are held accountable for competition success or whose agreed goals with performers match these aspirations. Given that not all coaches can operate in the best conditions, their options are as follows:

■   to incorporate the prevailing conditions into the planning of the process;
■   to adjust organisational, performer and personal goals to match the available inputs;
■   to take action, where feasible, to improve or ameliorate the resource position (including using the efforts of other officials, managers or others);
■   to contribute to attempts to ensure that the resources generally available to deliver performance sport are optimised. This means campaigning and promoting a coaches' perspective on relevant professional bodies, committees and agencies.

The term 'professional practice' has been used to describe the coach's extended role responsibilities (Lyle 1984a) – particularly constraint management. Even within performance coaching there will be a range of part-time to full-time positions, and a commensurate range of organisational responsibilities. It is reasonable to assume that the scale of the professional practice will vary with the magnitude of the coach's obligations.

Before investigating the relationship between the coach's role and those of the remainder of the role-set, there is one further coaching role that is best explained by considering the range of functional roles. First, it is possible for the strategic co-ordination to be exercised (along with constraints management), but with the direct intervention and much of the intervention support implemented by others. This 'chief coach' role is best illustrated in the American football 'head coach' role, in which a team of specialist assistant coaches deals with much of the direct intervention. Another parallel is the British soccer 'manager', who exercises the strategic co-ordination and constraints management roles of the coach but is often assisted by one or more individuals who are given the designation 'coaches'.

Second, it is possible that in some circumstances the strategic co-ordination and constraint management roles are shared, or even dominated, by other individuals. This helps to explain the role of the 'performance director' in relation to the coach. The performance director role in the UK has blossomed as National Lottery funding accountability has demanded a more strategic and systematic management of performance. This role represents an overview of objectives and programmes to ensure that they are commensurate with organisational policies and objectives, in addition to assisting with administration and management of resources.

The interaction between these roles – coach, head coach, manager and performance director – increases the potential for role confusion and conflict.

Question Box

There is a complex relationship between function, level of developed expertise and occupational position. Is this evident in coach education?

ROLE COMPLEMENTARITY BETWEEN COACHES AND SUPPORT PERSONNEL

For the purpose of this section, it is assumed that a 'team' approach to implementing the coaching process has been adopted. This is common in performance sport and is epitomised by top club or national squad support teams. In addition to the coach there could be an extensive range of personnel: physiotherapist, assistant coach, doctor, masseur, team manager, trainer, sport psychologist, video analyst, notational analyst, performance director, team captain and so on. In developing a conceptual framework, there is a need to understand the interactions within this role-set. A number of potential issues can be identified but perhaps these are best encapsulated in the following questions:

1   Does the presence of a large team of support personnel diminish the 'directing' role of the coach?
2   It is assumed that support personnel are composed of discipline specialists (medicine, science), generalists (managers, notational analysts, conditioning coaches) and sports-specific persons (assistant coaches, performance directors). How is decision making, particularly integrating and strategic decision making, affected by such a wide range of specialist inputs?
3   Which role functions within the coaching process are most appropriately complemented by the support team?

Again, bear in mind that the athlete is also likely to be an active participant in decision making.

Two constructs are important in bringing clarity to these interrelated roles. It is necessary to appreciate the distinction between a *support role* and a *replacement role*. In the former, the activities of the support team improve the coach's decision-making capacity by providing information (and recommendations). In the latter, the support team member provides a direct service, which replaces a delivery function that would otherwise be carried out by the coach (or conceivably not carried out at all). This is also made more complicated because these services are provided by personnel who are 'attached' to the team/squad/club, or by 'consultants' who provide specialist services to clients from many coaching processes

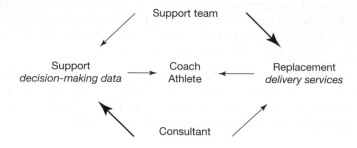

Figure 4.2 *The support and replacement roles of the coaching role-set*

(see Figure 4.2). 'Consultants' operate from sports injury centres, university sport science centres, private companies or centres of excellence.

It is understandable that the 'consultant' is more likely to provide a specialist service in a support capacity. That specialist is very unlikely to have a sufficiently detailed insight into the coaching process and may not be sport specific. Advice and recommendations based on data collected have to be weighed against many other interdependent factors. The replacement role may be more appropriately implemented by personnel attached to the club or squad. In the context of role complementarity, it is easy to understand how the consultant roles may become somewhat detached from the other roles. The replacement role may be found at all levels, from direct intervention to constraint management, but not at strategic co-ordination. The support role is more likely to impact at intervention support. Figure 4.3 is not intended to be comprehensive but does illustrate some of these supporting roles.

A number of potential conflicts arise within the coaching process role-set. First, in relation to the performance director's role, it is necessary to recognise the distinction between the execution of the coaching process and the management of the performance system within which the coaching process takes place. The performance director will be given responsibilities for the direction of the performance system, perhaps including identifying

Specialist	Support	Role function	Replacement	Role function
Sport psychologist	Player profiles	2	Crisis management	1
Manager	Sponsorship	3	Recruitment	3
Sport physiologist	Monitoring data	2	Training programmes	1/2
Sport analyst	Opponent profiles	2	Match strategy	1/2
Sport physiotherapist	Screening	2	Rehab. programmes	1/2

Notes: 1 = direct intervention, 2 = intervention support, 3 = constraint management

Figure 4.3 *Support team roles and role function*

WHAT IS COACHING ABOUT?

targets, selection of athletes, recruitment of coaches and other personnel, and resource management. A number of these functions will contribute to the coaching process but do not replace the strategic co-ordination of the process itself for the individual performer. Nevertheless, the potential for role ambiguity is evident.

Second, the coach's competition management role brings with it a potential time pressure to decision making. The extent to which support information can be made available in timely and applicable fashion during competition is an area for further study. The difficulties here emphasise the seemingly central but often isolated role of the competition coach.

Third, the availability of specialist assistance for elements of the delivery of the coaching process does not diminish the coach's role. Indeed, it serves to emphasise the key process skills identified earlier – planning, monitoring, decision making, crisis management, contingency management and regulation.

Fourth, anecdotal evidence and personal experience confirm that the contributions of sport scientists (and other specialists) can be less effective when not integrated into the coaching process. This can happen when the sports science programme is 'imposed' by a governing body and/or when the coach is unwilling or unable to utilise the information provided.

Fifth, examples can arise in which the advice of the support member conflicts with the goals of the team/coach. One example would be the advice on the implication of injury given by a doctor or physiotherapist during a competition. Although there will be clear cases of severe injury in which there is no question but that the specialist's advice must be taken, there will be many 'grey areas' in which there are a number of options. At least in theory, this can lead to an issue of 'who makes the final decision' (Lyle 1984b; Flint and Weiss 1992; Vergeer and Hogg 1999).

Sixth, on a number of occasions, reference has been made to an interpretation of the coach's role as that of a 'technical expert'. Where the coach is perceived as just one of a number of specialists to be 'brought in' to assist the athlete, there is potential for a lack of direction and role clarity (indeed, this suggests an ignorance of the coaching process). Such a situation may be more likely with individual sport athletes, but seems less likely with team sports.

Seventh, the effect on status of hierarchies and decision-making chains should not be underestimated. Highly trained discipline specialists may not feel comfortable, or that their professional interests are best served, by being part of a process that is integrated, managed and directed by a coach. This, of course, devalues the cognitive skills required for strategic co-ordination, in addition to the craft skills of the coach.

Eighth, role complementarity will be best achieved, and role clutter and conflict avoided, if stable teams of specialists are available to contribute appropriately to the coaching process. Direct intervention functions should not be replaced by personnel from outside this team, if at all possible.

The fewer individuals involved in the coaching process, the less likelihood there is of conflict and loss of focus. However, this has to be set against the contribution of specialists and the number of performers involved. It is difficult to imagine that in team sports or with medium to large squads of performance level athletes, a sophisticated coaching process can be devised and delivered without a team of support personnel. It is obvious that no one individual can provide the range of sophisticated, in-depth, focused and specialist performance analysis and enhancement required. For reasons of ethical values (athlete welfare), individualisation, practicality (the complexity of team training drills) and, most importantly, to access specialist expertise, it is necessary to take a team approach to the optimal execution of the coaching process in performance sport. A good deal of energy is expended on prescriptions for better communication between the coach and sport scientist. Further progress would be achieved by a recognition of their respective roles in relation to the coaching process.

ORGANISATIONAL IMPACT ON THE COACH'S ROLE

Role is normally defined in an organisational setting and refers to the expectations of an individual who holds a particular position within an organisation. Many of the comments made in the previous section will also apply here – for example, the availability of a support team, the need for extended professional practice and the management duties associated with a club or squad. Assertions made about 'head coach' roles and the concomitant functional roles are dependent on an organisational context. Therefore, it is important to put organisational constraints into the conceptual framework.

There are a number of factors that impinge on the coaching role: the sport sub-system, the structuring of roles, the intensity and scale of the coaching process, the characteristics of the organisation, and the availability of an extended role-set. These factors impact on the coach's role in a number of ways: the scale of the extended role responsibilities, the contractual obligations, the autonomy of goal setting, the consonance of values between the coach and the organisation, and accountability and reporting responsibilities. The terminology and constructs used demonstrate that there is an interdependency between the organisational demands, the boundary marker measures and the coaching role. This needs to be understood in order to appreciate fully the coach's practice.

The interdependence of these factors can be illustrated in a number of simple examples:

- *The university team coach*: a number of the resource requirements and support mechanisms may be in place, but the team personnel changes regularly and there is a seasonal effect because of vacation and examination periods. There may be conflict between university commitments and representative and club commitments. Organisational goals may be quite explicit but governance of the organisation may be problematic.
- *The professional club coach*: reward systems are in place and the recruitment process is established. Players are full-time and resources are generally available. Player movements are unpredictable, however, and organisational goals are not set by the players or coach. A support team is likely to be available.
- *The player coach*: incorporating the coach's preparation requirements into the team's training schedule can be problematic. Unless supported by a number of assistants, the direct intervention functions can be restricted. This includes competition

management. The coach's personal performance provides potential issues for selection, emotional response and interpersonal relationships.

- *Representative team coaches*: the total hourage for the coaching process may not be extensive, since the coach meets with the team on a regular although infrequent basis. The coaching process is focused on tactical and immediate psychological preparation, although the coach tries to influence technique development over time. Selection and developmental pathways are very important.

These are merely creative examples. They use a team sport context to illustrate how boundary markers such as intensity, frequency and duration can be affected. The comprehensiveness of the coaching process (reflected in performance expectations) may be limited by the organisational characteristics. Resources, the emphasis on performance outcomes (success), and the social context will be determined by the structure within which the coach operates.

Figure 4.4 provides a summary of the factors involved. However, there are a number of further insights into the coach's practice, as shown below:

- One of the types of role conflict is that between the coach's value system and the expectations of the organisation. This is dealt with at length in a later chapter, but it can be noted here that the conflict is more likely in some organisations than others. This seems likely to be related to the reward system and perceived pressures from outcome accountability.
- Organisational roles also have an informal dimension. The nature of the 'contract' will impact on matters such as club loyalty, social interactions and leadership 'style'.
- The term 'assistant coach' is one determined by an organisational context and is not an indication of novice status. It is true that many assistant coaches will be relatively

	Element	Exemplars
Organisational setting	Agency	Club, university club, national squad, centre of excellence, independent squad
	Provision sector	Public (local authority, school, HE), Voluntary (NGBs, clubs), Commercial (subscription clubs, camps, schools), Professional
	Sport sub-system	Recreation, participation, performance
	Organisational policies	Competition success, recruitment, resources, values
	Role-set	Minimal to extensive support team
	Organisational position	Part-time, full-time, player-coach, assistant coach, representative squad coach, consultant, head coach
Performers	Age / stage	Age groups, young adults, mature adults
	Intensity / scale	Full-time, full-time education, part-time, employed
	Form	Development, performance, excellence, elite

Figure 4.4 *Organisational role determinants*

inexperienced and will aspire to a more autonomous position. However, an assistant coach in performance sport, and with a large-scale organisation, should not necessarily be thought of as a 'beginner' in status or capacity. Interestingly, there is some research evidence that assistant coaches exhibit different role behaviour (Solomon *et al*. 1996).

To reiterate: the role of the sport performance coach is the direction and control of the coaching process. This can be exercised at a number of functional levels, from direct intervention to strategic co-ordination, and by a range of personnel structures, from the individual coach to the extended support team. The role is determined by the nature of the coaching process, which, in turn, is determined by a range of contextual and environmental factors. The outcome is a range of potential coaching roles to accompany the similar range of coaching processes. The role of the coach, particularly in the relative balance of functional roles, and relationships within the role-set, is significantly underresearched.

THE UNIQUENESS OF THE COACHING ROLE

The focus on the coaching role suggests that, like the unique combination of boundary markers that constitute performance coaching, there is something distinctive about it. It is reasonable to ask, therefore, what makes it distinctive.

First of all, the personal characteristics and individual qualities of the coach have to be distinguished from the role characteristics. The individual can play many roles but what is different about the coaching role? There are a number of elements of sports leadership practice in which the coach might be considered to be unique: behavioural style, knowledge and skills, range of experience and values framework.

As to personal characteristics, surveys of coaches indicate a number of characteristic features (Hendry 1972; Gould *et al*. 1990; Tamura *et al*. 1993; Lyle *et al*. 1997). These may become part of a stereotype of the coach – either more achievement-orientated and single-minded or more altruistic and selfless in contributing to the development of sport and individuals. However, there is no reason to believe that any particular combination of characteristics is a necessary prerequisite for successful coaching. It may be true to say that some combination of personal qualities may predispose individuals to become coaches. It seems unlikely that personal characteristics are the distinguishing feature of sports coaching.

Behavioural style is given much more detailed attention in subsequent chapters. There is no reason to believe that communication or leadership styles are distinctive in sports coaching compared to other sport leadership roles. The variety of roles, the mix of team and individual sports, and the very varied dispositions of athletes make it unlikely that any one 'style' will be prevalent or distinctive.

Knowledge is a more likely source of distinctiveness. Surprisingly, this is not to be found in the sports-specific knowledge that might be expected in the coach. Technical knowledge, discipline knowledge, knowledge about human development, and applied knowledge such as training methods and planning might be shared by a variety of experts, from sports scientists and teachers to sports instructors. However, the coach will have a cognitive and craft knowledge, which is centred on the integration and co-ordination of knowledge. This may not be a unique form of knowledge or expertise, but it is distinctive in that no other sport leadership role requires it. This demonstrates the pre-eminence of propositional and procedural knowledge (dealt with later) over declarative knowledge.

Concerning experience, there are a number of sports in which successful coaches have not always themselves been experienced, high-level performers. However, although it is obvious that it is an advantage to be an experienced coach, this may have to be the result of education, continuing professional development and self-development. A number of assertions have some weight. In team sports or sports involving rallying and 'feeding', it is very common for the coach to have been a performance athlete. There is an argument that says that the experience is more valuable for the insights into the demands and reactions to top-level sport. Although this has face validity, the need for performance experience can be overcome, given time, in most sports.

Values and ethics, again, will be dealt with in greater detail. However, it seems likely that there will be a matching of coaches' predispositions and the demands of the circumstances in which they find themselves. In performance sport, it is often perceived that a means–ends value framework is prevalent and that self-interest is the overriding value. Nevertheless, it cannot be demonstrated that this is a requirement nor that coaches do anything other than display a full range of value positions.

As for skills, in earlier sections the skills required by coaches were described. Delivery skills such as communication, organisation, demonstration, rallying etc. are hardly unique. Much more attention has been paid to the skills of planning, monitoring and regulating the coaching process. Although these skills are not unique, their combination in the circumstances of performance sport is different from those of other sports leaders. Competition management skills are certainly unique to the performance coach in their emphasis within the coaching process.

Although it was difficult to argue that there was much about the sports coach that is unique, it should be remembered that it is not the individual coach but the coaching process that is unique. The demands of the performance coaching process place a heavy emphasis on integrating and co-ordinating skills and abilities. It is very likely, therefore, that it is the combination of demands and qualities that makes the coach different. The distinctiveness is the attempt to control or manipulate as many of the variables that affect performance as possible. This attempt, in turn, relies on a set of meta-cognitive capacities and a set of craft-based skills that are unique to the sports coach within sport leadership roles. The fact that there is often a team of individuals working with the performer makes this role more challenging and provides a potential for inadequately co-ordinated performance management.

 Critical Concept

It is not the individual coach but the coaching process that is unique.

The extent and nature of the coaching process determines the role of the coach. This is reflected in the 'contract' between coach and athlete, whether formal or informal. This word is a useful reminder of the key elements of the coaching process and the coach's role. The acrostic CONTRACT describes a combination of factors that characterise the uniqueness of coaching.

Complexity	The range of interrelated and interdependent variables that contribute to performance enhancement, the individuality of the performer and the contested nature of the environment result in a complex process.
Organisation	Stresses the co-ordination and management of diverse elements of the coaching process.
Negotiation	This is a reflection of the coach's mediating role between the performer's and organisation's aspirations and achievements, between the desirable and the achievable.
Training	The characteristic feature of the coaching process is that preparation outweighs competition. The training session, in its many guises, is the natural environment of the performance coach.
Regulation	The process nature of coaching identifies regulation as a key element. Regulating progress relies on planning, monitoring, analysis and contingency management.
Accountability	In attempting to reduce the unpredictability of performance, coaches are setting targets for which they can be held accountable. Nevertheless, this accountability must be evaluated in the context of environmental circumstances and performer liability.
Control of variables	This is the key feature of coaching that makes it different from the efforts of other sports leaders. In the context of full-time athletes, this will become a substantial life-style management exercise.
Targets	One of the characteristics of systematic coaching is the setting and regulation of progress through targets. This is helpful, not only to regulation, but also to motivating performers and to evaluating outputs.

Although the role of the coach has an element of individual difference and ideology about it, perceptions of professional practice should start here and it should also be the basis for education and training. Understandably, role is also the starting point for resolving conflict between coaches and support personnel and for debating the centrality of the athlete in the coaching process. Despite this, there has been very little development of the concept of role in the sports coaching context. At this early stage of occupational crystallisation, role expectations will be dynamic, and considerable variety can be anticipated in the coach's implementation of the coaching process. This is influenced by organisational factors.

The four functional roles are a very important conceptual and analytical tool. Indeed, strategic co-ordination is the distinguishing feature of the coach's role, although expertise in the other functional roles is required. Strategic co-ordination will always be the role of the performance coach, although some aspects of the direct intervention, intervention support and constraint management may be undertaken by others – such as assistants, sport scientists or team managers. This strategic role has been likened to that of a

WHAT IS COACHING ABOUT?

manager. Schembri said that 'Head coaches at the Australian Institute of Sport, as programme managers, are increasingly having to manage both the coaching and off-field specialists who form the large technical team that guides the development of the athlete' (1998: 7). Earlier, Peter Coe, coach and father of Sebastian Coe, said, 'I realised at once that, above all, coaching was a matter of management' (1985: 10). In an interesting attempt to model the coaching process using a 'soft systems approach', Ledington and Wootton (1986) conceived of the coach as a systems manager. Frank Dick has emphasised the strategic role of the coach as the ability to synthesise the disparate elements of advice into a coherent and practical programme, and has speculated on the most effective structuring of the role-set for elite athletes (Dick 1997c).

The strategic co-ordination and management role reinforces an emerging theme throughout the book. Performance coaching requires higher-order cognitive functions in addition to craft-based intervention delivery. This also reinforces the centrality of decision making as the key skill for performance sports coaches. Much of the cognitive functioning is tacit and not easily verbalised: it is rarely part of coach education and depends on situated learning and experience. Nevertheless, it is important to correct the perception of the role of the coach as tracksuited intervention. Although extremely important, it is one part of a complex coaching role.

SUMMARY

This chapter will have familiarised you with the following:

- the importance of role in understanding fully the coach's practice;
- a set of commonly used concepts and terminology with which to analyse role;
- the role of the coach when used as an ideological statement about the purpose of coaching;
- the four functional roles for the coach – direct intervention, intervention support, constraints management and strategic co-ordination – and the benefits of this framework for analysis and comparison;
- the extent to which coaches may or may not exercise fully each of the four functional roles;
- the issues arising from an extensive role-set surrounding the performance athlete – in particular, the distinction between a support role and a replacement role in implementing the coaching process;
- the effect of organisational factors on the coach's role;
- an argument for the distinctiveness of the coaching role.

Reading

There are no texts that extend beyond the material covered in this chapter. Students are recommended to read more widely about the concept of role and to apply this to novel situations in sports coaching.

PART2
HOW DO COACHES BEHAVE?

CHAPTER FIVE

▼　**MODELLING THE COACHING PROCESS**

■　Introduction　　　　　　　　　　　　　　　　　79
■　What is Meant by a Model?　　　　　　　　　　80
■　Problems in Model Building　　　　　　　　　　84
■　An Evaluation of Existing Models　　　　　　　85
■　Models: Application, Constraints and Implementation　91
■　Summary　　　　　　　　　　　　　　　　　　94
■　Projects and Reading　　　　　　　　　　　　94

INTRODUCTION

This chapter focuses on the coach's behaviour: how it can be represented for the purposes of analysis and modelling, and how the available literature on the subject has described the coach's practice. The problems of model building are emphasised and the attempts of model builders to date are described and evaluated against a set of principles. Key amongst these is the extent to which the model builders have managed to relate the essential components of the coaching process to the coach's behaviour or practice. This quest is consonant with the objective of developing a conceptual framework around the coaching process. Often, a first stage in setting out a conceptual framework is to attempt to model practice. It will become obvious that this is not an easy task and is made more difficult by the 'processual' and multivariable nature of sports coaching.

The chapter begins with a clarification of what is meant by a model and identifies some of the difficulties in model construction. A number of models of sports coaching from the literature are then described and evaluated. The chapter closes with an examination of how models can be used for analysis, dealing with the vexed issue of application and reality constraints.

In summary, the following statements represent the current 'state of play':

■　There are no all-embracing models of the coaching process that have received consensual agreement (Sherman *et al*. 1997; Abraham and Collins 1998; Potrac *et al*. 2000).

- Models of the coaching process do not play a large part in coach education and training.
- The 'coaching episode' is easier to model than the extended process and this has influenced the literature.
- The balance between the advantages of the generic model and the advantages of sport-specific models has not been resolved.
- There are very few models 'of' coaching that have been derived from rigorous research. Côte *et al*. (1995a) is an exception, and their model is discussed later in the chapter.
- The shortcomings in the literature identified earlier – absence of assumptions and lack of conceptual vocabulary – are evident in model building.

A number of models are reviewed in the latter part of the chapter (Franks *et al*. 1986; Fairs 1987; Côte *et al*. 1995a; Sherman *et al*. 1997). Each of these models has something useful to offer but each exemplifies the difficulties and shortcomings of model building in sports coaching. Ledington and Wootton (1986) confirmed the value of modelling but reinforced the difficulties involved. There are also many examples of 'part-models' – detailed accounts of sub-processes within the coaching process (for example, see Saury and Durand 1998 for an excellent example of this), but these do not amount to models.

It would be reasonable to ask why so much time is being devoted to models of coaching when it is clear from the outset that there are few good exemplars and the general tenor of the critiques of extant models will be critical. The capacity to devise appropriate models is one measure of the health of the conceptual development of the field. The intention of this chapter, therefore, is not simply to review existing attempts but to contribute to future developments as well.

WHAT IS MEANT BY A MODEL?

The outcomes of the sports coaching process are observable; that is, in athlete performances and athlete and coach behaviours. However, the coaching process itself is a construct, an abstraction. The purpose of this abstraction (the conceptual framework) is to provide a mechanism for the better understanding of the observable practice. A model is used to describe the components of the phenomenon (for example, the coaching process) and the relationship between the components.

 Critical Concept

A model is a representation of the relational aspects of (usually) complex phenomena by using symbols or simplified descriptions that help to conceptualise the phenomenon itself.

Most individuals would be familiar with the notion of a replica model – that is, a smaller representation of a physical object – often capable of being 'taken to pieces' to demonstrate 'how it works'. On the other hand, models of the coaching process are symbolic models. These may appear to have a different function but really they are designed for much the same purpose. Models are valuable for

- description and scoping,
- explaining relationships between components,
- analysing practice by 'comparative' methods,
- providing templates for research and education, and
- predicting outcomes.

The potential for predicting outcomes by replacing default values in a model with real measures is an appealing prospect. The more that the relationships in a model can be specified and the components quantified, the more likely is prediction. However, first, it will not come as a surprise to learn that the great majority of sports coaching components cannot easily be quantified; and second, that the 'direction' of arrows or lines on a diagram have an apparent simplicity. However, they imply *causal*, *sequential* and *conditional* qualities, the accuracy of which may not yet be justified by research. Third, it may be possible to predict performance 'gains' in some individual (usually power-repetitive technique) sports, although the environmental effects are difficult to control and measure. It may also be possible to predict competition outcomes based on the differential human and material resources available. On the other hand, there have been few attempts to predict the outcome of a coaching process. This seems likely to be a result of the problem in controlling the enormous range of variables that influence performance. Subsequent evaluation will demonstrate that the models available have been more concerned to describe, rather than predict.

Modelling the sports coaching process should be part of any analysis of coaching behaviour and performance, and is central to evaluating effectiveness. A key feature of modelling is that it normally embraces a set of assumptions about performance, performance enhancement, social interactions and the coaching role. In addition, it may or may not be possible to incorporate notions of individual 'achievement strategies'. Despite this, or perhaps because of it, there are few (if any) good models of the sports coaching process and certainly none that have achieved consensual agreement or application. One of the objectives for this chapter is to develop a capacity to examine in a critical fashion any attempts to model the sports coaching process.

It has been recognised that models are representations of phenomena, the complexity of which is difficult to represent solely in words. A visual/spatial/relational representation allows an enhanced appreciation of the phenomenon and its qualities. It is important at this point to acknowledge that the term 'model' is used for a range of representations, ranging from simple diagrams to mathematical and complex modelling that allows some degree of prediction. There are also many limitations in building and displaying models. Amongst other problems, it is not easy to represent complex interactions, continuity of process, variation in scale and variations in practice. The most commonly used two-dimensional representations have inherent limitations.

Critical Concept

Models are generalised representations and are not causal at the level of the individual.

Type	Feature	Purposes
Diagram	Visual representation, reinforcement, modest relational qualities, usually simplistic, abstract concept.	[Understanding]
Model	Represents structure but indicates the relationship of the parts.	Understanding [Analysis]
Operational model	Represents a function or process; shows 'how it works'. Model 'of', usually derived from practice or research.	Understanding Analysis Prediction
Ideal model	Idealised representation; shows 'how it *should* be'. Model 'for', but should be able to say what the assumptions for the model are.	Understanding Analysis Prediction Planning
Planning model	Represents intentions; somewhere between operational model and ideal model. Real-life parameters built in.	Understanding Analysis Prediction Planning
Also Conceptual model	Helps to reflect/represent relationships between concepts and/or ideas. Useful for setting up research. Doesn't describe a real-life event or process.	Understanding Analysis

Figure 5.1 *Common types of models*

In order to scrutinise the literature more easily, it would be helpful to categorise the various types of models and the purposes for which they might most appropriately be used. Figure 5.1 describes the common types of models.

Care must therefore be taken with the casual use of the term 'model' when authors are intent merely to give a visual reinforcement of their ideas. This is evident in 'lists' or diagrams of sub-categories of phenomena, which have no explanatory powers and no sense of relationship between components.

Models '*of*' the coaching process are derived from a description and analysis of coaching practice. Of course, the variety in practice would pose problems for generating an all-embracing model but this process has the advantage of a strong relationship between principles and practice. The model-'of' approach is very like the 'case-building' approach in the social sciences. On the other hand, the model '*for*' the coaching process begins from a set of assumptions about sports coaching and builds a more idealistic or conceptual model for practice. The model builder may not expect the model to be found in practice in exactly its idealised form, but it provides a useful analytical tool for identifying the issues that are worthy of further attention.

HOW DO COACHES BEHAVE?

Models are used for a variety of purposes. They may model intentions at the planning stage or be used to evaluate practice. They may also be used to help understand the implications of practice. For this reason it is important that the coach should be able to make judgements about the worthiness or appropriateness of a model. The following questions would be a valuable beginning in determining the usefulness of a coaching process model:

- Is it comprehensive? Does it attempt an all-embracing description of the process?
- Is it understandable? Are the key features easily discerned?
- Is it accurate/representative? Does it have an immediate sense of being valid?
- Does it describe all variations in practice? (This, of course, would be an ambitious task.)
- Does it build towards an outcome? Is it predictive (Operational and Planning Models)?
- Is it sufficiently detailed to be discriminating and, therefore, useful for analysis?
- Does it apply to all situations? Have contextual features been built into the model?
- Is it clear how the process described represents practical / concrete manifestations of sports coaching behaviour?
- How well is progression/continuity represented?
- Can it be quantified (mathematical models only)?
- Is the nature of the relationship between component parts (if A then B) established? Have the linkages been described in terms of direction, strength and causal condition?

Given this demanding list of questions, it would be reasonable to wonder whether there are any good/useful models. Clearly, this is not an easy business! At this stage in the evolution of sports coaching as a concept, theory and profession, there would appear to be no acceptable models with universal application. Part of the problem is the interrelatedness of the variables that influence performance and performance enhancement. At a simplistic level of analysis, the comparison of practice and performance to the model may allow the athlete and coach to decide where planning and implementation may have gone wrong. If a 'good' model is used for analysis, it may be possible to say, 'Therefore, this should have been the effect.' Although this sounds feasible, it is clearly not common practice at present and the major limiting factor is the absence of a suitable model.

Question Box

Models are generic representations. They are not 'used' by coaches but are available for analysis purposes. Nevertheless, this raises the question of whether the principles embedded in the model are (1) used in coach education, and (2) sufficiently understood by coaches to be used for evaluation purposes.

PROBLEMS IN MODEL BUILDING

There are some general problems that model builders will have to overcome in modelling the coaching process:

1   The coaching process is not an inert system. The element of human behaviour invokes issues of volition and cognitive organisation and decision making, which are difficult to represent and replicate.

2   The scope of the coaching process involves direct intervention in competition and preparation, intervention support, constraints management and a meta-cognitive integration and co-ordination that is largely a mental exercise. Although the coaching process may be individualised, it often applies to large groups of performers.

3   Many of the variables that influence performance and performance enhancement are interdependent. However, this is a complex pattern of interdependency with variables co-acting, interacting and sequence dependent. In addition, the process is mediated by a similarly complex set of short-, medium- and longer-term goals and objectives.

4   Despite the best attempts of the sport scientists, performance enhancement is not a linear process, nor is the output/improvement related to inputs (training) in a constant fashion. Whilst simple measures of performance components such as strength or power may be more predictable and manageable, complex game skills with opponent interference are much more difficult to track.

5   The model builder must choose between modelling a generic core process that is manageable, and attempting to create a sufficiently all-embracing and sophisticated model that resonates with practice. Core process models may be useful analogies but may not be sufficiently detailed or 'applied' to be helpful in analysing practice.

6   The picture that is emerging is that of a coaching process that is largely a cognitive exercise, both in planning and in expert execution. Illustrating this cognitive activity and integrating it with more observable activity is a significant challenge for the model builder.

7   One further challenge is the paucity of systematic data collection (particularly given the potential quality of data available) by coaches or researchers. The result is an absence of insight into relationships between process components and the consequent failure to integrate this into a model.

It is also important to pay attention to one further problem. Performance sports coaching is a process, and the serial and dynamic nature of a process is difficult to capture in a model. In addition to the issues identified above, it will be necessary to incorporate the essential features of a process, which can then be used as an evaluation tool. Figure 5.2 identifies the components of a process and the consequent coaching issues to be integrated into a model of practice.

The overall coaching process is also composed of a number of sub-processes (for example, personal development, physical conditioning, injury prevention, sponsorship and promotion, club development and goal setting). These are distinctive and complex and, although there is a high level of interdependency, the sub-processes might often be quite self-contained. The need for co-ordination and integration has already been identified and highlighted. In the context of model building, the diverse and somewhat fragmented nature

Process component	Evaluation	Sample coaching issue
Initiation	What is the catalyst for beginning the process? How is this related to performance development systems?	Is this stage dependent on the talent identification process? What are the criteria for establishing the contract?
Development	What is the essential nature of the process? How can this be demonstrated in the model?	Adaptation of the athlete is the goal of the coaching process. To what extent is this compatible with other objectives?
Operation	How can the different forms of delivery be illustrated and integrated?	Can the model overcome the tendency to focus on the direct intervention stage?
Progression	Process implies a cyclical aspect to the model. How can this be displayed? Is there a feedback mechanism for controlling progression?	Has there been sufficient research on the threshold criteria applied by coaches to regulate progress?
Monitoring	Are monitoring stages built into the model? How responsive is the model to changes in status?	Is coaching practice sufficiently systematic to generate monitoring data and to be able to incorporate this into practice?
Contingency	Is the model able to incorporate unplanned variance in performance and changes to the environment?	How stable is the environment in particular sports? Dos this influence the degree of forward planning possible?
Evaluation	Does the model work towards an outcome? How is this 'goal direction' incorporated into the model?	Evaluation of the coaching process is central to measuring the effectiveness of the coach.
Termination	Is a 're-consideration of the "contract" stage built into the model?	Which criteria are used to decide on the appropriateness of continuation?

Figure 5.2 *Process components and coaching issues*

of the coaching process stresses once again the coach's strategic role and the central role of planning and decision making.

The difficulties of model building have become clear and, although the principles through which existing examples might be evaluated have been established, the demands are very challenging. The chapter continues by presenting and evaluating a number of attempts to model the process. The examples have been chosen because they illustrate some of the difficulties involved and because they are cited most often in the literature.

AN EVALUATION OF EXISTING MODELS

This section describes a number of models of the coaching process (Franks *et al.* 1986; Fairs 1987; Côte *et al.* 1995a; and Sherman *et al.* 1997) and assesses their strengths and weaknesses. Each of the examples is presented in diagrammatic form and there is a summary analysis of their usefulness and the extent to which they fulfil the principles identified earlier. In each exemplar the implied question is 'How strong is the model's explanatory power and how useful would it be for understanding and analysing performance sports coaching practice?

The key factors model, by Ian Franks and colleagues (1986)

The first example is quite distinctive because it does not really purport to illustrate the entire coaching process. Franks *et al.* (1986) set out to propose a means of assessing coaching effectiveness. In this case, therefore, there is an implied model, which has to be interpreted from the authors' paper. Their assumptions are evident and focus on direct intervention, giving the model an episodic emphasis that is built around skill development (see Figure 5.3).

The interesting contribution of the model is the identification of key performance criteria and their use to regulate progression. The key elements of performance are identified in a quantitative fashion (both in competition and training), and training is planned around an incremental and differentiated improvement in these factors over time. The priority given to key factors can be varied according to perceived needs following competition. The coach's role is interpreted as a planner and manager of direct intervention.

The constant evaluation method and the attention to a range of key factors suggests that the model would be most appropriately applied to league sports in which there is a regular cycle of competition and preparation, and performance is complex and not susceptible to absolute measurement.

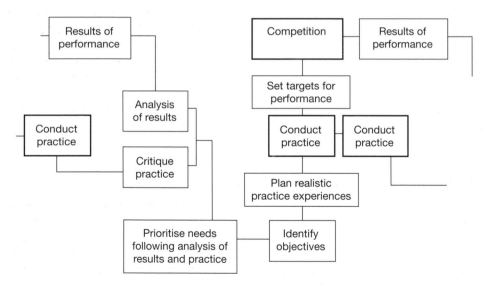

Figure 5.3 *Coaching process model (adapted from Franks et al. 1986)*

Evaluation

Strengths	*Weaknesses*
The use of data on key performance factors as a regulation and progression mechanism	The model is not comprehensive
Recognition of incremental improvement in performance	There is a down-playing of the variability in performance from session to session
Attempt at quantification by 'scoring' performance factors	Coaching behaviour is not related to performance improvement
Some contextual relationship to regular league sports	The detail in the paper focuses on the coach's observable behaviour
There is an episodic validity for performance sport	The complexity of performance is over-simplified
The assumptions are reflected in the model	The linkages between stages are not established

Summary

The example could be best described as a partial process model because of its emphasis on skills learning and direct intervention. It is a model 'for' coaching since it has not been derived from empirical studies on coaching practice but appears to display a face validity for performance coaching in league/tournament sports. Nevertheless, it makes a number of interesting contributions to conceptual development: the focus on regulation and progression, and the contingency element of planning based on competition demands and progress in key performance factors. The explanatory power of the model is high – albeit within the boundaries delineated by this sub-process, and the model would be useful for analysis purposes.

The objectives model, by John Fairs (1987)

The next example is taken from John Fairs (1987), who describes a five-step process model of coaching (see Figure 5.4), based on an interpretation of the coaching role that reflects a problem-solving approach. There is little doubt that this is an 'objectives model', and the author is very specific that coaching should be considered a 'process' – it is 'not a haphazard, trial and error affair but involves a series of orderly, interrelated steps' (1987: 17). There is no evidence that the model is based on an aggregation or analysis of coaching practice and it is, therefore, a model 'for' coaching.

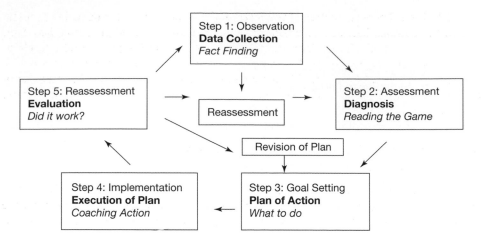

Figure 5.4 *Coaching process model (Fairs 1987)*

Evaluation

Strengths	*Weaknesses*
The process nature of coaching is emphasised	There is no attempt to be all-embracing or even specific to coaching. It does not have an immediate sense of being a valid or useful representation of the coaching process
The cyclical nature of the process is conveyed	There is no sense of longer-term planning (the problem correction approach focuses attention on the coaching episode)
Some accompanying assumptions were identified	There is no detail on the relationship between component stages. Regulation of progression within and between stages is not detailed
It is simple and easily understood	There is no contextualisation
	There is no differentiation between competition and preparation, nor of the component parts of performance

Summary

The model fails many of the evaluation criteria but it is perhaps rather harsh to be so critical. The paper in which the model is presented is not a detailed academic work but illustrates a simple principle about working to objectives and re-evaluating these in a cyclical fashion. There is no attempt to illustrate the complexity of the coaching process. Indeed, the balance between core generic principles and detailed processes has been weighted so much to the former that the model provides neither insight nor understanding. Given the absence of 'reality relationship', it is obvious that the model will have a very limited usefulness. Nevertheless, this simplified objectives approach may be more useful for individual direct intervention sessions in which less ambitious and more specific objectives can be identified.

The 'mental model' coaching model of Côte and colleagues (1995a)

The model of Côte *et al.* (1995a) is a valuable exemplar since it was derived from empirical data. The experiences, opinions and insights of expert gymnastics coaches were garnered through in-depth interview procedures, and from these data a model was devised (Figure 5.5).

There are a number of distinguishing features of what the authors term a 'conceptual model'. There is a prioritising of coaching process components and an acknowledgement that there are significant limitations in the extent to which teaching paradigm conceptualisations of coaching adequately represent its complexity. The distinction between core and peripheral process elements is similar to the distinction between direct intervention/ intervention support and constraints management. However, the most interesting contribution is the centrality in the model of the coaches' 'mental model' of athlete potential.

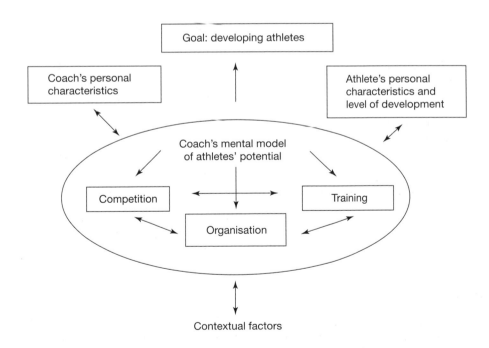

Figure 5.5 *Coaching process model (Côte et al. 1995a)*

This places the focus beyond the observable behaviour of the coach and reinforces the cognitive nature of performance sports coaching.

The authors' claim is to have produced a conceptual model within which existing research studies can be assembled and integrated. However, this seems a little generous given the lack of detail on the relationship between the constructs. The authors acknowledge that much more detail is available from the expert coaches' responses than is presented in the paper.

Evaluation

Strengths	Weaknesses
The model is derived from empirical data	It is not immediately obvious that this is a process model. The authors use the phrase 'constantly monitored and adjusted' but the dynamics of the process are explored in insufficient detail
The 'mental model' element has great potential for explaining coaching practice	As a conceptual model (perhaps simply a diagram), it is not immediately applicable to practice
	Factors are represented rather than the relationships between them described
	There is insufficient detail to differentiate between coaches and thereby analyse practice

Summary

The richness of the empirical data has not been fully represented in this particular conceptualisation of the coaching process. The emphasis may have been more on the coaches' knowledge structures but this has limited the process elements of progression and regulation. Nevertheless, the mental model construct points usefully to the mechanism for operationalising the coaches' expertise. The limitations of conceptual diagrams/ models for analysis purposes are illustrated in this example but there is some potential for explaining behaviour. The advantages of simplicity and reduction to core constructs have to be set against the absence of sufficient process detail to represent adequately the complexity and scope of performance coaching.

The 'sport instruction' coaching model of Sherman and colleagues (1997)

This model is treated differently because of the approach and intentions of the authors. Although their paper offers a diagrammatic representation of the 'instructional model', it is not the model itself that is of interest here, but the assumptions on which their model is based. This is an example of the model being appropriate to the prior assumptions but the assumptions themselves not being fully representative of sports coaching.

The authors correctly identify deficiencies in some previous models. Their response is to focus on a part of the coaching process, noting that coaching 'involves the instruction of motor skills' (1997: 104). They therefore propose an instructional model with key stages: achievement, aptitude, learning, instruction, achievement evaluation and instructional evaluation. In defence of this, they say that 'the instruction role of coaches has been termed in the sports coaching literature as a "coaching process"' (1997: 106), but they do also note that 'one of the many requirements and roles of sport coaches is the instruction of motor skills' (1997: 121).

This provides an opportunity to examine the assumptions made by the authors:

- The comment about the coaching process being synonymous with the instruction of motor skills is not one that I would share and it does illustrate very well the need for a shared conceptual vocabulary.
- The terms 'learner' and 'novice' are used extensively throughout. This and the absence of any attention to preparation for competition clearly situate the paper within (at best) participation coaching.
- 'Performance' is interpreted rather narrowly with technique elevated above other components.
- The centrality of the instructional role may well deserve its pre-eminence, but the complexity of performance, the factors influencing performance, the coaching process and the coaching role have been lost in the 'reductionist' approach.

This is not intended to be too critical an evaluation of the paper, in which the authors have made a convincing case for increased attention to the instructional process. Nevertheless, the failure to deal with participation/performance coaching and the reluctance to identify their model as a sub-process of the direct intervention role limits the model's contribution to building the conceptual framework.

MODELS: APPLICATION, CONSTRAINTS, IMPLEMENTATION

The next chapter describes a proposed model of the coaching process. However, before that, some consideration is given to the development and application of models. The clear message thus far is that the importance of modelling the coaching process has been established but that, to date, attempts have fallen short of what is required. It is worth stressing that, notwithstanding the inherent complexity of the coaching process, models can never reproduce the subtlety and nuances of real life and there is a danger of expecting too much. The model should be fit for its purpose. A second point is that model building and use should be a dynamic affair. Broadly, the process could look like this:

1   begin with assumptions,
2   develop the model,
3   test the aptness of the model by comparing to practice,
4   modify initial assumptions,
5   re-design the model, and
6   retest.

This then becomes an iterative process with the model being constantly refined either through comparisons with practice or by being informed by more specific research output.

There are three principal uses for models and these are re-emphasised here:

Education and training	An accepted model and interpretation of the coaching process should be the basis for coaching education and training. However, it is not evident that detailed models or the output of research on performance coaching have yet become the basis of coach education in the UK (Abraham and Collins 1998). As an example, the model and conceptual framework may point to the importance of cognitive skills and the development of expert 'shortcuts' in decision making. How is this incorporated by the coach educators?
Research	This is expanded upon in a subsequent chapter. For the moment it is enough to say that the model can help to identify the questions to which the researchers should turn their attention. For example, which decision-making heuristics are used by coaches of team sports during matches? Which criteria are employed by coaches to evaluate satisfactory progression towards training targets? Parts of the model might be assessed against the practice of expert coaches in a range of sports to test the applicability of the model.
Analysis and understanding	Often analysis is carried out retrospectively in order that the lessons learned can be incorporated into future practice. This may be part of personal development or may be part of an accountability exercise to evaluate the coach's performance. Data on coaching practice and contextual resource features are compared to the model with the intention of understanding success or failure. This can (perhaps more easily and sensibly) be done on sub-processes within coaching practice, for the purpose of understanding and developing expertise.

Analysis of the patterns of issues that arise from researching into coaching practice and the discontinuities from the model would aid a general understanding of performance coaching practice. That this hasn't happened on a systematic scale points to the paucity of research, the failure to communicate widely and the absence of a useful model.

In the context of the above, it is reasonable to ask what developments might be expected in model building. Figure 5.6 incorporates some speculation of the future of model building.

HOW DO COACHES BEHAVE?

Models 'of'	Models 'for'
Greater attention to research in coaching (partly as a result of increased resourcing) should lead to more modelling based on empirical investigations of practice.	Models for coaching will continue to be the 'bridge' between academic disciplines and coaching, e.g. psychology, decision making and coaching behaviour.
It is unlikely that detailed and all-embracing models of the coaching process will be the focus. Rather, that research and subsequent models will be targeted on sub-processes.	Models 'for' will continue to be used as templates for research and to reflect theory development. These will become increasingly refined as empirical findings become available.
Models of novice and expert practice will become important features of education and professional development.	Models 'for' will be used to analyse practice. However, as the models become more sophisticated, attention may well turn from components and structure to quantifiable relationships and thresholds.
Comparative model building will be encouraged. This may be cross-cultural or merely across sports.	Simplified models may be used to understand the influence of different sets of constraints on the performance coaching process.

Figure 5.6 *The future of model building in sports coaching*

Two comments that are sometimes heard when discussing models are (a) that they cannot be put into practice and (b) that they are pointless without understanding the context of practice. This raises a number of issues:

■ Models are to be used in the ways described in this chapter. They are not designed to be adopted by individuals, although the models can help with analysis and subsequent changes in practice.
■ All coaching practice is idiosyncratic and unique. It is the complexity and uniqueness that brings challenge to its study. Nevertheless, there are patterns of behaviour and these can be charted. Two matters are relevant:

  1 Models 'of' usually involve some aggregation and 'averaging' of practice in order to generalise.
  2 Highlighting the dissonance between individual practice and the models is a very valuable mechanism for identifying the elements of practice worth investigation.

■ The issue of sport specificity is likely to be solved in the future by the creation of a 'family of models'. Individual/team/elite/performance/representative models will follow from increased attention and understanding.
■ The charge that constraints must be taken into account is a powerful one. This is partly what is meant by suggesting that future research will be focused on relationships between components. In other words, we know what the decision is that needs to be taken but what do coaches do in a variety of resource situations? How do restricted competition access, athlete injury or underachievement of training targets affect decision making in various situations?

The answer is not to create a huge number of variations of models but to focus on contingency planning, the criteria used by coaches to make decisions, and the coaches' access to an effective repertoire of solutions. These will increase our understanding of how the context influences coaching practice.

The way forward is not to argue about the component parts of the coaching process. There will be a fair measure of agreement over these, although some models will be more detailed than others. Attention must be focused on the coaches' practice that reflects the implementation of the model. This is why the examples of decision criteria, thresholds for progression and contingency factors are constantly emphasised. Inevitably this reinforces the central theme of the conceptual framework thus far, that coaching is essentially a cognitive exercise with elements of craft delivery.

SUMMARY

This chapter will have familiarised you with the following:

- the current status of modelling the coaching process;
- a definition of a model and common presentation of models;
- the distinction between models 'of' and models 'for' coaching;
- questions with which to judge the usefulness of models;
- the problems inherent in model construction;
- the elements of any process that need to be incorporated into a coaching model;
- examples of critical appraisals of existing coaching models, including strengths and weaknesses;
- issues of implementation and application;
- likely developments in model construction.

PROJECTS

- Engage in the creative process. Devise a possible model of a sub-process within coaching and invite six coaches to amend/elaborate on your model.
- Using the models reviewed in the chapter, identify three key features from each and consider how practice could be changed to accommodate these features.
- Assumptions are important in model building. Review four research articles and catalogue their assumptions about the coaching process. Consider whether these assumptions would be useful in model building and demonstrate why.
- Choose two components of the coaching process and consider in depth the relationship between them and how this might be represented in a model.
- Select one process characteristic (e.g., contingency, progression). Consider how that characteristic could be incorporated into a coaching process model.

Reading

There is no supporting reading on the construction or analysis of models. Those models reviewed in the chapter can be accessed in the original source but the summary here is sufficient. Saury and Durand (1998) is a good example of more specific enquiry into components of the coaching process that can be built into a model.

CHAPTER SIX

▼   A PROPOSED MODEL FOR COACHING

■   Introduction   96
■   Prior Assumptions for the Proposed Model   97
■   Identifying the Building Blocks   99
■   The Model   106
■   Operationalising the Model   107
■   Summary   115
■   Projects and Reading   115

INTRODUCTION

In the previous chapter the nature of models was explored and a number of examples of models 'of' and 'for' the coaching process were examined. The models available have some significant limitations, although their potential value for describing and communicating a conceptual framework for sports coaching can be taken for granted. This chapter consists of a proposed model for sports coaching, which is intended to make a contribution to academic study in this field.

1   The proposed model both builds on the conceptual framework elaborated thus far, and is also a key part of it.
2   It is necessary to reiterate that, as a model for coaching, it is a template to be used to compare to practice, and to contribute to a gradual refining of our understanding of sports coaching.
3   There is a short evaluation of the model in the final passage of the chapter. However, it should be recognised at this point that the model has many of the weaknesses of those already described. Nevertheless, it is intended to be more comprehensive and detailed than previous attempts.

The most essential part of this introduction is to explain the approach taken to initiating and building the model. The principle underlying the model is that of the 'ideal model'. The use of the ideal model is a feature of the work of seminal sociologist Max Weber (Albrow 1990). It can be argued that models of practice that are developed from aggregating the behaviour of many, many examples of that practice will provide an accumulative snapshot of the phenomenon, but will have limited value for describing, or perhaps understanding, the practice of the range of individuals who make up that population. The model describes the behaviour and practice of an 'average' person, who does not actually exist. One answer is to construct an 'ideal' model, which is based on the action that would be taken in the rational and informed pursuit of appropriate objectives in constraint-free conditions. Insofar as the model is based on the rational pursuit of objectives, it should make use of the many sub-disciplines and sub-processes that are required to understand coaching practice.

In constructing the model, the model builder would not expect it to correspond exactly to reality but it would have an obvious and testable validity for those in that field. As already explained, the value of the model is that it can then be contrasted with observation of coaching practice, and the differences and discontinuities are highlighted for further study. The ideal model also provides a vehicle for the aggregation of existing studies on coaching practice. Following the principles of model building and the requirements of the ideal model, the proposed model will have four parts:

1   assumptions about the sports coaching process, on which the model is based;
2   identification of the sub-processes and 'building bricks' from which the model has been constructed;
3   an appropriate representation of the component parts of the model and the inter-relationships between them;
4   The dynamics of the model and how the process is operationalised. (This element of the model is not presented in full in this chapter as it forms much of the content of the subsequent chapter on coaching practice.)

PRIOR ASSUMPTIONS FOR THE PROPOSED MODEL

This is an important set of statements. Not only does it represent the basis for constructing the model but it also provides a means of critically evaluating the model and the emerging conceptual framework. It is also important because other writers have been criticised for not making explicit the assumptions on which their research is founded.

1   Sports coaching is a culturally acknowledged practice of leadership in sport that is intended to facilitate individuals/teams to improved performance in sport competition.
2   Sports coaching is a process, the effect of which is dependent on the integration of the whole being greater than the sum of its parts. Partial implementation reduces its impact on performance outcomes.
3   The performers' involvement is normally sport specific and recognised by membership of and association with that sport's agencies, organisations and competition framework.
4   Sports coaches manage a process based on the rational pursuit of identified performance objectives, although the process may have other concomitant and socially valued developmental and personal objectives.
5   The essence and scope of the coaching process is circumscribed by a number of factors: duration, frequency, continuity, stability, progression, long-term planning, goal orientation, competition objectives and control of variables.

6   The preparation/training phase of performance improvement is effected by strategic improvements in the component elements of sport performance. Over time, this will create a potential (and more or less predictable) improvement in competition performance.

7   The direct intervention element of the coaching process will incorporate principles of teaching and learning behaviour, and practice that will facilitate improved sport performance.

8   Implementing the coaching process in a systematic fashion will facilitate optimum improvement and performance.

9   Performers are committed to the process and engage voluntarily (or within a desirable reward environment) in pursuing agreed and/or beneficial goals.

10 The limitations in performance capacity and the extent of the improvement in sport performance are constrained by the performer's genetic capacities and early environmental experiences, including physique and intellect.

11 Improvements in sport performance are difficult to predict because of the range of factors influencing performance, including the number of and complexity of inter-relationship between variables and the non-mechanistic response by performers to training stimuli.

12 The assessment of coaching effectiveness is determined in part by relative and absolute measurement of outcomes.

13 The implementation of the coaching process is constrained by the resources available, such as funding, equipment, facility access and appropriate competition. This also includes human resources, such as the skills and knowledge of the coaching team.

14 The intensity of the interaction characteristic of the coaching process is most often, but not exclusively, marked by empathy between coach and performer, which is likely to enhance the process.

15 The core elements and assumptions of the coaching process are not negated by the very wide range of behavioural styles, ideological approaches or value frameworks adopted by performers and coaches.

16 Although core processes remain constant, the balance of performance component priorities and the coach's role in competition management are influenced by sport specificity.

17 The range of skills and knowledge required to implement fully the coaching process implies that the process can be most appropriately facilitated by a team of coaches and other specialists.

18 The sports coaching process is best conceptualised and modelled as having four levels or stages: direct intervention, intervention support, management of constraints and strategic co-ordination and integration.

19 The defining feature of performance sports coaching leadership is the strategic integration and co-ordination of the process. This defines sports coaching as a cognitive process.

20 The fullest expression of the sports coaching process is to be found in circumstances in which the intensity of performance preparation and the accompanying committed engagement and resourcing are appropriate to the optimum achievement of performance objectives.

Question Box

These assumptions can be divided into those that are sociocultural, about performance, about the nature of the process and about effective practice. Are the assumptions internally consistent? Do they reflect performance sport?

IDENTIFYING THE BUILDING BLOCKS

These 'building blocks' are a further set of assumptions (see Figure 6.1). Rather than the previous set of assumptions, which delineated the coaching process, these starter concepts identify those constituent parts of the model of the coaching process that are necessary to 'bring it to life'. They may be thought of as implementation assumptions. These features of the model will not be obvious in any diagrammatic representation of the process but they are necessary for it to be implemented. This also gives these components some potential value as evaluation criteria.

The information platform
Coaching expertise
Performer capabilities
Analysis of performance
Operationalisation
Systematic development
Planning
Goal setting
Regulation procedures
Monitoring procedures
Preparation and training programme
Competition programme
Individualisation
Personal and social meaning

Figure 6.1 *The building blocks of the coaching process*

The multiple variations in and between the building blocks go some way to explaining how the model can accommodate differentiation and contextualisation between coaching processes without losing the core pattern evident in the model. It may be useful to think of the coaching process as a 'wall constructed of building blocks'. The same building blocks are used in each wall but they are of different sizes and quality, and constructed differently by each coach. Each of the components is described in some depth.

Critical Concept

The same elements of the coaching process are used in each 'wall' but they are of different sizes and quality, and constructed differently by each coach.

The information platform

Information is the fuel required to feed the implementation of the process. Planning, decision making, regulating, monitoring and evaluating in a systematic and logical fashion depend on the availability of the necessary and appropriate information. An enormous amount of detailed information is generated about the athlete's or team's performance and this is used in the planning of training schedules. However, there is a wealth of other 'intelligence' that has to be available: opposition characteristics and form, developments in technical and tactical knowledge, competition programme and venues, and, of course, information about the performers themselves – social, educational, historical performance record and so on.

- It is useful to distinguish between awareness and intelligence gathering, and the information/data that has to be generated in the implementation of the coaching process. The latter requirement highlights an important part of the coach's practice.
- A feature of coaching practice will be the generation, storage and retrieval of this potentially vast range of information. Modern methods of electronic storage and retrieval will assist the coach.
- There is a fine line between information and the coach's capacity to make use of it and to understand its implications – the latter being better termed 'knowledge'.

Question Box

Is evidence of the generation, storage and use of information/data a valuable way of determining whether or not the coach operates in a systematic fashion?

Coaching expertise

The knowledge and skills of the coach will be a key feature of the implementation of the coaching process, and the form and nature of the process are likely to be shaped by these capacities and the coach's personal characteristics and values. Each of the four levels of the process, from direct intervention to strategic integration and co-ordination, requires a distinctive set of skills and knowledge. The matrix of cognitive and craft skills will be exercised in communication, management, leadership and decision-making contexts, sometimes requiring speedy action and at other times with considered reflection. Coaches may also require sport-specific skills and expertise, although this is very sport specific and may also depend on role. Knowledge can be usefully subdivided into three categories: sport-specific knowledge (technique, tactics, equipment, performance developments and so on); established principles of practice (including training theory, coping strategies, planning, injury prevention, learning and teaching strategies); and sub-discipline knowledge (such as sport psychology, exercise physiology and sport biomechanics.).

■　In terms of being a building block for the coaching process, it is assumed that the necessary skills and knowledge are present within the coaching team and among specialists available, and not only the individual coach. In practice, however, the performance coach is required to exercise or understand the full range of expertise (without some of the more specialist and detailed knowledge and expertise of the support team experts).

■　The delivery of the coach's expertise involves a complex series of professional short-cuts and decision making, dependent on tacit knowledge and routines, but open to crisis management or more considered reflection as required.

■　The coach's knowledge, in the sense of its exercise or use, can also be usefully categorised into 'declarative' (knowledge about), 'procedural' (knowledge how to), and 'propositional' (what will happen if).

Performer capabilities

In practice, the coaching process is meaningless without individual performers or teams and they are, therefore, a crucial and indispensable building block. The performers' current and potential capabilities determine both performance goals and achievement, although this is not an easy judgement to make. The complex interaction between genetic endowment, environmental influences and learning, technology and the vagaries of specific performances make prediction of achievement very difficult. This is evident in talent identification and recruitment procedures, which remain somewhat subjective exercises. Nevertheless, while hereditary factors may set the limits of performance, the quality of the coaching process will determine how close to those limits the performer will reach.

■　A degree of individualisation is implied in the delivery of the coaching process. This is made much more difficult for coaches who are working in team sports.

 Critical Concept

Hereditary factors may set the limits of performance. The quality of the coaching process will determine how close to those limits the performer will reach.

Analysis of performance

Improvement of sport performance is the central purpose of the coaching process, and a detailed knowledge and understanding of performance is essential for almost all stages in the process – from target setting, prediction and monitoring progression to training programme design, and planning strategy and tactics. One of the assumptions on which the coaching process is based is that systematic and co-ordinated improvements in individual components of performance, and, of course, rehearsal and repetition of the total performance under appropriate conditions, will lead to improved competition performance.

■ Although sport performance can be expressed in terms of result, time, score, position and so on (and this is useful for recording progress and measuring outcomes), it can only usefully be understood and accounted for in terms of the component parts of the performance.

■ Sport performance has a number of component parts, which are always present: primary components (technique, physical, tactical, strategic, event-related, psychological, attitudinal) and secondary components (equipment, general psychological disposition, medical condition, social interaction).

■ The balance between primary and secondary components (e.g., on the dependence on equipment or medical status) will differ between sports.

■ Coaches will attempt to ensure that explanations for performance are couched in terms of stable, controllable factors (tactics, physical condition) rather than unstable factors (opposition tactics, weather and effort). The preparation programme will be designed to influence directly the stable factors and to prepare performers to cope with less predictable factors.

■ Coaches will often distinguish between the outcomes of performance (comparative result) and the outputs of performance (achievement in components, or absolute measures).

 Critical Concept

Systematic and co-ordinated improvements in individual components of performance, and, of course, rehearsal and repetition of the total performance under appropriate conditions, will lead to improved competition performance.

 Question Box

Is a threshold level of knowledge required before becoming a performance coach? Is the novice performance coach already a sport specialist?

Operationalisation

The coaching process becomes evident in coaching practice. This involves the behaviour and practice of performer and coach, and the translation of planning and intentions into preparation and competition. The detailed operationalisation of the process is individualised and contextualised, but it can be recognised in three management functions: practice management (planning and directing training sessions and other forms of preparation); competition management (preparation, selection and direction); and programme management (such as administration, organisation, finance and liaison).

- The balance of practice and competition management duties will be very much influenced by the sport and the availability and contribution of support personnel.
- The extent of programme management is dependent on the organisational context within which the coach operates.

Systematic development

The assumption of a rational approach and the purposeful integration of the contributing performance variables towards an identified goal result in a need for systematic progression towards those goals. Improvement in performance is intended to be stable, predictable and, of course, manageable. In addition, there is a scientific foundation (or principled practice approach) to performance enhancement. It is not intended that this should (or could) result from chance or unplanned activity. Taken together, this points to progression being based on attempts to control the variables influencing performance and to implementation decisions being based on evidence, principle and accuracy.

- Nevertheless, there may be some sport-specific parameters that challenge the capacity to act in a systematic fashion in the implementation of the coaching process.
- When discussing coaching practice, it will become evident that this is one of the building blocks that is used with great variation by each coach.

Planning

As a result of the adoption of a rational and systematic approach to improving performance and the assumption that coaching involves an intention to reduce the unpredictability of performance, planning is an essential and central element of the coaching process. Planning involves a predetermination of practice, which is intended to capture the sequencing, level and nature of activity necessary to achieve goals. Planning has its own principles of good practice and these incorporate principles from other sub-disciplines involved in improving and sustaining performance. The output from planning also provides a regulation and evaluation mechanism.

- Planning follows a recognised set of procedures: status review, goal setting, structuring of targets and objectives, implications for performance components identified, pre-planning model devised (extent of the programme), and preparation (including performance components) and competition cycles identified. This template is then used to devise workloads and activities for shorter cycles and individual sessions.
- Planning models are quite distinctive for league sport activity and for target sports (long periods of preparation). Contingency planning may be an important feature of planning in sport.

Critical Concept

Planning involves a predetermination of practice, which is intended to capture the sequencing, level and nature of activity necessary to achieve goals.

Goal setting

Goal setting is a planning exercise and necessary to give direction and purpose to the coaching process. The targets set are also an important part of the management of progression, achievement, success and failure by the athlete. Acknowledgement of the goals set will also impact on the purposeful engagement of the athlete in the learning process. Goal setting provides an integrative element that links the athletes' potential and aspirations, environmental and organisational resources and aspirations, and the operationalisation of the process. The goals and the preparation and performance needed to reach these goals drive the planning exercise.

- There will be distinctions drawn between outcome goals (related to results and public measures of success) and output goals, which are best described in terms of performance components and, if possible, absolute measures of performance or performance improvement. Goals can also be described in process (such as adherence to training) and product terms.
- It may be necessary to reach an accommodation between personal and organisation goals and this is very evident in team sports.

Regulation procedures

The process nature of coaching brings with it a requirement for regulating that process. It can be assumed that variation and change are inevitable: achievement against targets will be variable, the environment is changeable, and ensuring the benefits of systematic application of training principles requires constant adjustment of workloads. Regulation implies a continuous process of achieving a best fit between planning and goal setting, the current and projected status of the athlete, and evolving circumstances. Regulation is the action that follows from monitoring to ensure that the objectives are likely to be achieved.

- There are some general sub-processes that should ensure regulation – planning, goal setting and monitoring, for example.
- Perhaps more challenging is to identify and quantify the thresholds, catalysts and decision-filters that constitute the decision-making criteria by which the coach exerts control over the process.

Monitoring procedures

Many of the features of the coaching process – rational approach, planning, performance analysis and progression – are based on the premise that sufficient and suitable data are available on which to make judgements. The operationalisation of the coaching process therefore assumes that there is a continuous process of monitoring, not just in competition but also in training and preparation.

■   The range of monitoring mechanisms will include video recording, athlete responses, telemetry, notation, field procedures (heart-rate, timing), and laboratory measurement when appropriate.
■   A further implication is that the data gathered will be stored in an organised and retrievable fashion.

Preparation and training programme

The improvement or maintenance of performance implicit in the coaching process cannot be achieved in the longer term by participation in competition alone. The need to isolate performance components, to provide opportunity for rehearsal and practice, and to control workload intensity is achieved by a series of preparation (or training) sessions. The adaptation of the performer in performance components (physical capacity, technique, decision making, patterns of play, emotional resilience, amongst others) and the integration of those component changes are achieved through a planned series of activities. It is partly this emphasis on preparation that distinguishes the performance sportsperson from the less committed participation sportsperson.

■   Preparation involves a very full range of activities, including recovery activities, strategy discussions, individual psychological preparation, rehearsal competitions, and so on, in addition to the more obvious 'training session'.

Competition programme

Involvement in sport competition is assumed in the characteristics of the coaching process, although clearly this involvement can vary significantly in level, scale and intensity. Competition scheduling and the relationship between competitions and goals set have a very significant influence on planning and periodising the yearly (and beyond) programme. Competition results are also used to measure progress and success. The very nature of sport competition means that the intended goals in one coaching process are actively contested by the athletes and coaches associated with another coaching process.

■   The selection and scheduling of competitions will be important in some sports, and imply a degree of flexibility. For other sports (notably team league sports), the competition framework may be predetermined and to some extent (success in cup competitions leading to a prolonged competition programme, for example) difficult to predict.

Individualisation

One of the basic principles in the operationalisation of the coaching process is that it will be individualised to the needs of the performer. The extent of this individualisation will depend on factors such as the size of squads and team groups, sport specialisms (events, distances, positions), the extent to which the individual's needs have been identified, and the degree of systematic interpretation and implementation of the process. Although the use of training principles and other principles of practice may result in 'recipe'-type planning and delivery, it is assumed that the coaching process will operate most effectively when individualised to the performer.

■ All coaching processes will be unique. Not only do individual performers and groups of performers differ in their aspirations and potential, but the resource context of the process (including other performers) will also differ.
■ Coaches will also have particular approaches to the operationalisation of the process. The coach's style and values are discussed in later chapters.
■ The specificity of the sport will further divide coaching processes and coaching practices, depending on factors such as the coach's role in competition.

Personal and social meaning

Dealing with processes and sub-processes can tend to mask the fact that the coaching process is essentially an interpersonal activity. The coaching process takes place in personal and social space and its operationalisation impacts on both the individuals concerned and the social world around them. The values, idiosyncrasies and personal qualities of individuals are reflected in interpersonal behaviour and are exacerbated by perceptions of success and failure. The performer's (and coach's) psychological state forms part of their performance readiness, and it is hardly surprising that this is linked to emotional responses. In addition, the individual's engagement in the process has a personal meaning in terms of commitment, self-identity and potential satisfaction. Once again these are challenged by perceptions of success and failure and by social interaction throughout the process. The coaching process also occupies a social space and this brings with it elements of social recognition, status, legal and ethical (social values) behaviour, and its operationalisation cannot be divorced from these social meanings.

These building blocks are a combination of the constituent parts, the facilitating procedures and the assumed activities that take place when the coaching process is operationalised. The next section illustrates the process.

THE MODEL

The third part of the model is a visual representation of the component parts of the coaching process and the relationships and sequencing between components. Figure 6.2 illustrates the model in a two-dimensional diagram. At this point it is worth reiterating that the model is more detailed than the others available but it also demonstrates a number of the weaknesses of the model 'for':

1   The chief of these is that the component parts and sub-processes are identified but the relationships between them (including the means by which these relationships are effected) cannot easily be illustrated in such diagrams.
2   Nevertheless, there has been an attempt to emphasise the feedback circles and decision points within the process. The procedures for executing this decision making will be dealt with in the next chapter.

The model of the coaching process can be summarised in the following way (and treated as a Critical Concept):

> The sports coaching process is a cyclical series of activities centred on a dynamic set of performance goals. The process is serial and continuous. A variable pattern of coach interventions, athlete activity and organisational activity is devised to respond to a set of external constraints and personal and performance goals, which are time dependent. A flexible model of expectations, based on current status and identified performance targets, is generated and used to regulate the process. Constant feedback loops and a series of threshold decisions points regulate the model.

OPERATIONALISING THE MODEL

Coaching practice forms the substance of the next chapter and deals with the detailed operationalisation of the model. It has already become clear that this is not a model that the novice coach will attempt to adopt but one that informs education and training, and is valuable for analysing and reflecting on practice. Nevertheless, there are a number of features of the model that should be emphasised.

The control box

Part of the model is reproduced here in order to focus attention on the regulation process (see Figure 6.3). In previous chapters there has been an accumulation of ideas (about integration, co-ordination, mental models, decision making and the coach's overview of the process). This section of the model is the control box that regulates the process. An essential feature of moving from a novice to expert coach is the gradual development of the capacity of the control box.

A series of threshold decisions helps the coach to control the myriad potential decisions to be taken and to integrate the great range of data that is constantly presented. Feedback loops from training and competition (and from interaction with the athlete) come to the control box where the feedback both informs current status evaluations and is evaluated against the performance model, existing planning intentions and any external environmental circumstances that may have influenced performance. In most cases, the cognitive computations will fall well within acceptable limits and the coaching process interventions continue as planned. In some cases, there will be too great a difference

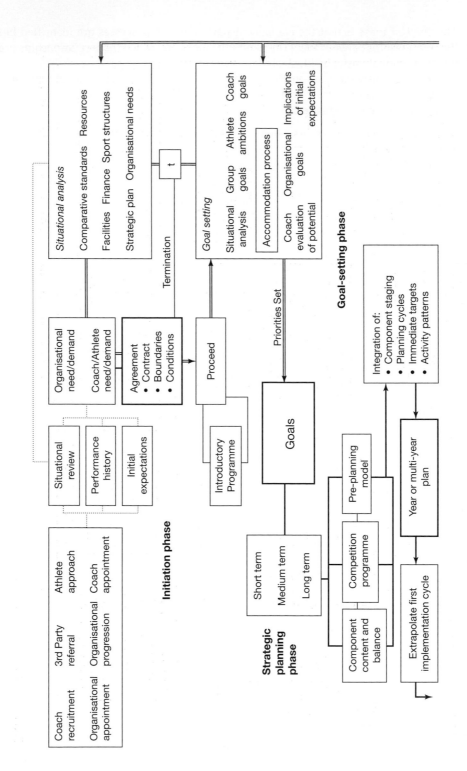

Initiation phase

Situational analysis
Comparative standards   Resources
Facilities   Finance   Sport structures
Strategic plan   Organisational needs

Organisational need/demand
Coach/Athlete need/demand

Agreement
• Contract
• Boundaries
• Conditions

Termination

t

Proceed

Introductory Programme

Situational review

Performance history

Initial expectations

Coach recruitment   3rd Party referral   Athlete approach
Organisational appointment   Organisational progression   Coach appointment

Goal setting
Situational analysis   Group goals   Athlete ambitions   Coach goals

Accommodation process

Coach evaluation of potential   Organisational goals   Implications of initial expectations

Goal-setting phase

Priorities Set

Goals

Short term
Medium term
Long term

Pre-planning model

Competition programme

Component content and balance

Strategic planning phase

Integration of:
• Component staging
• Planning cycles
• Immediate targets
• Activity patterns

Year or multi-year plan

Extrapolate first implementation cycle

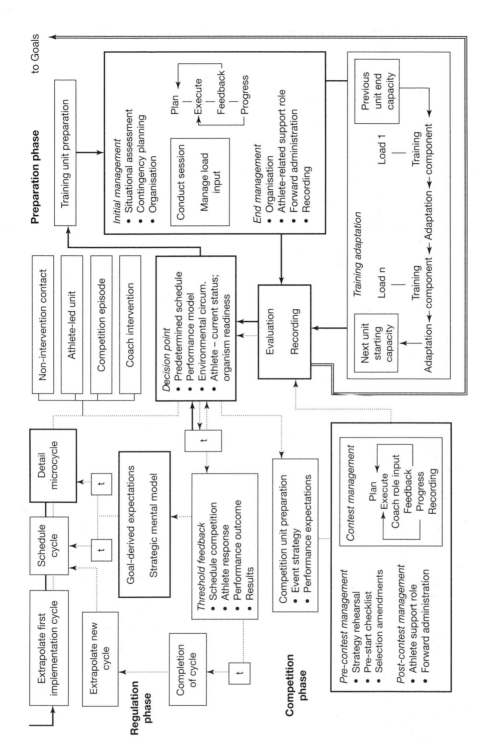

Figure 6.2 *The coaching process*

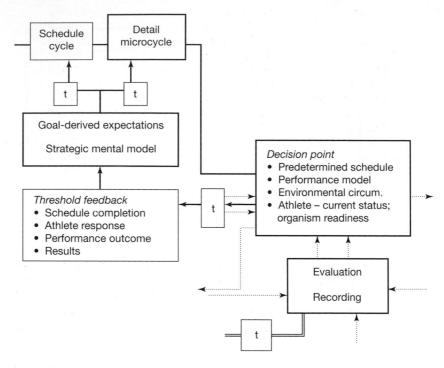

Figure 6.3 *The control box of the coaching process*

between the anticipated and actual achievement. If this persists, a threshold is breached and the coach will effect changes to the programme of interventions (or possibly alter the level of expectations).

The system of thresholds allows the coach to use efficient and effective professional shortcuts (dealt with in the next chapter). There is a hierarchy of threshold decisions, some of which are capable of being effected within modest contingency planning and some of which require more substantive re-planning. The hierarchy moves from sessional interventions that require adjustment to the training loadings, to the next stage, in which accumulative breaches lead to deliberative re-scheduling of preparation cycles, and finally to the point at which goals may need to be adjusted. The breaches of the thresholds can be in training, in competition and in process elements of adherence/resourcing and so on.

Thresholds

One of the weaknesses acknowledged in the model is the absence of detailed relationships between component elements or stages of the model – partly threshold values, but also the effect of changes in one element on others (the influence of organisational goals on individual goal setting, or the impact of coaching behaviour on competition performance). It is one of the purposes of the coaching process model that it should be used to generate research on such questions.

Coaches	Athletics	Volleyball	Swimming
1	1 week	Wait as long as possible	1 session
2	1 week	If major, 2 games	Quickly
3	Immediate action	Short a time as possible	Less than 1 cycle
4	Immediate action	2 weeks	4 weeks
5	Less than 4 weeks	If critical, constant attention	2–3 days
6	2–4 weeks	3 training sessions	1 week
7	4 weeks	½ a season	3–4 weeks
8	8 weeks	¾ season	Investigate immediately
9	2 weeks	Immediate action	2–3 sessions
10	—	—	2 weeks

Source: Lyle 1991; Lyle 1992

Figure 6.4 *Threshold responses by coaches in three sports*

Figures 6.4 and 6.5 demonstrate the sort of findings that can be used to illuminate coaching practice. Two examples are given, each of them from some earlier work by the author (Lyle 1991; Lyle 1992). The tables are composed of questions posed to experienced coaches about how they would deal with 'threshold issues'. The responses were not quantified, and are provided merely to illustrate that it is possible to particularise these decision stages.

Figure 6.4 details the responses of coaches to the following question: 'For how long would the non-achievement of training targets be allowed to continue before taking steps to alter the situation?'

Although used merely for illustration, these data were given by practising, experienced coaches. For the most part, coaches were concerned to take fairly immediate or short-term action, although the range of responses is extensive and there is a sense of not wanting to react too immediately.

In the second example, coaches were asked the following question, which was couched in terms of a mental model of performance: 'How significantly would the likely performance differ from the predicted one before there would be a change of expectations?' This question probes the threshold values required to change goal-derived expectations. The responses were collated in textual form and again display a wide range of values (see Figure 6.5).

There are some clear sport-specific differences and also some significant differences between coaches. It would seem that coaches are reluctant to change – perhaps a recognition that fluctuation is normal, or perhaps that too much change is unsettling for the performer.

What is reinforced from these data is that coaches operate idiosyncratic practices and that a good deal of further research is required with successful, expert coaches.

Coach	Athletics	Volleyball	Swimming
1	Not change if possible	Try to hold on	Would need to be significant
2	Threshold (not specified)	If 2 games don't match image, change	Leave as long as possible
3	Leave as long as possible	Try to leave	Intuitive action when not achieving
4	Leave as long as possible	Would have to be very significant	Very small
5	Leave as long as possible	Pretty far off course	Significantly
6	I have faith in planning	Until manifestly obvious	Not much
7	When obvious to the athlete	One session	Keep going if possible
8	Leave to right itself	If critical or bad (unexpected) result	Quite a lot
9	—	—	Significantly

Source: Lyle 1991; Lyle 1992

Figure 6.5 *Coaches' responses to performance deficit*

Sport specificity

The coaches' responses used in Figures 6.4 and 6.5 point to sport-specific differences in operationalising the model. Coaching practice in different categories of sports is dealt with in the next chapter. However, as an idealised conceptual model, it is designed to apply to all coaches and coaching processes. Of course, when the actual practice is mapped onto the model, the resultant pattern will be different for all coaches and most sports. It is partly this diversity that necessitated the ideal model approach.

If the model is not appropriate for describing a particular coaching practice, this should be evident in the assumptions or building blocks. Remember also that the process is described in some detail, and it has already been acknowledged that a partial application of the model is possible. Research is likely to show that the key phases are emphasised and balanced differently across sports. Figure 6.6 lists the key stages in the model.

Initiation
Goal setting
Strategic planning
Regulation
Preparation
Competition

Figure 6.6 *Principal model phases*

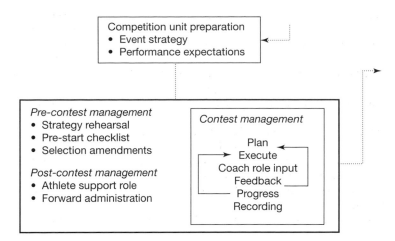

Figure 6.7 *Generalised competition phase*

Sport-specific differences will lead to differential emphases on these stages of process components. Given the process nature of the coaching process, these stages are interdependent and cyclical. They form a useful reference point for identification of competences, for research and for education.

Adapting the model

One of the intentions of working with the conceptual framework is that the model should be adapted continuously, as evidence of practice becomes available. The next example shows how the generalised model conceptualisation of part of the competition phase can be made more sophisticated when evidence of coaches' behaviour is incorporated. Figure 6.7 reproduces the section of the model dealing with the competition phase. With further investigation (Lyle 1998b), this might be re-conceptualised more usefully (and accurately), as represented in Figure 6.8.

The more sophisticated model identifies the threshold decision points and, perhaps more interestingly, the distinction between a confirmed competition strategy and an emergent strategy. The competition role input is, of course, very dependent on the sport and the coach's role in competition. It is this gradual refinement of the model that will lead to a better analytical tool, a more accurate model and, ultimately, a better understanding of coaching practice.

The model is another way of saying, 'This is what I think coaching is about'. It is also a vehicle for research and a reflection of the fruits of that research. This model began as an ideal model and was the catalyst for an investigation into the mechanisms for professional shortcuts – the control box and its attendant processes of cognitive modelling, thresholds, routine and recipes.

The model should be treated in the same fashion as the others reviewed. Therefore, the strengths and weaknesses have been identified as in the table below:

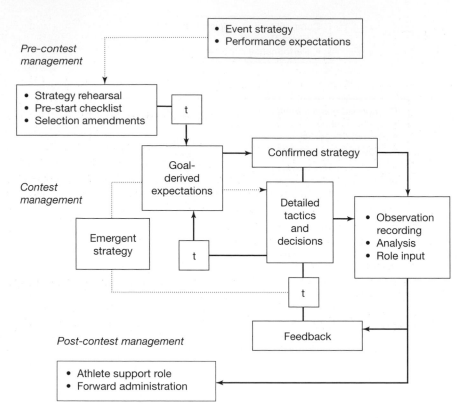

Source: Adapted and interpreted from Lyle (1998b)

Figure 6.8 *Upgraded model of the competition phase*

Strengths	Weaknesses
Assumptions identified	Complicated
Key building blocks identified	Relationship/linkages not sophisticated
Detailed	Too ideal
Useful for research	Generic (immediate applicability compromised)
Comprehensive	Individual stages not detailed
Demonstrates the need for strategic overview	
Process emphasis	

Inevitably (although this is a criticism), the model is stronger in structure than function. In other words, demonstrating the model in action is problematical. The next chapter focuses on coaching practice and how the model is operationalised.

SUMMARY

This chapter will have familiarised you with the following:

■ a model for the sports coaching process based on the concept of an 'ideal model';
■ the prior assumptions on which the model is predicated – which can be used to critique the model;
■ the building blocks of the model – the information platform, coaching expertise, performer capabilities, analysis of performance, operationalisation, systematic development, planning, goal setting, regulation procedures, monitoring procedures, preparation and training programme, competition programme, individualisation, personal and social meaning;
■ a graphical representation of the model;
■ a number of features of the operationalisation of the model:

  – the control box
  – the use of thresholds to exemplify the relationship between various elements of the model
  – the sport-specificity of the model
  – an example of the upgrading of the model based on research findings, and
  – an analysis of the strengths and weaknesses of the model.

PROJECTS

■ Select a component part of the model. Devise an investigation to test the aptness of the model in practice. Re-design the model in line with your findings.
■ Review the prior assumptions. Select three or four and investigate their impact on the model. What would be the impact of a change in these assumptions?
■ Design an investigation into the comparability of two sports in the way that coaches from those sports 'build the wall'. Attempt to measure the emphasis given to individual building blocks by the two groups of coaches.
■ Select two component parts of the model. Design an investigation to identify the nature of the relationship between the components. This might require an investigation into coaching practice in different circumstances, or coaches with different levels of expertise.

Reading

The model has been devised by the author in order to stimulate debate, analysis and research. Therefore, there is as yet no appropriate supporting reading relating to its analysis or criticism.

CHAPTER SEVEN

▼   COACHING PRACTICE

■ Introduction   116
■ Systematic Coaching Behaviours   119
■ The Picture from Research   125
■ Planning the Process   125
■ Implementation Behaviour: Explaining Coaches' Expertise   131
■ Coaching Practice: A Condensed Description   142
■ Sport Specificity in Coaching Practice   144
■ Summary   146
■ Projects and Reading   147

INTRODUCTION

Attention to the developing conceptual framework should supply answers to the basic question, 'How can the practice/behaviour of sports coaches be described, analysed and explained, and thereby better understood?' Thus far, that part of the framework dealing with key characteristics, purposes, role and boundaries has produced a broad template for coaching behaviour but it is necessary now to go beyond the obvious and superficial. It is not sufficient to describe the coach's intended behaviour as facilitating improved performance and managing the resultant programme. This is of very limited assistance for evaluation and in structuring coach education. The role of the coach is implemented through four sets of behaviours: direct intervention, intervention support, managing resources, and meta-functions co-ordinating the process. What is required is to translate this into more detailed analysis of practice, comparing actual practice with how coaches might be modelled to behave.

A number of supplementary questions arise immediately: Is coaching practice sport specific? Is coaching behaviour stable and consistent across varying circumstances? What is the balance of influences between social context, personal predisposition and process characteristics? What is the impact of coaching boundary changes on coaching practice? This list has the feel of an unfulfilled research agenda rather than a list of chapter contents!

Nevertheless, the capacity to analyse coaching practice in detail depends on a sound conceptual awareness of the coaching process and, in turn, provides a number of additional properties for the emerging conceptual framework:

- a language of analysis for describing coaches day-to-day practice;
- a more definitive descriptive capacity for analysing coaching practice – establishing the relationship between coaching practice and athlete/team performance is problematical; being able to describe fully the coaching practice element is a contribution towards resolving that issue;
- professionalisation assumes the capacity to describe professional practice and to recognise those factors exerting the greatest influence on it;
- an acknowledgement of the relationship that exists between the time and place circumstances of individual processes and the generality of the conceptual framework;
- identification of the relevant factors to be taken into account when predicting behaviour and potentially evaluating coach effectiveness (dealt with in a later chapter).

Not surprisingly, the task is not an easy one and there are a number of potential barriers. First, there have been few, if any, attempts to aggregate and consolidate the evidence of research into coaching behaviour. The focus of the research has been on observable intervention skills, such as communication and feedback styles, and much less so on the cognitive skills involving decision making, such as session management, manipulation of training drills, contingency planning or contest management. The failure to investigate such behaviours has limited the depth of understanding about coaching practice, which in turn has constrained enquiry. Research has asked questions about coaches' behaviour but rarely about the balancing and prioritising of behaviours that become accumulated into coaching practice. Second, the problem of investigating coaches' decision making is exacerbated by the tacit nature of the knowledge base. Coaches appear to use intuition and professional 'tricks of the trade' to make their tasks manageable. Salmela (1995) expresses the view that such tacit knowledge can be verbalised by coaches but, even so, it challenges the investigative skills of the researcher.

The third problem area is the specificity of coaching practice to individual sports. This is given some attention in this chapter. Despite the earnestly argued tenet in this framework that sports coaching is a generic process, it is immediately clear that the realisation of generic principles is very different in, for example, archery, badminton, rugby union and swimming. The intention is the same but the coaches' practice will be different.

The fourth issue is the uniqueness of each coaching process. The point has already been made that there is no ideal practice and no average practice. The number of potential

---

 Critical Concept

There is no ideal practice and no average practice. The number of potential variables, and the 'degrees of freedom' within these variables, is extensive. Descriptions and analyses of coaching practice must, therefore, be understood in their unique context.

variables, and the 'degrees of freedom' within these variables, is extensive. Descriptions and analyses of coaching practice must, therefore, be understood in their unique context.

Based on those aspects of the conceptual framework already constructed, there are a number of features of the coaching process that bear upon the extent to which descriptions of practice can be understood in a generic or contextualised manner:

- The patterning of contributory variables is very complex. Each of these impacts on the performer/performance but can be varied by the coach and by external agencies. Coaching practice is about managing these variables and influencing the circumstances affecting the process to as great an extent as is possible.
- It would be unreasonable to expect coaches to 're-invent' practice for each group of athletes or each season – despite the obvious variety in aspirations, abilities and character. Nevertheless, performers will have a particular combination of genetic disposition, stage of performance development, and technical idiosyncrasies to require individualised treatment. Coaching practice, therefore, will have to balance sufficient specificity with a 'routinised' practice.
- This principle is also evident in the environmental contextualisation of the coaching process. The coincidence of performers, competition, resources, organisational structures and goals results in a process that must be understood in its 'time and place'. There is also a discipline imposed by the competition structure.
- Finally, coaching practice will be influenced by the uncertainty element of the coaching process. There are a number of factors – ranging from the contested nature of competition to the physiological, psychological and emotional responses of the performer (and coach) – that make the 'unfolding' of the coaching process somewhat unpredictable.

 Question Box

There is no doubt about the need for specificity of design and delivery and yet there is clearly a generic coaching process and 'process skills' element. How does coach education deal with this?

The coaching process is characterised by uncertainty, complexity and uniqueness. The fact that this makes it difficult to describe and analyse has already been pointed out. The result, however, is that coaching practice has to deal with a continuum from the controllable and predictable to the unpredictable, the latter requiring more contingency, and possibly crisis, management. Once again, this reinforces the cognitive skills associated with contingency planning and solving problems. The description of sports coaching permeating this introduction to the chapter is clearly one that assumes performance coaching. When describing coaching practice, it is assumed that the performance coaching paradigm offers the most appropriate context for the all-embracing, comprehensive and expert expression of coaching practice. Participation coaching practice will embody this more comprehensive form to the extent demanded by the circumstances.

HOW DO COACHES BEHAVE?

Throughout the chapter coaching behaviour and practice have been used rather inter-changeably. Coaching behaviour should be used to describe coaching activity, responses and conduct that are related to one, or a restricted range of, tasks or issues. Such issues might involve leadership behaviour, feedback styles, demonstrating, recording, observing athletes, or managing a training session. Remember that this is not just observable behaviour but includes cognitive activity, decision making and associated outcomes as well. Coaching practice is the accumulation and contextualisation of those behaviours. Coaching practice, therefore, might focus on the common features of behaviour (perhaps interpersonal style or contingency planning), the balance of behaviours in comparison to role, the relationship between behavioural demands and the coach's skills, or the social/values context within which behaviour is displayed (ethical issues, for example).

This chapter focuses on the coach's behaviour and some of the common elements of practice, such as planning and decision making. The interpersonal and contextual analysis of coaching practice is given very substantive treatment in subsequent chapters. To begin with, there is an examination of the extent to which coaching practice can be said to be systematic. This is followed by a more detailed examination of the research evidence on coaching behaviour. Two specific issues are then covered: planning and decision making. The chapter concludes with a look at the sport specificity of coaching practice.

SYSTEMATIC COACHING BEHAVIOURS

When the ideal model of the coaching process was proposed, in the previous chapter, it assumed a rational, logical and constraint-free approach: in other words, a systematic approach to the business of coaching. Despite this, a common-sense perspective might begin with the view that this would be a very difficult practice to fulfil, and that some coaching processes are likely to be more systematic than others. Figure 7.1 illustrates this in a simple model.

The purpose of this section of the chapter is to examine the nature of more or less systematic practice as an 'overview' feature that will provide a reference point for more specific behaviours. In passing, it should also be noted that this may be a useful comparative evaluation tool for coaching practice. The first question is, What is meant by systematic practice?

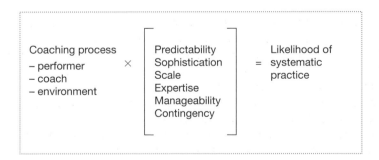

Figure 7.1 *Factors influencing the likelihood of systematic practice*

The characteristics of systematic coaching practice are that

- the process will be comprehensive in its coverage and attention to detail;
- actions will be planned, calculated and goal directed;
- there will be a marked degree of management or 'control' of the process, particularly through regulating performance preparations; and
- decision making is based on established principles of good practice.

In an earlier passage, sports coaching was described as an attempt to reduce the unpredictability of performance within specified boundaries of time, place and resource. The word 'attempt' is important. When dealing with human behaviour, it is not unreasonable to preface systematic with the caveats 'as possible', or 'within reason'. The description of systematic practice follows logically from that earlier statement. The argument has been presented in this way.

> In order to reduce unpredictability (which assumes tailoring to suit individual needs), the coach will attempt to control as many as possible of the variables affecting performance and their preparation. The systematic regulation of the process will involve planning, recording, monitoring, problem solving and calculated decision-making. In constraint-free circumstances, we might expect the coach to adopt a rigorous detailed approach to practice. This implies monitoring progress, compiling player profiles, measuring performance capacities and operating from predetermined plans and schedules. The coach's strategic goals are constantly evaluated through the monitoring and recording of the individualised workloads from each training session. Strategic and tactical decisions in competition are based on objective analyses of the performances of the performers and their opponents.
>
> Lyle (1998c: 69)

One of the key features of systematic practice is the attempt at quality control by the coaching team. The extent to which the quality of the process and its sub-processes are assured may also be a useful measure of accountability and efficiency. Note also that it is the quality of the output and not the outcome that is assured. Control, in this sense, implies '*management to best advantage*' and should not imply negative connotations. There is no suggestion that 'control of the performer' is a feature of systematic coaching practice. Indeed, quality management is a useful maxim for coaching effectiveness studies.

 Question Box

The use of the words 'control' or 'manipulation' is intended to be directed to the range of performance variables but is often interpreted as a negative feature of interpersonal behaviour. How could this confusion be better explained?

HOW DO COACHES BEHAVE?

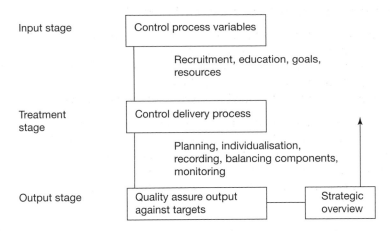

Figure 7.2 *Quality control stages*

Quality control occurs at a number of different stages. Figure 7.2 identifies these control stages using a simple input–treatment–output model.

There will also be a number of predictable features of the process (Figure 7.3) that will provide an indication of the likelihood of more or less systematic practice.

Identifying these potential barriers suggests that systematic coaching practice is a demanding exercise and will need to be evaluated in the light of what is feasible and realistic in the circumstances in which the coach and the athletes are engaged. However, there are further considerations. It is reasonable to expect that coaches will adopt a professional practice that is the most efficient and effective. The term 'systematic' should not imply that unnecessary procedures are employed or that coaches are constrained not to prioritise their time and effort. In describing and evaluating coaching behaviours, a number of common features should appear if the coach is to act efficiently in managing the process:

■ routinise regular practice where possible;
■ adopt option-reducing strategies for decision making;
■ prioritise record keeping;
■ focus attention through thresholds and key catalyst indicators to prevent over-monitoring;
■ avoid over-planning – maintain contingency approach;
■ retain flexibility and the human response approach.

However, these potential features of coaching practice are also tools for analysing evidence of coaches' practice. It is necessary to establish the extent to which coaches actually operate systematically. Before looking at some examples, it is important to point out that the term 'systematic' may have different connotations for the participation coach. Insofar as participation coaches are more episodic in their outlook and are less involved in longer-term planning, resource or competition management, it is possible for them to deliver sessions, and series of sessions, which are well organised and adhere to good principles

	Process feature	Potential barrier to systematic behaviour
Role	Part-time athlete or coach	Less impact of training principles
		Time pressures
	Number of assistants	Specificity of expertise available in full range of process
Complexity	Number of contributory performance components	Potentially enormous number of measurements and recording possibilities
		Specificity of goals, targets
Implementation	Individualisation	Problem of squad size, facility availability
	Workload management	Difficulty of measuring psychological, technical workloads
		Managing drills in complex sports
		Injury, illness, emotional response
	Monitoring	Maintaining an intelligence system
		Variable response to training loadings
		Interdependence of performance components
		Volume of data accumulated
	Human response	Emotion and effort as integral features of performance
		Reaction of performer to purely rational decision making
The sport	Pattern of engagement	Competition scheduling
		Competition role of coach
		Relative immutability of training cycles
Education	Coach expertise	Sufficiency of experience to assess and incorporate evidence-based decision making
		Evidence of good practice
Environment	Resources, finance, facilities	Impact of resourcing on option choices
		Impact of external agency goals and priorities

Figure 7.3 *Potential barriers to systematic practice*

of session structuring and management. It can also be assumed that the management of the programme is well organised. However, the absence of control of variables, the absence of instrumental preparation towards longer-term goals, and the lack of comprehensiveness in the programme signal that the term 'systematic' would be inappropriate.

 Question Box

Systematic behaviour is perceived not to be a feature of all coaching practice – even successful practice! Does this imply that recognising coaching practice is difficult or that successful athletes are not necessarily the product of effective coaches?

HOW DO COACHES BEHAVE?

How would the systematic approach be recognised? There are many possible criteria relating to the regulation of the programme. The following are examples of such criteria:

- the degree of adherence to predetermined plans;
- the quality and scale of record keeping;
- the individualisation of athletes' training programmes;
- precision in implementing training drills and exercises;
- the extent of workload monitoring and progress across performance components;
- the degree of incorporation of rigorously obtained evidence into programmes.

The chapter continues by examining two pieces of evidence on coaches' practice. In the first, Lyle (1991, 1992) investigated the self-reported coaching behaviours of thirty coaches of international performers, ten in each of athletics, volleyball and swimming. Figure 7.4 indicates the percentage of coaches who reported that they fulfilled the criteria described.

Criteria	Swimming	Volleyball	Athletics
Planning elements			
Written record of goals	20	10	0
Short-term goals identified	90	80	70
Long-term goals identified	90	30	90
Outline periodisation of the year	100	60	100
Plan for 4–5 weeks	100	70	90
Plan for one week	50	70	70
Use of pre-planning model	50	10	40
Total hours identified	40	38	40
Training targets identified	44	60	50
Competition targets identified	50	33	29
Monitoring elements			
Written plan for session	70	80	50
Written record of session	80	50	70
Workloads identified	90	40	80
Drills/exercises based on testing	90	0	0
Programmes individualised	40	20	80
Recording in systematic form	90	40	40
Close monitoring of personal training	50	30	20
Performance potential estimated			
– constantly	10	50	30
– each session	30	50	30
– at competition	90	80	90
– by objective testing	90	20	20
Sufficient data for goal setting	20	70	60

Source: Lyle (1991, 1992)

Figure 7.4 *Coaches' responses to systematic coaching criteria*

The evidence suggests that a number of criteria of systematic practice were clearly not fulfilled. The two tasks that stand out are the failure to monitor training programmes carried out when the coach is not present and the low incidence of individualisation of programmes. Although it is evident that planning is a central concern for these coaches, there are significant differences between sports and in recording and monitoring progress. Perhaps not surprisingly, competition performance is obviously a key factor for monitoring progress.

It should be noted, however, that this evidence can only be illustrative of coaching practice. There is no doubt that the coaches were 'performance orientated' but the coaches were almost all part-time, as were the great majority of the performers. The study needs to be repeated to assess the coaches' practice in less constrained circumstances. Nevertheless, it is valuable for highlighting areas in which completely systematic behaviour might be a problem.

In a similar investigation into the behaviour of hockey and swimming coaches, Cross (1995a, 1995b) found that there were a number of significant constraints to the implementation of the coaching process and that hockey coaches in particular exhibited a high degree of apparently less systematic practice.

The data collected in the studies were supplemented by in-depth interviews. These examples point to a conclusion that coaching practice is not best described as systematic in the sense that a rational, detailed application of principles to all components of performance in conditions of evidence-based decision making takes place, competition and training targets are always established and individualised training programmes are constantly delivered, monitored and recorded. On the other hand, coaching practice can be described as systematic in the sense that there is attention to planning, the approach is methodical, practice is based on principles of good practice, and there is set of procedures for efficient and prioritised monitoring, recording and decision-making behaviour. The findings can be described in a way that raises interesting suggestions about coaching practice, to which the chapter will return in a later section. It became clear that:

- there is a fairly detailed planning umbrella within which coaching action is determined;
- delivery activity is more likely to be applied contingently;
- monitoring progress and the decision making related to delivery is subject to a professional expertise, which is largely cognitive;
- the apparently intuitive practice of the performance coach (even within the rigorously applied schedules of some coaches) masks a complex set of cognitive processes which is the hall-mark of the expert coach;
- the 'shortcut' decision making is supplemented by a series of objective data and testing, and by competition outcomes.

Before exploring this cognitive activity in greater detail, it will be useful to evaluate the findings from research into coaches' behaviour.

THE PICTURE FROM RESEARCH

This book did not set out to be an aggregation of research findings on coaching practice. It has been clear from the outset that this is an attempt to establish a conceptual framework within which sports coaching can be better understood. Nevertheless, it is important to say a few words about why there is a very limited reliance on research into coaching behaviours. There are good reasons for doubting the efficacy of aggregating such diverse research:

1   One of the original reasons for writing the book and primary criticism of the literature is that the absence of a conceptual framework has limited the transferability and comparability of the findings.
2   The variation in the sample populations and the attendant variables is extreme: specific sport, age of athlete, philosophy/purpose (education, recreation, performance), practice/game/experimental intervention, expert/novice.
3   The research method also varies enormously: instrument used, intervention/naturalistic, number of coaches, descriptive/theory testing.
4   The majority of studies have employed systematic observation. This has focused attention on instruction, teaching/coaching contexts, and episodic interpretations of coaching.

The approach adopted in this section of the chapter is to be very selective. Where the construction of the conceptual framework has valued the support of specific papers, these have been acknowledged in the text. Figure 7.5 identifies a group of research studies with some indication of the sort of findings available. A further set of studies is also identified. These are very selective. They are dated only from 1990, and deal with elements of coaching behaviour and intervention practice related to the coaching process (rather than social context, interpersonal behaviour or career issues, which are reviewed in subsequent chapters). The intention is to point the reader in the direction of a body of research, then to establish the conceptual framework and invite the reader/student to conduct further analysis on the research from a fresh perspective.

PLANNING THE PROCESS

Planning is a specialised part of the coaching process and the capacity to progress from planning the session to planning for a multi-year cycle is a mark of the developing expertise of the performance coach. It is important to situate the planning process within the conceptual framework but this short section cannot do justice to the sophistication of planning practice in the space available. The emphasis given to the planning phase in the proposed model of the coaching process is testimony to its importance. Planning provides the link between aspirations, intentions and activity. It is a guide to day-by-day activity, provides a template against which changes can be calculated, and is a strategic overview of the process. As one of the defining characteristics of the coaching process, it is an essential element of performance coaching. In addition, there is a very strong link between planning and the earlier section on systematic practice. The criteria for evaluating practice as more or less systematic are firmly rooted in planning-led behaviour.

Study	Selected findings
Bloom, Durand-Bush & Salmela (1997)	Pre-competition practice relies on routines and the control of emotions
Bloom, Schinke & Salmela (1997)	Communication skills develop over time, reflecting changed role and interpersonal behaviour requirements
Bloom, Crumpton & Anderson (1999)	In contrast to beginner and intermediate level coaches, one-third of the coach's behaviours related to offensive/defensive strategies
Côte, Salmela, Trudel, Baria & Russell (1995a)	Coaches use hierarchical mental models that allow them to deal with problem solving
Cross (1995a, 1995b)	Swimming coaches exhibited more systematic practice than did hockey coaches, suggesting that team sports had particular challenges
Duke & Corlett (1992)	Basketball coaches' time-outs were dictated most by the players' physical status
Jones, Housner & Kornspan (1995)	Experienced coaches use contextual information more so than inexperienced coaches
Jones, Housner & Kornspan (1997)	Expert coaches make fewer changes to plans and have more alternatives available
Jones, Potrac & Ramalli (1999)	Coaches exhibited more instructional and hustle behaviours in contrast to managerial/ questioning/ positive modelling behaviours when in their teaching role
Liukkonen, Laakso & Telama (1996)	There is less humanistic behaviour as the level of competitive involvement increases; individual event coaches are more responsive than team coaches
Lyle (1992)	Coaches operated in an apparently intuitive fashion; they had a systematic planning shell but implementation was much less precise
Miller (1992)	The most prevalent behaviour of coaches was instruction: the greatest time was spent in silent observation
Salmela (1995)	Coaches use meta-cognitive models of the coaching process to regulate practice. These cognitive structures can be verbalised by coaches
Saury & Durand (1998)	Coaches use routines and cognitive anticipation based on flexible plans
Solomon, Striegel, Eliot, Heon, Maas & Wadya (1996)	Head coaches focused more on high expectancy athletes and mistakes: assistant coaches fulfilled more reinforcement and encouragement roles
Trudel, Côte & Bernard (1996)	Observation was an important aspect of behaviour; interaction behaviour was directed to players on the bench and in transition

See also

Black & Weiss (1992)
Burke, Peterson & Nix (1995)
Chase, Feltz & Lirgg (1997)
Hardy & Howard (1995)
Lacy & Goldston (1990)
Laughlin & Laughlin (1994)

Potrac, Jones & Armour (1997)
Salminen & Liukkonen (1996)
Seagrave & Ciancio (1990)
Trudel, Guertin, Bernard & Boileau (1991)
van der Mars, Darst & Sariscany (1991)
Vangucci, Potrac & Jones (1998)

Figure 7.5 Selected research studies on coaching practice

Critical Concept

Planning provides the link between aspirations, intentions and activity. It is a guide to day-by-day activity, provides a template against which changes can be calculated, and is a strategic overview of the process.

The purpose of this short section is to describe the different types of planning undertaken by coaches and to relate these to other aspects of the conceptual framework. In order to do this, the section is focused on planning principles, the influence of the competition cycle, types of planning and their associated skills, and a number of special features that are process-related.

Planning is generally taken to have two related meanings. The first is an overall approach to setting targets, reconciling various activities, establishing priorities, managing resources, maintaining focus on improvement and progression, and achieving goals. The second, perhaps more role-related, specifically refers to designing the athlete's/team's preparation programme – short-handed to 'the training schedule'. For performance coaches, the term 'training schedule' can be assumed to involve all of the direct intervention programme and not solely the physical preparation programme.

Planning is based on the premise that workloads can be manipulated and administered within a set of principles that will ensure that adaptation takes place in the athlete's capacity for performance. Performance is broken down into components (technical, tactical, psychological and physical) and progression in each component and in combination of components is achieved by regulating intensity, volume and other features of the work. Activity necessary to adapt energy systems, technical development, and other components is emphasised in particular phases of the training programme: some activities being precursors to others, and balances being struck between general training, specialised training, rehearsal, stabilisation/maintenance, competition and recovery. The differentiation is achieved by periodising the planning period. This means identifying major phases of the 'season' and subdividing into contributory phases. There are principles available to schedule micro-cycles (often 6–10 days) such as standard, competitive, impetus and recuperation (Bompa 1999).

 Critical Concept

Planning is based on the premise that workloads can be manipulated and administered within a set of principles that will ensure that adaptation takes place in the athlete's capacity for performance.

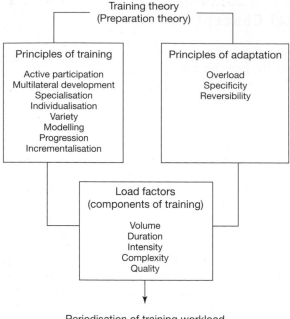

Figure 7.6 *Training theory principles*

Given the assumptions about the coaching process identified previously, it would not be surprising to see principles of good practice such as progression, integration, targeting and flexibility, applied to the planning process. However, there are some training theory principles (see Figure 7.6) within which the planner will operate.

Training principles are dealt with very well by Bompa (1999), and an excellent publication by the National Coaching Foundation (NCF) (Crisfield and Houlston 1993) provides an exemplar of the process to be followed. There are a number of respected writers in this field (for example, Balyi 1998a, 1998b). It is generally accepted by these writers that the 'training schedules' element of the planning process rests on experience and good practice, rather than on the findings from rigorous research. For this reason, biographical accounts of coaching practice often contain elements of good practice about athlete preparation (for example, Francis 1990).

In order to understand why planning practice might vary between coaches, it is necessary to appreciate that planning is dependent on the competition cycle and the discipline that this imposes on the planning process. Figure 7.7 illustrates how sports can usefully be subdivided into three competition categories.

Planning can be thought of as the direct intervention strategy. Given the varying contexts occasioned by the above competition patterns, coaching needs to have available a repertoire of planning types to suit the demands of a particular context. These options are best considered as variations on the 'pure', principled and systematic form of planning.

Competition category	Characteristics	Planning issues
Target sports e.g. rowing, swimming, athletics, gymnastics	Tendency to on- and off-season; major competitions can be distinguished from minor ones; extended period of preparation; often individual sports	Few constraints to cyclical planning; detailed planning 'shell' with periodised cycles; action plans for 4–6 weeks; coach's intention is to adhere to plan; maintenance period depends on competitions
League sports e.g. hockey, soccer, rugby, netball	Extended and regular competition programme; results are aggregated for success; often team sports; normally performance composed of multiple components	Longer-term planning is more difficult; priorities influenced by the result and imminence of competition; contingency and crisis planning common; detailed planning is unlikely beyond short cycles.
Circuit sports e.g. skiing, tennis, golf	Extended competition programme but results are normally not aggregated; major and minor competitions, with some interdependence; multiple performance components	Maintenance of 'form' with peaks for identified targets; planning for overall progress; comparative performance; longer-term planning shell with short-term competition preparation; contingency planning likely

Figure 7.7 *Planning issues related to competition cycle*

They are *recipe, contingency* and *episodic planning*. The systematic form assumes extensive data, working from first principles on workloads, creating new drills and exercises and constantly monitoring to provide the evidence on which to base all subsequent workloads. This is a very demanding practice and unlikely to be efficient use of time.

In recipe planning, the coach employs training prescriptions from a store of experience and a repository of observations, workshops, publications and shared practice. The 'plans' are known to have worked in the past in similar circumstances and allow the coach to 'routinise' practice. The experienced coach will be able to contextualise generic plans, and will expect a contingency element to practice.

It should be noted that there are some dangers inherent in recipe planning: the novice coach may apply the recipe without any contextualisation. This approach may stifle innovation and change.

Contingency planning is not a complete approach to planning but is a form of planning that can be applied to a greater and lesser extent. The contingent element is the degree to which intentions can be carried out in the light of environmental conditions (weather, facility access, equipment), athlete condition (illness, injury, availability), or goal reassessment (impact of results, performer reactions). The amendments to activities may be made at the beginning of the session (pre-session contingency) or as a result of emerging circumstances during the session (in-session contingency).

The danger of excessive contingency planning is that the benefits of the original plan are lost because of the changes made. Taken to its extreme, the coach may adopt a 'wait and see' approach that fails to achieve the accumulative and aggregative benefits intended by planning to principles.

The episodic planning approach attempts to combine some of the benefits of longer-term planning with shorter-term competition horizons. Episodic planning is best illustrated in team, league sports in which the (usually) weekly competition preparation dominates the planning. Longer-term progress is maintained by attending to 'key features' of performance (Franks *et al.* 1986) on a regular basis, but short-term goals (strategic rehearsal) often monopolise preparation. There is also the considerable problem of balancing the maintenance of physical condition with the demands of specific occasions.

The most obvious danger is that the very short-term demands are attended to at the expense of longer-term progression and balance, particularly for younger, developing performers.

Question Box

There is no doubt that planning, of all sorts, is important. Given the likelihood of contingency and partially fulfilled schedules, the most important record to be kept is that of 'work done', not 'work planned'. Would this be a change in coaching practice?

To some extent these planning models are complementary. Whatever the model employed, there are skills required by the coach to devise and execute the plan:

- identifying the performance requirements of specified goals;
- creating a strategic planning overview of the year/planning period;
- extrapolating activity requirements for major preparation and competition phases;
- interpreting recipes;
- identifying and setting precise workloads;
- obtaining and using performance component data;
- session design;
- dealing with crisis and contingency;
- recording and monitoring for subsequent micro-cycle/session design.

This, of course, is in addition to executing the direct intervention activity itself.

There are a number of process-related planning issues:

1 Planning is not an activity that is easily adapted to being a shared experience, although athletes will absorb principles over time and may be able to demonstrate a degree of autonomy as they mature.

HOW DO COACHES BEHAVE?

2   Flexibility and accommodation to opportunistic factors is both expected and antici-
    pated in the coach's planning behaviour. When writing about 'overtraining', Fry *et
    al.* (1991) say that 'coaches must be flexible and . . . training programmes are merely
    a framework from which to work' (1991: 53).
3   In some sports, planning is dominated by physical conditioning. In these often
    individual, power-based sports (including swimming, rowing, canoeing, some athletics,
    cycling) planning can be very sophisticated and adherence to principles and to the
    predetermined schedule is taken much more seriously than in game sports. In these
    sports, the procedures for tapering and peaking are very important, as is the preven-
    tion of over-training (Cross and Lyle 1999b).
4   Part of the problem in game sports is that identifying loading factors in technical,
    tactical and psychological training, and in competition, can be very difficult. Intensity
    is problematic in exercises and drills, and volume and duration are often used
    synonymously.

Planning practice re-emphasises the complexity and uniqueness of the coaching process.
The next section examines how the coach copes with this complexity in everyday practice.

IMPLEMENTATION BEHAVIOUR: EXPLAINING COACHES' EXPERTISE

There have been many indicators of coaching behaviours and practice thus far –
descriptions of direct intervention, planning behaviour, the model of the coaching practice,
and the many research findings cited earlier in the chapter. This important section in
the chapter offers an explanation for how coaches fulfil their role in the coaching
process. This explanation should go a good deal of the way to explaining the day-to-day
practice of the performance sports coach and defining what is meant by the distinctive
expertise of the performance sports coach. The list of functions/behaviours is extensive,
but well understood. Coaches plan sessions, select teams, devise competition programmes,
set goals with athletes, discuss resources with club officials, recruit new performers, keep
records, maintain rapport with athletes, assist performers with life management issues,
engage in self-development, organise and run training sessions, liaise with other experts,
and so on. In terms of the developing conceptual framework, the intention in this section
is not simply to chart all of these behaviours but also to explore and provide an explanation
for *how* the coach manages to cope with such an extensive list of responsibilities. The
ideas in this section are the result of research into coaches' behaviour (Lyle 1991, 1992,
1998b) and twenty years of experience as a coach and in coach education. Of course, the
ideas have also been informed by the literature (notably, Salmela 1995) and many, many
discussions with colleagues. The emerging framework was first described in Lyle (1998c)
and Lyle (1999a).

The explanation given for the coach's behaviour is intended to incorporate a number of
assumptions about the coaching process and coaching practice (these have been rehearsed
and argued elsewhere in the book):

1   The coaching process is dynamic and complex. There are many uncertainties and the
    'production' element of the process cannot be guaranteed. The process is contested

insofar as the outcome goals are often sought after by others and process, output and personal goals are mostly pursued without the active co-operation of opponents.

2   There are many aspects of the external environment that cannot be controlled by the coach or the athlete.

3   Performance coaching practice will demonstrate a level of expertise that can be classified from novice to expert.

4   The distinguishing feature of coaching practice is cognitive behaviour. The behavioural output element of this is most evident in problem solving and decision making. However, even the craft delivery elements of coaching practice (conducting training sessions, for example) are managed by a continuously refined mental model of athlete performance.

5   Coaching practice is almost always conducted in conditions that are less than ideal. The most obvious example of this is that coach–athlete 'contracts' are rarely one-to-one. Coaches normally work with teams, squads, or groups of performers.

6   The coach needs to find a balance between the over-burdensome, perhaps even impossible, detail of completely systematic practice and the need for principled, efficient and effective action. This also has to be a set of behaviours that allows the athlete to cope with the subsequent demands, that permits a degree of human frailty and variability, and allows sufficient 'space' for the interpersonal nature of the coaching relationship to flourish.

7   Coping strategies will, therefore, be capable of dealing with uncertainty, but also of enabling coaches to have a degree of routine and habituated activity that will bring stability to the coach's practice and the athlete's expectations.

The issue is not that the coach's task seems difficult, or even impossible. Coaching behaviour can be taken as a given, in the sense that performance coaches are engaged with their athletes and, in general, a degree of effectiveness can be assumed, since performers characteristically improve their performances over time. The issue is threefold. First, there are very few attempts to explain coaching practice. This is normally attributed to the tacit nature of the coach's knowledge and expertise, and interrogating this is, therefore, a difficult task. Salmela (1995) acknowledges the tacit nature of much of the coach's knowledge frameworks but believes that coaches can verbalise them.

Second, the conceptual and theoretical underpinning has not been in place to support this form of enquiry. And third, the 'intuitive', 'artform' explanation of coaching has been used to explain the unexplainable. The recognition that mental activity is at the basis of coaching activity has been dealt with by recourse to an explanation that does not require further elaboration. There has been a regular interest (Dick 1977; Cain 1980; Woodman 1993; Borrie 1998) in the 'coaching is an art' argument as a substitute for an appropriate account of coaching expertise.

A satisfactory account of coaching practice will need to explain:

■   the apparently intuitive decision making of the coach;
■   coping with changes in the environment;
■   coping with fluctuations in performance;
■   maintaining focus on goals;
■   managing the interdependence of consequences;

- balancing stability and innovation; and
- maintaining an overview of short- and longer-term implications of action.

(In passing, it should be noted that not all coaches will display developed expertise at this level – there will be those who are less than expert. In addition, there will be novice and developing coaches who are 'learning their trade' – something for the chapter on coach education!)

The conceptual framework around which an account of coaching practice is built will deal, in the remainder of the chapter, with the following, integrated elements:

1 intuitive decision making;
2 decision making based on 'interactive scripts' (constantly updated anticipation of situation and appropriate action);
3 knowledge structures;
4 thresholds and catalysts;
5 mental models (related to goals and to management of intervention); and
6 contingency planning.

Each of these is described in turn and then aggregated into an account of coaching practice.

Intuitive decision making

The word 'intuition' often appears in conjunction with descriptions of coaches' actions. What is implied is recourse to an unexplained, and perhaps unexplainable, cognitive process in which the coach does not appear to be using a considered, option-based approach to decision taking that depends on developed expertise. This is not the case. Although there will be cases in which there is an intractable problem and the coach may, as a last resort, select a solution knowing that there is no principled basis for its selection, the great majority of 'intuitive' actions are simply 'cognitive shortcuts'. These represent part of the tacit, propositional and procedural knowledge that Salmela (1995) suggests that coaches can verbalise, although it may have been unconscious and unexplained at the time (Easen and Wilcockson 1996).

Claxton explains intuition as an outcome of non-conscious neural associations, part of an 'intelligent unconscious' (1998: 220). In untidy problem-solving situations, key prompts within the coach's awareness of the problem trigger off neural activity in which associations are formed within the matrix of memory and knowledge structures. This matrix includes previous solutions and linkages between prompt and action. The outcome is that the coach may be able to make decisions about appropriate action without this becoming a conscious process.

It will be obvious that intuition explained in this fashion depends on a store of experience and knowledge. Hammond *et al.* (1993) suggest that it is also dependent on the nature of the problem and they propose a continuum of types of decision, rather than a sharp dichotomy. However, Klein (1998) offers a simple explanation. In what can be a dynamic set of circumstances (characteristic of coaching), key patterns will be recognised by the coach, based on a non-conscious use of previous experience.

There is also a distinction in the literature between creative intuition, which is slower, and the 'speedy association' of routine, repetitive and operational decision making (Wierzbicki 1997). Wierzbicki's definition of intuitive decisions as 'quasi-conscious and sub-conscious information processing, leading to an action, utilising aggregated experience and training' (1997: 69) begins to put in place an understanding of coaches' behaviour that does not rely on the 'coaching must be an art' argument. What it does point to is the importance of being able to recognise similarities and patterns in coaching situations characterised by large numbers of cues, perceptual evaluation, uncertainty and brief time exposure (Hammond *et al.* 1993; Sloman 1996).

Question Box

Intuition has been used as a convenient 'hook' for the absence of an explanation of coaching practice. Is it surprising, therefore, that status, education and expertise in coaching are problematical?

Decision making based on interactive scripts

This short section reports on research carried out into the nature of the cognitive organisation best describing coaches' non-deliberative decision making (Lyle 1998b). The context for the research was the non-deliberative (time-pressured) decisions taken by expert volleyball coaches during matches. This is not the more deliberative, slower, 'effortful' decision making described by Boreham (1994). The games were videotaped, and a stimulated recall procedure was used to elicit the coaches' accounts of decisions taken during the games. Figure 7.8 illustrates the four potential models of decision making used to structure the coding framework (described in Lyle 1999c, with extended reading sources).

In the investigation, the interactive script model accounted for almost two-thirds of the decision incidents (Figure 7.9).

The schema model was not employed extensively but predominantly involved time-out decisions (generally threshold score decisions). The schema script model was prevalent in tactical decisions that were susceptible to decisions based on rule association on an 'if this happens, I will . . .' basis. The case script model was not employed significantly but the interactive script model appeared to best describe the coaches' decision-making

Critical Concept

Coaches attempt to reduce the non-deliberative element of their decision making, partly to reduce uncertainty and partly because of the reduced range of options available to them.

	Mechanism	Solutions	Coaching
Schema model	A knowledge framework is activated by pattern recognition.	There is a close link between recognition and predetermined responses.	Coaches have an automatic reaction to situations: e.g. threshold breaches of scoring differences, emotional responses by athletes or breakdowns in drills.
Schema script model	An unfolding 'script' or process is recognised from the 'enabling conditions'. This includes forward projections.	Reading the enabling conditions provokes a match to associated script solutions stored in memory.	Coaching expertise is in reading the conditions (not novices) but not too early. Coaches recognise enabling conditions as causes rather than outcomes of problems, which trigger apparently intuitive solutions.
Case script model	The reading/recognition process triggers a specific case script	Recognition acts as a catalyst to the solution adopted previously in that specific case.	Because of its complexity, coaching seems unlikely to create exactly similar cases. However, individual athlete behaviour may do so.
Slow interactive script model	The generalised script is recognised from the enabling conditions, but these are subject to constant updating.	There is a closer, quasi-conscious linkage between options and the anticipated changes in the script. Options are constantly factored into the script.	Coaches will attempt to reduce uncertainty by anticipating events and associated actions. Forward modelling makes up for the lack of time to make decisions.

Figure 7.8 *Potential models of non-deliberative decision making*

	Incidents	%	Time outs	Substitutions	Tactical incidents
Schema model	7	10	6	–	1
Schema script model	11	16	2	1	8
Case script	1	1			1
Interactive script model	43	61	16	22	5
Other / not attributable	8	11	1	2	5
Totals	70	100	25	25	20

Source: (Lyle 1998)

Figure 7.9 *Results of the allocation of decision making incidents to potential models*

behaviour. Overall, there was a clear attempt by coaches to reduce the non-deliberative element of their decision making, partly to reduce uncertainty and partly because of the reduced range of options available to them.

Before attempting to summarise coaches' decision behaviour, it is worth pointing to the consonance between the findings of the investigation and the model of decision making described by Klein (1998). His recognition-primed decision model is framed within the 'naturalistic decision making' (NDM) paradigm. This refers to contexts in which there is uncertainty, complexity, time pressure, limited data available and in which it is inappropriate to try out options. Empirical work is situated in the natural contexts within which individuals operate (typically, fire-fighters, air traffic controllers, and others) and seeks to explain how people make decisions under those 'pressured' situations.

Putting together a number of ideas from NDM, the following is a speculative account of how individuals make such decisions. Situational assessment permits recognition of the problem. The individual builds a story based on the available evidence in order to diagnose the situation and hypothesise about future events. The future events are subject to mental simulations that include appropriate solutions. Where data are limited, assumption-based reasoning is used to 'fill in' the picture. Two-stage recognition may take place. The first is fairly automatic, and may be a 'quick test' to visualise the solution. However, a meta-recognition may then offer an opportunity for critiquing and correcting in the light of limited resources or a misreading of the situation. The decision making is non-compensatory: that is, all potential options are not subjected to an evaluation. Where there is time-pressure, there is more need for accurate pattern recognition and speedy diagnosis. However, individuals may need to trade certainty of diagnosis for impact of the solution. Solutions may, therefore, be selected for their 'coverage' rather than being optimal responses (termed 'weak' solutions or, perhaps, a default option) (see Cohen *et al.* 1996; Flin *et al.* 1997; Lipshitz and Strauss 1997; Zsambok and Klein 1997; Klein 1998).

 Question Box

Remember that this description is dealing with coaches' decision making that is non-deliberative; that is, there is little or no time to reflect. How do you react to it? Does it have immediate face validity?

This 'model' has been elaborated on at length because it has an obvious consistency with the emerging conceptual framework for the coaching process. Naturalistic decision making may prove to be a very valuable avenue for research into coaching behaviour. For the present, the findings from research and the literature can be aggregated into the following propositions about coaches' decision making as it underpins coaching practice (these ideas were first reported in Lyle 1999c).

Coaches' decision making

A good deal of decision making by coaches is 'slow and deliberative' (Boreham 1994). This refers to planning and scheduling decisions, and allocation of resources. However, many intervention and delivery decisions are made without apparent deliberation, as are decisions within contest management. This 'effortless' decision making is one of the marks of the expert.

The overall approach of the coach is to *manage uncertainty* and *retain control* within the dynamics of the situation. This means acting optimally in terms of data gathering, predicting/anticipating/assuming, and having solutions/responses to hand. For the expert coach, experience has been converted into usable decision-making tools.

Decision making, as it is implemented, has to cope with a number of factors:

1   Decisions impact on individuals and the individual's reaction/response will be an added factor (emotion, pride, disappointment, ego and so forth).
2   It cannot be assumed that coaches' decisions are unaffected by the same human emotions. Research is required into the impact of psychological factors on coaches' decision making.
3   Variability in performance, environment, interpersonal relationships, and external constraints (education, life-style).
4   Decisions in or relating to competition are taken in a *contested arena*. It can be assumed that many competition decisions will be actively contested by other coaches working to their and their athletes' goal agenda.

A number of principles, which may be applied to most decisions, may form a useful research agenda. The following propositions need to be tested.

1   Decisions taken early increase uncertainty and require weak solutions. Decisions taken later may reduce impact.
2   Effectiveness is linked to reducing option choices. It is important to 'narrow' option choices. (NDM actually proposes that the solution 'emerges' because of good situational analysis, rather than as a 'selection' issue.)
3   Decisions will be influenced by personal preferences.
4   Heuristics (rules for making choices) are likely to be based on 'good practice', rather than derived from 'rational, logical rules'.

In the light of the above, coaches will apply heuristics that optimise, rather than maximise (because of the inherent uncertainty – contested, limited resources, emotion, strategy, difficulty in predicting): heuristics that minimise the number of options and maximise the 'coverage' of possible solutions. Lipshitz and Bar-Ilan (1996) suggest that in such circumstances it is appropriate to diagnose early, delay decisions and choose inclusive solutions. (It may be that this is what experience has taught coaches to do!)

Decision making is triggered by the recognition of a pattern of behaviour or circumstances. This is matched with a 'catalogue' of problem patterns and an action decision may follow. The coach has built up knowledge structures with attendant variation and resultant actions – schemata. The triggers themselves need to be established for a range of contexts in all sports (although some will be general) – again, research is required. In the volleyball research cited earlier, the competition triggers, or key factors, were target scores, momentum changes, loss of playing rhythm, loss of mental composure, and clusters of points.

Pattern recognition is extremely important, whether in training sessions or competition. Early and accurate situational analysis reduces the options required. This is not an easy task. The familiar list of factors – dynamic, complex, contested, human reaction and others – make 'reading the game' or 'understanding the players' a difficult task. Decomposing these complicated pictures may also be a mark of the expert (Chi *et al.* 1988; Siedentop and Eldar 1989; Berliner 1994).

Prediction is difficult. The coach will construct a 'story' from the observed history of the action and take into account the enabling conditions (the status of each of the contributory elements). This is measured against the bank of existing 'scripts' and the unfolding events are predicted. However, the forward script will have a degree of variation built into it, along with probabilities and computed solutions. This is the interactive script model. This process of weighing options before they happen might be termed 'anticipatory reflection'. The coach then maintains a constant scanning process to update the emerging script, with action taken if one of the thresholds in the key factors is breached.

The expert coach can engage in pre-emptive and preventative action because of the accuracy and speed of situational analysis. Novice coaches may need to engage in more 'remedial' activity. The expert coach will also be more accurate with the 'assumptive reasoning' required to infer the forward behaviour of performers or opposition performers or coaches.

The coach's behaviour will appear intuitive because the action decisions have (if all goes well) been anticipated or have been recognised fairly quickly and matched to script and solution – perhaps after a first test and subsequent confirmation or correction.

The behaviour will also seem to be routine because the action decision is only necessary when the threshold is breached, and solutions to problems have already been converted into accessible solutions and 'indexed'.

In summary, the coach constantly scans the coaching process-related activity. Situational analysis, based on pattern recognition and key triggers, leads to diagnosis and hypothesising future events. If the diagnosis is that training, competition or process goals will be negatively affected, the coach may decide that action is required. A number of action decisions may be triggered in a rule-based manner by a sufficiently serious event. Otherwise the pattern recognition process has led to an interactive script, which is updated constantly. A simulation model is devised to anticipate forward activity and this model has a number of solutions computed for different outcomes. If the situation requires action, one of the solutions is activated. The 'strength' of the solution depends on the certainty of the diagnosis and the probability of accurate prediction. A constant process of scanning, modelling and decision taking follows. Some situations/decisions may become routine or 'default' actions and may also be idiosyncratic.

The coach's simulation model, planning model and performance model (anticipated progress on key elements of performance within the context of goals and targets) constitute the 'mental model' referred to earlier in the text. Certainly, the model of decision making proposed above reinforces the cognitive nature of the coach's practice. The integration of these models with the management of intervention, personnel, resources and interpersonal behaviour requires a form of meta-decision making (the fourth level of coaching practice), which is, as yet, far from adequately understood.

Question Box

It is worth noting that speedy decision making is required not just in competition but in directing training exercises and resolving problem situations as they arise. Once again, how is this integrated into coach education?

The next four elements of the conceptual framework relating to implementation behaviour have already been referred to on a number of previous occasions and the treatment necessary at this point is quite brief.

Knowledge structures

Knowledge can be placed in the following categories:

Declarative knowledge knowledge about things; knowledge that . . .;
Propositional knowledge relationships between concepts: if . . . then; 'production rules', perhaps abstract and applicable to novel situations;
Procedural knowledge knowing how to.

Abraham and Collins (1998) provide an excellent account of the knowledge structures in coaching. They differentiate between two knowledge domains: the first to do with managing the training environment, and the second concerned with sport-specific technical knowledge. The authors question the type of knowledge used in coach education, particularly for novices. There is a danger in providing too ready an access to procedural knowledge without the supporting background to allow for reflection, application and flexibility. They make the relevant point that coach education shows little, if any, evidence of having incorporated findings from research. Propositional knowledge is certainly required for planning and procedural knowledge will be evident in craft elements of practice. However, the important issue here is not simply the kind of knowledge but how this is structured and accessed.

Knowledge is structured and stored in abstract cognitive frameworks known as schemata. A schema has been described by Evans (1989) as a knowledge structure which is 'induced or learned from experience, contains a cluster of related declarative and procedural knowledge, and is sensitive to the domain and context of the current focus of cognitive activity' (1989: 84). Schemata are individual, context-related, hierarchical, mental representations of the world, and derived from experience (Côte *et al*. 1995a). However, knowledge is stored as both abstractions and specific instances. The relationships between

phenomena are gradually refined through experience into a matrix of relationships (sometimes said to be stored in 'frames') that can be used to bring understanding to an event/occurrence, once recognised. Knowledge is also stored in scripts – that is, a particular kind of knowledge structure that relates to sequences of events (Custers et al. 1996).

There are a number of issues for coaching practice:

1   Coaching knowledge is recognised to be tacit – that its, not written down or expressed (Salmela 1995). Nevertheless, Salmela suggests that coaches can verbalise this tacit knowledge. Hoffman et al. (1995) describe how knowledge can be elicited from experts. The tacit knowledge of experts, which is thought to characterise their behaviour becomes evident in routinised cognitions, declarative knowledge becoming procedural, and intuitive access to knowledge structures.

2   Knowledge will be a key element of expertise. Features of this are:

- domain-specific knowledge;
- procedural knowledge employed by novices, with propositional knowledge used to 'speed things up' by experts;
- more elaborate schemata by experts (Schempp 1998).

3   It cannot be assumed that coaches and athletes will have shared meanings about knowledge and relationships between phenomena, given the reliance on experience and the idiosyncratic creation of schemata. This suggests that communication is important and that decision making will be more successful if explanations are shared.

4   The most important issue is education. Although there is some understanding and insight into knowledge structures, there is far less wisdom on how these are developed. Experience will, with time, lead to the creation of knowledge structures. However, education is intended to forshorten and make more successful the period of experience. This will be dealt with in a later chapter.

Thresholds and catalysts

It has already been suggested that the coach scans the environment constantly. However, to bring a sense of reality and proportion to the coach's task, it must be assumed that much of this is subconscious and that not all events and occurrences could lead to action decisions. In order to bring a sense of structure and priority to the task, a system of thresholds operates to identify where action is required. Being able to focus on the most meaningful elements of the display helps coaches to recognise the 'patterns' in coaching contexts (Randel et al. 1996).

The recognition of patterns in behaviour and events is linked to catalysts, or key features, which draw attention to priority matters that are likely to impact on the coaching process. Obvious examples are injuries, emotional outbursts, poor performance, non-adherence to training targets, and specific sport-related competition catalysts. These features may exist, but at what strength? How bad does it have to be before action is required? There is little empirical evidence on this subject. In a previous section in this chapter evidence was cited from research by Lyle (1992). This must be a focus for future researchers.

Mental models

The term 'mental model' is used because cognitive activity has been referred to in this unspecified way in previous chapters. Côte *et al.* (1995a) use the term 'mental model' for their generalised description of coaches' cognitions. However, it is likely that there are at least three models used by coaches (see Figure 7.10).

The simulation model involves a prediction of future events but, crucially, incorporates monitoring and constant amendments. The coach cannot be prepared for everything, but through good situational analysis the expert coach may well be able to reduce the number of likely outcomes and happenings and have solutions available to cope with these. The phrase 'coping strategies' is often used. The use of the simulation or interactive model helps the coach to identify the necessary action decisions. Coping strategies may imply that coaches use favourite tactics to resolve difficulties or that some generalised strategies are used for a number of problems (weak solutions).

Model	*Structure*	*Function*	*Operation*
Goal model	The goal model is an overview of the planning process. Mechanisms for achieving goals are planned in a deliberative fashion and changes to this are made as progress, environment and resources alter.	The model includes the performance targets required to achieve the goal. Changes to goals may result from non-achievement of subsidiary goals. The goal planning process includes a number of 'what . . . if' variations, because of the inherent uncertainty and contested nature of sport.	Although the goals will often be identified, it would be rare for the detail to be specified.
Performance model	The performance model itemises what would be expected from the performance in order to achieve the goal. This includes time scales, targets, component contributions and, importantly, anticipated progression.	The performance model is necessary for planning and for identifying threshold decisions. The progression expectations and goal impacts are fed into the simulation model.	This model is evident in planning schedules but the details are most often tacit.
Simulation model	The model consists of 'scripts' that anticipate future events on the basis of past experience and the 'story so far'. The scripts contain action solutions for events that threaten desired progress or success.	The simulation model is described in the decision-making section. The model is used to deal with the uncertainty in the coaching process and to assist with non-deliberative decision making.	These models are tacit, although it may be that coaches can verbalise them.

Figure 7.10 *Coaches' mental models*

Verchoshanskij (1999) offers some support for a component of the performance model. He describes how a 'virtual image' of the training process is created, based on training principles. The simulation model looks forward but has a degree of reflection about it. Eraut (1994) suggests that this reflection incorporates 'proceeding in a state of continual alertness' (1994: 145). Beckett (1996) also deals with anticipative action. In 'hot action' (that is, non-deliberative decision making), he describes this as 'an anticipative conversation with our practices' (1996: 149).

The above models are interconnected insofar as the goal model informs the performance model, which in turn informs the simulation model. Conversely, feedback and impact from practice will be identified in the simulation model and will impact on the performance model and goal achievement. The development of these models clearly has enormous implications for coach education and the extent to which coaches and athletes share their inherent assumptions.

Contingency planning

Contingency planning has been used as a generalised term for short-term amendments to plans and schedules, usually with an implied sense of being 'forced' onto the coach. It will be useful to clarify what is meant by this term. Contingency planning is used in two contexts:

1   as a part of normal planning procedures, in which changes in the availability of facilities, illness, weather, travel and a range of other factors need to be incorporated into the organisation of training, the schedules and workloads themselves, and perhaps into goals and targets; and
2   as part of the management of the intervention programme and delivery. This might be thought of more as 'adaptation to an unfolding script'. The changes here are the result of less-deliberative decision making, and follow from unanticipated events, under-achievement in performance, or simply uncertainty.

Contingency is accounted for in the decision-making model described earlier in the chapter. However, the terminology might be more recognisable as 'action decisions taken as a result of threshold stimulated problems or unforeseen events'. One of the dangers of acknowledging the contingency element is that it may be used by coaches as a reason (excuse?) for not planning in great detail in the first place. This deserves further research. A second issue is that it is necessary to follow up in a considered way the effects of contingency planning. This makes it important to have a record of the competition, training or planning as it happened and not as it was planned.

COACHING PRACTICE:
A CONDENSED DESCRIPTION

Some summary statements can be made about coaching practice before examining the very important issue of the sport specificity of practice. These are presented in list form.

■   The practice of performance sports coaching is encapsulated in the four levels of direct intervention, intervention support, constraints management and strategic co-ordination.

- The coaching process model identifies key stages: recruitment, goal setting, planning, delivery, monitoring and contest management. These are complemented by continuous processes such as administration, counselling, organising and personnel management.
- The role of the coach influences practice. Club coaches, squad coaches and representative team coaches will each have different sets of role responsibilities. The main areas of difference will be in managing and liaising with support personnel, liaising with National Governing Bodies, and with owners, committee members or performance directors.
- The role of the coach will also be illustrated in the balance of responsibilities undertaken. Some coaches may emphasise their technical and tactical direction because support personnel focus on physical conditioning. Similarly, some coaches may exercise a more strategic, planning role, with support science personnel contributing to each of the components. It is less likely in performance sports coaching that the coach will exercise all of the component parts of the process.
- Coaching practice is dominated by particular combinations of planning and delivery. This is sport specific.
- Coaching intervention behaviour is characterised by a variety of leadership styles, feedback modes and interpersonal behaviour.
- Coaching practice is characterised by apparently intuitive behaviour. The emphasis is on cognitive styles of decision making and information management that make for effective and efficient practice. This means optimal methods of data collection, monitoring and decision making.
- Coaching practice depends on the implementation of planned activity designed to achieve performance changes that will satisfy athlete and organisational goals. Most coaches will 'periodise' the preparation and competition period and plan performance component improvements within training theory principles.
- Some planning is very detailed, and well-tested recipes for improvement can be implemented with minor modifications for athlete condition and disruptions to the schedule. Monitoring data are incorporated into the planning of detailed micro-cycles and there are clear training and competition targets.
- Some planning is less precise, largely because the conditions for implementation are less controllable. In these cases, micro-cycle and sessional plans are more dependent on shorter-term horizons, often dominated by competition needs. Workloads and training targets are less precise and there is a greater element of contingency planning.
- Coaching practice relies for the most part on coaches' knowledge structures that are tacit. Many decisions by coaches (amendments to drills, evaluation of success in exercises, amended workloads, tactical decisions, targets in training, amendments of programmes, psychological approaches to individual performers, team selections and so on) are taken in an apparently intuitive manner. That is, they are generally capable of principled explanation afterwards but, at the time, were taken without apparent deliberation. This has very significant implications for coach education (Lyle 1998c: 75).
- Coaching practice is informed by knowledge structures organised into schemata and scripts. These are activated for decision-making purposes by a series of catalysts (key features) recognised from a constant scanning of the coaching milieu. Some action decisions are unhurried and deliberative – problem solving or planning may be a more

apt description. Other action decisions are triggered in a more reflexive way or with a minimal deliberation. There is little time for a rational selection of alternatives, and anticipatory modelling eases the coach's decision alternatives.

- Coaching practice has the potential for almost limitless detail in planning and monitoring and recording of athlete activity. In addition to good planning, coaches implement an efficient practice regime:

  - a system of threshold values to indicate sufficiently worrying behaviour or performance, based on targets and a performance model. Variability is expected and anticipated;
  - regular monitoring regimes supplemented by reacting to critical incidents;
  - the use of training and preparation recipes that have had a record of success in similar circumstances in the past;
  - routinised activity; and
  - contingency planning, as required, to ensure the currency and appropriateness of activity.

  Saury and Durand (1998) conducted a qualitative investigation into the knowledge structures of expert sailing coaches. Their findings complement the description of coaching practice offered in this chapter. They found that coaching was a cognitive exercise in which coaches used routines and 'cognitive anticipation' to cope with the constraints of training efficiency, temporal situations and uncertainty in performers and weather.

- It has been argued that coaching is a largely cognitive exercise and that the craft elements of intervention and management are also dependent on cognitive models for efficient practice. In relation to decision making, it is possible to identify some of these cognitive skills and expertise:

Pattern recognition	Diagnosis and hypothesising
Situational analysis	Storytelling
Decision framing; option narrowing	Assumptive reasoning
	Anticipatory reflection

These elements of decision making are supported by appropriate knowledge structures, including elements of procedural craft knowledge.

It was important, in the context of this developing conceptual framework, to identify generic aspects of coaching practice. Nevertheless, it is also clear that there are quite distinctive differences in practice between sports, and the final section of the chapter addresses this issue.

SPORT SPECIFICITY IN COACHING PRACTICE

Developing a conceptual framework has inevitably emphasised the common generic elements of the coaching process. Nevertheless, one of the recurring themes within the text is the variability in the coaching process and much of this stems from the nature of the sport itself. The conceptual framework must therefore be able to account for variability in practice in relation to sport specificity. Consider the distinctiveness of performance routine sport such as gymnastics and ice dance, with their technical rehearsal demands, in comparison to the repetitive, uncontested, volume training of long-distance athletes, cyclists and rowers. These can be contrasted with the drills-led interactive practices of team sports such as basketball and hockey. Each of these sports brings its challenges and different coaching practice.

Sport characteristic	Sport example (compare)	Impact on coaching practice
Role in competition	Basketball with athletics	Expertise required in contest management; high level of intervention; presence required; coach dependency in decision making; level of independence fostered in performers; active engagement in competition with attendant emotional demands.
Performance profile (race, game, performance)	Swimming with hockey with rhythmic gymnastics	Control of performance outputs, target setting; interactive tactics; psychological preparation for uncertainty; focus on opposition performance; coach's competition role; specificity of preparation/rehearsal.
Team/individual	Netball with archery	Complexity of processes; control of variables; level of individualisation; amount of data; methods of communication; control of interactive workloads; specificity of goal setting; selection.
Competition pattern (league, target, circuit)	Ice hockey with athletics with golf	Periodisation of year; goal setting; impact of illness/injury; variability in threshold values; monitoring horizons.
Equipment dependence	Rugby union with motor racing	Need for technical expertise; control of variables; psychological preparation.
Environmental conditions	Sailing with badminton	Stability of planning intentions; ease of communication; delivery style; ease of monitoring.
Balance of performance components	Cricket with rowing	Priority given to major components – tactical capacity, physical conditioning, technical development, etc.; complexity of process – planning, monitoring; incremental versus systematic progression.
Interactive role in training	Volleyball with skiing	Constancy of feedback; management of workloads; skill required for feeding/control; communication control; use of support team; monitoring and evaluation.
Characteristics of performers (age, gender, disability)	Gymnastics (elite age) with soccer (elite age)	Leadership style; physical and psychological maturity into planning; life-style support issues; interpersonal relationship issues; communication; independence.
Development profile	Soccer with handball	Performer reward environment; availability of funding; support personnel; sport science support; recruitment; education opportunities.

Figure 7.11 *Sport-specific factors in coaching practice*

In which elements of the coaching process will there be differences? Figure 7.11 provides more detailed examples of differences in coaching practice. However, these can be summarised as follows:

- Differences are most likely in the direct intervention roles. Differences in managing the external environment are more likely to be dependent on organisational structure and level of engagement. It is possible that the strategic co-ordination role will be more demanding in team sports with large coaching teams and support personnel, and with organisational goals to be satisfied.
- The three elements of coaching practice – planning, involvement in exercises/drills, and a competition role – are central to sport specificity. Many of the differences between sports lead to one or more of these functions.
- Workload management is a key concept. Earlier sections have highlighted the continuum between carrying out training and competition intentions with some degree of predictability and the variability in precision expected in interactive and contested sports. Sports with high levels of tactical decision making and degrees of freedom in technical execution require more workload management and feedback.
- The phrase 'coach dominated' is often used for those sports in which the competition role of the coach involves decision making that has a significant impact on the pattern of the game/sport. Conversely, there are sports in which observation of the external environment is less significant and can be accomplished, in many cases, by the performer. It is not unusual in a number of sports, and for athletes of some experience, for the coach's role to be 'reduced' to adviser or occasional consultant.

In the chapters that follow, the emphasis changes from the structure of the coaching process and the implications for coaching behaviour and practice to the interpersonal dimension of the coaching process.

SUMMARY

The chapter will have familiarised you with the following:

- the issue of generic versus specific/contextualised descriptions of coaching practice;
- the terminology linking coaching behaviour and coaching practice;
- the definition of systematic coaching practice, the factors in the coaching process influencing systematic practice and how this might be measured;
- an example of coaches' adherence to systematic coaching practice criteria;
- selected examples of coaching behaviour research;
- planning models and their relationship to coaching practice in sports characterised by different competition patterns;
- a brief review of coaching process assumptions;
- an explanation for apparently intuitive decision making by performance coaches and a review of potential models of decision making in non-deliberative situations;
- a summary of decision-making behaviour by performance coaches;
- details of three mental models employed by coaches;
- a summary description of coaching practice; and
- a review of the features of specific sports that influence coaching practice.

PROJECTS

This was a lengthy chapter and the potential for investigating coaches' practice is enormous. The range of possible projects is almost limitless. Try to select studies that involve and invoke elements of the conceptual framework.

- Repeat the study of Lyle (1992). Improve the criteria of systematic practice and select two sports to compare.
- Carry out a study into coaches' decision making during training sessions. Video coaches' management of a drill/exercise and, using stimulated recall, analyse the subsequent accounts of the decisions made to regulate the practice. Establish the key criteria.
- Carry out a content analysis of planning documentation. Using a case study, observe a coach over a period of four weeks and compare the planned interventions with the athletes' activity.
- Select two examples from Figure 7.11. Design an investigation to demonstrate the importance of the selected sport characteristics for explaining differences in coaching practice.

Reading

The coverage within the chapter is quite extensive and any reading must inevitably be selective. The following sources provide a stimulating insight into aspects of coaches' practice, based on empirical research: Lyle (1992), Salmela (1995), Côte *et al.* (1995a), and Saury and Durand (1998). Francis (1990) is a first-hand account of a coach's work with a world-class athlete. Woodman (1993) and Abraham and Collins (1998) provide useful summaries of coaching practice.

PART 3
COACHING AS AN INTERPERSONAL RELATIONSHIP

CHAPTER EIGHT

▼ A QUESTION OF STYLE AND PHILOSOPHY

- Introduction   151
- Coaching and Interpersonal Relationships   153
- Coaching Styles   156
- Philosophies of Coaching   165
- Summary   172
- Projects and Reading   173

INTRODUCTION

There is no doubt that performance coaches are conscious of the interpersonal dimension of the coaching process and that this interpersonal behaviour has the potential for a range of positive and negative effects on the performer. The length of time that performance coaches spend in interaction with performers makes it difficult to believe that coaches could be unaware of the human dimension to coaching, from both performer and coach perspectives, and within the dynamics of personal characteristics, values, aspirations, motives and achievement. Nevertheless, the danger of focusing on performance and performance outcomes, and the potential for emphasising organisational rewards and goals above individual interests, have highlighted the human and interpersonal aspects of coaching as areas of concern. Coaches are aware that the practical implementation of values in the public arena brings with it a degree of societal scrutiny. The social context within which such a concern finds expression is dealt with in a subsequent chapter.

The interpersonal behaviour of the coach encompasses:

1 communication;
2 social relationships;
3 intervention delivery style;
4 decision making;
5 rewards and goal management; and
6 leadership.

Although coach–athlete directional behaviour is assumed, the athlete is a central player in interpersonal relationships. Coach to coach (and other support personnel) behaviour will also be important.

This chapter focuses on the interpersonal element of the coaching process and builds on the conceptual framework by offering a conceptualisation of what is commonly termed 'coaching style', and providing a perspective on values within which the coach's practice can be better understood. The attempt to devise and describe the generic coaching process, models of coaching, and the role of the coach has acknowledged that the coaching process is varied in implementation and practice. This chapter explains some of that variation and the impact on those concerned. However, the central message is more than that the human element of coaching practice produces variety. The interpersonal dimension of the coaching process is fundamental to that process and wide-ranging in its impact on effectiveness, athlete satisfaction, implementation practice, and coach and performer roles. Relationship issues should not be thought of as 'add-ons' to the coaching process. They are central, significant and, often, key to the satisfactory maintenance of the coaching contract.

 Critical Concept

The interpersonal dimension of the coaching process is fundamental to that process and wide-ranging in its impact on effectiveness, athlete satisfaction, implementation practice, and coach and performer roles.

The following simple statement of assumptions applies throughout the chapter. First, performance sports coaching is an interpersonal phenomenon. It is unlikely that the boundary markers and key concepts can be fulfilled without this. (Nevertheless, this allows for practice, which is considered less than ideal, in which there is limited face-to-face contact: for example, training schedules for middle- and long-distance athletes being communicated by post. However, as will be demonstrated, there may be some coaching processes in some sports that rely less on face-to-face contact in interactive intervention, although not diminishing the counselling and other interpersonal exchange that is necessary in coaching practice.)

Second, interpersonal exchange (IP-exchange) is shaped by a number of factors, including the coach's and athlete's value systems, personal characteristics (including age, maturity and personality traits), sport specificity, and organisational context. IP-exchange has an impact on *performance, athlete satisfaction, development and welfare*, and *coaching practice*.

Third, the evidence on IP-relationships and their influence is limited. There are many anecdotal accounts (and autobiographies of coaches and athletes can be very valuable for this purpose) of IP-exchange in coaching practice, but research evidence has largely

COACHING AS AN INTERPERSONAL RELATIONSHIP

been limited to athlete satisfaction studies. The richness of evidence required to describe IP-exchange has not suited the predominant behavioural research paradigm.

Lastly, the foundation of opinions on IP-behaviours and their benefits is often based on belief systems (sets of values) rather than evidence of impact/effect on performance or personal development. The conceptual framework should be able to account for coaching practice that is determined by such an ideological stance. This is important in analysing coaching processes but evaluation is made more difficult by the 'ought to be' element of ideological approaches. It should be possible to describe and explain why coaches (and athletes) perceive particular coaching behaviours to be more appropriate. However, it may not be possible to demonstrate that any one approach to IP-exchange is the most beneficial.

COACHING AND INTERPERSONAL RELATIONSHIPS

One of the features of the coaching process that highlights the place of IP-relationships is the multiplicity of goals. Coaches often have a value framework that includes the personal development of the athlete. The performance goals can be assumed for the performance sports coach, but these are often accompanied by equal/secondary/even prime goals, which focus more on elements of personal development. Even where these are not explicit, a default position of not damaging the interests of the performer can be assumed. This chapter will show that it is most often the IP element of the coaching process that is perceived to threaten the achievement of personal development goals.

It must not be assumed, however, that it is only the non-performance goals that are threatened or enhanced by IP-behaviour. Given that the attempted control of variables is central to the performance coaching process, it would be strange indeed if the human dimension and its contribution to performance were ignored. A good deal of sport research has focused on the technical and scientific enhancement of the athlete's performance. Naturally, this has embraced the athlete's psychological, physical, technical (and other) differences, dispositions and abilities. There would be no argument against the human element of performance, demonstrated in (for example) psychological preparation for competition. However, it requires no great leap of faith to accept that the implementation of the coaching process, which inevitably involves a relationship between the coach and the performer(s), will constitute a set of variables that demand attention.

This is reinforced if the nature of performance is considered. Performance can be thought of as consisting of stable and unstable elements. Stable elements are the developed and learned abilities associated with physical and technical capacities. However, performance, in training and competition, is also influenced by emotion, perception of effort, motivation/ activation, identity, ownership, and other social-psychological factors that constitute a less stable element. Managing these factors is part of reducing the unpredictability of performance and they are influenced by the nature of the IP-behaviour between coach and athlete.

Question Box

If we accept that heredity sets the limits of achievement but coaching practice determines the level of achievement within these limits, the interpersonal dimension may be impacting on the small increments of performance that determine success. Is this too strong a statement?

Question Box

Sport performance 'on the day' is subject to some variability. It seems quite likely that interpersonal factors will impact at this stage. Is sufficient attention paid to the management of competition and the coach's role in it?

It is not possible to adopt a completely value-free approach to any analysis of sports coaching. The chapters to date have emphasised a rational approach to an all-embracing coaching process, which attempts to manage the variables that influence performance. Nevertheless, it has been acknowledged throughout that coaching involves people and is an IP-relationship and that this is a fundamental assumption about coaching. The value position adopted in this analysis is as follows:

■ Reducing sport performance to a mechanistic concept is inappropriate. It is wrong not to emphasise the IP-dimension in the coaching process.
■ Added value is obtained from attending to the IP-relationships in the coaching process.
■ Coaching practice may be accompanied by a set of goals, purposes and values that emphasise competition, achievement and external outcomes. However, these should not be achieved at the expense of the interests of the individual performer.

Before moving on to the main sections of the chapter, Figure 8.1 elaborates on a number of brief statements that will set out the relationship of IP-exchanges to the conceptual framework.

It may seem from this opening section that the claims about the IP-relationships element of the coaching process are less assertive than those in previous chapters. There is an element of truth in this – perhaps reflecting the lesser attention given by researchers and their difficulties in finding causation between IP-behaviour and athlete performance, or indeed, between IP-behaviour and the athlete's personal 'development'. The following list of questions sets a research agenda that is far from completed:

1 Which aspects of coaching practice are enhanced by mutual empathy between coach and performer(s)? Does a shared commitment to goals create empathy? Are some coaching styles more likely to foster empathy than others?

Framework issues	IP-relationship
Pervasiveness	The coaching process model deals with stages and sub-processes. It is assumed that the process is goal-directed and that attention to goals pervades the process. Similarly, the IP-relationship between performer(s) and coach is pervasive throughout the process: not only in direct intervention but also in recruitment, goal setting, planning, etc. The IP-relationship can be thought of as the 'oil' that makes the process work.
Role	The role of the coach finds expression in IP-relationships. The extent of the athlete's engagement in a number of directional and decision-making functions is a question of role and style and IP-behaviour reflects this.
Boundaries	Empathy (2-way) between coach and performers is often cited as a feature of performance coaching. However, the nature and strength of the IP-relationship can be based on a number of factors – personal liking, respect for knowledge and experience, organisational structure.
Individualisation	The individuality that the athlete and coach bring to a coaching context will shape the process and be visible in the IP-exchanges among other behaviours. This is not surprising, and reflects personality, education, experience, values, and the context within which they operate. However, 1 IP-relationships are a means to an end insofar as they can be shown to impact on performance and preparation for performance. 2 IP-relationships are also an end in themselves insofar as they represent an aspect of the personal growth and development that exemplify some motives and value frameworks in coaching. 3 The conceptual framework should be able to distinguish between value-led behaviours and evidence-based behaviours.
Analysis and description	There is a tendency to portray IP-behaviours at either end of a continuum of 'person-centred' or 'performance-centred' modes. First, these extremes are unlikely to describe adequately the subtleties of IP-behaviour. Second, this perpetuates a dualism between performance and the person that is not reflected in the complexities of the coaching process.
Recruitment	The emphasis is understandably on direct intervention and other aspects of the coach's role and practice. However, it is important to acknowledge that IP-behaviour will influence coach education, coach recruitment and selection, and professional development.
Social context	This chapter focuses on the IP-exchange between coach and athlete and recognises that the coach's values framework is central to this. However, values have an element of context-specificity and the social and organisational context within which the coaching takes place will partly explain coaching practice. There is no attempt to separate individual and social context, merely to accord them sufficient depth of treatment. The social context is dealt with in a subsequent chapter.
Participation/ performance	It is tempting to distinguish between these 2 types of coaching on the basis of IP-behaviour – perhaps suggesting that there will be a more person-orientation within participation coaching. However, this reflects differences in goal orientation and individual motives for coaching. (Lyle *et al.* (1997) demonstrated differences in the motive to 'help young people' between coaches of more and less able performers.) Nevertheless, Salmela (1995) found that experienced and expert coaches had a very athlete-centred approach to the role, and the distinctions are likely to be quite complex.

Figure 8.1 *The relationship between the coaching framework and interpersonal characteristics*

2   It may be difficult to boost an individual's perceptions of self-worth in performance sport contexts in which relatively few performers have continuing success. How can IP-behaviours contribute positively to developing such a sense of self?

3   A sense of ownership by the performer(s) over the coaching process, and concomitantly greater degrees of understanding and awareness, may be difficult to achieve in conditions in which the coach's strategic overview is sometimes tacit and often contingent. How can control and management of variables be exercised alongside greater ownership for the athletes?

4   Self-determination and decision making in competition is encouraged in athletes. Is this developed by appropriate choice of preparation exercises or coaching styles, or both?

The factors influencing IP-relationships are extensive, and Figure 8.2 provides a useful summary.

Personal factors	Power differences	Coaching role	Social context
Maturity	Maturity	Decision making	Organisational values
Knowledge	Knowledge	Power of selection	Reward environment
Motives	Gender	Recruitment	Organisational mores
Aspirations	Communication	Goal management	Media expectations
Gender	Experience	Communication needs	Code of ethics/conduct
Experience	Credibility	Competition role	
Status	Status		
Value framework			

Figure 8.2 *Factors impinging on interpersonal relationships*

COACHING STYLES

'Coaching style' refers to the distinctive aggregations of behaviours that characterise coaching practice. The vocabulary used includes the terms 'authoritarian', 'autocratic', 'democratic', and 'person-centred'. The concept is common in coach education and in non-academic writing on coaching. However, there is also a considerable body of rigorous academic research on leadership styles in coaching (see Kuklinski 1990, and Douge and Hastie 1993 for a review). Coaching styles may be a useful mechanism for describing and analysing coaching practice or it may be a superficial way of caricaturing the most obvious elements of the coach's behaviour patterns. Insofar as coaching styles are a reflection of the coach's value framework and determine much of the IP-behaviour, they cannot be ignored in the conceptual framework. The doubts raised earlier about the link between coaching behaviours and performance remain, but this section will demonstrate that 'style' has substance and is a fundamental aspect of coaching practice. Further doubts are raised, however, over the assumptions made about adopting coaching styles and their polarisation into style categories.

Coaching style is not simply about instructional behaviour, although the use of behavioural observation instruments to investigate leadership behaviour has focused attention on direct intervention. As an analytical tool, coaching style also has the potential to offer an understanding of IP-relationships, social exchange, decision-making behaviour, communication, goal management and so on. For these reasons, coaching styles should be part of the conceptual framework and certainly not treated in a trivial or superficial manner. However, the following brief review of issues and questions suggests that there have been limitations thus far in the way 'style' has been conceptualised.

Style review

One of the most taxing questions is whether a coaching style is a relatively stable group of behaviours or a more transient approach that can be assumed by coaches as the situation demands. Is an 'authoritarian' style determined by experience and a psychological disposition or is it a learned capacity (perhaps through coach education)? Indeed, given the tacit nature of much of coaching practice, is coaching style a conscious aspect of practice? The prevailing style ideology may be both appropriate and effective, but can it be assumed that all coaches are able to adopt it? Perhaps more importantly, should all coaches adopt the same style, even allowing for idiosyncratic interpretation?

Second, the emphasis on social and personal values underpinning coaching behaviour raises the issue of coaching styles being defended on the basis of 'should' and 'ought' rather than a rational assessment of impact. As discussed in the introduction to the chapter, this may be more relevant to some goals and purposes than others.

Third, coaching style is an aspect of IP-behaviour (and a little more). This means that coaching style involves two-way interaction with athletes and points to the danger of focusing too directly on solely the coach's behaviour. Although much leadership style research has featured athlete satisfaction as the dependent variable, there has been little research into the effects on other athlete characteristics.

Fourth, Douge and Hastie (1993) refer to congruence between coaching styles and athlete preferences in their review of coaching effectiveness. They acknowledge that IP-relationships are linked to leadership style, but do not propose effectiveness criteria that associate style and performance. The authors do, however, perpetuate the uncritical assumption that leadership styles can be adapted by coaches.

Fifth, the research paradigm employed has focused attention onto observable behaviours, largely in the instructional setting, or on satisfaction responses to behavioural options – for example, Salminen and Liukkonen (1996). Given the scope of the coaching process, this may have considerably underestimated and under-reported behaviour in non-intervention contexts. Much of the perception about style comes from biographical accounts, self-reported accounts, critical incidents, and inductive reasoning from isolated intervention observations.

Sixth, there is no evidence that coaching style (in its generic and aggregated sense) influences performance. It would be very difficult to refute an assertion that coaches and athletes have had successful performance outcomes with the full gamut of coaching styles. Typical research might focus on elements of practice such as decision taking, use of questioning or feedback, and relate this to athlete satisfaction. It is assumed that the satisfied performer is better motivated, committed and so on. However, this is some way short of demonstrating an association between style and performance.

Seventh, participation coaches may be more interested in the participant's immediate satisfaction and continuation in the sport, and the coach's communication and delivery style is likely to be much more influential in that context. It is reasonable, therefore, that coach education should focus on delivery and communication for the novice participation coach and, in the absence of experience, present a delivery and organisational style that is inclusive, participative, animating and stimulating.

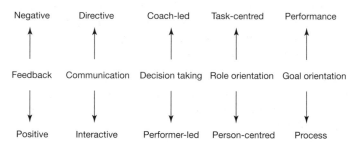

Keywords: performance–orientated; authoritarian; autocratic; directing; dictatorial

Coaching practice is characterised by:
- the primacy of the coach in decision taking
- a dominating, directive approach to IP-behaviour
- the transmission of knowledge, teaching and learning assumed to be one way
- coach-determined rules, rewards, standards and application
- rigidity and lack of personal empathy

Autocratic Coaching Practice

Negative	Directive	Coach-led	Task-centred	Performance
Feedback	Communication	Decision taking	Role orientation	Goal orientation
Positive	Interactive	Performer-led	Person-centred	Process

Democratic Coaching Practice

Coaching practice is characterised by:
- a participative decision-making style
- an interactive communication process
- human values incorporated into goals and evaluation
- the active involvement of the athlete in the teaching–learning process
- flexibiltiy, empathy and support in personal relationships

Keywords: person-centred; humanistic; sharing; democratic; caring; interactive

Figure 8.3 *The distinctions between autocratic and democratic coaching practice*

COACHING AS AN INTERPERSONAL RELATIONSHIP

Eighth, much of 'styles' research has used opportunity samples. At the same time, it seems very likely that there is a relationship between organisational/social context and the values and traditional practices on which styles are founded. Much more research is needed in performance sport contexts and in naturalistic settings. This need is based less on the level of performance and much more on the complexity, scope, intensity and multi-goal nature of the performance sport setting. In such settings, coaching style is likely to be a more complex phenomenon (and much more difficult to investigate).

The debate about coaching styles is often polarised into a comparison between extreme, but simplified, conceptualisations of styles. The contrast is generally between the more authoritarian/autocratic and the democratic/person-orientated styles. It is important, therefore, to examine those concepts in greater detail. Figure 8.3 is adapted from Lyle (1998c).

Clearly, these extreme positions have been exaggerated for effect. Even if accurate, it is unlikely that any coach's practice would be appropriately described by these models. It is worth reiterating that coaching style should not only be applied to direct intervention – managing training session, competition management, directing exercises and drills – but also to the approach taken to support activities such as planning and goal setting, and critical incidents such as crisis management and under-achievement. For this reason, it is difficult to imagine that stereotypical descriptions such as these are sufficiently refined as to capture the subtlety of coaching practice.

A further exemplar was provided by Tutko and Richards (1971), who suggested a more all-encompassing categorisation of coaching styles, and included personal qualities and situational consequences. Although this is not based on research findings and has something of a bias to psychology, it is reproduced in Figure 8.4 to illustrate some further examples of aggregated coaching behaviours.

These categories are based on the authors' experience, but there is no sense of context and they make too many assumptions to be suitable for the conceptual framework. However, their purpose is to stimulate ideas and they do point the way to a more varied and rounded conceptualisation of style.

 Question Box

Why is style important? The categories above may describe individuals rather than the totality of coaching practice. However, is style to be left to personal whim or are some approaches more effective, more appropriate and more successful than others? Where is the evidence? If it's too important to be left to chance, how have selection, recruitment and education dealt with this?

Leadership style is part of the coaching literature that provides the academic underpinning for coaching styles. Much of this research has been carried out in North America and has given the area some academic credibility. However, the insight into and impact on

THE AUTHORITARIAN STYLE
Discipline, punishment, rigid schedules, distanced from performers, organised and well planned, dominates the coaching team and performers.

Advantages	Disadvantages
well organised	defeat taken badly
good spirit in victory	sensitive performers not handled well
physically well prepared	anxiety high in performers

THE INTENSE STYLE
Endless planning, very good knowledge, never satisfied, motivates by example, may have difficulty with crises, similar to authoritarian but less harsh on performers.

Advantages	Disadvantages
coach supports hard work	performers put off by demands
coach works very hard	emotional outbursts from coach
prepared from competition	less motivated performers overlooked

THE EASYGOING STYLE
Dislikes schedules, appears lazy, displays few pressures, may not seem to take sport seriously, not easily disturbed by competition.

Advantages	Disadvantages
little pressure within team	coach criticised as not interested
performers receptive to suggestions	pressure not handled well
performers feel independence from coach	performers may not be in top physical condition

THE BUSINESS-LIKE STYLE
Well organised, detailed schedules, constant evaluation, relationships may be cool, treats coaching as science, coach craves knowledge.

Advantages	Disadvantages
performers up-to-date on technique	performers feel like pawns
sound and organised strategy	team spirit not emphasised
performers have confidence in coach	emotionally motivated performers may be overlooked

THE NICE-GUY STYLE
Liked, considerate, flexible with schedules and problems, positive motivation, opposite of authoritarian, personable, concern for welfare of performers.

Advantages	Disadvantages
cohesive team	coach may be seen as weak
relaxed atmosphere	socially inhibited performers overlooked

Source: Adapted from Tutko and Richards (1971); first appeared in Lyle (1998c).

Figure 8.4 *Coaching styles (Tutko and Richards 1971)*

COACHING AS AN INTERPERSONAL RELATIONSHIP

performance coaching practice has been limited. The seminal work was carried out by Chelladurai (Chelladurai and Saleh 1980; Chelladurai 1984), and the resulting Leadership Scale for Sport has been used in many investigations and studies have been replicated in many different situations. The Leadership Scale has five dimensions: training and instruction behaviour, democratic behaviour, autocratic behaviour, social support behaviour and rewarding behaviour. Kuklinski (1990) provides a summary of the research findings to that date, identifying three sets of explanatory variables: player (experience, aspirations, gender), coach (experience, age), and situation (the nature of the sport, environment).

An example of a specific study is Dwyer and Fisher's (1990) investigation into wrestlers' leadership preferences. The wrestlers preferred positive feedback, quality in training, quality and clarity of instruction, and coaching practice low on autocratic behaviour. However, there is also some evidence that performers do not prefer the more democratic approach in IP-relationships (Terry 1984; Gordon 1988). This seems likely to be a reflection of the team/individual dimension in direct intervention.

As suggested at the beginning of this section, the research on leadership styles in coaching has contributed little to understanding coaching practice.

- There is no doubt that some key variables have been identified and general preferences established for a range of coaches and athletes. However, the positivistic survey paradigm, the lack of context specificity, and the opportunistic sampling have limited the richness of the data.
- The absence of control of contextual variables (performance level, experience, maturity, organisational role, reward environment and so on) within and across studies has resulted in generally conflicting evidence. An example of this is the evidence on gender and preferred leadership style (see Fasting and Pfister 2000).
- The application of the evidence into coach education and coaching practice has also been limited. There are a number of reasons for this. The first is the lack of 'firmness' in the findings. The second is the fact that the findings do not apply equally to all members of a group or team. The third is that it involves an assumption that leadership behaviour is learned and flexible.
- Few of the studies adopt a critical perspective in relation to coaching process boundaries and socially and organisationally determined power relationships. The factors that may prove insightful include reward dependency, coach outcome accountability, social cohesion and stability, and the intensity of the coaching process.
- There is no doubt that identifying athlete satisfaction or preferred styles provides valuable information, but a simple catalogue of likes and dislikes does not delve deeply enough into important questions about coaching practice:

  - What is the extent of the difference between actual and preferred (by performers) leadership behaviours in performance sport?
  - Are some behaviours more important than others?
  - What action do athletes take when practice is other than preferred? How much of a difference does there need to be?
  - Does this impact on performance?
  - Do leadership styles alter in different aspects of the coaching process?

Figure 8.5 illustrates the factors involved in determining leadership practice. These factors are reconciled by individuals into a preferred leadership style. These styles can be categorised as humanistic, directive, instrumental, systematic or adaptable.

What, then, are the implications for the conceptual framework of an analysis of coaching styles? The overall conclusion must be that the potential for categorising and analysing coaching practice and the prevalence of leadership/coaching style research in the literature signal that coaching styles must be part of the conceptual explanation. Nonetheless, there are a number of constraints. The first is that there is a lack of conceptual clarity between IP-behaviour, leadership and coaching style. IP-relationships are a central feature of coaching practice and figure prominently in definitions of leadership and coaching

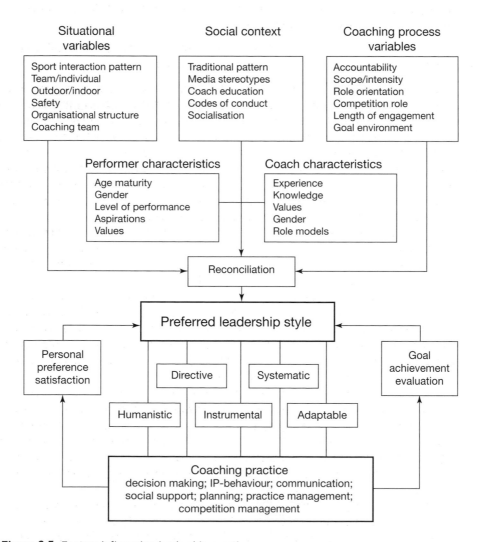

Figure 8.5 *Factors influencing leadership practice*

COACHING AS AN INTERPERSONAL RELATIONSHIP

style. Indeed, it would be reasonable to argue that they are the catalyst for differentiating between coaches' practices. Leadership has the advantage of being a wide-ranging construct and implies an aggregation of behaviours. Coaching styles should be understood to embrace all coaching practice and not simply observable intervention behaviours. More importantly, the failure to define coaching styles in the language and role demands of performance sport has greatly limited their value to date.

The second constraint is that the vocabulary is not sufficiently role-specific and, although the reduction to parent categories (such as autocratic-democratic) may have some value for classifying coaches' practice, the descriptors might benefit from having multiple dimensions. A third constraint is that the typology of coaching styles is as yet quite rudimentary. The typology suggested in Figure 8.5 – humanistic, directive, instrumental, systematic, adaptable – is merely a proposal and more work is required in classifying behaviour in the performance sport context.

A number of salient points can be made about the explanatory power of coaching styles for understanding the coaching process and its implementation:

1   It cannot be assumed that, once identified as appropriate, coaching styles can be adopted readily by all coaches. In any case it is not immediately obvious that coaching styles can be identified in this way. One must assume that a degree of personal preference, idiosyncrasy and the diversity of prior experiences will mean that the coaching practice of all coaches will be recognisably different.
2   Coaches' individuality should be encouraged. However, there is a need to distinguish between levels of impact of aspects of coaching practice. Some aspects of individual behaviour may be classified as 'stylistic' and presentational. Others are core processes and impact more significantly on the athlete's experience.
3   It can be assumed that there will be some congruence between organisational expectations, traditional practice, athlete preferences and coaches' practices. What is less clear is whether this is a process of self-selection, gradual adaptation, education, or a means–ends computation by the coach.
4   It can also be assumed that a process of *compensatory judgements* takes place. In other words, all persons concerned will weigh up the advantages and disadvantages in the mix of styles, preferences, goals and achievements. The absence of an overtly person-centred approach (if that was valued) might be compensated for by the coach's considerable experience and knowledge. Put simply, many performers may be more interested in achievement than IP-behaviour.
5   A more profitable approach may be to identify elements in the coaching process on which behaviour is known to have an effect. While this may seem obvious, the corollary is that there is less benefit in aggregating these behaviours into one composite style. Thus, an interactive, person-orientated approach to social support is signalled; active engagement in the learning process should be expected (Mosston and Ashworth 1990); and a directive approach to practice and competition management may be effective in interactive team sports.
6   Despite the delivery and communication emphasis in the early stages of coach education, it seems unlikely that coach education is responsible for the development of coaching style. Many performance coaches rely heavily on their own experiences

as performers, and are recruited directly from active participation. A 'social learning' process is a much more likely explanation for the way that coaches assimilate coaching style, often from other, more expert and experienced coaches (Lave and Wenger 1991).

7   The final point is that there would appear to be a genuine mix of effectiveness and appropriateness (that is, based on an evaluation of values) in dealing with coaching styles. One of the dangers is that, in the vacuum of research on effectiveness, the weight of value-led argument can be persuasive.

 Question Box

The capacity to assimilate leadership options may be best achieved through social learning. This has implications for the selection of coach mentors and for senior coaches more generally. This assumes adaptable leadership behaviours. Are they adaptable, and have we considered this as a part of the formal training of coaches?

There is a danger of overestimating the authoritarian approach, often stereotyped in performance sport. Salmela (1995) carried out in-depth interviews on twenty-one expert performance coaches and his findings are very illuminating. The coaches in the sample had carried forward from their own participation a set of personal qualities – 'extreme passion, intensity and a drive for excellence' (p. 6) – that characterised their coaching activities. The coaches' 'personal models of coaching' developed over time, and 'became increasingly flexible, orientated towards the personal development of the athletes over the rest of their lives and attempted to empower them towards taking personal responsibility for their performances and their lives' (p. 7). The overall impression is of coaches who are able to bring a sense of perspective to developmental and performance goals, at the same time retaining a personal set of values and standards.

Saury and Durand (1998), working with expert coaches, found that athletes and coaches shared control of training, citing negotiation and shared responsibilities. Côte *et al.* (1995b) found an interpersonal intervention style characterised by giving responsibility, being supportive, gaining respect from gymnasts, asking for quality training and keeping an appropriate personal distance. Similarly, Saury and Durand (1995) identified coaches who adopted an empathetic attitude towards athletes, employed tactful negotiation during training, defined a margin of autonomy for athletes during training, and used a 'communal reference point' to exchange knowledge and experience.

In a very interesting paper, d'Arripe-Longueville *et al.* (1998) illustrated how athletes and coaches negotiated their interpersonal relationship. The dynamics of the interaction could be classified as authoritarian. Coaches stimulated rivalry, entered into conflict, displayed indifference and showed preferences. The athletes countered by showing diplomacy, soliciting coaches directly, diversifying information sources and bypassing conventional rules. Both coaches and athletes adapted to power distribution within the elite sport system.

This more optimistic view needs to be reinforced by similar work carried out in some of the commercialised, media-dominated professional sports. Nevertheless, it points to the centrality of values in determining behaviour, and the chapter now turns to the relationship between the coach's value framework and behaviour under the heading of philosophies of coaching.

PHILOSOPHIES OF COACHING

The assumption underlying this section of the chapter is that coaching behaviour reflects a set of values about coaching, sport and human relationships more generally. This set of values or values framework has been termed a 'coaching philosophy' (Lyle 1999b). In fact, coaching practice may not correspond to stated 'philosophies' and it is important, therefore, that the conceptual framework of the coaching process is able to account for the relationship between values and practice. This section examines the values under-pinning coaching behaviour and provides a set of conceptual tools with which to analyse and understand this aspect of coaching practice.

Values are the means through which individuals evaluate their experiences and lead to some things being regarded more highly than others. A complete set of values provides a meaningful context for an individual's activities and those of others. In this sense then, values legitimate behaviour. Values are general conceptions about what individuals find important in their world and, although they can change over time, are quite stable. They are more deeply held than opinions and beliefs, which change more easily, and have less influence on behaviour.

Coaching practice is assumed, therefore, to be a reflection of values held by the coach: some individual, some shared. As a result of value judgements about good/bad/appropriate/ of worth among others, and given the fact that behaviour can be influenced either con-sciously or unconsciously, there is a potential for conflict. Figure 8.6 illustrates in a simple way that there is potential for conflict in a number of areas.

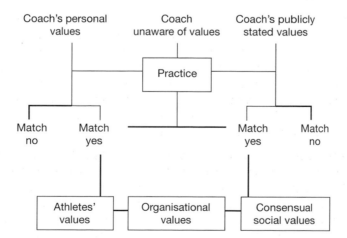

Figure 8.6 *Potential linkages between values*

The potential mismatches are shown by the bold lines. Where there is a tension between values and practice, or two sets of values, a number of possibilities exist. Behaviour can be changed, values changed gradually, or the individual can be unhappy or unsatisfied. This would, of course, assume that coaches (and others) were sufficiently self-reflective to be aware of their values and how they related to practice.

Before looking at how all of this can happen, it is worth noting that:

■ Lack of congruence between private and publicly stated values can be deliberate. Coaches may well be aware of the need to espouse values that match the expectations of others.
■ Where there is conflict, a measure of agreement can be negotiated through good practice.
■ Differences in value frameworks need not be so significant as to cause conflict.
■ In the absence of self-analysis, coaches may be unaware of the particulars of their behaviours and believe, inaccurately, that their actions conform to their stated values.
■ The development of values through early experiences, education, sport involvement, coach education and occupational socialisation (both for athletes and coaches) is likely to predispose individuals into sport contexts in which their values systems are more likely to be consonant. (Note that this is proposed in a context of relatively unexplored research territory.)
■ Conflict is more likely between organisational values and coaching values, or between the coach's value framework and more general conceptions of appropriate values in sport as expressed by those outwith the sub-culture.

The first point made above is that private values may not reflect public pronouncements. Part of the explanation for this is that statements of values may be tailored to either (1) what the coach perceives the demands of an employer or organisation to be, or (2) what the coach perceives 'should' be said – that is, commensurate with prevailing ideologies. There is an obvious danger here of a mismatch between the coach's preferred behaviour and stated values. This will be most evident to the athletes. It does point up the more general issue that coaching philosophies might become ideological (conforming) statements rather than guides to individual's behaviour and preferred practice – and by implication are poor measures of coaching practice.

A *coaching philosophy* is generally not expressed in the vocabulary of values themselves. Rather, these ordered statements are couched in terms of principles related to behaviour (that is, an element of context and implication). Taken as a whole, a coaching philosophy should provide a set of guiding principles for coaching practice, and, at the same time, identify those values that are felt most strongly. The range of practice elements is likely to be quite broad: performance sport, the role of the coach, the rights and responsibilities of the individual, desirable interpersonal behaviour, and relevant issues such as cheating or winning or intensity of commitment. A set of introductory comments about coaching philosophies will help to define the boundaries of the conceptual analysis.

Critical Concept

A coaching philosophy should provide a set of guiding principles for coaching practice, and, at the same time, identify those values that are felt most strongly.

Guiding principles of coaching philosophy

A 'philosophy' about a particular sport (which is really a technical/tactical model) should not be confused with a coaching philosophy. A coach's technical/tactical model might be based on a set of beliefs about the advantages and disadvantages of specific preparation methods, offensive /defensive strategies, or desirable performer qualities. However, this would be one element of the coach's knowledge structures and is probably based on the efficacy of the choice for performance achievement. A coaching philosophy is a more comprehensive set of values about the coach's behaviour and practice. It is possible that there might be some overlap between sport performance models and more general values.

A process of self-reflection (which in practice may actually involve others) is necessary to identify a values framework and is a growing part of coach education. The framework is also an essential element in analysing practice since it has an explanatory power. Coaches must, therefore, come to realise that a complete understanding of practice is not possible without identifying the coaching philosophy. One method of initiating this analysis is to carry out a review of 'critical incidents' in coaching practice.

Thus far there is no understanding in a coaching context of how values change over time or of how particular kinds of experience might impact on the coach's values framework. There is clearly a research agenda relating to the effects of education, maturity, respon-sibility, success, organisational authority and other factors on the development of values. Values do not change quickly, and it seems unlikely that coaches can, or would want to, adapt these deeply held constructs in a superficial way. It may lead, however, to coaches' public pronouncements being different from their personal values.

Values connote a sense of worth, of commitment and of conviction. Although there may be some values (such as self-determination or fairness) that command some universal respect and acceptance, it will be obvious that values are subject to social construction and there will be an element of social acceptance, or otherwise, in individual values. Some values may command less social consensus (meritocracy, competition) but be part of a prevailing occupational or sub-cultural ideology.

Values frameworks may contain 'core' and 'peripheral' values, although this has also not been subject to any depth of research (see Lyle 1999b). Core values for performance coaches may be centred on adherence and commitment to programmes and achievement. However, others' core values may be about athlete development and fairness. The relation-ship between core values and coach education is under-explored.

A coaching philosophy that is not derived from practice is merely a speculative set of intentions that have not been tested in implementation. It is not clear that this would have any purpose – other than, perhaps, an ideological statement about preferred values.

 Question Box

It is not unusual for coaches to express statements about how behaviour and practice 'should be'. Is it possible to 'borrow' a philosophy from others or from education, or must it come from experience? Can a non-coach have a coaching philosophy?

Since there is a measure of social acceptability, there must be a means of evaluating the values themselves. Figure 8.7 lists a number of criteria against which values can be judged, although it becomes evident that the same value would not be rated acceptable by each criterion.

As mentioned above, a value/practice that is judged appropriate in terms of traditional practice or means–ends rationality may not be considered good practice when judged against more general moral standards. Nevertheless, coaching is an interpersonal relationship, and it would be strange indeed if the values relevant to coaching were not similar to many other social relationships. However, it must be remembered that there will be some particular processes, tensions and challenges that are brought about solely by an engagement in the coaching process. Some of these will merely be contextual and derived from the purpose of coaching, but about which there are value choices. Others

Criterion

Rationality	The value is judged against the impact that the consequent practice would have on the purpose of the endeavour – in this case, improving and sustaining performance. Empowerment in decision making could be argued to result in more effective crisis behaviour by performers.
Moral standard	The value reflects consensual moral and ethical standards. This involves recourse to notions of human and civil rights, and standards of acceptability of public behaviour. Values associated with not cheating or honesty are examples.
Performer congruence	There may be congruence between the value framework of the coach and the athlete(s). The coach may, of course, recruit athletes who share similar values. Research is required to identify those values that most influence evaluation of compatibility.
Contextual relevance	The coach's values may be considered appropriate when judged against the social and organisational mores within which the coaching takes place.
Traditional practice	The values, or behaviour, through which they become evident are reflective of the traditional practice of those coaches achieving consensual recognition.

Figure 8.7 *Criteria for evaluating coaching values*

involve 'testing the edges' of acceptable practice/values. These relate to gaining an unfair advantage or engaging in practices that may not be in the interests of the athletes (doping, cheating and intimidation). This is dealt with in the chapter on ethics.

One argument would be that the coach's values would be demonstrable in all behaviour and practice. The coaching philosophy is, after all, a coherent group of statements about values and practices that are representative of the individual's approach to coaching. The range of behaviours associated with the coaching process has been elaborated in several parts of early chapters. While the generalisability of values seems a reasonable argument, a better understanding of an individual's coaching philosophy will be gained by focusing on specific aspects of the coaching process. Therefore, in analysis, it would be beneficial to focus on the following:

Recruitment practices
Goal setting
Interpersonal communication
Professional standards
Qualities valued in coaches
Selection principles
Rewards and discipline
Intervention behaviour
Setting and maintaining standards
Balance of personal and organisational goals

Leadership role
Emphasis on competition results
Decision making
Relationship with officials
Individualisation
Behaviour under competition pressure
Outcome evaluation
Personal motives for coaching
Attitude to rules and regulations

It would be inappropriate to present a complete example of a coaching philosophy. First, there is a danger that it is treated as an exemplar of good practice, and, second, that it is too sport specific. (Those that are published generally have a prescriptive element rather than representing a rigorous analysis of practice and used for self-development purposes (Crisfield *et al.* 1996; Martens 1997; for an exception, see Lyle 1999b: 33). However, good examples of the coaching philosophies of expert coaches can be found in Cross (1990) and Felgate (1997).

The statements that follow are intended merely as exemplars and have been extracted and adapted from a variety of values frameworks (adapted from Lyle 1998c):

> I will encourage players to be satisfied with their own levels of performance rather than to measure this against other players.

> In matters related to personal behaviour, I believe that the coach should lead by example. The coach should ensure that behaviour reflects status in sport and society. Punctuality, integrity, diplomacy and standard of dress are all important in this role.

> Players have a right to be consulted on all matters relating to strategic elements of team development.

> Final resolutions of problems and the absolute right to make on-the-spot decisions are the prerogative of the coach.

Criterion	Evaluation questions
Indicator of practice	Is there sufficient linkage between each of the statements and the specifics of coaching practice? Would it be possible to use the value framework as a guide to expected practice?
Consistency	Is there consistency between each and all of the statements? Are there examples of contradictions between statements or values (an example might be between athlete self-determination and coach's directive leadership practice)?
Aspiration	Is there any reason to believe that the statements reflect aspirations rather than actual practice? Is there a sense of 'what is expected'? Are some of the values (e.g. autonomy, equity) difficult to achieve in the given circumstances, and therefore more a statement of aims? One indicator of this is a statement written in the 'third person' – i.e. 'coaches should . . .'.
External context	Has the context within which the statement will apply been made explicit? Is there any indication that the philosophy is intended to be context-free? (Is that possible?)
Breadth	How comprehensive was the statement? Is there sufficient coverage of the coaching process to give a full understanding of coaching practice? Has the coach attended to both core and peripheral values?
Value clarity	Is there sufficient indication of the value that underpins the practice statement? The values are not always identified and there may be some confusion over the 'motive' for a particular practice. Is an 'open discussion policy' a reflection of athlete autonomy, a control mechanism, or a diffusion of values mechanism!
Situational specificity	Are any of the implications of the stated value made clear? In which circumstances would the practice be adhered to? An example might be a statement that 'I will be honest with performers'. Would it be inappropriate to use encouraging words if the athlete was performing badly? How honest is it reasonable/possible to be in matters of selection and recruitment?

Figure 8.8 *Evaluation criteria for coaching philosophies*

> Winning is an important goal but should be achieved within a framework of the rules and laws of the sport.

The next question to consider is how aggregations of such statements or coaching philosophies can be analysed and evaluated (not whether the underlying values are good or bad!). Figure 8.8 suggests a number of criteria for evaluating coaching philosophies.

Lyle (1999b) presents the results of a content analysis of the coaching philosophies of more than forty senior coaches. His analysis of 'meaning units' within the coaches' statements found an even distribution between: reasons for coaching, the coach–athlete relationship, the coach's characteristics, the role of the coach, and operational matters (1999b: 34). The operational element was less concerned with day-to-day intervention than with general statements about cheating and ethics. A keywords analysis was carried out and a process of aggregating synonymous terms and then reducing the inclusive constructs led to a similar list of concerns: athlete development, relationships, coaches' qualities, coaching ethos, the coach's role, goals and operational style (1999b: 36). The final analysis identified the values inherent in each statement. This list is reproduced in Figure 8.9.

COACHING AS AN INTERPERSONAL RELATIONSHIP

Personal growth	30	Instrumentality	9
Concern for well-being		Goal direction, planning	
Education		Efficiency, quality	
Respect for Others	20	Independence	6
Consistency, loyalty, trust,			
honesty, integrity			
Partnership	19	Equality of treatment	6
Co-operation, agreement			
Democracy, consultation			
Self-improvement (coach)	17	Adaptability	5
Self-determination (athlete)	17	Teamwork	5
Autonomy, understanding			
Empowerment, ownership			
Fairness	16	Application	5
		Commitment, discipline	
Professionalism	14	Non-extreme behaviour	4
Enjoyment	13	Reward for effort	3
Individuality	11	Accountability	2
Openness	10	Responsibility	1
Leadership	10	Conformity	1
Role model			
Supportiveness	10	Control	1
Empathy, accessibility			
Facilitation, help, giving			

N = number of Meaning Units in coaches' statements

Source: (Lyle 1999: 35)

Figure 8.9 *Identification of values by Meaning Unit*

It should be noted that Lyle acknowledges that the coaches in this opportunity sample had produced the value frameworks in an educational context, and that relatively few were performance coaches of elite/top-level performers. This may account for the very noticeable person-centred approach. A similar exercise is required with a more targeted group of performance coaches.

Other terms that might have been found are 'responsibility', 'achievement', 'excellence', 'balance' and 'equity'. It would also be useful to discuss coaching philosophies in interview format and to explore responses to problem scenarios. In such circumstances values such as *pragmatism* and *expediency* might be more evident.

How should a coaching philosophy be constructed? Figure 8.10 suggests a likely procedure.

When particular patterns of values are held by significant numbers of individuals and these are promoted as a coherent 'approach', it could be said that they represent an ideology – that is, a system of ideas and values about coaching. The following short chapter focuses on one particular set of values – termed a humanistic approach to coaching practice.

1 Provide an introduction that makes explicit the context within which the statement has been constructed or for which it is intended.

2 Describe motives for becoming a coach and whether or not this has changed. Identify core values and priorities.

3 Describe an interpretation of the role of the coach.

4 Focus on interpersonal relationships with performers. What is key about these relationships?

5 Describe developmental constructs that are intended to be fostered in athletes.

6 Derive a series of principles from a review of several critical incidents.

7 An 'operational' set of practices can be identified from reconstructing typical activities and how they are conducted.

8 Step outside the sporting context and review practice/relationships in the context of more generally held values about people and conduct

9 Review values to decide whether there are any situational compromises in their application.

10 Review 'difficult' issues for all relationships: abuse of power, trust, harassment, discrimination. Firmed-up positions should be reflected in statements.

11 Sport has an explicit set of rules and a less explicit set of expectations about conduct in relations to these. Clarify values in relation to these.

12 Consider professional context and expectations in relation to standards, education, development and conduct.

13 Review the statement made for the correspondence between practice and aspiration.

14 Consider the presentation of the framework in the light of the potential readership. Has the statement been amended to meet the expectations of the reader? Is the coach comfortable with this?

Figure 8.10 *Steps towards constructing a coaching philosophy*

SUMMARY

This chapter will have familiarised you with the following:

- interpersonal relationships as a dimension of the coaching process;
- the place of interpersonal relationships in the conceptual framework of the coaching process;
- unanswered questions about interpersonal behaviour;
- a review of current thinking on coaching styles;
- the distinction between autocratic and democratic coaching practice;
- the factors influencing coaching styles and a proposed typology of coaching styles;
- the value of coaching styles for understanding coaching practice;
- examples of literature suggesting that coaching styles are complex and cannot be oversimplified in performance sport;

- the place of values in analysing and understanding a coaching philosophy;
- a means of evaluating values, a focus for analysing values in coaching practice, and criteria for evaluating coaching philosophies; and
- how to construct a coaching philosophy.

PROJECTS

- Use Figure 8.10 to devise your own coaching philosophy. Enlist the help of an observer to evaluate whether your practice and philosophy are consonant.
- Adopt the typology of styles – humanistic, directive, instrumental, systematic, adaptable. Establish criteria for these and carry out a qualitative or quantitative survey investigation to characterise the styles of behaviour of a population of coaches.
- Carry out a case-study investigation with one experienced performance coach. Try to elicit explanations and elaborations for style behaviour for which you have accumulated some observational evidence.
- Analyse a selection of coaching philosophies. Choose your sample to facilitate an investigation into a particular variable – team/individual, novice/expert, etc.
- Investigate the adaptability of coaching styles. Create a matrix of style behaviour criteria and use these to establish the similarities/differences in the style behaviour of 3–4 coaches who operate in both participation and performance contexts.

Reading

Lyle (1999b) gives a useful review of coaching philosophies. Kuklinski (1990) reviews leadership styles and the associated evidence. Saury and Durand (1998) and d'Arripe-Longueville *et al.* (1998) will give a flavour of the complexity of interpersonal relationships in performance sport. Potrac *et al.* (2000) argue for coaching as a social and interpersonal phenomenon.

CHAPTER NINE

▼ **A HUMANISTIC APPROACH TO COACHING**

■ Introduction   174
■ Basic Assumptions   176
■ Humanistic Coaching Practice   178
■ Discussion of Issues   183
■ Summary   186
■ Projects and Reading   186

INTRODUCTION

This short chapter focuses on one particular set of values that have come to be acknowledged as a benchmark for behaviour in participation coaching, and as a comparator for coaching practice in performance sport. The 'humanistic approach to coaching' is a person-centred philosophy or ideology that emphasises the empowerment of the individual towards achieving personal goals within a facilitative interpersonal relationship. The set of values intrinsic to this approach has its rationale in what is considered appropriate for human beings and for their best interests: a sense of being 'correct' rather than effective. To some extent, therefore, such an approach has the 'moral high ground', and its tenets are used as benchmarks against which to measure coaching practice. Part of the focus in this chapter is the extent to which the humanistic approach is appropriate for performance sport.

 Critical Concept

The 'humanistic approach to coaching' is a person-centred philosophy or ideology that emphasises the empowerment of the individual towards achieving personal goals within a facilitative interpersonal relationship.

The humanistic approach represents an ideology within sports coaching. A set of values and practices become accumulated and assimilated into a relatively coherent perspective on what sports coaching 'should be like'. When these values are shared by significant groups of people, this ideology then becomes part of coach education (Crisfield *et al.* 1996; Martens 1997), the coaching literature (Smoll and Smith 1996; Gervis and Brierley 1999), and codes of conduct (NCF 1996; NCF/NSPCC 1998), and informs judgements about coaching behaviour and practice. Although it is not given attention in this chapter, it should be recognised that ideologies can be said to advantage those who hold and perpetuate them. This may mean merely satisfying a personal set of deeply held values and beliefs. However, there is also a potential commercial advantage from promoting an ideology. It is also the case that to become a prevailing ideology there needs to be acquiescence from those who exert power and influence within some social sphere. Some further critical analysis is required on the relationship between influence/power, ideology, and interest in the promotion of coaching ideologies.

There is little doubt that the humanistic approach to sports coaching has become the prevailing ideology in youth sport (De Knop *et al.* 1996; Donnelly 2000b). This is partly a response to perceived excesses in coaching practice in youth sport but also a reflection of age-related educational values. It is much less clear that its attendant practices can be, or indeed should be, applied to performance sport.

It is hardly surprising that there is a range of belief systems. The social phenomenon of sport stretches from school education to the Olympic Games, from professional sport to recreational pastime, and from young children to adult veterans. There are many motives for being engaged in sport and a range of social externalities to drive sport policy. It is possible, even likely, that competing ideologies are more suited to particular contexts. However, the humanistic approach to sports coaching has become dominant and must, therefore, be given detailed attention in any attempt to understand the coaching process. There are a number of reasons for this attention.

1   It has been acknowledged previously that the interpersonal element of the coaching process is very important in shaping coaching practice. The humanistic approach is very much shaped by the nature of the interpersonal relationship between athlete and coach.
2   The truly humanistic approach can be interpreted as being at one end of the continuum of autocratic-democratic styles. Insofar as it represents an 'extreme' style, it is worthy of study.
3   The conceptual framework, which provides the rationale for the book, needs to incorporate any factor that significantly influences practice. However, perhaps more importantly, if a set of values challenges the assumptions on which the framework is based, this demands attention.
4   Although the humanistic ideology has become prevalent in the rhetoric of youth sport and the early stages of coach education programmes, a number of questions remain:

    (a) To what extent is humanistic practice widespread in coaching practice?
    (b) How easily can humanistic coaching principles be put into practice?
    (c) To what extent might humanistic coaching practice be appropriate in performance sport?

(d) To what extent is the ideology based on research evidence of effectiveness, on principles of good practice, or on a belief system?

BASIC ASSUMPTIONS

To begin to answer these questions, it is necessary to examine the assumptions on which the ideology is founded. The humanistic approach makes a number of presumptions about sport and individual development:

1   Competition goals are important, but not more important than the interests of the individual.
2   The development of the individual will take place if experience and activity are characterised by empowerment, engagement and self-determination.
3   Sport experiences and achievements are only one part of an athlete's life and have to be set in the context of many other important human experiences (among them, education, career, family and health).
4   The performance sport context is a specific social arena and has its own set of values, motives and goals. These must be understood in the context of other value frameworks.
5   Sport should not be conceptualised merely as performance. In other words, the individual should be recognised rather than the achievement/score/result.
6   Sport performance should not be 'narrowed' to its technical aspects. It is important to consider the emotional, psychological and social components.
7   Sports coaching is an interpersonal phenomenon and is built around an interpersonal relationship.
8   The individual performer's growth and development is determined to a significant extent by the nature of the interpersonal relationship between coach and athlete – in particular, its facilitative qualities.

These assumptions about sport and humanism were established in a series of papers in the 1970s and 1980s (Sage 1978; Whitson 1980; Danziger 1982; Lombardo 1987), and are evident in the work of Orlick (Orlick 1990; Orlick and Botterill 1975). Lombardo (1999) provides an up-to-date account of humanistic principles. At first glance these presumptions appear to apply most appropriately to participation sport. It is necessary, therefore, to examine their relevance to performance sport, which is the context for the conceptual framework in this text. Inevitably, this involves generalising somewhat about the characteristics of performance sport. First, much of professional sport is caricatured as being driven by commercialism, an instrumental approach to achievement and morality, and a lack of concern for ethical standards and conduct. This is reinforced by a reward system for both coaches and athletes that has emphasised outcome success. As a result, coaching practice is performance-orientated and values competition success much beyond concern for individuals. It has to be acknowledged that this is rarely, if ever, expressed explicitly as being 'at the expense of athlete welfare'. Second, engagement in the 'fast track' of performance sport is perceived to require an almost total commitment by the individual athlete. The dominance of this 'central life interest' will often work to the disadvantage of many other aspects of the athlete's life. Clearly, this is gross exaggeration of professional and top-level sport, and paints an extreme picture that does no justice to the individuals involved. Nevertheless, it is obvious that there is a lack of immediate consonance between the humanistic presumptions about sport and this, albeit overstated, description.

 Question Box

The balance between athlete welfare and competition success is rarely discussed in print. Is it possible that National Lottery funding and enhanced life-style management have encouraged athletes to accept the traditional disincentives of elite sport participation?

Performance sport provides media role models for young people. One of the major criticisms of youth sport is that performance sport characteristics and attitudes (and, in addition, the less beneficial aspects) have been incorporated by coaches and parents (Cahill and Pearl 1993; Coakley 2001). This is evident in the practices associated with selection and early maturity, narrowness in preparation, overemphasis on competition success, lack of concern for health and long-term physical well-being, and downplaying the elements of fun and enjoyment. Once again this is evidently an extreme view and the literature is dominated by North American examples. Nevertheless, such practice challenges the assumptions on which the humanistic approach is based.

A major thrust of the humanistic coaching ideology is the nature of the interpersonal relationship between coach and athlete. The previous chapter focused on coaching/leadership styles and identified a range of styles from directive to more person-centred. The evidence cited pointed to a tendency in some coaching contexts towards an authoritarian, autocratic style. The characteristics of this practice include a limited degree of self-directed behaviour for the athlete, a 'one-way' relationship, performance rather than personal goals, and a lack of individuality and creativity. This dependency culture is at odds with the humanistic approach, which emphasises that the athlete should not lose control of the process.

As with many social relationships there is potential for an abuse of power in the coach–athlete association and a disregard of human values that would clearly not benefit the athlete. There is also a whole range of ethical issues (see the following chapter for a fuller treatment), such as cheating, harassment, doping, competition behaviour, and so on, that call into doubt the rather optimistic assumptions made by humanists about sport.

There is no doubt that this is a rather overstated refutation of the assumptions identified earlier. The intention was to point up the basis for a subsequent argument that the humanistic approach is very challenging to adopt in many of the circumstances that apply in contemporary sport, both participation and performance. A number of possibilities exist: (1) the assumptions are not justified; (2) the assumptions are not an accurate reflection of sport and it is unlikely that humanistic ideology will be found in practice; and (3) the humanistic ideology should be supported to mitigate some of the excesses of behaviour described. However, coaching practice may already have adopted and may reflect some of these principles. Reference has already been made to Salmela's (1995) findings, which demonstrated that expert coaches in top-level sport were concerned for athletes' development and adopted largely person-centred approaches (for an example, see Cross 1990).

HUMANISTIC COACHING PRACTICE

In order to look at the implications for coaching practice, it is important to understand the concepts involved in humanistic practice. Humanistic psychology embodies an active consciousness in individuals that has a capacity to organise and integrate experience and learning. This is in contrast to more mechanistic stimulus–response behaviourism or the early-years determinism of psychoanalytical theories. Humanism is said to be an 'optimistic' theory of behaviour since it assumes that individuals have a facility to 'become' – that is, they have an (infinite) potential for change and growth. This facility is an active one, is forward directed, and can be shaped by conscious motives. Lombardo (1987: 16–18) identifies a number of principles on which humanism is based:

1   the importance of personal interpretations of human experience;
2   an holistic view of human beings;
3   the centrality of freedom and autonomy; and
4   an acceptance that experience is individually defined.

The key to the theory is that the capacity for growth and development is facilitated only (or at least, more so) in circumstances that are favourable. This means opportunities for active engagement, self-determination and creativity, and in circumstances of improvement, progress and achievement. The key value is autonomy. Personal growth and development is, therefore, an appropriate goal in its own right in any human endeavour, including sports coaching.

It is also important to note that personal growth and development can be a continual process and is not restricted to young persons. Indeed, Cross (1991) has pointed out that the mature athlete may be more able to enter into a meaningful partnership. However, the participation of many young people in sport and their commitment to it emphasise the appropriateness of such goals. The eventual goal is individuals who have developed their powers in a balanced and integrated way. In an early paper, Botterill (1978) described an individual who is 'psychologically mature, stable, keeps things in perspective, copes well with difficulties, and is adaptable, cool, independent, self-confident and self-disciplined'. It would be very difficult to argue against this as a worthwhile aim, not only in sport, but in life more generally. Activities can be described as worthwhile if they have the potential to engender the necessary qualities of self-determination, self-control and individuality. These are obviously ambitious targets, not only for sport, but

 Critical Concept

Coaching activities can be described as worthwhile if they have the potential to engender the necessary qualities of self-determination, self-control and individuality.

Idealised constructs

Idealised coaching practice

Idealised constructs		Idealised coaching practice
Achievement context Sense of purpose Range of emotions Variety in IP-relationships Creativity Commitment & discipline Problem solving Independence	Goal setting	Goals are focused on personal development and processes rather than performance outcomes.
	Goal setting	Accountability and reward are evaluated against personal goals rather than organisational goals.
	IP-behaviour	The coach acts as a facilitator and resource for learning rather than transferring expert knowledge.
	Purpose	Opponents are considered to be contributors to goals rather than constraints.
	Behaviour	The coach focuses on the subjectiveness of the sport experience (emotion and interpretation) rather than performance behaviour.
	Behaviour	Standards of conduct and adherence are determined by self-discipline and collective authority.
	Behaviour	Evaluation is determined by internal/intrinsic measures rather than external measures.

Figure 9.1 *Simplified model of humanistic practice in sport coaching*

for education, family life and all social relationships as well. The issue is how (and if!) coach–athlete relationships and coaching practice can contribute to such worthy aims.

As has already been shown, performance sport has a perhaps unique set of challenges to humanistic coaching practice. However, there is no doubt that sport has the potential to facilitate personal growth and development. Figure 9.1 is a speculative, idealised matrix of constructs for humanistic behaviour applied to coaching practice.

Lombardo (1987) identifies the following key coach behaviours:

- response to change;
- developing 'real' freedom for athletes;
- clear goals;
- gradual relinquishing of control;
- providing problem-solving opportunities; and
- individualisation of the coaching process.

Whitson (1980) focused on three areas: instruction (perhaps now termed 'mentoring'), cognitive and emotional development, and personal relationships.

The behaviours identified above are merely exemplars of the catalogue of facilitative practices that could be calculated to assist individuals towards personal growth and development. It has been implied throughout, however, that, taken together, these may be unrealistic. This may, of course, be a result of the bias of the author, the limitations of current practice, or the limitations of coach education and a more general lack of awareness of the potential of such behaviour. Clearly, there is quite considerable complementarity with the democratic style of coaching/leadership described in the previous chapter. Nevertheless, there would appear to be a contradiction for which a resolution will be offered in the summary of the chapter: sport has enormous potential for personal growth and development if it is centred on these aims but, by definition, performance sport does not have this essential purpose. There is no doubt that many individuals (perhaps the great majority) benefit from their involvement in sport, even the partially limiting performance sport variety.

 Critical Concept

Sport has enormous potential for personal growth and development if it is centred on these aims but, by definition, performance sport does not have this essential purpose.

It might be argued that individuals will grow and develop despite the inherent limitations of the performance sport context – indeed, some individuals (the successful ones!) might benefit enormously. It must also be acknowledged that the majority of coaches are intent on balancing accountable performance goals with the interests of performers. The next section examines how this can be incorporated into good coaching practice.

 Question Box

We have an intuitive sense that the majority of individuals are not harmed by their sport experience – even given the excesses of youth and elite sport. However, positive personal growth goes beyond this. Is this a matter for individuals or is a cultural shift required?

Adapting practice

A detailed account of a coaching philosophy that can be characterised as humanistic can be found in swimming coach John Hogg's (1995) work on psychological skills. Hogg describes how the coach's practice should evolve from a more directive relationship with younger performers to a progressively sharing relationship, and, ultimately, independence for the performer. This purposeful but incremental empowerment of the athlete provides opportunities for personal growth and development. This evolving relationship is demonstrated in Figure 9.2 (Hogg 1995: 12.9).

The early stage of coach dependency is necessary during a period when basic skills are being taught, safety is important, and valuable routines and habits are being acquired. As the sharing stage develops, opportunities are taken to develop self-direction in decision making. As the performer moves into maturity, a gradual independence (and accountability) is developed. The athletes learn to manage their own engagement in the coaching

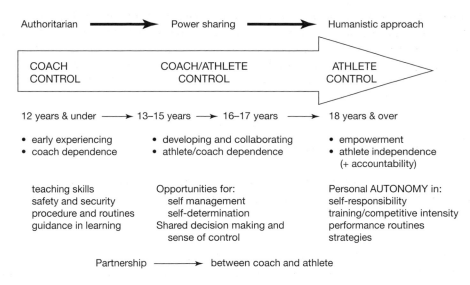

Authoritarian ➡️ Power sharing ➡️ Humanistic approach

| COACH CONTROL | COACH/ATHLETE CONTROL | ATHLETE CONTROL |

12 years & under ➡️ 13–15 years ➡️ 16–17 years ➡️ 18 years & over

- early experiencing
- coach dependence

- developing and collaborating
- athlete/coach dependence

- empowerment
- athlete independence (+ accountability)

teaching skills
safety and security
procedure and routines
guidance in learning

Opportunities for:
  self management
  self-determination
Shared decision making and
  sense of control

Personal AUTONOMY in:
self-responsibility
training/competitive intensity
performance routines
strategies

Partnership ➡️ between coach and athlete

Source: Hogg 1995:12.9

Figure 9.2 *Illustration of a shift in coaching paradigms*

process. (This perhaps explains the views of coaches who claim that they need not spend time on 'motivating' athletes. They are self-motivated and monitored.) Hogg argues the case for a humanistic approach and provides exemplars of appropriate behaviours in swimming coaching. The summary diagrams, for example, comparing the authoritarian and the existential humanistic paradigm, and the reference list, provide a very valuable insight into coaching practice in general and an idealised humanistic model in particular.

Cross (1990) uses the terms 'collaborative' and 'non-manipulative' to describe the humanistic practice of an expert swimming coach. In a later paper (Cross 1991), in which he advocates the use of such an approach, he characterises appropriate behaviour as creating an 'open' and 'no-blame' culture. The features highlighted are the following:

1 understanding athletes;
2 adapting to athlete needs;
3 communicating well;
4 motivating well; and
5 consistent behaviour.

Cross suggests that senior athletes are more suited to this form of partnership. He does go on, however, to point out that in his research athletes gave a less positive interpretation of existing coaching behaviour than did coaches.

Although much of the approach is centred on the adoption of appropriate values, it is necessary to consider the practical means by which the athlete can become involved in the process. It is worth repeating that within this philosophy personal growth should not be a concomitant or accidental outcome, but an actively promoted objective.

Adopting humanistic practice may well be an issue of security for coaches. Just as athletes become increasingly able to cope with responsibility, this will also happen to coaches. Is this an approach to be adopted by novice performance coaches?

There are a number of elements of direct intervention practice that cannot easily be devolved to the athlete. Practice management tasks, such as directing exercises/drills, providing immediate feedback, contingency planning and non-deliberative decision making are best implemented by the coach. However, athletes can be encouraged to become more aware of sessional planning skills and decisions, to engage in monitoring and evaluating the programme, to discuss progress in achieving goals, and to share tactical and strategy issues. In addition, coaches could (should!) devolve intervention adherence to the athletes: scheduling issues, time management, session discipline, recording duties, and routine injury prevention activity.

Athletes can also become involved in intervention support activities. The most obvious of these is goal setting and planning, including competition schedules. However, it may be more rewarding to involve the athlete in resource issues, organisational management, coach education and working with younger athletes (perhaps with a proviso that this does not impact on the time required for training).

The key factor is the quality of the interpersonal relationship. It is necessary for the coach to seek to develop an IP-style that does not become uni-directional, stifle creative thought, depersonalise the athlete, or abuse the authority of expertise or role. Exemplary behaviours can be described in simplistic terms – for example, positive feedback, and the use of questioning or listening. However, the suggestions that follow are much more challenging. They have been adapted from a seminal text by Carl Rogers (1961) and represent the characteristics of a helping and caring relationship. This adaptation of Rogers' characteristics was first published in Lyle (1998c: 116), and adapted further in Lyle (1999b: 39).

- Be trustworthy, dependable and consistent – but be real! Recognise your own feelings in your relationship with performers and as circumstances arise.
- Express these to the performers. Do not hide your feelings but specify the cause of your feelings.
- Always maintain an attitude of caring, interest and respect. Never depersonalise the performer.
- Be secure enough to allow the separateness of the performer. (This has a strong resonance for coaches who try to keep performers to themselves or limit interaction with other experts.) Let the performer(s) develop a separate identity.
- Try to recognise and understand the performer's feelings and emotions as well as their behaviour.
- Do not base your interactions on a threat of exercising some power or authority (whether this is team selection, maturity, greater knowledge or simply your approval).

■ Accept the performers for what they are becoming. Do not be limited by your perceptions of their past or present.

IP-behaviour based on these principles may have the potential to be truly liberating for the performer, but experience suggests that it would be difficult to adopt in its purest form. A simple guide is the extent to which these behaviours come easily in other caring roles – partner, teacher or parent. Perhaps most striking is the need to address the coach's behaviour in order to create the facilitating and supportive atmosphere necessary to allow the athlete to grow and develop.

DISCUSSION OF ISSUES

Some factors could militate against a less controlling approach by coaches:

1 *A perception by coaches that the role of the coach is a 'directing' one* This is only one interpretation of the coach's role, but it would be true to say that it can be inferred from the 'control of variables' approach advocated in earlier chapters. The term 'control' implies only that all the factors should be taken into account. However, the control of variables can be achieved by a partnership between athlete(s) and coach.
2 *The previous experience of individuals both as performer and coach* This suggests that the humanistic approach is not universal. The response might be to increase awareness and education, rather than to perpetuate common practice.
3 *A perception that athletes wish coaches to adopt a directing approach* There is some research evidence to support this in addition to anecdotal evidence (Chelladurai and Arnott 1985; Chelladurai *et al.* 1989). It is not surprising that athletes would say, 'I have enough to do without assuming some of these responsibilities'. Once again, however, this may be a function of lack of awareness of opportunities and benefits. Similarly, a claim that athletes are not sufficiently aware or knowledgeable to engage in the coaching process is perhaps more a reflection of a lack of education and lack of involvement of them by the coach. Breife (1981) identifies the unwillingness of performers to accept the responsibilities associated with the democratic approach as the main difficulties with the humanistic approach.
4 *There are some sports in which a coach-led approach is appropriate and effective* It is undoubtedly true that team sports and interactive games have a training and competition regime in which a degree of direction is a practical necessity. There may also be some sports (for example, martial arts sports) that are characterised by a style of coaching recognised and negotiated by both coaches and athletes (d'Arripe-Longueville *et al.* 1998).
5 *A social context and reward environment exist in performance sport in which accountability forces coaches to be reluctant to share responsibility* It is difficult to see how this can be overcome. The coach's accountability need not obviate a sharing approach, but in such circumstances it is unlikely that the personal goals that would benefit would be the first priority for the coach. This does not deny, of course, the fact that many coaches of top-class performers are operating in the humanistic tradition.
6 *Personal growth and development is difficult to measure and is not a realistic objective* There is a measure of truth in this and it may explain the preference of humanists for

process goals. Accountability in terms of outcome goals is certainly problematic with such goals. Although there are many anecdotal accounts of changes in athlete behaviour, stable change is medium-to-long-term and happens normally in an incremental fashion. This goes some way to accounting for the complementary nature of personal growth and development goals – that is, perceived as long-term aims but within a set of specific performance goals with shorter-term horizons.

Despite these barriers, there is an argument that suggests that performance athletes would be better performers if the personal qualities developed by sharing responsibilities and taking some control of their engagement in the coaching process were applied in the sporting context. Athletes who are self-disciplined feel a sense of ownership of the programme, have agreed and developed goals and targets, and athletes who are mature and cope well with crises have a personal capacity that can only enhance their performance potential.

Much of the writing referenced throughout the chapter adopts a polemical stance; that is, it offers an implied challenge to the perceived orthodoxy of coaching practice. It is important to note that the assumptions about the purpose and key features of the coaching process are often different. This is often about the priorities between purposes and goals. 'Winning' can be redefined (Danziger 1982: 121) and stress placed on intrinsic rewards. This points to the fact that the humanistic approach to coaching is a belief system. It represents a coherent set of values and beliefs about human beings, human relationships and sport. It is not a question of 'proving' that it is a more effective style of coaching for performance sport, because that proof does not exist. Nevertheless, there is plenty of evidence from education, counselling, psychology and other fields that certain kinds of relationships are effective in developing self-confidence, self-determination and so on. The issue is that personal growth and development of this kind does not feature as a priority for most performance coaches. The response of coaches would appear to be that the 'good' coach recognises that some elements of shared control are appropriate (Côte *et al.* 1995b; Saury and Durand 1995; Saury and Durand 1998) and that this goes as far as the maturity, accountability and practicality will allow. It certainly seems to be the case that the interpersonal relationships aspect of the coaching process, for most coaches, is perceived to be an enabling rather than constraining factor.

The picture must not be painted too rosily. In circumstances in which coaches have powers of selection, accountability is obviously outcome orientated, and in which significant financial implications may result, the controlling element of the coach's role may be much more evident. There is also an element of predisposition (or personality) and personal interaction skills that might limit the quality of interpersonal behaviour. Coaches who feel insecure may be less willing to 'share'. This perhaps explains the apparent lessening of autocratic behaviour as coaches mature and become more experienced.

It seems unlikely that the benefits associated with this approach will be achieved by a piecemeal adoption of relevant behaviours. Nevertheless, any coaching practice that reflects the person-centred approach would be applauded by its proponents. Many coaches will implement this practice without being aware of the ideology or many of its values. The criteria of good practice are very demanding when set against traditional practice in many sports. Coaching contexts in which coaches deal with individual sports, in which athletes' optimum performance occurs in adulthood, and in which performers are traditionally well educated, may be more susceptible to the humanistic approach. This will also be influenced by the previous experiences of the athletes.

Question Box

Humanistic principles are appropriate but perhaps provide an underlying philosophy for practice. It is not reasonable to expect a completely humanistic approach (is it?). Perhaps behaviour should be measured by these standards, or do you think that they should act as a warning light?

The issue of trust identified by Cross (1995b) had previously been incorporated by Hemery (1991) into a scenario in which the authoritarian style within direct intervention is tolerated (and perhaps even welcomed) because of the level of trust generated by a caring, concerned, committed and honest approach in IP-behaviour more generally. This is a very useful idea and a very important concept with which to understand coaching practice. It demonstrates that coaches and athletes are aware of the tensions between success and welfare and can reach an accommodation:

> This principle of consensual authority has much to commend it since it may allow the benefits (effectiveness, efficiency) of technical leadership to be exercised in concert with a more developmental approach overall. Thus a coach's practice may not adhere to the full range of humanistic coaching principles all of the time, but the developmental intentions go beyond the superficial and personal development may still be a priority.
>
> (Lyle 1999b: 42)

Critical Concept

The authoritarian style within direct intervention is tolerated (and perhaps even welcomed) because of the level of trust generated by a caring, concerned, committed and honest approach in IP-behaviour more generally.

The humanistic approach to coaching involves a demanding set of behaviours for the coach, if the ideology is to be adopted wholeheartedly. It is not an approach or style that can be adopted passively – it requires proactive and continuous immersion in relevant IP-behaviour and coaching practice. It may be perceived as more demanding in its extreme implementation than in a compromise solution that exists between control and sharing. There is a good deal of rhetoric about such practice. Coach education undoubtedly espouses these principles but their implementation in performance sport (particularly in some professional team sports) is significantly constrained by prevailing values and practices.

Nevertheless, such evidence as exists suggests that experienced performance coaches and athletes are able to fashion a partnership that allows elements of controlling behaviour within a genuine concern for the welfare and interests of the performers. This is yet another area about which far less research has been conducted than is warranted by its importance.

SUMMARY

This chapter will have familiarised you with the following:

- the basic assumptions and principles of a humanistic approach to sports coaching;
- the relationship between elements of interpersonal behaviour and the humanistic approach;
- constructs with which to analyse coaching practice;
- examples of humanism in coaching practice;
- factors involved in determining whether or not coaches adopt humanistic coaching practice;
- a realistic interpretation of the balance between humanistic coaching principles and performance sport goals;
- the importance of trust between athlete and coach as a basis for both shared responsibilities and directive intervention behaviour.

PROJECTS

- Use the constructs in 9.1 to create criteria for an analysis of practice. Observe 4–6 training sessions and carry out an analysis of training behaviour by the coach.
- Construct a short questionnaire based on 2–3 humanistic principles. Design an investigation to test the assumption that maturity/sport specificity may influence athletes' attitudes to preferred behaviour.
- Carry out a case study on a performance coach. Use a semi-structured interview to focus on relationships with the team/athletes. Emphasise the issue of athlete welfare and identify any contradictions between goals and behaviour.
- Identify 3–4 performance coaches. Investigate 3–4 critical incidents for each coach. Construct an account of each, based on performance versus welfare goals, and appraise critically the degree of humanistic practice.

Reading

Hogg (1995) is an excellent account of applied practice. Cahill and Pearl (1993) is a repository of issues arising when young persons are involved in intensive sport. Orlick (1990) is an example of a humanistic ideological approach to achieving in sport. D'Arripe-Longueville *et al.* (1998) is a realistic example of the balancing of performance and welfare goals.

PART 4
COACHING IN ITS SOCIAL CONTEXT

CHAPTER TEN

▼   COACHING AND SOCIAL CONTEXT

■ Introduction   191
■ Sports Coaching and Social Enquiry   193
■ Social Issues   195
■ Status and Professionalisation   198
■ Commentary   206
■ Summary   207
■ Projects and Reading   207

INTRODUCTION

In the first chapter reference was made to the need to provide a critical appreciation of sports coaching in its social context. Just as with any social phenomenon, sports coaching practice will have been shaped by social structures, power relationships and social trends and will, in turn, have contributed to those emerging social patterns. Specifically, performance sport cannot be immune to the social space that sport occupies. Today, sport is characterised at a macro-level by globalisation, commercialisation and capitalisation, political significance, media-reliance, emphasis on triumphalism, spectacle and personality (Kew 1997; Maguire 1999; Cashmore 2000).

Sports coaching is recognisable in social life as an occupational grouping, as an accumulation of social structures and processes within sport, and as a series of symbols and social values associated with the coaching construct. More particularly, it can be interpreted as a form of social interaction and interpersonal relationship. The mere fact that coaching is an interactive human phenomenon means that the social weight of coaching practice will be worthy of study.

Critical Concept

Sports coaching is recognisable in social life as an occupational grouping, as an accumulation of social structures and processes within sport, and as a series of symbols and social values associated with the coaching construct.

It would be very surprising if sport had not been subject to considerable sociological enquiry, partly because of the more general social issues it embraces (gender, race, commercialisation, social equity) and partly as a vehicle for illuminating social theory. (There are many, many texts over the past thirty years that would attest to academic interest in the sociological analysis of sport. Recent examples are Jarvie and Maguire (1994) and Horne *et al.* (1999).) However, sports coaches operate within this social setting and have received far less attention (Potrac and Jones 1999; Schempp 1998; Cusdin 1996). Coaching exists in a social world that imbues meaning and significance beyond that created by the individual. The coaching process contract has a specificity of relationships, organisation, geography, structures and processes that can be described both within their macro-social setting and at a more micro-social level of interrelationships. However, it would perhaps be inappropriate to suggest that there was a significant agenda of coaching-related issues that currently exercised sport sociologists. Indeed, one of the most interesting, but under-researched, lines of enquiry is the extent to which coaching practice contributes significantly to the maintenance of the *status quo* (or indeed has an emancipatory potential) in controversial issues such as sporting ethics, racial inequality, perceptions of the sporting body or gender imbalance.

In a recent contribution, R. L. Jones (2000) makes a strong case for a sociology of coaching as a counterweight to the previous conceptualisation of coaching along 'bio-scientific fragmentary lines'. However, the emphasis is on coach education rather than coaching practice. This tends to under-value the breadth of knowledge displayed by practising coaches and over-value training theory and compartmentalised sub-discipline knowledge. Nevertheless, there is an excellent account of the need to educate coaches to be aware of the social matrix within which they operate – socially informed decision making based on the social environment, social relations, practical realities and the individual 'habitus' of accumulated 'social capital' (previous experiences, education, upbringing, social expectations and so on). Jones also points to the social construction of knowledge and 'received wisdom' within coaching, but suggests that coaches can forge their individual perspectives through awareness of competing perspectives, informed action and critical reflection. Despite this entirely appropriate advice for coach education, Jones fails to treat coaching as a problematic concept. There is no distinction between participation coaching and performance coaching and an appreciation of the components of the coaching role (from direct intervention to strategic co-ordination) would have emphasised the 'holistic' understanding intended (Potrac *et al.* 2000). There is an assumption of the 'coach as teacher' which limits the analysis. (This is a rare excursion into criticism and it is not intended that it should decry in any way this valuable contribution to what is a sparse field. However, it was important to make the point about the necessity of applying a suitable conceptual framework in order to situate arguments.)

Question Box

There would be little argument that coach education has neglected the social component. Would it not be true to say, however, that this is only one of a number of missing pieces of the jigsaw?

In this short chapter I cannot hope to do justice to such a broad field of enquiry and to the issues involved. It would be very ambitious to address completely the lack of attention to social analysis in coaching. The objectives for the chapter are to:

- balance the attention given to the 'scientific model' of the coaching process;
- delineate the issues involved – that is, to set a social agenda; and
- demonstrate that a full understanding of the social context requires the insights that can only be provided by an appreciation of the conceptual framework within which the coaching process and the social context find meaning.

The chapter provides an introduction to the area, with a particular focus on the social status of the coach and coaching, and is complemented by the following three chapters, which expand on motivations and recruitment, the dearth of women coaches and coaching ethics.

SPORTS COACHING AND SOCIAL ENQUIRY

Sociology provides an explanation of how society functions and attempts to predict social behaviour. Within this, there are a number of competing theoretical paradigms that offer distinctive perspectives on the social world. Each of these operates from a set of assumptions and priorities about 'how the world works' and the role of individual 'agency' in creating that world. This balance of structure and agency is at the heart of the contrasting interpretations of the social world. Not surprisingly, these different theoretical positions adopt distinctive modes of enquiry and issues agendas.

For example, the sport sociology of the 1960s and 1970s (particularly in North America) was dominated by a structural-functionalist perspective that emphasised order and cohesion in society, and focused on the structures and processes that were perceived to bring stability to society – education, the family, religion, politics and the workplace (see Ball and Loy 1975; Loy *et al.* 1978). In an interesting social analysis (from a functionalist perspective), Lombardo (1999) compares coaching behaviour and the 'powerful socialising agencies' of the time and finds congruence in their authoritarian principles.

Another trend in sport sociology was the Marxian analysis. This found similarities in the work ethic in sport and society and perceived an increasingly commercialised sport participation and spectacle to be contributing to inequalities in control over and access to resources in society (Brohm 1978; Hargreaves 1986). Although rarely expressed in these specific terms, it was implied that the practice of sports coaching contributed to characteristics of quantification, technology, meritocracy, and was a palliative to alienation from the work ethic.

A more recent approach has been the figurational sociology of the Leicester School (Dunning *et al.* 1993; Maguire 1999). This 'developmental approach' is particularly concerned with the historical power relationships that have shaped sporting phenomena. Although again tending to more general interpretations of sport, the application of this approach to coaching is hinted at in the 'figurational' treatment of sports coaching summarised by Cusdin (1996), in which she charts the 'coachification' of modern sports (see also Kew 1997). The potential relationships between sociological perspectives (including those mentioned above) and sports coaching are elaborated on by Jones (2000). An anthology edited by Coakley and Dunning (2000) gives an excellent summary of the field.

Hylton and Totten (2001) describe four 'dominant' perspectives:

- *Functionalist* A consensus view of society in which sport fulfils an integration function. (Sports coaching may be interpreted as reinforcing consensual values within society.)
- *Neo-Marxist* A conflict view of society in which the 'masses' are subjugated by the dominant groups. Sport reinforces the interests of the dominant groups, largely in economic matters, although it is perceived as an arena for challenge to these groups. (Sports coaching may be interpreted as reinforcing differences in achievement between individuals and acquiescing in limiting athlete control.)
- *Feminist* A perspective on society in which a patriarchal society produces a male-dominated social order. Sport is perceived to reinforce masculine values. (Sports coaching reinforces these values and provides a clear demonstration of inequality of attainment, although it also provides a location for resistance and challenge to that position.)
- *Postmodernist* Society is argued to have become less certain and structured in its values and social order. Diversity in sport provision creates an opportunity for individualism and expression. (Sports coaching has rarely, if ever, been interpreted from this perspective, although Rail (1998) points to the need for coaches not to be hidebound by preconceived notions of appropriate behaviour.)

Perhaps the most important point to be made about these general social perspectives is that, despite the potential for increasing understanding, they have not yet been applied to an analysis of sports coaching in any rigorous fashion. What can be assumed is that theorists will interpret coaching practice as reinforcing or challenging each of these theoretical perspectives: it will never be neutral. However, the problem is more specific. Where sports coaching is exemplified, it is treated as a uni-dimensional subject and practice. The most obvious limitation is a failure to distinguish between participation and performance coaching. Thus sociology of sport texts slip seamlessly between participation coaching in analyses of dysfunctional social values in youth sport (Donnelly 2000a), and the assumption of performance coaching in analyses of nationalism or abuse of power. Studies of performance sport itself rarely distinguish between professional spectator sports and other forms of top-level sport. In the absence of research dissemination and appropriate attention from writers, the vacuum is filled by coaching stereotypes in which autocratic, elitist, rational-scientific behaviour is assumed at the expense of more sophisticated and diverse practice.

One further issue is the sub-cultural specificity of practice, although this has to be contrasted with the influence of globalisation on coaching practice (migration of coaches, availability of knowledge). The most obvious example of this is the assumption of the North American high school/collegiate coaching model in sport sociology. Potrac and Jones (1999) is a good example of this. However, this is clearly very different from the Eastern European practice that characterised a good deal of the rational/scientific approach, embraced by what Lombardo (1999) calls 'the professional model of coaching'. This model is much closer to the systematic, control model of coaching described in earlier chapters.

It is worth pointing out again that this is a very superficial account of enquiry into the social context of sport. It is also the case that analyses of social contexts are contested in terms of perception of reality, interpretation and explanation. Sports coaching is, as yet, not sufficiently mature as an area of study to provide the evidence necessary to carry out comparative sociological interpretations of practice. However, this is not the focus of the text, and it is more important to point to the extent to which a greater understanding of sports coaching concepts would enlighten these analyses.

 Critical Concept

Sports coaching is, as yet, not sufficiently mature as an area of study to provide the evidence necessary to carry out comparative sociological interpretations of practice.

SOCIAL ISSUES

A number of social issues impinge on coaching practice, and the most important of these have been emphasised in the three chapters that follow. Social issues can be subdivided into those in which broader social issues find expression in sports coaching and those that are particular to sports coaching itself. In the first category, it is important to acknowledge that such issues do exist more widely and that practice in sports coaching cannot be divorced from practice in other fields. In fact, understanding and explanations from other social contexts may shed light on issues such as racial inequality, gender bias, moral standards, or power and authority. In the second category, it is also the case that issues such as professionalisation, socialisation and role conflict will be informed by exemplars from similar occupations or sub-cultures.

It would be difficult to provide any substantive list of issues, but the following is representative of the most significant issues:

■ the relative absence of women coaches in high-level sport;
■ recruitment pathways into coaching: social characteristics, qualifications and motives;

- the exercise of power between sports coaches and administrators in sport;
- socialisation into sports coaching: social learning and formal education;
- the professionalisation of the occupation of sports coaching;
- status and perceived social standing for sports coaches;
- coaching practice and the reinforcement of dominant social values;
- the congruence between the ethics of sub-cultural social practice and social values;
- the language and symbolism of sports coaching;
- leadership practice as a power relationship within sport teams;
- (social inclusion) sport policy and participation coaching practice; and
- coaching as an arena for alternative practice and resistance to dominant values.

It will have become clear that diverse methods of enquiry are necessary to garner the evidence necessary to address the issues identified above. Survey evidence, observation and interviews are commonplace. However, there is also a place for participant observation, reflective accounts of practice, stimulated narratives, life histories and biographies. These are necessary to provide the richness of subjective interpretation and meaning with which to understand interactions, relationships, motivations and significance. Potrac and Jones (1999), in summarising the case for coaching as a neglected area for sociological enquiry, make a plea for ethnographic methods of research in order to place the emphasis on the coach as practitioner. They identify in detail three specific issues – the relationship between gender and coaching, the under-representation of minority groups, and teacher-coach role conflict. However, they go on to suggest that increased attention is required to social issues 'related to power, domination, resistance and group sub-cultures' (1999: 2). This is a welcome addition to the field but it is also a good example of a failure to differentiate between participation and performance coaching sub-cultures, and between the occupation-specific literature of North America and other coaching contexts.

Sports coaching can be considered to be a particular set of sub-cultures (assuming that there are distinctive sub-cultures for participation coaching, sport instruction, professional sport, performance club coaching, and NGB representative coaching), although there may be extensive similarities between some of them. The key features of sub-culture analysis is the extent to which members create and defend boundary markers, diffuse values, and recruit new members (Donnelly 2000a). This is yet another area that requires more extensive research. It is clear, however, that the clarity of the conceptual framework is necessary to provide a conceptual terminology within which to understand boundary markers.

 Question Box

The sub-cultural features of performance sport may be very important both as determinants of social cohesion and as markers for 'acceptable' coaching behaviours. Do coaches build walls around their areas of expertise and security?

Lombardo (1999) identifies a number of social trends that he considers influential in shaping coaching practice with young people, including pressure to specialise at an early age and the employment of unqualified coaches. A similar analysis of the trends influencing performance coaching practice is required. This might include (in the UK):

- an increasing percentage of the population in full-time further and higher education;
- increased public accountability for professions and occupations;
- a proliferation of initiatives in national sport development;
- the enhanced technological capacity occasioned by computers;
- more systematic talent identification programmes;
- the globalisation of knowledge;
- an increasing gap in practice, standards and resourcing between community and performance sport;
- certification of education and training;
- continued impact of National Lottery financing on athlete commitment, and support for minority sports;
- a continuing media-led cult of personality; and
- the significant earnings-potential gap between sports and between a small number of elite sportspersons and the rest.

Trends such as these need to be absorbed by coaches as part of the social reality within which they operate. This suggests that there is a hierarchy of levels of social knowledge and awareness:

1 taken-for-granted assumptions about the social world;
2 current trends in performance sport practice;
3 features of the social environment in sports coaching;
4 awareness of specific organisational cultures and social group relationships;
5 social awareness of self, self-identity, previous experiences and 'social capital'.

This is an ambitious array of knowledge and awareness to which the coach should become sensitised. Further debate is clearly needed about whether this is part of coach education or social learning more generally. Features of the social environment in sports coaching might include:

- public accountability;
- outcome measures of effectiveness;
- multiple social roles;
- hierarchical social structures;
- positive reward environments;
- highly structured and specialised roles;
- competition and achievement orientation.

A further area for study, which has perhaps been under-researched, is the influence of organisational structures and culture on behaviour. There is a considerable body of evidence on the relationship between organisational variables and many aspects of individual behaviour (Slack 1997). However, this has focused on administrators, professional and volunteer, rather than coaches. It has already been acknowledged that coaches can operate for National Governing Bodies (NGBs), large sports clubs, within self-contained coaching groups, and, of course, within one-to-one relationships. This is exacerbated by the performance system within which the coach and athlete operate (Lyle 1997b, 1999d) and the dynamics operating within coaching teams. Much of the North American literature on the high-school/collegiate coach could be relevant, in terms of recruitment, advancement, appraisal, role conflict and so on. Nevertheless, there is less evidence available on voluntary sector and professional sport sector organisational behaviours in the UK, as they apply to coaches.

One particular social issue is the use and abuse of power. Gruneau (1993) acknowledges that power is important in all relationships. The limits and boundaries of the relationship form the constraints within which conscious agency is exercised. However, there is a need to examine, in any social setting, a number of tensions: for example, the abstract (or potential) of power versus the structured freedom of hegemonic forces; or conscious constructions of power relationships versus internalised constructions. The exercise of power by individual coaches often takes place within further realms of institutional boundaries (Foucault's 'technologies of surveillance'), and is evidenced in decisions about, for example, selection and recruitment. This has implications for coaches' accountability.

Lukes's (1974) three dimensions of power identify the control of the agenda of decision making as crucial and he maintains that differences are likely to exist between the interests of the power holder and those over whom power is exercised. Any debates within coaching philosophies about devolving decision making/autonomy to athletes must therefore be evaluated against the availability of information to the athlete, the control of the agenda of decision making (what to decide about), and the negotiation over needs and interests (whose needs prevail?).

There is no doubt that performance sports coaching involves a complex set of power relationships and that this gives a potential for a reconceptualisation of coaching styles and interpersonal relationships. Abuse of power is also evident in sexual and psychological harassment of athletes by coaches.

STATUS AND PROFESSIONALISATION

A crucial issue in social context is the importance accorded to the occupation of sports coaching and the individuals within it. This is related to the measures taken by those within the occupational grouping to mark and improve their status and to protect it from challenge. The chapter therefore examines the concepts of status and professionalisation, and how these are better understood in the light of our developing conceptual framework.

Status has a number of meanings, each of which can be applied to sports coaching:

■ Status is a statement of the relative value given to something within a hierarchical ranking. This is often applied to occupations – the division of labour – and statements of social value are accorded to occupations relative to other occupations. Professional occupations such as those of doctors and lawyers are accorded greater social value than manual assembly-line workers or bus drivers, for example.

■ Status is used to describe a position within an organisation or informal set of social relationships. This also has an element of ranking but implies a more complex set of

COACHING IN ITS SOCIAL CONTEXT

role relationships. It is less about comparison with others and more about the rights and responsibilities accruing to that position. The coach's role within the club or NGB could be described in this fashion.

■ Status also applies to differentiation between individuals within a social group or occupation. In this sense, individuals achieve social worth by either acquiring or achieving status in criteria valued by the members of the group. The most obvious examples for the coach are jobs with the most prestigious clubs, or competitive success.

Status (of all kinds) is important, since it brings with it a number of tangible and less tangible benefits. Prestige, power and authority, rewards and resources, and attractiveness to initiates will be reflected in the value placed on the activity. This will also be evident at the level of the individual, where a sense of self-identity and self-worth will be influenced by these 'external' measures. Since there are benefits to be had from higher status, occupations will take measures to improve this, sometimes through advocacy, improved regulation, increased exclusivity, levels of education and training, or selective levels of service. This is the process of professionalisation. As with other aspects of the coaching process or coaching practice, the emphasis in this treatment of the subject is less with the actions required to improve the situation and more on the concepts required to understand it better.

Two constructs are useful for helping to understand status. First, ascribed status is conferred on individuals by virtue of certain characteristics that they possess. This refers to membership of groups based on features such as gender, race or occupation. Thus occupational prestige and social esteem are ascribed to occupations relative to others because of the value placed on that occupation. The statement by an individual that 'I am a school teacher' or 'I am a sports coach' brings with it an ascribed social status.

Second, achieved status is not conferred because of membership, but accorded to an individual because of acknowledged achievement within the group. This creates a ranking or 'pecking order' between individual coaches. Within the coaching 'profession' status is gained by being associated with successful athletes/teams, by occupying coaching positions with prestigious clubs, by appointment to national representative or Olympic teams, or by attaining recognised 'levels' of achievement (for example, through certification).

 Question Box

The Coach of the Year awards (NCF) are an entirely appropriate part of the promotion of the 'profession'. However, does this merely reinforce the emphasis on achieved status?

In the discussions that follow, a case will be made that sports coaches have paid insufficient attention to the professionalisation of their occupation. This is another way of saying that ascribed status has been less important at an individual level than achieved status. Perhaps this is understandable, since benefits accrue to the individual coach, both esteem and reward, from achieved status. Clearly, this raises issues about professionalisation, but also about the availability of mechanisms for appropriately acknowledging (and understanding) coaching practice. It also adds a further perspective on the earlier discussions within the IP-behaviour and humanistic philosophy sections on the relative 'weight' given to performance and personal goals.

At various times and for various purposes (evaluating trends in employment, for example) occupations have been classified. This is one indication of social worth. Hierarchical classification implies within its levels factors such as education and training, complexity of tasks, skills required, need for judgement, and so on. These classifications change over time, and sports coaching is a good example of this. In the Registrar General's Social Class Index sports coaching was interpreted as sports instruction and classified as a skilled manual occupation for which a university degree was not required. Although acknowledging that there is an element of craft and sport-specific skill involved in the coaching process, this characterisation of coaching is at odds with the conceptualisation described throughout this text. However, the updated Standard Occupational Classification (Office for National Statistics 2000) classifies sports coaching in its 'Major Group 3' – associate professional and technical occupations. These are described as requiring 'an associated high level vocational qualification, often involving a substantial period of full-time training or further study. Some additional task-related training is usually provided through a formal period of induction' (2000: 12).

An interesting aspect of this is that the tasks associated with the occupation specify the anticipated 'coaches teams or individuals by demonstrating techniques', but also 'monitors and analyses technique and performance and determines how future improvements can be made' (2000: 133). This subtle change in classification is likely to be recognition of greater awareness of the role, increased education and training, increased 'scientification' of practice and the value placed on sport itself. The introductory chapter on the historical development of sports coaching acknowledged its historically low status but also recognised that there has been relatively little research into the development of coaching as an occupation.

Before moving to an examination of the professionalisation of sports coaching, it will be useful to summarise a number of the factors that have influenced the social status placed on sports coaching as an occupation:

1   The most obvious feature is that traditionally the majority of sports coaches have been voluntary and part time. Until recently, this also characterised the majority of performers, even at a high level. In the eyes of the general public, therefore, it may have been difficult to shed a 'leisure activity' tag.
2   A higher media profile for Olympic sports, continuing interest in professional sport, an increase in the number of full-time coaches, a greater acknowledgement of the science of performance, and, in particular, attempts to 'professionalise' the occupation may, in time, influence the coach's ascribed status.
3   There is a public perception (fuelled by media exposure) that the key factor in coaching appointments is previous 'playing' experience rather than education, training and apprenticeship. This does not help to raise the status of the profession.
4   Although the coach in team sports receives some, often considerable, recognition, there are many other examples in which the coach is not seen to take part in the

competition itself and is not acknowledged in medal ceremonies, etc. This 'hidden role' does not assist with positive exposure for the profession. On the other hand, some media coverage (admittedly, very much based on soccer in the UK) highlights the peremptory hiring and firing of coaches/managers, and the media has shown little interest in the 'mechanics' of the coaching process itself.

5   There are a relatively small number of appropriate role models for the profession.
6   The point was made in the first chapter that the competition role of the coach in sports in North America (baseball, US football, basketball, ice-hockey) has given coaches a profile that is not matched by that given to coaches in traditional sports in the UK (soccer, rugby, cricket, netball, hockey). This has to be added to the traditional and respected high-school/collegiate occupation of sports coach. The full-time status, lengthy education and training, opportunity to travel, and importance of sport in former Eastern-bloc Soviet countries also accorded coaches a higher status. These examples are a reminder that status is culture-specific.
7   Although working with children and young people generally accrues high status, the participation coach perhaps suffers from comparison with the schoolteacher, who, while not perhaps given the status considered appropriate within that profession, is nevertheless considered to be a high-status occupation. The 'adjunct' status of the coaching role for physical education teachers has not helped raise the status of sports coaches.

Many of these issues are about the boundaries of coaching and role confusion. A good deal of time was spent on this in earlier chapters, with emphasis on concepts such as

■   the unwelcome focus solely on the direct intervention role;
■   the strategic co-ordination and planning component of the role;
■   the emphasis on higher-order intellectual skills; and
■   the distinction between participation and performance coaching.

It would also be necessary to acknowledge that the links between coaching practice and performance outcomes are not yet firmly established, and that the range of coaching styles and the multiplicity of goals may confuse the perception of the coaching role. Nevertheless, the clarity brought by a greater understanding of coaching process boundaries and the coaching role will not only help to explain and understand status values, but also to focus on those aspects of occupational development necessary for enhancing the profession. This is an appropriate point, therefore, at which to turn to the concept of professionalisation.

Professionalisation

Professionalisation refers to the process through which an occupational grouping develops and strengthens the extent to which it is characterised by criteria reflecting a mature, crystallised, sophisticated, refined and socially approved occupational activity. One way of interpreting this is to say that the occupation comes closer to the profile of those occupations already accepted as 'professions'. It is appropriate, therefore, to examine characteristics of a profession and how sports coaching measures up to this comparison (Lyle 1986; Treadwell 1986).

Professions can be characterised in a number of ways: by the nature of the professional's role, the organisation and structuring of the occupation, or the characteristics of the professional's practice. Downie (1990) has emphasised the demands on the individual practitioner:

- expertise based on a broad knowledge base;
- a relationship with clients protected by legitimated role practice and demonstrating integrity of purpose;
- a social motivation beyond individual client cases;
- independent judgements not constrained by the state; and
- breadth of education (i.e. beyond training, within a values framework).

These characteristics and the social value attached to the work of the kind implied by these demands bring the practitioner professional (that is, highly valued) status.

Middlehurst (1995) identifies four generic features of professional practice:

1   considerable expertise (mastery) in an acknowledged occupational specialisation;
2   a need for extended education, emphasising intellectual skills;
3   an element of independence and judgement in the work; and
4   an ethics-based code of practice.

It is clear from these lists that there would be some measure of agreement on the basic criteria of professional practice. The profession is evaluated on the extent to which these criteria are structured into the occupation. For that reason, professionalisation is often reduced to a small number of consequent criteria: a professional body to oversee standards and assure independence; a licensing system for membership; a distinctive body of knowledge; demanding education qualifications (involving a period of training); and a career structure with identifiable levels of expertise at each 'level'. However, Middlehurst goes on to identify the criteria of 'professionalism' (1995: 36):

- technical and theoretical expertise and the authority and status flowing from such expert and highly valued knowledge, understanding and skill;
- the establishment and the exercise of trust as a basis for professional relationships (with clients and between professionals);
- adherence to particular standards and professional ethics often represented by the granting of a licence to practise;
- independence, autonomy and discretion; and
- specific attitudes towards work, clients and peers, involving dedication, reliability, flexibility and creativity in relation to the unknown.

This list goes beyond simply technical expertise, and writers may try to focus on what they consider the essence of professional practice. Beckett (1996), for example, points to discretionary judgements – that is, decision making and problem solving – as one of the key features. Hodkinson (1995) also steers the focus beyond simple boundary maintenance to a definition of professionalism as empowerment and self-development of individuals.

No matter how they are expressed, it is clear that there is a demanding set of criteria that designates professional status. However, the notion of a profession is a more complex concept. Hugman (1991) gives examples of three categories of professions:

1 traditional professions with strong organisation, stringent membership criteria and considerable autonomy (such as medicine and theology);
2 client patronage professions in which contractual agreements determine the scale and extent of the expertise required (such as accountancy and architecture);
3 state-mediated professions, in which their autonomy and independence is limited by state controlled policy and resources (for example, teaching and nursing).

 Question Box

Which model should sports coaching use as an exemplar? The instructor might be best thought of as a client patronage practitioner, whereas the teacher/coach is often funded by the state. Is the performance coach more of a manager?

The vocabulary applied to this area often distinguishes between the traditional and pseudo-professions – that is, the newer occupations that aspire to professional status. However, more intensive media scrutiny and an awareness of clients' rights to quality of service have challenged even traditional professions in areas such as accountability and quality assurance (Burrage 1994). Lyle has summarised the characteristics of professional practice:

> Professional practice is characterised by skilled behaviour, not normally available to members of the public, which is developed over an extensive period of education and training and is conducted within identified codes of ethics and conduct. Professions are concerned to protect their boundaries and mark their territories through control of access accreditation of training, professional bodies and the licensing of practice.
>
> (Lyle 1998c: 134)

This short summary of professionalisation prepares the way for an evaluation of the occupation of coaching in its social context. Put another way, how does coaching practice measure up to the criteria identified above? Figure 10.1 is a rather generalised account of the degree of fit between coaching and these criteria; in other words, there has been no attempt to draw together detailed evidence for these statements. However, the substance in each of the assertions is dealt with in sections throughout the book.

It would be very difficult to escape the conclusion that sports coaching in the UK is significantly distant from achieving the criteria necessary for profession status. Some progress in identifying the knowledge and skills required to implement the coaching process does not compensate for the lack of professional infrastructure and the absence of scale in the occupations related to performance coaching. This does not mean that sports coaching cannot be acknowledged as a highly specialised occupation and that coaches cannot demonstrate the characteristics of professionalism that were highlighted earlier in the chapter.

Critical Concept

It would be very difficult to escape the conclusion that sports coaching in the UK is significantly distant from achieving the criteria necessary for professional status.

Criterion	Evaluation	Score
Education	There has been some advance in university-level education in sports coaching and NVQ developments have enhanced NGB programmes in breadth and form. However, the quality of education and training is very variable. The key issue is that there remains no threshold, accredited educational qualification that admits members to the 'profession'.	Weak
Body of knowledge	There is a knowledge base in the scientific sub-disciplines underpinning sport performance. In addition, there is a body of sport-specific technical knowledge. However, the body of knowledge and skills on which coaching practice is founded is less crystallised. Some elements are based on teaching principles but the meta-cognitive, strategic co-ordination of the coaching process has not yet been adequately packaged.	Moderate
Boundaries	The boundaries of the coaching role are not distinctive. Lack of conceptual clarity has contributed to a failure to provide a clear account of the occupational roles that would be embraced by a 'coaching profession'. This may be ameliorated by an emerging awareness of the performance coaching role. Key to this, however, is the absence of a 'licence to practice' that denotes boundary maintenance.	Weak
Professional practice	In general, a professional service is rendered to a client with a degree of detachment; that is, the advice/service is provided in the best interests of the client but not influenced by a personal consideration. This may be at odds with the IP-relationship advocated in the section on person-centred coaching. Would an extended, intensive, mutually empathetic relationship between athlete and coach militate against a professional role?	Moderate
Career structure	There are a number of limitations in professional development occasioned by an uncrystallised career structure:	Weak

- The scope and scale of performance coaching positions is not yet extensive (*Note 1*).
- Differentiation between practitioner, teacher and subject developer roles is not yet apparent.
- Structural differentiation with appropriate training/knowledge requirements at different levels is not yet in place (*Note 2*).
- Although informal 'apprenticeships' may take place, coaching does not yet have the (usually) extensive formal noviciate during which the licence to practise is obtained.

Values framework	Most commentators agree that a profession operates within a set of values that are formalised and monitored. There are a number of examples of codes of ethics and codes of conduct in sports coaching (*Note 3*). However, these standards are not imposed by a professional body and the sanctions are not related to the right to practise. A subsequent chapter explores the ethical standards in coaching. In that chapter, it is suggested that there is no substantive set of ethical standards in performance coaching.	Weak
Professional body	*This is a key element in professionalisation*. In the UK, there is no professional body to regulate sports coaching. The functions of licensing, accrediting training, applying sanctions, establishing good practice and protecting members are exercised imperfectly or not at all.	Very weak

Notes:

1 There are many more participation coaching 'positions' (albeit the great majority of these are voluntary and part-time). It is obvious that the criteria identified above are not applicable to these roles, although they may, of course, constitute a significant occupational grouping. It is also important to acknowledge the absence in the UK of the teacher/coach profession evident in North American high schools, colleges and universities.
2 To some extent the NVQ/National Standards framework should provide a basis for this. However, the framework does not necessarily match the occupational dynamics within the 'profession'.
3 In the UK, the best known is the Code produced by the National Coaching Foundation (NCF 1996).
4 The National Association of Sport Coaches (NCF) exercises some of these functions. However, it is not an independent body that is able to self-regulate, which is one of the features of a profession.

Figure 10.1 *An evaluation of sports coaching in relation to criteria of professionalisation*

Some of the issues surrounding professional status can be related directly to elements of the conceptual framework. The chapter concludes with a brief summary of these issues.

First, individuals are part of a profession because they 'profess' to have knowledge and skills that cannot be exercised by the general public, but which are necessary and valued. In an earlier chapter, an attempt was made to identify the expertise that was distinctive and different in sports coaching. The conclusion was that, while drawing from sub-disciplines and sport-specific knowledge and craft, the performance coach had a set of intellectual skills that centred on the strategic co-ordination of the coaching process and involved planning and managing preparation and competition programmes. It was an intellectual expertise that recognised the complexity of the coaching process. Whilst this is a strong basis for the development of professional status, it is also true to say that the embryonic state of knowledge of coaching expertise and its translation into coach education means that a good deal of work needs to be done to establish the distinctiveness of coaching practice.

Second, in the emerging conceptual framework, it was concluded that participation and performance coaching were not part of a continuum but distinctive roles. Although there would be some attractiveness in using participation coaching as the 'lower tier' of the 'profession', the characteristics of participation coaching are enormously removed from professional status (educational requirements, absence of control, no boundary criteria, minimum specialist knowledge and so on). More work is required on entry to performance coaching and the initial stages of becoming socialised into such positions.

Third, the chapter on the role of the coach attempted to bring some clarity to the role of the performance coach. Nevertheless, it was acknowledged that some role confusion remains in relation to the link between the coaching process and performance outcomes, the coach's leadership role within the coaching team, and the difference between effective and successful coaches. This raises the spectre of confusion about the professional contribution of the sports coach, and yet a profession would be expected to be very clear about the service being offered and for which its members can be held accountable. Although a clear conceptual framework has been argued in this text, it would be fair to conclude that coaching practice as yet lacks this clarity of purpose.

Fourth, the conceptual framework dealt with the key issue of expertise/decision making that seemed to be based on intuition and the extent to which this could be incorporated into systematic coaching behaviour. An explanation was presented for the professional shortcuts that were characteristic of expert practice. However, this apparently 'untrained' practice and the insistence by some writers on persisting with the argument that coaching is an art form does not create a model of professional behaviour. The myth of initiation into esoteric knowledge needs to be dispelled and replaced by a more adequate explanation for expertise in performance coaching.

COMMENTARY

Sports coaching creates a social context for practice, and operates within a broader social framework, to which it contributes. There is a set of social dynamics created by the coaching team, the performer–coach relationship and the organisational parameters within which the coaching process is implemented. There are also social dynamics in sport and society more generally and therefore issues about status, achievement, commercialisation, drugs in sport, among others, will impact on sports coaching and sports coaches.

There is no doubt, however, that this is a very under-explored field but one with great potential. Sports coaching has rarely been subjected to sociological analysis and this has contributed to a less complete understanding of the coaching process than should be the case. The preliminary sketch of the area given earlier in the chapter suggests that the area would be a rich one for analysis from differing theoretical perspectives. One concomitant of the absence of theoretical exploration is that such writing as is available is issues-led. This explains the constant emphasis on gender issues and ethical issues, and the lesser emphasis on micro-level power relationship issues.

An 'holistic' appreciation of the coaching process will include all social contexts, and part of the conceptual framework around which the coaching process is built should, therefore, comprise the social networks and values within which it is implemented. It is a plausible argument that coaches will be more effective if they take into account the social circumstances (at all levels) that are impacting on the coaching process. However, it may be a little harsh to expect this from performance coaches when social awareness does not yet form a sufficiently important part of coach education. Jarvie (1990) argues that the incorporation of sociological knowledge into coaching programmes will lead to a better understanding of IP-relationships, develop reflective practitioners, enhance personal development and improve awareness of social context (1990: 8).

This chapter on social context is now complemented by three short chapters on specific issues: motivations and recruitment into coaching, gender and coaching, and ethical issues.

SUMMARY

This chapter will have familiarised you with the following:

- the social dimension to understanding sport and sports coaching;
- a very brief account of sport sociology and the range of theoretical perspectives adopted;
- the social issues and trends likely to influence sports coaching;
- the potential of power analysis as a tool for understanding social interaction in sports coaching;
- the difference between ascribed and achieved status;
- factors influencing the social status placed on sports coaching as an occupation;
- the characteristics of a profession and of professionalisation;
- an evaluation of the current position of sports coaching measured by indices of professional status; and
- the links between the conceptual framework and the development of the occupational role of sports coaches.

PROJECTS

- Carry out an analysis of a coach education curriculum. Select 2 NGBs and appraise their coach education materials for content relevant to the social dimension.
- Analyse the government's policy for sport (Department of Culture, Media and Sport/DfEE 2001). Present an argument for the extent to which coaching practice reinforces the government's priorities.
- Choose 3 or 4 criteria of professionalisation. Compare developments in sports coaching to practice in 2 other established professions. Make recommendations.
- Interview 6 performance coaches. Construct a matrix of power/influence exercised by the coaches within their clubs/NGBs.

Reading

There is an extensive literature on the sociology of sport. However, very little of this is directed to sports coaching. Jones (2000) presents an argument for a sociology of coaching, although not exclusively situated in performance sport. Lombardo (1999) provides a catalogue of issues likely to impact on coaches. An historical account of the status of professional development (and an extensive series of associated papers) can be found in Lyle (1986). More general issues concerned with professional development are usefully summarised in Eraut (1994).

CHAPTER ELEVEN

▼   **MOTIVATIONS AND RECRUITMENT IN SPORTS COACHING**

■ Introduction   209
■ Review of Evidence   212
■ Conceptual Issues   216
■ Summary   219
■ Projects and Reading   219

INTRODUCTION

This is the first of three short chapters each of which focuses on one important aspect of the social context of sports coaching. This chapter examines the motives for becoming coaches and the recruitment mechanisms through which performance coaches are mobilised into coaching. An assumption can be made that sports coaches are motivated by a range of factors, although there may be a discernible pattern. This, in turn, will have implications for recruitment. Identifying personal qualities, motives, experience and 'predisposition' will focus attention onto likely populations from which coaches can be recruited.

Recruitment is an important issue:

■ Maintaining social space depends on recruiting and retaining an adequate supply of coaches. The nature of that social space is also determined by the composition of the coaching workforce.
■ Status and professionalisation issues are linked to the characteristics and quality of the initiates.
■ The social space of individual sports is partly a factor of their achievements in scale and relative competition success. Sports coaching is acknowledged to be a central feature in the matrix of factors that bring about this success.
■ National sport policy objectives are related to an appropriate supply of suitably educated and trained coaches. This is based on an assumption that growth, development and standards of performance are influenced by the 'quality' (and quantity) of the coaching available.

■ Recruitment is inextricably linked to selection. Quite rightly, attention is often focused on recruiting initiates into coaching, but availability or selection for important club or national squad positions is also an important part of the conceptual framework within which recruitment should be understood.

One very specific issue that arises is that the availability of suitable coaches reflects upon the quality and status of a sport at any given time. This chapter is being written at a time when coaching positions with the England soccer team, England cricket team, British Lions rugby union team, England women's soccer team, and national coaching positions in swimming, rowing, basketball and ice hockey are occupied by coaches from overseas. This implies that there are no coaches in the UK who have the qualifications and experience to fulfil these National Governing Bodies' (NGBs') objectives. Therefore, the recruitment of coaches reflects not just individual motives, education and training, and experience but also perceptions of the quality of coaching practice as influenced by the environment within which coaches operate.

 Question Box

The employment of overseas coaches in prominent positions is justified in terms of the experience required to deal with the elite athlete. However, there is a balance of advantages and disadvantages. How would you interpret the balance of individual quality and catalytic impact versus an absence of role models, perception of 'glass ceiling', lack of development emphasis on UK coaches, and absence of long-term planning?

The recruitment of coaches is more complex than simply having a pool of coaches with the appropriate education and training. Figure 11.1 identifies the factors involved. This

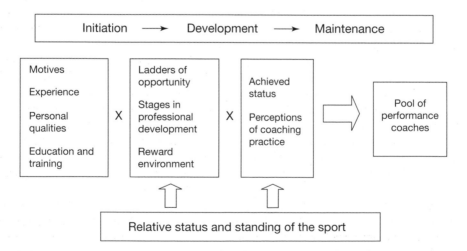

Figure 11.1 *Factors involved in the recruitment and maintenance of performance coaches*

COACHING IN ITS SOCIAL CONTEXT

is not simply a matter of initiation: a suitable reservoir of coaches is required to satisfy development needs and this requires more strategic planning.

As with many of the issues raised in these chapters, and at the risk of repetition, there is a limited literature on recruitment and motives in performance coaching with which to support the ideas and principles identified. There is a substantial literature on coaching motivations in North America and a number of national surveys. However, examination of these will demonstrate that the focus is most often on participation coaches. For this reason the emphasis within the chapter is on identifying the questions that need to be addressed.

There appear to be a number of particular issues:

1   *The social composition and balance of those individuals recruited into coaching*   The gender composition, racial balance and opportunity for social inclusion in coach recruitment are problematical issues and will be affected by the policy and actions taken by those with responsibility for recruitment.

2   *The career reward environment*   The traditional pattern of coaching deployment has been largely a part-time, voluntary one. However, this picture is perhaps over-influenced by the vast number of participation coaches. Nevertheless, performance coaches have often been part-time. One of the effects of the limited literature is that performance coaches have not been targeted in surveys and the payment/commitment of performance coaches cannot be stated with certainty. However, it might be assumed with some assurance that performance coaches often receive some payment for their time commitment but also that coaching is also an avocation that can be afforded only by some groups of individuals. An interesting speculation is that increasing rewards (perhaps from National Lottery funding and increasing professionalisation of sport) may, in future, alter the composition of those who are prepared to give the time required for increasingly full-time commitment.

3   *There is a relationship between individual motives and recruitment mechanisms*   This may seem obvious, but the implication is that recruitment becomes less supply-orientated and more demand-orientated. In other words, recruitment policies have to be less focused on education and training programmes and more focused on identifying those with the predisposition to become performance coaches.

4   *Supply and demand issues are not straightforward*   This is a more complex issue than it may appear to be. At first glance, the relationship receiving attention is that of the organisation coach. However, the coach–athlete relationship was acknowledged as a starting point in the coaching process model described in an earlier chapter. In professional sport clubs coach–player relationships are often problematical and can lead to either party leaving the club. In many other performance sport contexts the relationship is less formal and the matrix of coach credibility, coach–athlete compatibility, and athlete recruitment influences selection and recruitment to higher-status positions. A good deal of work is required in this area. The uncrystallised nature of the profession means that the recruitment pattern does not mirror the initiation into first-career positions following qualification and a gradual progression through increasingly higher level or status positions. Experience suggests that relatively few positions are obtained by selection. There is some evidence that opportunity factors play a substantial part in the transition stage from performer to coach.

5   *Education and training are linked to motivation and recruitment issues*   This is another obvious statement but the concomitant implications may not always be acknowledged in practice. Is education and training related to the positions in which performance coaching initiates can be expected to operate? What experience are those with a predisposition to performance coaching likely to have, and how is this incorporated into the training programme?

 Question Box

In a sport with which you are familiar, state the recruitment policy (if there is one). Is it assumed that coaches will migrate from participation coaching? Is the coach education programme used as a recruitment mechanism? How is it advertised?

These issues suggest subtle questions that are not answered in current research, particularly in the existing surveys on coaches' characteristics. There are also strong links between motivations and recruitment and many of the conceptual framework issues raised in earlier chapters. The most obvious of these is the participation/performance coaching distinction. The key question is whether performance coaches are recruited from the ranks of participation coaches. However, there are many other issues, such as between motive and perception of role, motive and coaching style, recruitment and skills and knowledge, role elements and initial expectations, coaching philosophy and recruitment, and so on. In order to begin to address some of these issues, the chapter now reviews the existing evidence on coaching motivations and recruitment avenues.

REVIEW OF EVIDENCE

Without wishing to begin this section on a negative note, it is necessary to offer some evaluative comment on the quality of the evidence on motivations and recruitment:

- The sample populations are not directly comparable and there has been relatively little control of the stratification of the populations.
- With few exceptions, the questions/criteria offered for selection are not comparable. There is also a disappointing level of rigour in the constructs employed. (In one example, 'fun and enjoyment' is descriptive of one construct, as is 'pride and achievement'. However, if 'enjoyment' refers to immediate satisfaction, it need not be equated with 'fun'. Achievement might connote many associated elements other than pride and vice versa.
- The evidence available points to a number of sport-specific factors. It seems clear from the surveys conducted that they have been influenced by the original sampling frame and also the response rates from particular sub-sets.

Data for motivations for coaching in the UK are contained in a report entitled *A Four-Country Study of the Training for Sports Coaches in Australia, Canada, the United Kingdom and Japan* (Tamura *et al.* 1993). The scale of the data on which the UK evidence

The five most popular 'reasons for coaching' were:

■ fun and enjoyment	85%
■ continue in sport	52%
■ pride, achievement, success	48%
■ skill in teaching	38%
■ fitness and health	31%

Note: Coaches were able to select three reasons
Source: Tamura *et al.* (1993)

Figure 11.2 *Motivations for UK coaches in the four-country study*

The four most popular 'reasons for coaching' were:

■ natural progression from competition	39%
■ general interest in sport	24%
■ as an interested parent/relative	15%
■ came from teaching	13%

Source: English Sports Council (1997)

Figure 11.3 *Motivations for UK coaches in the ESC 1993 Survey*

is based is quite limited (83 'advanced' coaches and 165 'novice' coaches). The most popular reasons for coaching are shown in Figure 11.2. The sampling techniques and the apparent bias in the response rates have produced a rather skewed profile: 50 per cent of the female coaches had been coaching for less than five years; 14 per cent of the female sample had been coaching in their specialist sport for less than a year; 51 per cent of the female coaches considered themselves to be professional coaches. The most disappointing part of the report is that the data for the novice and advanced coaches has been aggregated.

Similar data were collected in the English Sports Council (1997) *Survey of Coaches 1993*. This was an extensive survey of 24 sports with almost 1,500 responses from coaches. The most popular reasons for coaching are shown in Figure 11.3. Unfortunately, the responses from coaches who worked with beginners are again aggregated with those working with international athletes. In addition, 'routes into coaching' have been confused with 'main reasons for coaching'. Nevertheless, some useful data are produced.

This is obviously of more interest in terms of recruitment avenues. In a later table in the report, respondents indicated the factors that motivated them to continue:

1 Helping others to improve	39%
2 Enjoyment	29%
3 Making a contribution to sport	19%
4 Achievement/success	8%

(English Sports Council 1997)

Motive	Borders Region (%)	Tayside Region (%)	Grampian Region (%)	Highland Region (%)
To continue participation	71	65	47	67
Parental motive	14	15	23	18
Teaching motive	8	18		

Source: CLR 1992, 1994a, 1994b; Slainte Ltd 1993

Figure 11.4 *Coaches' responses to selected recruitment motives*

Motive	Proportion (n=177)
Continue participation	45%
Parental route	19%
Education/teaching	10%

Source: Sports Council 1994

Figure 11.5 *Motives expressed by coaches in the TOYA study*

A series of studies (Centre for Leisure Research 1992, 1994a, 1994b; Slainte Ltd 1993) was carried out in Scotland in the mid-nineties to inform and underpin the creation of regional coaching development strategies. These had a common format and the data are comparable (Figure 11.4). They demonstrate a fairly consistent pattern.

The Training of Young Athletes project undertaken by the Sports Council produced a specialist report on the coaches of the children involved in the project ('TOYA and Coaching', Sports Council 1994). Figure 11.5 shows the motives for entering coaching cited by the coaches of the young athletes in the study.

Lyle *et al.* (1997) surveyed coaches in seven sports (602 responses: 47 per cent response rate) as to their motivations for coaching. The coaches had at least an NVQ Level 2 award in their specialist sport: the majority operated within clubs and worked with intermediate levels of performer. Of the coaches who worked with elite level performers 70 per cent had been coaching for over ten years. In addition, these 10+ years coaches were more likely to have been attracted by 'continuing their interest in competitive sport'.

The general findings were not surprising. In response to a question about motive, 95 per cent cited 'general interest', 89 per cent 'putting something back into sport, and 96 per cent 'helping young people'; 87 per cent indicated that finance was not a factor in their motive for coaching. Of more interest were some of the recruitment findings. For example, 72 per cent of the coaches indicated that their motive/recruitment was not related to their own children. However, there were sport-specific factors. In swimming and athletics, over 50 per cent of those coaches related entry to coaching to parental status, saying that it was at least of 'some importance'.

There is a trend towards sport-specific differences in recruitment avenues. For example, the TOYA and Coaching report (Sports Council 1994) found that 19 per cent of coaches had cited the 'parental route' into coaching. However, in swimming and gymnastics the proportion jumped to 30 per cent of coaches. Also, the proportion of 'parent coaches' was higher in athletics, swimming and rugby union (English Sports Council 1997). This is not surprising given (1) the younger age groups in the sport, (2) the dependence on parents for transport, and (3) (perhaps) less need for prior experience. Nevertheless, the aggregation of participation and performance coaches in the surveys means that they have to be treated with some caution. On the other hand, 75 per cent of rowing coaches in the English Sports Council (1997) report had been competitors. In both the Lyle *et al.* (1997) and ESC (1997) reports, team sports (basketball, hockey, netball) coaches were linked with a 'from teaching' route. Both the Lyle *et al.* (1997) and TOYA (Sports Council 1994) studies found that tennis 'coaches' cited financial remuneration as a motive. One very interesting finding from the English Sports Council (1997) investigation was that a higher proportion of senior coaches had backgrounds as performers.

There is also evidence from more qualitative studies. Salmela (1995) interviewed twenty-one expert performance coaches with an average of over ten years' experience. The key findings were that coaches had had an 'intense involvement' (not all at the highest level) in their sport and mentors were a very significant influence at an early stage of coaching. Lyle (1998b) interviewed twelve expert performance volleyball coaches (average age 40, with 80 per cent having 10+ years of experience). Only one coach had 'emerged' from the coaching awards programme using it as an entry route. The clear picture was of a (perhaps not quite seamless) transition from playing to coaching, although there was some evidence of the transition being unplanned. In earlier studies, White *et al.* (1989) and West and Brackenridge (1990) each interviewed women coaches in five sports. Two principal findings are of interest: first, there was a pronounced link to their experience as performers; second, there was a 'drift' factor in the coaches' entry into coaching.

A number of summary statements can be formulated:

1 It is a significant weakness of the existing surveys that their participation and performance coaching populations have not been disaggregated.
2 There is some evidence that recruitment is principally from those who wish to maintain their involvement in sport.
3 There is tentative evidence that performance coaches have generally been performers and that a profile of intense commitment is evident.
4 There is an overwhelming sense that coaches perceive their entry to coaching to have a 'helping others' motive.
5 There are clear sport-specific differences. This is very pronounced (to the extent of an inverse relationship) in parental and teaching recruitment avenues.
6 The implication from the evidence is that the motive and the recruitment avenue are linked. However, some of this complexity has been lost in the survey approach.
7 Research is required into all elements of recruitment:

   (a) A targeted approach to populations of performance coaches is required.
   (b) If coaching is 'selective' from performers, it is necessary to identify the pre-disposition to the opportunity when presented.
   (c) There would appear to be a combination of motive and opportunity at play. The 'opportunity' is made up of a series of factors, the interaction between which requires further research: predisposition, experience, mentoring, need, selection and so on.

(d) In addition to sport-specific issues, the gender of coaches will almost certainly impact on recruitment. (This is dealt with at length in the chapter following.) For example, the transition from competition to coaching for male coaches of female athletes may involve a different set of factors.

(e) Lyle *et al.* (1997) speculate on a number of useful theoretical perspectives through which to explore recruitment. One particularly appropriate approach may be the Sport Commitment Model of Scanlan *et al.* (1993). It was suggested that the factors involved in coaches' commitment to the role will be: delayed enjoyment; the presence or absence of sport-related alternatives; the concept of power as an attractor; personal investment; and the concept of obligation as a motivator.

CONCEPTUAL ISSUES

The purpose of this section is to identify the links between motivations and recruitment and some of the conceptual issues about the coaching process that have emerged as the details of coaching practice have been developed.

Participation-performance coaching

Distinctions have been drawn between these two forms of coaching practice in terms of intensity, athlete motivation and the degree of application of systematic principles. One of the key conceptual issues was that the participation and performance coaching roles were not on a continuum; that is, performance coaching is generally not a progression from participation coaching. Some of the evidence described in the previous sections demonstrates that performance coaches differ in their motives and recruitment patterns. The most striking issue is their performance sport background and a desire to maintain and continue in this. This, of course, has implications for coach education.

An interesting issue that links recruitment and education is the situation (perhaps best illustrated in soccer in the UK), in which there is an assumption that the performance sport background, particularly a successful one, is the sole criterion for predisposition for coaching/managing.

Transition versus recruitment

This is an important issue. Participation coaches may be influenced by promotional campaigns and the provision of coach education courses. In other words, they are 'recruited' into coaching. One obvious attractor is the participation of the prospective coach's children in the sport. However, in performance coaching, the general picture is one of *transition* from active engagement in sport – and one that is already characterised by intensive commitment. To some extent this transition can be a managed process. Some of the factors already identified are:

1　The likelihood of 'drift' into coaching and the importance of opportunity factors.
2　The importance and catalytic effect of mentors in influencing individuals into coaching.

3   A form of (intentional or unintentional) preparation by the creation of structured opportunities to 'apprentice' within the coaching role. This involves 'assistant' opportunities, working with specialist groups, working with development squads etc.
4   Situated learning (see Lave and Wenger 1991) occurring during the transition period. The prospective coach gradually acquires knowledge and insight via their contact with coaches. Added responsibility is given as this knowledge and skill develops, and eventually the coach is accepted into the occupational sub-culture. This needs to be articulated with the more formal coach education programme.

Coaching process boundaries

Part of the conceptual development focused on 'levels' within the coaching role (direct intervention, intervention support, constraints management and strategic co-ordination) and the 'completeness' with which the coaching process is implemented. The evidence on motivations and recruitment reinforces the distinctions between those who (intend to) implement the whole process and those, generally participation coaches, whose engagement is less intensive.

A number of reports draw attention to the link between a financial motive and tennis coaches. This is interesting, as it reinforces a perception that many of these individuals are, in fact, tennis instructors; that is, they give lessons on tennis but do not implement the whole coaching process.

One caveat on finance, careers and coaching is that the surveys on which the chapter is based were completed before the effects of greater National Lottery funding for performance sport had impacted on coaching. This is clearly a fertile area for research.

Coaching as an interpersonal relationship

This concept has been explored in some depth, and there is clear evidence that general factors such as helping others and assisting athletes to reach their potential are common motives for coaches. One particular construct that was given attention earlier was the question of coaching style. It was speculated that coaching style was relatively stable, based on values and influenced by previous experience of influential coaches and mentors. There is some evidence from the survey results that performance and participation coaches may have different sets of values, but certainly have different sets of experiences. To some extent this reinforces the fact that performance and participation coaches, whilst most likely centred on athlete welfare, have distinctive linkages between style/behaviour and the performance demands of the role.

Skills and knowledge

The evidence on motives and recruitment highlighted the relationship between the parental route into coaching in some sports (notably swimming, gymnastics and athletics) and the teaching/education route in many team sports. This is largely explained by the extent of non-school club provision (in the former case) and traditionally school-based provision for younger players in the team sport example. However, the issue here is the prominence given in earlier chapters to the skills and knowledge required within the coaching role. In some sports the engagement may be a very practical one: feeding, demonstrating, and appreciating interaction between participants. This may help to explain the more limited reliance on these skills in other sports (swimming, gymnastics and athletics) and the potential for recruitment from outside the performer base.

Cognitive models

A key concept in understanding how coaches operate was their cognitive organisation, and more specifically their mental models, with which to make sense of the past and anticipate the future. The models are part of the developed expertise of the coach and allow the coach to operate efficiently, given the complexity of the coaching process. In recruitment terms, the interesting issues are the experiences necessary to develop these models – perhaps more so at the early stages of performance coaching. If it is assumed that these cognitive abilities are shaped from situated learning as a performer, from interaction with mentor/expert coaches, from trial and error in practice and from coach education, this determines the sort of background that will be most facilitative and, therefore, has implications for recruitment.

Recruitment populations:
sport-specificity – socio-economic group

Performance coaches are generally expert in one sport. When allied to the need for experiential knowledge and characteristics of intensive involvement, this simple fact has enormous implications for circumscribing the population from which the recruitment stream of performance coaches may be drafted. This is a factor that will be considered in the following chapter, on female coaches. One further issue is that several studies have demonstrated that performance coaches are more likely to have experienced higher education (Gould et al. 1990; Tamura et al. 1993; Lyle et al. 1997). To some extent this reinforces the 'coaching as a cognitive exercise' approach advocated in this text. It is certainly a recruitment issue, although more research is required on sport-specific populations.

Disengagement

This short review has focused on recruitment rather than 'burnout' or disengagement from the coaching role. Once again, most of the literature on this subject is North American. It is largely a US phenomenon, arising from institutional pressures and role conflict. An example of relevant research, and a very good review of the field, is Kelly et al. (1999).

It seems clear that not enough is known about the recruitment pathways of performance coaches. For the most part, coaches appear to come from the performer base, already experienced, specialised and committed. The actual mechanism through which they make the transition into coaching needs much more research. The balance of mechanisms – choice, serendipity, drift, selection – needs to be evaluated against recruitment success and the expressed motives of the coaches. Performance coaches are not recruited into sport; they are mostly recruited from sport.

The surveys to date have produced some useful data on the characteristics of coaches, but the failure to disaggregate the participation coaches from performance coaches has significantly weakened the extent to which the information is useful for policy purposes. A richer source of evidence is required on coaches' motives. While it is useful to know that most coaches have been motivated by a sense of helping others, it is disingenuous not to explore the achievement motive in a performance sport context. There is no doubt that a balance of athlete welfare and achievement motives will exist. One avenue that requires exploration is that the recruitment of coaches from the performer pool means that these values have matured during the individual's long exposure to performance sport. Occupational socialisation is already happening to the nascent performance coach.

Perhaps the most important issue is that the sifting/selection process is going on during the athlete's career as a performer. Why are some athletes predisposed to continue as coaches? Do we know enough about what makes a good performance coach to influence that sifting process? Is it an informal process or should there be a more formal developmental process? This has important implications not only for coach education but also for the professionalisation issue. The particulars of recruitment to performance coaching may impact on the stages of professional development – really suggesting that the initial novice stages have in many instances already been experienced.

SUMMARY

This chapter will have familiarised you with the following issues:

- why recruitment is an important issue for sports coaching;
- the factors involved in maintaining recruitment to the pool of performance coaches;
- supply and demand in sports coaching;
- the evidence from national surveys on motivations for entering coaching;
- the limitations to existing research and the questions needing to be asked;
- the range of conceptual issues that impinge on understanding motivations and recruitment: participation/performance, transition mechanisms, process boundaries and personal characteristics; and
- the implications for coach education and professionalisation of selective recruitment from the performer reservoir.

PROJECTS

- Conduct semi-structured interviews with 10–12 performance coaches. Construct the interview schedule to explore recruitment mechanisms and create case examples for different avenues.
- Create life histories for 3–4 experienced coaches. Explore the catalysts for entering coaching, the perceived rewards, the motives for changing roles within coaching, and their sport background. Use the analysis to identify issues for further research.

- Select one sport. Construct a questionnaire based on qualifications, experience and expressed motives. Conduct a survey across levels of coaching in that sport and build a matrix to show the relationship between stages in professional development and the variables surveyed.
- Carry out any of the suggested projects but focus on a particular group of coaches – for example, women coaches, disabled coaches or coaches of disabled athletes, coaches from ethnic minorities, or coaches with a very successful record as a performer.

Reading

Tamura *et al.* (1993) provides useful data for analysis and comparison. Perhaps the most accessible survey data can be read first hand in Lyle *et al.* (1997). This also reviews some of the literature and is a useful source of further reading. The literature on the recruitment of women coaches is dealt with in the next chapter. In the absence of research on performance coaches, a useful source of evidence are biographies of coaches/managers. Sik (1996) is a good example of this.

CHAPTER TWELVE

▼ ## WHERE ARE ALL THE WOMEN COACHES?

■ Introduction   221
■ Women's Participation in Sport   223
■ Review of Evidence   224
■ Possible Explanations   226
■ Conceptual Issues   229
■ Commentary   232
■ Summary   232
■ Projects and Reading   233

INTRODUCTION

As the evidence will demonstrate, there is a dearth of women coaches in performance sport, and women coaches are under-represented more generally in coaching (Fasting and Pfister 2000). Although it can be argued that the coaching process as a concept is gender-neutral, its implementation takes place in a social and cultural context and produces a skewed gender ratio. The institution of sport and its many sub-cultures can clearly be described as male dominated and this has received considerable attention in the academic literature (Hargreaves 1994; Clarke and Humberstone 1997; Scraton and Watson 2000). Despite recent increases of women in participation in active recreation, it is argued in the literature that opportunity and access are denied to women through a combination of overt, structural and hegemonic discrimination. In particular, elite sport, and the demands and values associated with it, are perceived to constitute a masculine arena in which women coaches do not play a significant role. Indeed, Hargreaves (1994) suggested that 'coaching remains one of the most prestigious areas of sport which embodies grossly unequal gender relations' (1994: 199).

 ## Critical Concept

Elite sport, and the demands and values associated with it, are perceived to constitute a masculine arena in which women coaches do not play a significant role.

The purpose of this chapter is to examine the issues associated with women's participation as coaches in the UK and to seek explanations for their under-representation. Given the orientation of the book, it will also be important to investigate whether aspects of the conceptual framework related to the coaching process enhance insights into these explanations. One possibility is that the conceptual interpretation and representation of the coaching process, as described in this book, is not neutral but has been constructed within masculine assumptions about coaching, its purposes and characteristics. Clearly this was not intended and the presumption is that 'gendering' is a social construction.

As will have become a familiar theme for readers, there is a substantial literature on gender aspects of coaching but this is predominantly based on North American inter-scholastic and intercollegiate coaching and the emphasis on institutional and employment issues limits its relevance (Hart *et al.* 1986; Knoppers 1987,1988, 1992; Hasbrook *et al.* 1990; Acosta and Carpenter 1994; Pastore and Meacci 1994; Wilkerson 1996; Barber 1998; Fasting and Pfister 2000). There has been far less empirical work on gender aspects of coaching in the UK (White 1987; White *et al.* 1989; West and Brackenridge 1990; West *et al.* 1998).

The issue of under-representation is important for a number of reasons:

- Any factor that reduces the number of coaches available to work in sport is a concern. It can also be argued that it reduces choice and therefore the quality of coaching.
- From a promotional point of view, the dearth of women coaches, particularly in senior positions, leads to fewer role models with whom to encourage recruitment into sport and into coaching.
- If there is evidence of manifest discrimination, this is an ethical issue that should be tackled and policy action implemented to redress the situation. Of course, institutional or structural discrimination requires similar policy action.
- There would be less likelihood of abuse by male coaches in women's sport if more women coaches were available (White 1987).

 Question Box

Although perhaps not resolvable in this chapter, an interesting policy question over which to ruminate is whether women coaches must inevitably reflect the situation in sport more generally or whether they can act as a catalyst for change. Which needs to come first?

The first stage is to examine briefly some aspects of women's participation in sport more generally and its impact on recruitment into coaching.

WOMEN'S PARTICIPATION IN SPORT

Studies of women in sport argue that sport is part of a patriarchal society and one in which the practice of sport reinforces and reproduces male dominance. A complete review of the field is beyond the scope of this chapter, but a selective review of some evidence will demonstrate that the explanations for there being fewer women coaches are symptomatic of the more general, 'subordinate' position of women in sport. Also, leadership positions more generally are a focus for attention in women's studies.

Figure 12.1 was constructed from data contained in the COMPASS 1999 report into sport participation patterns in European countries (COMPASS 1999). The figures are intended merely to be indicative. The report does make it clear that participation statistics vary according to the criteria employed. However, they do suggest that some official measures of participation are optimistic and highlight the differences that exist between males and females. The key figures are the sub-totals for what might be described as performance sport (categories 1 and 3). The female figures are just 30 per cent of male participation in these categories.

	Category	UK (%)	Male (%)	Female (%)
1	Competitive, organised, intensive	4.5	7.9	1.6
2	Intensive	12.6	15.2	10.3
3	Regular, competitive	4.1	5.9	2.6
	Sub-total categories 1 and 3		13.8	4.2
4	Regular, recreational	5.7	5.2	6.0
5	Irregular	18.6	19.6	17.8
6	Occasional	20.4	18.6	21.9
7	Non-participant	34.2	28.5	39.0

Source: COMPASS (1999)

Figure 12.1 *Male and female participation in sport by participation category*

Question Box

One interpretation of the data in Figure 12.1, and a possible strategic option, is that the focus for increased numbers of women in leadership positions should be in forms of coaching other than performance sport. However, would that (1) reinforce the male stereotype, and (2) reduce the availability of role models?

Hall *et al.* (1991) summarise a catalogue of explanations for women being under-represented in sport. Although this is a North American source, the factors identified provide a valuable template for understanding women's participation and organisational progress more widely. They identify the following reasons:

- stereotypical notions about women's competence despite their qualifications and expertise;
- questions about background, motivation and commitment;

- an emphasis on achieved rather than ascribed status (having to prove themselves);
- the prevalence of male symbols and values;
- a presumption about family responsibilities;
- the maintenance of a male *status quo* through the exercise of power by existing elites and a formal and informal social and professional network;
- the absence of affirmative action to address the needs of women in sport.

These factors build upon the early experiences of young females, in which family and educational socialisation place less emphasis on sport than for their male counterparts. Whilst this may be less pronounced than was previously the case and changes in family structures and employment practices have increased opportunities, the participation rates retain a 'female deficit'. Fasting and Pfister (2000) suggest that male dominance in coaching has to be understood in the culture of sport and the gendered power structure in both sport and society (2000: 103). This will influence not only the coaches themselves but also the perceptions of the athletes about the coaching role. Fasting and Pfister review a number of more specific explanations:

1   that men use sport to reinforce their male hegemony (perhaps because of its reduction in other spheres);
2   that women are marginalised in areas in which they do not occupy the principal leadership roles (and that this becomes self-perpetuating);
3   that the 'system' is reproduced in the image of the dominant group; and
4   that 'female deficit' is not an explanation for the disparity – in other words, the explanations do not lie in the characteristics of women coaches themselves (although they acknowledge that lack of confidence may be a factor).

REVIEW OF EVIDENCE

Evidence from the Sports Council (1993) demonstrates a general trend towards fewer women coaches as the level of coaching award increases (see Figure 12.2). This reinforces the perception that female coaches are more prevalent in participation than in performance sport.

Level of award	Gymnastics	Badminton	Volleyball	Tennis
5	24	0	8	21
4	39	19	–	20
3	55	22	13	31
2	70	24	16	24
1	78	36	35	22

Note: Figures are in percentages
Source: Adapted from Sports Council (1993) and updated from Sports Council, unpublished report (1995)

Figure 12.2 *Percentage of women coaches by level of coaching award*

COACHING IN ITS SOCIAL CONTEXT

Award	Male (%)	Female (%)
Advanced	13.7	4.2
Senior	41.3	16.7
Intermediate	34.8	62.5
Elementary/introductory	10.0	16.7

Notes: n = 419

The sample was intended not to consist of inexperienced coaches and the elementary section is therefore small

Source: Lyle *et al.* (1997)

Figure 12.3 *Type of NGB award by gender*

Year	Athletes		Coaches	
	Male (%)	Female (%)	Male (%)	Female(%)
1976	73	27	96	4
1980	68	32	91	9
1984	68	32	96	4
1988	64	36	90	10
1992	61	39	92	8

Source: Sports Council (1993)

Figure 12.4 *Percentages of female coaches in the UK Summer Olympic squads*

The figures are all the more worrying since the sports selected are those with a strong base in women's participation. Although the evidence from such surveys are very dependent on the sampling techniques, the evidence is convincing. Figure 12.3 presents a similar set of statistics that were identified by Lyle *et al.* (1997) in a review of coaches' recruitment patterns.

Coaching Matters (Coaching Review Panel 1991) identified the failure to attract women into coaching as problematic and involvement was said to be 'negligible'. One statistic quoted was that only 14 per cent of the membership of the British Institute of Sports Coaches at that time were women.

The number of female coaches appointed to British Olympic teams provides further evidence of the disparity in appointment to senior positions. Figure 12.4 points to the stark contrast between the percentage of women athletes and that of women coaches.

A general perception that there is an under-representation of women in coaching appears to be borne out by the data available. In participation coaching and in the output of initial stage coaching certification there is a balance between men and women. The position may be summarised as follows: 'Women are under-represented in senior coaching positions and in higher categories of coaching award in comparison to men and in comparison to their participation statistics.' The position can also be illustrated in specific sports. In researching for an investigation into volleyball coaches in England (Lyle 1998b), it emerged that, at that time, the registered coaches of all Division 1 Men, Conference A and B Women, and all Senior and Junior International team coaches were male. Further examples in soccer are given by Fasting and Pfister (2000).

 Critical Concept

Women are under-represented in senior coaching positions and in higher categories of coaching awards in comparison to men and in comparison to their participation statistics.

POSSIBLE EXPLANATIONS

Five factors are generally adduced as contributing to the circumstances described above. These are: low expectations; the limited scale of performance sport; absence of social support; recruitment patterns; and lack of social flexibility. First, *low expectations*, which arise as a result of a number of factors which contribute to female performers not experiencing a 'preparation phase' whilst still performers. This is a combination of an absence of role models and role exemplars, and an absence of social support for the 'situated learning' that accompanies early commitment to the role. These factors are combined into a simple model in Figure 12.5. A simpler way of expressing this is that women may not have conscious and unconscious messages passed to them that suggest that they should consider becoming a coach. They may then fail to develop a commitment to the role. A failure to prepare for potential responsibilities – for example, by a developing relationship with a mentor coach – means that they are then unprepared when or if the opportunity arises.

Low expectation can also be generated by the expectations of athletes. In an early study by Parkhouse and Williams (1986), male and female high-school basketball players favoured male coaches when win/loss and coaching qualifications were controlled. Weinberg *et al.* (1984) found that male athletes preferred male coaches but female athletes' attitudes towards male and female coaches did not differ. More recent studies show a general tendency towards a preference for male coaches in both male and, to a

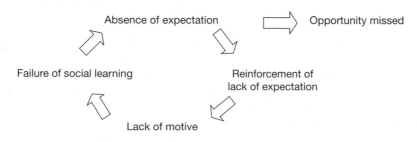

Figure 12.5 Low expectation model of preparation for coaching

lesser extent, female athletes (Patriksson and Eriksson 1990; LeDrew and Zimmerman 1994). Fasting and Pfister (2000) found some evidence that elite female soccer players preferred female coaches because of their approach and the fact that male coaches 'did not take them seriously'.

The second factor is *the limited scale of performance sport*. The previous chapter on recruitment noted the likelihood of a recruitment avenue directly from performance sport and with a motive of retaining interest in competitive sport. The scale of performance sport for women was shown earlier in the chapter to be considerably less than for men, and this must have an influence on the size of the population from which recruitment takes place. This is possibly exacerbated by two other factors: (1) the age range of participants in popular female sports such as gymnastics and swimming may negatively influence transition to coaching; and (2) the fewer rewards generally in female sports have resulted in less professionalisation.

Third is the *absence of social support*. The cumulative effect of male domination is evident in the lack of social networks and support mechanisms available to women. The relatively small number of coaches and officials, the subsequent lack of influence, power and authority, and the failure to provide formal support structures are likely to affect recruitment (motive), maintenance (isolation) and retention (security).

The fourth factor is *patterns of recruitment*. Selection (that is, for employment positions) is an issue in the North American literature, in which researchers find evidence of differential or discriminatory practices (Acosta and Carpenter 1994; Pastore and Meacci 1994). However, some of the evidence reviewed in the previous chapter suggested that entry to coaching and many appointments, particularly in the voluntary sector, may be the result of 'drift' – that is, influenced by existing club opportunities, informal invitations, assumed leadership and coaching roles, serendipity and mentor grooming. This is likely to be evident in both male and female entry to coaching but, once again, the preponderance of men in influential leadership positions may disadvantage women. This is also likely to be the case in selection for representative team/squad posts.

The previous chapter provided some evidence of male–female differences in recruitment patterns, although there was some consistency in motive. Hart *et al.* (1986) reported that women coaches chose a coaching career to extend their involvement in competition, and for the opportunity to work with skilled athletes. These motives were confirmed by Pastore (1991) for both men and women. Lyle *et al.* (1997) identified general factors common to both males and females but with some differences in extreme responses: female coaches were less likely to be attracted by continued involvement in competition but more likely to be attracted by helping young people.

Fifth is *lack of social flexibility*. An assumption is often made that women will be responsible for the domestic and child-rearing duties in families. This undoubtedly restricts their social freedom and flexibility, and these expectations lead to a lack of access and opportunity in leisure, including sports coaching (and similarly in education and employment more generally). This may be merely a traditional perspective but it seems likely to be one factor that remains influential. Some of the concomitant outcomes – lack of financial resources, skill deficit, and early exit from performance sport – may also influence recruitment and progress in coaching.

These factors can be found to varying degrees in the research studies. Hasbrook *et al.* (1990) examined stereotypical gender-role assumptions about coaches – that there is a lack of qualified women coaches and that they often experienced time constraints because of family commitments. These beliefs were unfounded (although it has to be remembered that recruitment may be affected to a greater extent than perceptions of employed coaches warrant). Hasbrook and colleagues account for the preponderance of male coaches through the prevalence of a male coaching stereotype: 'coaching is viewed as requiring one to be aggressive, competitive and firm rather than soft, feminine and yielding' (1990: 259). Staurowsky (1990) interviewed ten female coaches of male athletes. The coaches reported that they were perceived as not as tough as their male counterparts and that relationships with officials and other coaches were characterised by a lack of authority and awkwardness. However, Barber (1998) found that there were few differences between men and women coaches in terms of perceived competence.

West *et al.* (1998) use Witz's (1990, 1992) model of occupational closure to bring an insight into the evidence of interviews with twenty women coaches across five sports. They found evidence that the creation of a masculine role gender-perception, an emphasis on performance sport achievements, and informal networks were used to produce occupational closure by the dominant male group. That is, they engaged in mechanisms that demarcated the role and excluded it from women coaches. The women coaches engaged in 'countervailing measures' to resist closure – emphasising their achievements, obtaining qualifications and identifying niche roles (particularly with children). This seems a particularly useful analytical tool but the failure to distinguish participation and performance coaching (and athlete backgrounds) limits this particular analysis. One of the issues to arise is the link between previous performance and perceptions of coaching competence. Although this is often presented in fairly crude 'gendering' fashion, based on levels of performance, subsequent discussion will demonstrate that coaching expertise may, in some sports, be significantly influenced by mental models rooted in performance.

Question Box

Although it might be argued that the coach's mental models depend to some extent on performance experience in some sports, the interpretation of coaching as a largely cognitive exercise should render it gender neutral. Agree?

Another very interesting speculation from the research is that women coaches also engaged in 'closure' – both by emphasising their suitability for niche markets (more effective than men because of their empathy, style, philosophy and so on) and their achieved status (to effect closure against other women coaches).

CONCEPTUAL ISSUES

Previous chapters have dealt with the essential characteristics of the coaching process, the role of the coach and the range of value positions to be found in coaching. In none of these was there any inherent characteristic that marked out coaching as a male preserve. Nevertheless, it has to be acknowledged that elements such as control, commitment, intensity, direction, leadership, competition orientation, achievement orientation, and a scientific approach to performance, which underpin this interpretation of the coaching process, can be recognised as masculine values in sport and in social life more generally. On the other hand, there would seem to be no doubt that the social construction of the coaching process and coaching practice marks it as a gendered activity. A number of possible explanations for women's under-representation as sports coaches have been suggested, and it is likely that these work in concert to produce the current circumstances. It is necessary now to examine whether the conceptual framework can provide insights into some of the issues raised.

 Critical Concept

The social construction of the coaching process and coaching practice marks it as a gendered activity.

The evidence on women coaches in the UK (White *et al.* 1989; West and Brackenridge 1990; Lyle *et al.* 1997; West *et al.* 1998) has focused on the social circumstances in which the coaches operate. The coaching process in these studies has not been treated as problematic and it is not possible, therefore, to describe in detail the coaching practice of women coaches. In particular, the key distinction between participation and performance coaching has been ignored. Figure 12.6 displays a matrix of factors contributing to women becoming coaches, and individuals are likely to 'pick their way through' the matrix.

One obvious point is that the process of entry to coaching may not be greatly different for male and female coaches. However, further research is required to establish these patterns. It seems likely from existing research that two principal routes exist. The first is from parent/teacher/general interest into participation coaching and is much the greater in scale. The second is from competition sport into performance coaching. The point has already been made that the transition between these forms of coaching is not easy and, indeed, the relationship between the requirements of performance coaching and the explanations identified earlier may be a fruitful avenue for research into the dearth of women coaches.

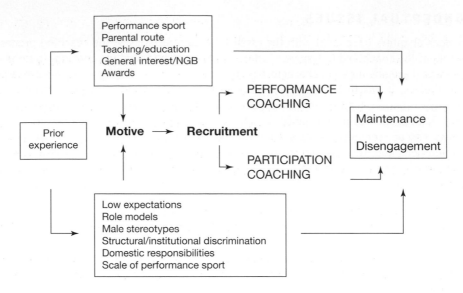

Figure 12.6 *Factors influencing the engagement of women coaches*

🗒 **Question Box**

The transition into coaching for women is a good illustration of the failure to appreciate the lessons to be learned from conceptual analysis. Many commentators talk of the reduction in women coaches as the performance level of the athlete increases. However, this fails to account for the fact that there is little transition from participation to performance sport, for either athletes or coaches. In other words, the explanation has to lie solely in performance sport not in the transition, which is difficult and generally unlikely in any case! Does this help to focus research?

The transition stage into performance coaching with its intensive demands will not come as a surprise to performance athletes, whether male or female. However, the intensity of commitment may reinforce the stereotypical perception of female coaches being unable to commit to the role because of personal and social circumstances.

Systematic observation studies in North America have provided some evidence of differences between the practice of male and female coaches. Given the limitations of these studies, it is hardly surprising that the emphasis is on direct intervention. Millard (1996) established differences in the amounts of technical instruction, encouragement and control behaviours between male and female coaches, even after controlling for age, experience and playing experience. One issue that is rarely discussed is whether there is any differential required in coaching male or female athletes (Hamilton 2000). A general position would be that there will be differences between individuals and these are accounted for in the coaching process. The differences (if any) between male and female athletes are unlikely to be any greater than the range of differences in either group.

The coaches in West and colleagues' (1998) study were typical in that they reported that males questioned female coaches' playing experience and knowledge of their sport. This could, of course, be part of the male demarcation of the coaching role but it may also be the case that some of the mental models on which the coach's expertise depends are in their formative stages during the coach's playing experience and also the transition phase. It must also be recognised that there are sport-specific differences in the use of performance models – factors such as interactive sports, the coach's role in competition, team/individual sports, and strategy sports have been identified previously. The effect of this is:

- to reinforce the advantages of recruiting from competition sport;
- to emphasise the need for 'assistantships' as support mechanisms during the transition phase;
- that coach education cannot assume the parity of 'performance models' (lack of sensitivity to this may place additional pressure on women (and male) coaches with lesser competition experience).

It would be inappropriate to label coaches by their previous playing experience (although this appears to be common). Nevertheless, in the early stage of transition into performance coaching, there may be some material benefit from a considerable prior experience.

In earlier chapters, relationships were drawn between levels of role and the key skills required. Emphasis was placed on decision making, and process skills of planning, monitoring and regulating the various elements of the coaching process. These are clearly not gendered skills. Although demonstration is unlikely to be a significant requirement in much of performance sport, there are a number of sports in which rallying or feeding is an important component in practice management. The coach may need sufficient playing ability to challenge the performer. Women coaches who are perceived to have less performance ability than male counterparts may be disadvantaged by these perceptions. It seems likely that this issue is over-emphasised, but it may help to explain the relative absence of female coaches in some male sports and contribute to the incursion of male coaches into women's sports.

In a chapter to follow, the issue of evaluating coaches is examined. One of the general conclusions is that there are few, if any, satisfactory ways of evaluating coaches' effectiveness. Wilkerson (1996) alludes to this in suggesting that, because there are few criteria for evaluating, comparing and selecting coaches, particularly when appointments to women's sport are made, a recourse to quantification (of results) favours the existing pattern of deployment (that is, fewer women coaches).

To some extent, then, the stress on social factors and the number of women coaches has masked the potential for conceptual issues to contribute to explanations for gendered coaching practice. However, there is relatively little evidence of differential practice. The observational studies have shown some evidence of differences of emphasis in direct intervention behaviour. There is some momentum behind the notion that women coaches are a little more person-centred in orientation, and perhaps, therefore, receptive to more humanistic coaching practice. This would not be surprising in participation sport. In performance sport there is little evidence at all, but none to suggest that (when some of the extremes of behaviour are factored out) women coaches differ appreciably from their male counterparts.

COMMENTARY

The relative lack of women coaches is part of the larger picture of women's under-representation in sport and leadership positions more generally (White and Brackenridge 1985). The fact that women coaches form a substantial part of the participation coaching workforce must not be overlooked, but it is clear that in performance sport, and in particular with elite groups and representative sport, women coaches are greatly under-represented. This has an impact on the prominence of women role models to encourage women both into sport and into coaching.

The key issue is that recruitment from performance sport is required and this has a limited scale. However, a climate of low expectations has been created in which women's transition into coaching has been bedevilled by the protectionism of male coaches and the dominant male groups in sport more generally. A taken-for-grantedness has become established in which coaching is perceived to be a male enterprise and early socialisation into the coaching role is not an expectation for women performers.

There is a very limited non-North American literature available, and much of this has an emancipatory tendency in which the numbers of coaches and the search for sociological explanations for differential access and opportunity have dominated. However, detailed research on recruitment mechanisms, populations of performance coaches, and women's coaching practice and behaviour have been overlooked, and an integrated picture is not possible without this evidence.

SUMMARY

This chapter will have familiarised you with the following:

- the issues surrounding the dearth of women coaches in performance sport;
- factors involved in women's under-representation in sport more generally;
- some evidence of women coaches being under-represented at more advanced levels of certification and in positions of leadership;
- a range of possible explanations, including low expectations, the limited scale of performance sport, absence of support networks, discrimination in recruitment practices and lack of social flexibility;
- details of a particular explanation based on 'occupational closure';
- links between conceptual issues and an understanding of women coaches' recruitment, particular factors being the lack of transition from participation to performance coaching, and the difficulty of evaluating coaches' effectiveness.

PROJECTS

- Interview 6 performance coaches. Semi-structured interview schedules should focus on the transition from playing to coaching. Explore the specific details of the decision-making process. Identify issues for further research.
- Select one sport. Devise a matrix of coaching positions and illustrate the balance of men and women coaches. Chart all of the assistant positions and support personnel, where appropriate.
- Identify 3 sports and interview 10 senior women performers in each. Examine their intended future in relation to coaching. Identify the factors involved in their goals.
- Repeat any of the research studies cited in the chapter, particularly on women performers' attitude to male and female coaches. Situate the investigation in club sport.
- Devise a case study on the literature and materials associated with the coach education programme/workshops and recruitment literature of one selected sport. Based on content analysis, examine the language and symbols used for evidence of gendered assumptions.

Reading

There is an extensive and critical literature on women in sport, although little of this makes explicit reference to sports coaching. The historical position is summed up in West and Brackenridge (1990) and the Sports Council (1993). Wilkerson (1996) and West *et al.* (1998) are stimulating reading on explanations for the dearth of women coaches. For an up-to-date piece of research with a valuable summary and review, read Fasting and Pfister (2000).

CHAPTER THIRTEEN

▼   **COACHING AND ETHICAL PRACTICE**

■ Introduction   234
■ Ethical Issues   235
■ Problem Areas   239
■ Conceptual Framework Issues   241
■ Codes of Ethics and Codes of Conduct   242
■ The Legal Dimension   244
■ Professional Sport: A Suitable Case for Treatment   245
■ Summary   247
■ Projects and Reading   247

INTRODUCTION

The purpose of this chapter is to examine the relationship between the values inherent in the coach's practice and their social significance in terms of the extent to which the practice is considered appropriate and acceptable. Coaching practice can be subjected to social evaluation and sanction. The judgements range from those behaviours that are illegal to those that are morally unacceptable or offend more contextualised ethical practice. Once again, it will be suggested that a greater insight into the issues will be afforded by appreciating the conceptual issues involved. Although there has been a good deal written about appropriate and inappropriate coaching behaviour, there has been little or no analysis in relation to the conceptual framework surrounding the coaching process. The treatment has been issues-led: for example, child abuse, doping, or inequitable behaviour to athletes.

Morality is a judgement based on moral principles, about which there would be a degree of consensus. Moral principles are often expressed at a level of abstraction or generality and are guides to right and wrong behaviour. They may have their roots in religious or moral philosophy. Ethics, on the other hand, are a more or less coherent set of principles formulated around behaviour in a particular activity. Ethics tend to be expressed in terms of 'what behaviour ought to be', and it is not surprising, therefore, that ethics studies focus on apparently negative or inappropriate practice, attempting to establish the difference between acceptable and actual behaviour and the factors leading to challenges to this 'fine line'. This is perhaps the most appropriate issue to highlight: the interpretation, application and contextualisation of these principles is susceptible to social construction. In addition, these 'rules for social behaviour' may not be adhered to because of individual (or collective) values, predilections or conscious intentions to seek advantage.

 Critical Concept

Ethics are a more or less coherent set of principles formulated around behaviour in a particular activity.

As with other social issues, a field of study has developed in relation to sport, to which this short chapter cannot do justice. In addition to general texts (Morgan and Meier 1995; Arnold 1997; McNamee and Parry 1999), there is a substantial literature on specific issues: for example, sexual harassment (Brackenridge 2001), professional development (Haney *et al*. 1998), and performance-enhancing drugs (Houlihan 1999). This is further complemented by codes of ethics and conduct produced by NGBs or pseudo-professional bodies (NCF 1996; NCF/NSPCC 1998; IAAF 1999). The objective in this chapter is to illustrate and analyse the ethical dimension in coaching practice and its relationship to both social context and concepts associated with the coaching process. It should also be noted that there are many ethical issues associated with sports practice. It is reasonable to assume that not all of these are the direct responsibility of the coach. It is important, therefore, to establish the boundaries of the coach's responsibilities in relation to ethical behaviour, by the coach, the athletes and other individuals.

ETHICAL ISSUES

There can be no doubt that ethical issues are a contemporary concern for coaches and the developing coaching profession (and, indeed, may always have been so).

- The suspension of top athletes for failing drugs tests (particularly, nandrolone) appears to be a universal condition in some sports (Houlihan 1999).
- The revelations of widespread and systematic doping of performers in the former Eastern-bloc countries (and the findings of the Dubin Commission (Dubin 1990) in Canada) established a link between coaching practice and athlete behaviour (see also Francis 1990).
- A number of high-profile sexual harassment cases involving coaches have received media attention.
- The implementation of the Children Act has focused attention on appropriate behaviour in dealing with young persons.
- The courts are now dealing with a greater number of cases involving violence and discrimination (Hartley 1998).

Note: detailed accounts of many cases and incidents related to drugs, sexual abuse, inappropriate behaviour with young people and violence can be found in Gardiner *et al*. (1998), and in the journal *Sport and the Law* (British Association for Sport and Law).

Exemplar	Issue	Category
Encouraging or condoning intimidation in performance	Lack of respect for others	IO
Intentionally creating a dependency culture for athletes	Athlete welfare	PD, IP
Condoning the use of performance-enhancing substances	Cheating	IO
Allowing insufficient recovery from injury or illness	Athlete welfare	IO
Selection/recruitment on the basis of gender or race	Equity	SR
Sexual harassment	Athlete welfare	PD, IP
Failure to accept officials' decisions	Lack of respect for others	SR
Elitism in resource allocation	Equity	SR
Lack of opportunity for disabled performers	Equity	SR
Applying adult planning and workload expectations to young children	Athlete welfare	IGS
Delaying menstruation in young female athletes	Athlete welfare	IO
Acceptance of cheating in eligibility, technical specifications, recruitment regulations, etc.	Cheating	IO
Encouragement of partisan behaviour	Lack of respect for others	SR
Reward environment based on results	Lack of respect for others	PD, IGS
Failing to prepare athletes for disengagement from sport	Athlete welfare	SR, IP
Openly criticising fellow coaches or performers	Lack of respect for others	SR, IP
Over-committing young performers to competition	Athlete welfare	IGS

Figure 13.1 *Examples of ethical issues*

It would be useful to demonstrate the range of issues likely to concern coaches and coaching practice. Figure 13.1 categorises a number of examples of ethical practice according to their allocation in a speculative set of criteria based on a how/why/where question:

■   Interpersonal relationships (IP)
■   Power differentials (PD)
■   Influencing outcomes or performance (IO)
■   Social role (failure to maintain) (SR)
■   Inappropriate goal-setting (IGS)

Figure 13.1 and its exemplars are intended merely to be illustrative of the range of issues involved. There has been no attempt to prioritise them, and yet it must be obvious that those in which there has been an infringement of, for example, technical specifications or regulations are of less concern than those involving sexual harassment or potential injury. Athlete welfare must be considered more important than the regulations concerned with sport competition. Overall, however, it is useful to acknowledge that the issues falling under the banner of ethics will involve *legal matters* (harassment, treatment of young children, discrimination), *regulation* (eligibility, communication, drugs), and *behavioural codes* (autocratic behaviour, over-expectancy, honesty). The implication of falling into one of these categories is that sanctions will be different – criminal action, sporting sanctions, or 'professional' sanctions. One of the limitations caused by the absence of a professional body, discussed in an earlier chapter, is that there are few effective sanctions for unethical behaviour that does not infringe the law or NGB regulations. It is worth noting, however, that there is an increased tendency towards civil action in the courts for redress for inappropriate behaviour.

Question Box

It might be argued that athlete welfare issues should take precedence over matters of regulation. However, if asked to create a list of concerns, which would coaches identify as most pressing? An interesting research question.

Before examining the relationship between these issues and coaching practice, it is necessary to identify why the ethical dimension of sport and coaching should be such a concern. There are a number of reasons:

1   Ethical issues are likely to arise when interpersonal relationships are involved and particularly when there is a 'power differential' between the individuals. Sports coaching implies an interpersonal relationship, but, perhaps more importantly, it has a number of special features. Relationships are characterised by one or more of the following:

- differences in age and maturity;
- differences in knowledge and experience;
- differences in gender;
- intensity and duration of engagement;
- close physical contact;
- psychological dependency;
- emotional intensity.

2   Sport's contribution to the education of young people and its potential for enriching the personal development of participants is based on two presumptions:

(a) that sport has an inherent moral dimension insofar as it establishes rules for all competitors, precludes unfair advantage, has an element of self-regulation, and involves a 'spirit' of the sport that goes beyond the rules;
(b) that the conduct of sport provides opportunities for the display of moral qualities – respect, integrity, altruism, honesty and so on.

Any practice in sport that negates the individual's capacity to display these qualities or removes sport's inherent 'level playing field' is a challenge to the meaning of sport and raises ethical concerns. The previous point has an idealistic feel to it. It is clear that there are many individuals involved in sport (and not just in professional or elite levels of sport) for whom this idealism is misplaced. For them, the 'moral dimension' is not important and a rather more 'means–ends' approach to achieving success is prevalent. Nevertheless, this counter-culture merely highlights the ethical issues involved.

 Critical Concept

Any practice in sport that negates the individual's capacity to display moral qualities or removes sport's inherent 'level playing field' is a challenge to the meaning of sport and raises ethical concerns.

3 Perhaps the most obvious reason for problematic ethical issues being attached to sport is the combination of *competition* and *reward*. Performance sport is inherently competitive and is organised in such a way as to establish winners and losers. At the same time, there is a differential reward system, based on achievement, and society generally values success in sport, from community to national levels. The rewards are desirable, manifest and omni-present:

- Top-level performance sport has a globalised, commercialised, media-facilitated quality in which the financial rewards are significant.
- Rewards may also be expressed in less tangible ways. Status and social prestige accrue from success in sport at all levels.
- The effect of this is to shape individual aspirations, identity and satisfactions.

This has a particular resonance for coaches, who not only share this value system, but are successful by association with successful athlete and teams. The overall effect has been to intensify the meaning and implication of success, with a concomitant challenge to the moral and regulatory framework within which success is achieved.

4 It can also be argued that the intensity of commitment required for success is considerable – human and material resources, technical and scientific support, and life-style dedication. This may reinforce the desire for reward and the means–ends approach to achieving it. Potential conflict arises because coaches and performers are constantly stretching the boundaries of permissible action in order to maximise performance. The use of the term 'means–ends approach' is useful shorthand but the issues are more complex. Fry (2000) discusses the morality of coaches' decision making in relation to the means–ends argument.

5 Not all sport is like this. Much of sport is less intensive, at a participation or developmental level, involving young persons and/or more casual participants. This form of sport is much less reward-influenced, but nevertheless many of the characteristics of the coach–athlete interpersonal relationship remain and have the potential for abuse.

6 Professional sport and some high-level performance sport form a particular sub-culture with its own ethical behaviour. Research is required to examine in depth the nature of ethical practice at this level of sport in order to establish practice, rather than view behaviour from a more idealistic stance. It seems likely that there will be

COACHING IN ITS SOCIAL CONTEXT

a limited application of the 'spirit of the rules', an acceptance of pursuing improvements in performance by taking every advantage possible, and by challenging rules and regulations. Despite this, 'the single-mindedness of some sportspersons need not be accompanied by a complete absence of respect and dignity for opponents' (Lyle 1998c: 146).

Question Box

The acceptance of elite sport sub-cultural excesses of behaviour may be part of their appeal to spectators. Limits are understood and excesses punished. In other words, the actors accept a different set of assumptions. Is this amoral?

7   Brackenridge (2001) identifies the potential for abuse as stemming from the power differential between coach and performer but more specifically the dependency of athletes based on hero-worship and infatuation. Perhaps more significantly, she also highlights the relationship between sport, the attention to the body, the sexuality of the body and the coaching relationship. She suggests that the sexual politics need to be given more overt attention.

PROBLEM AREAS

Ethical issues arise when:

Power differentials are abused   Coaches may have the maturity, experience and knowledge to take advantage of their power. The power may rest in the exercise of these differences or in their control over recruitment, selection and advancement.

As significant persons in an athlete's life and as a respected (perhaps even revered figure), coaches are in a position to abuse the hero-worship often afforded to them by young athletes.

These power differentials are the basis of much of the sexual harassment perpetuated by coaches and reported in depth by Brackenridge (2001) and others (e.g. Tomlinson and Yorganci 1997; Nielsen 2001). It seems likely that sexual harassment is greatly under-reported in performance sport because of the coach's control over the athlete's career.

The expression of the coach's power can take many forms, ranging from harassment, bullying and intimidation to the exercise of control through decision making.

There will always be power differentials between coaches and athletes. However, the ethical problems arise when the coach disregards the 'informed consent' (Drewe 2000b) that is the basis of the coaching contract.

Attempts to influence results or performance

This leads to a series of actions by the coach and performer, most of which fall under the heading of 'cheating'. For example,

■ the use of performance-enhancing substances;
■ influencing officials by intimidation, gamesmanship or bribery;
■ circumventing regulations on eligibility or technical specifications.

Inappropriate assumptions applied

Ethical problems arise when the assumptions of the performance sport sub-cultural context are applied to other sporting contexts (specifically sport for young people).

It is not always made clear to young people that the behaviour of role models applies only to that sub-culture and that there are often safeguards to many of their heroes' excesses of behaviour.

Planning, training theory, competition demands, psychological and physical demands are placed on young athletes at too early a stage in their careers. In this way athlete welfare is disregarded for short-term gains.

Figure 13.2 demonstrates how these problem areas can be identified with elements of the coach's practice. The role of the coach in these ethical concerns needs to be emphasised. The coach's behaviour will consciously or unconsciously reinforce ethical or unethical practice. This will be achieved by acting as a role model for others, by reinforcing or condoning the behaviour of athletes either tacitly or by verbal feedback, through intentional action, and in more insidious ways through the values climate created by the coach's leadership.

Drewe (2000b) provides a very useful review of the range of issues with which the coach should be concerned. Elements of coaching practice may lead to quite specific concerns. One example is the requirement of athletes to continue to perform when injured (Flint and Weiss 1992; Vergeer and Hogg 1999), or the under-representation of black coaches (Patel 1999). Brackenridge's (2001) excellent work on sexual exploitation points to some specific aspects of practice that have the potential to facilitate harassment or abuse, but can also be the focus of coach education. She highlights the authority/power differential and identifies problematical aspects of performance: the extensive intensity and duration provides opportunity for 'grooming'; the reward environment intensifies the impact of the

The coach's demeanour and behaviour in the coaching role	Determining or condoning performer behaviour
This refers to:	This refers to:
■ Overt behaviour in relation to officials ■ Gender- or race-related language ■ Emotional control over victory and defeat ■ Cheating ■ Appropriateness of training methods ■ Technical demands	■ Encouraging performers to cheat ■ Reinforcing or condoning violent conduct ■ Promoting or condoning performance-enhancing drugs ■ Performer behaviour towards opponents and officials
The coach's interpersonal behaviour with performers	The coach's professional role
This refers to:	This refers to:
■ Sexual harassment and abuse ■ Over-demanding expectations ■ Absence of respect and dignity in behaviour and language ■ Inequitable treatment of performers ■ Confidentiality	■ Relationships with other professionals ■ Life-style advice to performers ■ Autonomy/dependence culture ■ Clarity of intention and purpose ■ Safety and well-being of performers

Note: This list first appeared in Lyle (1998: 147)

Figure 13.2 *Four elements of the coach's practice and associated ethical concerns*

exercise of power; and control of variables can be an excuse to enter 'difficult' areas about the body. There is now a very considerable body of literature on sexual harassment in sport, the greater part of which identifies appropriate and inappropriate coaching practice (Lenskyj 1992; Volkwein *et al.* 1997; Brackenridge 1997, 2001; Nielsen 2001).

CONCEPTUAL FRAMEWORK ISSUES

The early development of the conceptual framework stressed the nature of the coaching process and its essential purposes. This did not include an ethical dimension. This does not mean that the ethical dimension is unimportant. However, it is important to appreciate the purpose of such definitions and conceptual clarity. Just like the adoption of an inappropriate coaching style, the infringement of ethical principles does not negate the purpose of coaching – but it says something about the social and moral probity of those involved.

The last few chapters have stressed the social context within which coaching takes place. The role of the coach has a social dimension: responsibility should be exercised in a number of ways:

■ to others within the coaching contract;
■ to the sport, the organisation, the club and the NGB;
■ to the community.

The implication here is that adherence to a set of sport-related ethical principles is not sufficient. There is a need for proactive and positive practice for the common weal.

There are some moral principles that are unassailable: respect, integrity, equity, fairness. However, the application, interpretation and implementation of these in a set of ethical behaviours have been shown to be context-specific. Once again this highlights the distinctions between participation and performance coaching, with implications for recruitment, initiation, transition and education. The differences should not be exaggerated – abuses of power, seeking unfair advantage, intimidation and cheating are applicable in all contexts.

Leadership or coaching style is closely bound up with the notion of ethical practice, although it should be stressed that the excesses of coaching practice may be evident in all leadership styles. It is more likely that the implications of, for example, an autocratic leadership style or an over-emphasis on a scientific-rational approach for human values will be felt in more subtle ways.

A major issue is that sport is a 'contested activity'. As such, it involves seeking advantage over a competitor and this brings with it secrecy, strategy, active confusion, exploiting weakness, exploiting resources and influencing environmental circumstances. This can (and should) be carried out within a set of consensual ethics. However, there is a danger that the contested nature of performance sport is ignored or that commentators apply ethical standards that are unrealistic, in that they incorporate a developmental aspect, or 'greater good' element, that is at least contestable.

The levels of the coaching process (direct intervention, intervention support, constraints management, strategic co-ordination) can be related to the various types of ethical practice, although research is required to establish the exact pathways and connections. This is demonstrated in Figure 13.3.

Participation coaching is focused on direct intervention and it will be here therefore that ethical issues will arise, such as safety (including organisation and travel) and harassment. Coaches who operate in an instructional capacity may also be subject to scrutiny in the currency and quality of their knowledge and skills. Performance coaching has greater scale, commitment, emotional intensity and, of course, material reward. The intensity of interaction and the external evaluation of status and success provide opportunities for excesses in behaviour. A greater acknowledgement of the distinctions between participation and performance coaching would assist the literature on coaching ethics.

CODES OF ETHICS AND CODES OF CONDUCT

One of the essential characteristics of the professionalisation of an occupation is the availability of a code of ethics and a professional body to regulate the code and impose sanctions. It was noted earlier that, although a code of ethics had been produced by the National Coaching Foundation (NCF 1996), the 'profession' was unregulated and the code had more symbolic and educational than regulatory value. Nevertheless, there are also a number of specific codes.

The NCF Code (1996) identifies a set of principles, divided into those dealing with human rights, interpersonal relationships, commitment/contract, co-operation, integrity,

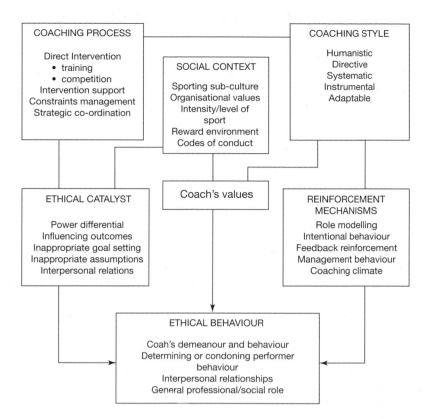

Figure 13.3 *Coaching style and ethical practice*

advertising/proficiency, confidentiality, abuse of privilege, personal standards, safety and competence. Taken together, the principles constitute a wide-ranging guide to ethical practice with which it would be difficult to disagree. Understandably, the principles are expressed in terms of aims and with a level of generality requiring some interpretation for particular instances. These principles are accompanied by an indication of acceptable conduct for members of the National Association of Sports Coaches. This interprets the earlier principles and highlights issues of public criticism of colleagues, misrepresentation, commitment, confidentiality, criminal convictions, disciplinary proceedings, personal misconduct and complaints procedures. These items are expressed as inappropriate behaviour that would constitute a breach of the code.

Clarifying the code of ethics is necessary to demonstrate to the public and to clients what behaviour can be expected of a member of the profession. Inevitably, codes of ethics and conduct tend to be written in a fairly minimalist fashion since they identify threshold criteria and focus on what is not appropriate. They say little, therefore, about the detailed and proactive qualities of good practice and their value, as descriptors of good practice is limited. McNamee (1999) argues that a code of conduct based on adherence to rules is too limiting and there is a need to go beyond rule observance. He argues for virtues-based conduct. Although he accepts that these codes have some value, he points out that they cannot of themselves ensure ethical behaviour. Lyle (1998c) concludes that the current state of professionalisation in the UK (including the failure to license the top coaches) limits the value of any precepts on coaching practice: 'the absence of a trust-based recognition and status for the work of coaches has precluded the implementation of a code of conduct in any meaningful sense' (1998c: 149).

THE LEGAL DIMENSION

Coaching behaviour can, of course, go beyond social and professional acceptability to overstepping legal standards. This area has become a specific field of study in sport (Moore 1997; Gardiner *et al.* 1998; Beloff *et al.* 1999; Grayson 2000). The purpose of this very short section is merely to acknowledge the legal aspect of coaching behaviour and to point to a number of implications for practice. The most important distinction for coaches is that between behaviour from which an athlete suffers a loss and the coach is held negligent in some way and those instances in which the coach breaks the law, such as financial impropriety, sexual harassment, misrepresentation or discriminatory action. Gardiner (1999) summarises the likely concerns for coaches as negligence, statutes, contracts, disciplinary matters, defamation and abuse.

A number of trends in sports and sports coaching have impacted on the potential for legal action:

- Sport has become increasingly commercialised and athletes' earnings (including salaries, prizes, sponsorships and grants) are larger and more identifiable.
- Legislation (in particular, the Children Act 1989) has implications for education and training, in addition to good practice.
- More coaches are employed in performance sport, and employment issues (dismissal, performance evaluation) are likely to become more prevalent.
- A tendency to self-employment/consultancy in the members of the coaching team (including sport scientists) has implications for legal responsibility.
- Single-issue legislation relates, for instance, to the handing and provision of some performance-enhancing drugs.

There are potential legal challenges at all levels of the coaching process:

- *direct intervention*: organisation of the working environment, management of injury, inappropriate interpersonal relationships
- *intervention support*: selection issues, quality of preparation, currency of technical advice
- *constraints management*: contractual issues, financial management, travel arrangements.

Where an incident occurs, negligence by the coach has to be established and a duty of care to the athlete seems obvious. However, coaches should take care to acknowledge the distinction between working for an NGB/club (where a contract is established) and operating as a coach to a self-sustaining 'squad'. In any case, insurance is vital and the value of a professional association is reinforced. Coaches must keep up-to-date with regulations and best practice in their sport. Each of the standard texts makes reference to the coaches' responsibilities (Moore 1997: 64–5; Gardiner *et al.* 1998: 152–8; Beloff *et al.* 1999: 118–19; Grayson 2000: 190–9). This is one of the occasions on which the distinction between teaching and coaching is not useful and direct intervention best practice applies to all such circumstances.

Nevertheless, there are differences between participation coaches and performance coaches. Participation coaching is likely to involve more novice athletes and young children with less defined goals and fewer material rewards. The focus will be on direct intervention. Performance coaches normally place greater demands on athletes but may operate with older and more experienced and skilled athletes. However, the rewards are more tangible and the impact on life-styles will be more significant.

PROFESSIONAL SPORT: A SUITABLE CASE FOR TREATMENT

Professional sport, particularly team sports, provides an exemplar of some of the issues raised throughout the chapter. It is a useful contribution to the discussion on the conceptual framework because it demonstrates the linkages between the coaching process, organisation objectives, sub-cultural expectations and coaching practice. This is a personal analysis and the statements are intended to stimulate debate. They should be considered as assertions to be refuted or confirmed by further research. There are many anecdotal accounts of practice in professional sport: these need more detailed analysis.

Education – professionalisation

Many coaches in professional sport do not have formal coaching qualifications and these are not prerequisites for entry to the profession. Status, credibility and effectiveness are judged by successful experience. The absence of structured career development stages has not assisted the recruitment, transition and professionalisation of coaching. Coaches are recruited almost exclusively from the performer base. High value is placed on lengthy experience, sport-specific skills and technical insight, to the exclusion of other knowledge and skills. There is a marked degree of occupational protectionism.

Role models – professional practice

Coaches in media sport act as role models and typify the profession. This emphasises overt behaviour, with impact on coaching ethics, assumed style and the balance of skills and competence.

Organisational goals – evaluation

Although many coaches may achieve considerable influence and power within their organisation, organisational goal setting is paramount and acts as a template for personal (coach, athlete) goals. Organisation goals are likely to be results-orientated, and this will influence rewards and evaluations of effectiveness and achievement.

Goals – planning, practice

The urgency of goal attainment leads to a short-term approach and is likely to impact on many aspects of the coaching process. Processes such as recruitment, development of young performers, competition preparation and the development of techniques may well be marked by shorter-term horizons, to the detriment of considered and systematic practice.

Goal attainment – ethical practice

The results orientation and the public nature of accountability may lead to an ethical climate in which individual welfare is secondary to organisational need and where it is considered normal to push practice to the limits that the regulations will allow. This is occasioned by the reward environment, unrealistic expectations and an acceptance of a sub-cultural interpretation of sporting ethics. Individuals are generally aware of the ethical practice within which professional sport operates. Coaches are recruited from within the ranks and this helps to perpetuate the sub-cultural values.

Coaching style – environmental constraints

Although a coach–athlete interpersonal contract will be established, the dominant factor may be an employer–employee relationship. Coaching styles are generally 'directive' but the coaching environment may encourage this: team sport scale and interaction of players, turnover of performers, accountability for results, influence of coaches on performers' careers and rewards. Evidence cited previously suggests that performers accede to this style, although they may not have had experience of any other. The humanistic orientation (concern for individuals, personal development, process orientation) is not emphasised. However, this does not mean that individual coaches do not operate without genuine concern for the welfare of performers or in an atmosphere of enjoyment.

Systematic practice – environmental constraints

Anecdotal accounts suggest that the coaching process is often implemented with a less than systematic approach. This may be a result of lack of training for coaches, the complexity of team sports, short-term goal horizons, gradual incorporation of sports science, emphasis on direct intervention. Coaching practice, however, is culture- and sport-specific.

The conceptual framework helped to provide an analytical account of practice that appears to be less than ideal. The practice is evident and the constraints are obvious – the key factors, perhaps, being coach recruitment and training and a short-term outlook in planning. Professional sport is a job for coach and athletes and much of top-class performance sport is also undertaken by individuals on a full-time basis. Care must be taken not to treat sport differently – not that the rules of social engagement do not apply but that participants are not charged with a level of moral responsibility that does not exist elsewhere. The important issue is not that the coaching process model or principles of good practice do not apply but that there is a conceptual framework within which an understanding and account of practice can be fashioned.

SUMMARY

This chapter will have familiarised you with the following:

■ an understanding of ethics and how they influence coaching practice;
■ a range of ethical concerns and how they might be categorised – interpersonal relationships, power differentials, influencing outcomes or performance, social roles and inappropriate goal setting;
■ the characteristics of sport and sports coaching that lead to potential ethical dilemmas;
■ the three principal causes of ethical problems: abuse of power, attempts to influence results and inappropriate assumptions;
■ the relationship between the coach's role and examples of problematic behaviour;
■ conceptual framework issues and understanding ethical practice;
■ codes of conduct;
■ an overview of the legal dimension of coaching practice; and
■ professional sport used as an exemplar of the complex interaction of conceptual issues, coaching process, environmental circumstances, sub-cultural practice and coaching practice.

PROJECTS

Ethical clearance should always be obtained for carrying out research. In this instance, it is likely that many projects will deal with sensitive issues and you should take care to discuss the design of projects with tutors. This may mean limiting the scope of the research until you have further experience. Certainly, you will wish to discuss prior disclosure, confidentiality, the 'rules of engagement' (that is, when to stop), and the prevention of any emotional or psychological discomfort or damage to coaches or athletes.

■ Using the list of concerns in Figure 13.1, create a questionnaire for coaches in which they rate each item. Compare the responses from two groups of coaches – male/female, novice/expert, or from two or more sports.
■ Create a scenario in which a coach faces an ethical dilemma. Present this to a group of coaches and record their responses. Analyse the responses in relation to appropriate/inappropriate coaching behaviour.
■ Use the 'critical incidents' approach to create a bank of short case studies on coaching practice. Appraise these, using a coding framework based on ethical practice.
■ Carry out an in-depth conversation/interview with a coach with whom you are comfortable and familiar. Explore an agreed range of ethical issues. Use the occasion to gain a further and deeper insight into a coach's accommodation with competing values and practice.

> ■ Use a code of ethics/conduct to create a systematic observation instrument. Use this instrument to compare the behaviours of groups – e.g. in dealing with different groups of athletes. (Note the caveat above.)

Reading

General texts such as Morgan and Meier (1995) and McNamee and Parry (1999) give useful accounts of the field, and exemplars of issues can be found in Gardiner *et al*. (1998). Brackenridge's (2001) book is exceptionally detailed and deals directly with coaching practice. There are interesting accounts in Drewe (2000b) and Francis (1990). Students should be familiar with the NCF Code of Conduct (NCF 1996) and McNamee's (1999) critique of such codes.

PART 5
A BASIS FOR PROFESSIONALISATION – THE WAY FORWARD

CHAPTER FOURTEEN

▼ EFFECTIVE COACHING AND THE EFFECTIVE COACH

■ Introduction   251
■ What is Meant by Effectiveness   253
■ Coaching Effectiveness Literature   260
■ Further Conceptual Issues   262
■ Alternative Approaches to Effectiveness   263
■ Commentary   270
■ Summary   272
■ Projects and Reading   272

INTRODUCTION

There are two pivotal statements that characterise the nature of this chapter. First, identifying coaching effectiveness is an important but seemingly intractable problem. The tenor of the arguments presented may seem a little negative, as if there are few answers. Unfortunately, the conclusion may be that the practical solutions available do not match the more impractical answers provided by increased conceptual clarity. Second, this issue is perhaps the best example in this treatment of the coaching process of an absence of adequate conceptual analysis. Swift (2001) offers a reminder that 'conceptual analysis is a fancy name for the job of working out what people mean when they say things' (2001: 42). The literature in this field is a prime example of the failure of authors to help the reader by enumerating the assumptions underlying their concept of coaching and effectiveness. The result is a lack of precision in terminology and approach, and a singular failure to relate effectiveness literature to any conceptual understanding of the coaching process. The purpose of the chapter, therefore, is to offer a conceptual analysis of coaching effectiveness: in other words, what do we mean when we use this term?

Critical Concept

The practical solutions available to assess coaching effectiveness do not match the more impractical answers provided by increased conceptual clarity.

The need to focus on evaluating the effectiveness of the coach and the coaching process seems undeniable.

- The 'contract' between coach and athlete and between coach and employer uses the term 'accountability'. Although establishing exactly what the coach is accountable for remains somewhat problematic, effectiveness is a measure of evaluation of performance that will figure in any account of liability.
- The professionalisation of the occupation of coaching would hardly be able to fulfil its responsibility for the regulation of standards and practice without a consensual understanding of effective practice.
- This is also true of coach education. It can be assumed that the output of coach education is an individual who is effective, and that the outcome is more effective practice. How has this been assessed to date?
- Insofar as effectiveness is an evaluation of the coach and of practice, it could be used to differentiate between coaches for purposes of recruitment, selection and reward. This is likely to lead to a discussion of the terms 'successful' and 'effective'.
- Given the orientation of the book towards establishing a conceptual framework for coaching, it would be strange indeed if the issue of what constitutes an appropriate measure of output/outcome is not debated. One of the rationales for establishing the conceptual framework is the capacity for analysis of practice. Effectiveness is key to this analysis.

To some extent there would be merit in trying not to make this issue more complicated than it need be. If a doctor says, 'Take this and you will get better', or if a lawyer says, 'The law should be interpreted this way, so act accordingly', and in each case the professional is proved to be correct, then effectiveness is being displayed. If a coach says, 'Train this way and you will be a better performer', a similar analogy might apply. However, there are some confounding issues:

1 Once again it has to be remembered that sport performance is a contested arena. The final outcome of performance is contested by others with similar goals.
2 Performance and progress themselves are not easily measured. This is particularly true of team sport performance.
3 The constraints within which the coaching process is operationalised are dynamic and extensive. Furthermore, many of the environmental constraints will not be under the control of the coach.
4 In the (admittedly simplistic) examples given above, there is a notion of threshold achievement. Part of the issue with sports coaching is establishing what the level of performance could or should be.

A BASIS FOR PROFESSIONALISATION

5   Although this analysis is focused on performance coaching with achievemer
     competition sport as a consensual purpose, the coaching process normally has
     of multifaceted goals. This makes goal achievement a difficult issue.

The conceptual framework began with a recognition that the coaching process was complex, and difficult to model and analyse. Although, in the context of environmental constraints, the contested nature of success, and the specific problems of evaluating performance in sport, it is easier to be critical than to provide solutions, it is necessary to move the debate beyond simply understanding why answers cannot be found. Improvements will always be possible in practice, but it can be assumed that some, most or all coaches are currently operating effectively. The practical problem for evaluation is deciding what to measure and how to measure it.

 Question Box

It may be easier to identify the ineffective coach. If competence is assumed, must effectiveness also be assumed? How would you disprove this? Consider this option as you read the chapter.

A useful starting point is to provide a summary guide to the arguments that follow. Effective coaching and successful coaching have been confused in the literature, as has effective coaching and the effective coach. Two approaches predominate: the 'good practice prescription' and the 'components approach'. In the first, 'effectiveness' is a general term for good practice in coaching behaviour; that is, a delivery measure, rather than an output-related measure. This is more likely to be a prescription than a research finding. In the second approach, individual aspects of coaching practice, or sub-processes within the coaching process, are identified and assumed to be either characteristic of or essential for effectiveness. These recommendations may be based on empirical research. Leadership studies are a good example of this, as are feedback practice and instructional behaviours. Overall, there has been a failure to draw specific relationships between behaviour and practice and performance outcomes (or indeed, personal development outcomes). The problem of dealing with the specifics of coaching process environmental constraints, for comparison purposes, has not been resolved.

The emphasis in this chapter is very much on the conceptual analysis of the issues. More detailed accounts of coaching behaviours (the components approach) can be obtained from Douge and Hastie (1993) and Cross (1999).

WHAT IS MEANT BY EFFECTIVENESS?

'Effective' can be defined as 'having the intended effect' – that is, achieving the desired purpose within the resources available. In this case, the purpose implies achieving performance goals within competition sport, and the resources available include the performers' inherent abilities. However, there is a distinction to be drawn between 'effective' and 'effectiveness'. 'Effective', as an adjective, implies 'the quality of a process or product that is generally known to be effective'. This has a certain potential or future aspect to its understanding. This goes some way to explaining the use of behavioural criteria – the components approach – to characterise that which is effective. 'Effectiveness', on the other hand, suggests that a judgement has been made, based on a measurement or assessment of some kind. The distinction here may be partly resolved by the introduction, at a later stage in the chapter, of the difference between capacity and performance when discussing the concept of what is meant by 'effective'.

Having begun with a simple definition, it is necessary to subject this to further analysis, by asking three deceptively simple questions:

1   How does the term 'effective' compare to 'successful' or 'competent' or 'expert'?
2   How easy is it to adopt a simple 'goal-achievement' approach in practice?
3   Are effective coaching and the effective coach essentially the same concept?

Comparison of Terms

Successful versus effective coaching

The term 'successful' is important because this population of coaches is often used as a benchmark group against whom to evaluate the use of particular behaviours (for example, see Claxton 1998; Seagrave and Ciancio 1990). It may also be a more easily measured criterion. Nevertheless, it is understandable that the common features of such practice should be of interest. Success has two connotations:

1   *The achievement of an objective*   This would appear to be the same as effectiveness insofar as it refers to the achievement of an (agreed) goal, whilst subject to the same constraints of definition and circumstance.
2   *Attainment*   Here, success is measured by the achievement of a publicly recognisable accomplishment. This normally implies one that is contested and outside the control of the individuals concerned. In this instance, success would be the same as effectiveness only if measured by publicly acknowledged outcome measures.

Success, therefore, is a mark of prominence achieved, in this instance, by competition success. Note, however, that this need not always imply the winning of competitions. Three corollaries are very important and are expressed in the following Critical Concepts:

 Critical Concept

Coaching success is measured by association with successful performers.

Critical Concept

The nature of the contribution of the coach to the coaching process cannot be inferred from successful coaching. (Consider the relative contributions, in different circumstances, of effective recruitment versus effective competition management, or a coach who 'inherits' a successful team.) However, repeated success may imply effective practice by a coach, particularly if achieved consistently in different sets of circumstances.

 Critical Concept

The sport-specific differences in the coaching process, noted in earlier chapters, may limit the value of using populations of successful coaches, unless these differences in practice are taken into account.

Conceptual analysis requires that a degree of clarity is brought to the terminology used. Thus, successful coaching is likely to have been effective (assuming the goals were accurate) but a lack of certainty about the exact contribution of the elements of the coaching process make it problematical to aver an 'effective coaching process'.

On the other hand, effective coaching may be successful. This is because the term 'effective' takes the contributory circumstances into account. Thus effective coaching is a measure of coaching performance within a given set of circumstances. The resources available to the performer and coach may not allow the achievement of relative success, but that need not imply that the coaching process was not effective. Evaluations of success are based on performance outcomes and do not acknowledge constraints (although, inevitably, it would be natural to comment on the relationship between them). Effective coaching performance takes place within an acknowledged set of constraints and, perhaps more importantly, within a given time, place and organisational setting.

'Competent' versus 'effective'

There are similarities in the use of the terms 'competent' and 'effective', and they may be used interchangeably in some contexts. The description of a process or person as competent is not a mark of high esteem. However, the use of the term to indicate a 'threshold achievement of competence to fulfil a role' may be useful, and this has a strong resonance with the use of 'effective' to imply achievement of the purposes of coaching. 'Competent' is a qualifying descriptor, and implies that the person has the necessary skills and knowledge to carry out the functions required of the role. The term is used within the competence-based education and training movement (Hyland 1994; Bridges 1996), and refers to a minimum level of acceptable performance. Insofar as those who wish to be deemed competent have to demonstrate their performance in the many sub-elements of performance, this mirrors the 'components approach' described earlier, in which the behaviours of successful/expert coaches are identified.

Jones *et al.* (1997) identified US national standards for coaching (similar to the UK's National Occupational Standards), but interestingly point out that there is a dearth of empirical research linking these competencies to coaching effectiveness. It may not be helpful, therefore, to describe coaching as competent. First, it implies as generic descriptor, a capacity, which may be difficult to test in a variety of circumstances. Second, it implies a quality of minimal effectiveness. There is no distinction between more and less competent and more and less effective. On the other hand, the term 'a competent coach' has some useful meaning, if only to signal minimum threshold values of functional competence. The descriptor, however, needs to be delimited by sport and level of performer. Coaches described as competent have a capacity for effective coaching performance if their competences are applied in an appropriate fashion to the environmental circumstances as they apply to that coaching contract.

 Critical Concept

Coaches described as competent have a capacity for effective coaching performance if their competences are applied in an appropriate fashion to the environmental circumstances as they apply to that coaching contract.

'Expert' versus 'effective'

The obvious starting point is that the term 'expert' implies a high level of effectiveness. Experts are so called because their expertise has been measured in some way. This may be in response to particular problems or technical requirements. It not only implies that some functional capacities are carried out well but also that experts have some abilities that novices don't have. In the earlier chapter on decision making, the experts' ability to recognise patterns in the environment and their cognitive organisation for dealing with such problems in an efficient manner was described.

In a seminal text, Glaser and Chi (1988) identify the characteristics of expert behaviour: better domain knowledge, recognition of meaningful patterns in their domains, faster operations, better short- and long-term memory, representation of problems at a more principled level, more time spent on analysing the problem and strong self-motivating qualities. These insights need to be used to a greater extent in distinguishing between novice and expert coaches. Professionals move through stages in development – novice, advanced beginners, competent, proficient and expert (Berliner 1994; Eraut 1994) – and the notion of effectiveness needs to be explored at each stage. Competent, effective coaches will exhibit high levels of processing ability, speedy access to procedural knowledge, use of routines, successful heuristics for unexpected problems – and so on. This must be achieved in an incremental fashion.

A BASIS FOR PROFESSIONALISATION

Otter (1994) sums up the dilemma (with 'coaches' substituted for 'teachers'):

> It is debatable whether newly graduated coaches could achieve competence in higher level occupations through their undergraduate study programmes, even when this includes periods of work placement. Such competence may not be achieved until the individual has demonstrated sufficient of the personal autonomy and responsibility which underpins competence in the professions.
>
> (1994: 4)

This is also a reminder that participation coaches are not novice performance coaches and that the stages of professional development have yet to be satisfactorily articulated.

Experts are also accorded the descriptor through public acclaim. Interestingly, this will involve competition success, but not solely. The expert is likely to have significant experience and 'successful' practice (Dodds 1994; Pieron and Carreiro da Costa 1996).

'Expert' implies that the person is highly effective in achieving a purpose (but note that this is sometimes a specialised function). It is noteworthy that, again, this implies a capacity for performance. The expert has an expertise that will be likely to produce effective coaching in varied circumstances. Indeed, that may be the mark of the expert.

Adopting a 'goal-achievement' approach in practice

The second question raised earlier was whether the simple 'effective means achieving goals' provided a useful analytical tool. As this section demonstrates, the issue may be one of interpreting goal achievement rather than the principle involved. Figure 14.1 summarises the issues involved: some of these are generic in nature and others are derived from the performance sport context.

The conclusion from the arguments summarised in Figure 14.1 is that there are some difficulties in implementing the deceptively simple concept that effective coaching means achieving the goals set by the athlete and coach.

Question Box

Despite what has been said, the effectiveness/goal achievement argument is attractive. The proviso is that the goals are appropriate. However, is there a tendency to think in terms of outcome goals when making this judgement?

It is also true that, although the interests and aspirations of the athlete and coach may be reconciled in the goal-setting process, there is a further set of influential individuals who may have different goals: parents, NGB, owners/employers. Given the conceptual confusion that exists, it is unlikely that they would all agree on definitions of effectiveness, but even the goal achievement measure would be militated against by potential goal conflict.

Issue		Explanation
Appropriateness	Generic	Effective goal setting is required before it can be used to measure effective coaching. The goal-setting process is not easy and reconciling individual athlete, coach and organisational aspirations with the resources available is problematic. Nevertheless, failing to achieve inappropriate goals is not a sound measure of effectiveness (other than in goal setting!)
Variation	Generic	(Output) goals are rarely dependent on one occasion and the goal-setting process will (1) set a range of acceptable achievement, and (2) be dynamic, as the year unfolds. Effective coaching may be tied to goal management more than goal achievement.
Output – outcome	Generic	The literature on goal setting extols the merits of internal/output goals. It would be naïve, however, to imagine that outcome targets are not prevalent in performance sport. There are so many factors outside the control/influence of the coach that the competition results measure is not a good measure of effectiveness (but of success, as discussed earlier in the chapter).
Multiple goals	Generic	Although performance coaching has a clear focus on performance achievement in sport, it is recognised that there is a balance between short-term/long-term goals, individual/team/squad goals, and personal development/performance goals. The context of sport and performance sport in particular is beset by multiple goals. Simple measures of achievement are therefore very difficult.
Causation	Performance	Improvement in performance is the basic performance sport goal. However, young athletes will often improve through maturation. It is not a simple matter to demonstrate stable performance improvement, nor that this resulted from the coaching process.
Threshold	Performance	It is very difficult to establish performance improvement thresholds. The issue of whether improvement could have been greater in other circumstances is difficult to resolve.
Achievability	Performance	There is a balance to be struck between setting targets that are meaningful in terms of challenge and progression and those that are achievable. Achieving 'easy' targets would not be a useful measure of effectiveness.
Measurement	Performance	Some performance component targets will be relatively simple to measure. Others, particularly in team sports will be much more difficult.

Figure 14.1 *Factors involved in the 'effective equals goal-achievement' approach*

Effective coaching and the effective coach – the same concept?

This is the question that has led to the most confusion in the literature, with the terms being used synonymously and with little precision. Setting out some assumptions may help to clarify the issue:

■ The simple presumption that effective coaching (achievement of performance goals) implies an effective coach can only be held for the one instance in which the judgement about the coaching process is made. This is effectiveness by association and nothing can be inferred about the coach's behaviour.

■ The coaching contract between the athletes and the coach (and the organisation) is the basis for the evaluation of effectiveness and is bounded by a specific set of parameters. Therefore, *effective coaching performance (evidenced in the achievements of the goal-directed coaching process) is bounded by time and place, and the constraints applying to that process*. It is assumed that the coach acted effectively – that is, *the accumulation of coaching behaviours produced the desired effect*.

■ To describe a coach as effective *implies a personal capacity or stable quality of performance*. This capacity will be demonstrated in a wide variety of circumstances. Such a judgement would need extended time and experience of practice to evaluate and may not therefore be easily demonstrated by the novice coach. It would also seem likely that the effectiveness would be specific to performance sport and any projection across other forms of sport or levels of performer would be problematical.

 Critical Concept

Effective coaching performance (evidenced in the achievements of the goal-directed coaching process) is bounded by time and place, and the constraints applying to that process. It is assumed that the coach acts effectively, that is, the accumulation of coaching behaviours produces the desired effect.

The position to be adopted, therefore, is that

1 coaching effectiveness is judged by evaluating instances of specific coaching performance;
2 the effective coach is one whose capacity for coaching effectiveness has been evaluated over time and circumstance;
3 the effective coach is almost certainly competent, will acquire and display expertise and may in time be termed an expert, and, in the appropriate circumstances, may be successful.

The apparent certainty in this summary continues to mask some important questions. Is there any evidence that coaches are effective in all aspects of the coaching process? This raises further issues. Which of the components of the coaching process or coaching behaviour are decisive/discriminatory in performance outputs or outcome? Is there a hierarchy of elements? Strategic co-ordination, decision making, technical knowledge, management of preparation or management of competition would all some claim to be priorities. Is effectiveness shared across the support team? How is 'priority effectiveness' incorporated into coach education? Before attempting to provide some further contributions to the debate, it is necessary to review the findings from the literature and to address some additional conceptual issues.

COACHING EFFECTIVENESS LITERATURE

The literature is characterised by a number of different approaches. The two most useful and relevant sources are Douge and Hastie (1993) and Cross (1999). Abraham and Collins (1998) also provide an overview of the literature. Each of the former provides an overview of the field, reviews the literature and deals with some of the conceptual issues. The remainder of the sources fall into one of two camps: the first involves identification of appropriate behaviours, and the second is an experimental approach. In the first, coaching effectiveness is used synonymously with 'good practice' and the intention is to describe 'appropriate behaviour' (Douge 1987; Howe 1990; Crisfield *et al.* 1996; Jones *et al.* 1997). In these sources the term 'effective coaching' is assumed rather than defined. In the second approach, coaching effectiveness is one of the variables in research into coaching practice. Given the problems of measurement alluded to throughout the chapter, it is not surprising that coaching effectiveness is evaluated largely by athlete opinion (for example, Laughlin and Laughlin 1994; Cross 1995b).

Douge and Hastie (1993) used developments in coach education as a starting point for reviewing evidence in leadership style, personal development, behavioural observation research, athlete opinion analysis and context-specific practice. The paper is valuable for a summary of sources but does not adopt a critical approach, does not deal with the concept of effectiveness and, as with much of the literature, treats the coaching process as unproblematic. Cross (1999) deals with the concept of effectiveness and reviews a number of potential measures. Particular attention is paid to the notion of 'value-added' as a criterion of effectiveness. Cross deals at some length with the components approach and identifies coaching behaviour that is thought to lead to effective practice, including style/philosophy. However, the question is posed as to whether component behaviour recommendations will be effective in all situations. He also acknowledges the variety of stakeholders likely to have views or an interest in effectiveness. He recognises the problems involved: 'It is extremely difficult to construct an all-embracing definition of coaching effectiveness that satisfies all coaching situations' (1999: 61).

There is a further body of literature that has been concerned with the identification of criteria to represent the coaching process in order to measure performance in an organisational setting (Maclean and Zakrajsek 1996). Naturally, these papers tend to focus on organisational and administrative aspects (Barber and Eckrich 1998). The same conceptual difficulties apply to this field as they do to others. Nevertheless, there are some interesting papers. Maclean and Chelladurai (1995) make a useful distinction between product and process criteria.

The literature on effectiveness demonstrates a number of features that are concept-related:

1   Effectiveness is most often equated with 'good practice' (closer to 'developed compe-
    tence' rather than success), but (a) the context is rarely made specific, and (b) the
    link between the practice and output is assumed rather than measured.
2   Effective coaching was generally measured as athlete response to a battery of coach
    or coaching process characteristics. Given that the athletes' perceptions were involved,
    the focus was not unnaturally on direct intervention behaviours.
3   The emphasis on client satisfaction with coaching practice has to be recognised as
    but one measure of effectiveness. More valuable would be the follow-up question of
    why the athletes were satisfied – consonant style, comfort, goal-attainment, success
    etc.
4   Complementing the comments made earlier in the chapter, there are few, if any,
    attempts to use output or outcome measures as a criterion for coaching effectiveness.
    (One of the reasons for this in research is the use of non-performance sport sample
    groups, for whom performance goals would be less likely to be available.)
5   The confusing mix of performance/participation coaches results in the motives or
    goals being similarly confused. There is an assumption that skills teaching, personal
    development and competition advantage are part of the mix, but the balance of
    priorities is rarely identified.
6   Empirical investigation is characterised by the components approach. Coaching
    performance in a particular behaviour would be compared to athlete satisfaction or
    differentiated by 'winning' versus non-winning coaching records (Lacy and Darst
    1985; Claxton and Lacy 1986). There is no attempt to reconcile the behaviour under
    investigation against the potential contribution of other factors.
7   There is a clear emphasis on the teaching/episodic paradigm in research (Lyle 1998a).
    There are a number of reasons for this: the use of systematic observation instruments,
    the use of North American high-school/collegiate samples, the participation coaching
    emphasis, the borrowing of hypotheses from education practice and a focus on the
    direct intervention role. The relevance of direct intervention studies of this kind is not
    in doubt but the weight to be given to this aspect of the role for performance coaches
    has not been established in all sports or against other performance-related coaching
    practice.

The research itself has a number of characteristics. First, the quantitative positivistic
paradigm in evidence is suited to a reduction of the coaching process to measurable
elements; second, its survey instrument approach inevitably loses the richness of individual
practice; and third, it fails to analyse (rather than describe) the practice of peer-acclaimed
coaches. The absence of a conceptual framework within which to situate effectiveness
studies has contributed to the fact that these studies have not accumulated into a body of
knowledge that has significantly influenced practice. It ought to be said that the problems
inherent in measuring performance gains and achievement without incorporating the
constraints applying to individual coaching processes is a very significant limitation.

Question Box

One of the problems in using goals is that they are dynamic and constantly adjusted. They are achieved over an extended period and accommodation is made to the emerging circumstances (including results) applying to the athletes. There is a tendency, therefore, to always achieve goals! How can this be resolved for research?

FURTHER CONCEPTUAL ISSUES

Before examining some possible ways forward, there are some further conceptual matters that need to be resolved. Each of these is introduced by a question.

1   *Is there any evidence on the practice/behaviour that discriminates between effective and ineffective coaching?* There is no evidence on the elements of coaching practice that are the most important, other than opinion. There is no easy way of corroborating that the characteristics of, for example, successful coaches have been appropriately catalogued and that the characteristics identified were those that contributed most. Perhaps the answer is that the 'shot-gun' approach to good practice (that is, identifying all of the components of good practice) is useful for establishing a state of 'not being ineffective'. In the language used earlier, a capacity for effectiveness has been established, but the performance still has to be implemented and evaluated within the constraints of that process. Performance coaching, paradoxically, may allow coaches to have a range of strengths and weaknesses (given the athletes' development and the contribution of coaching teams).

2   *What will be guaranteed to produce competition performance improvement in given circumstances?* There is no obvious research answer. The survey approach to this issue is perhaps not the most appropriate and more qualitative, case-study approaches are required to establish good practice in given circumstances. It seems likely that performance will improve for most athletes with relevant preparation: the issues are by how much, in what context, and at the right time. This raises the concept of 'adaptability', which is used by some authors as a key criterion (e.g. Woodman 1993). Effectiveness is the extent to which the coach can adapt proven (!) methods to the athlete and the circumstances. This is discussed in the 'competence approach' later in the chapter.

3   *Will there be differences in assessing effectiveness in participation and performance coaching?* The general development of the conceptual framework will have pointed to the obvious differences between the episodic participation approach and the much more complicated multivariable performance sport context. The effective delivery of a session (Thorpe 1987) is different in kind from the management of the interacting variables over an extended period and towards performance sport goals. Nevertheless, effective delivery of the programme will be important for all coaches.

4   *Can every coach be effective?* This is a good question! There is no reason why all coaches should not have the capacity to be effective; that is, to work with performers

A BASIS FOR PROFESSIONALISATION

to reach their intended results (although clearly not all performers can be successful in terms of public measure of success). However, is it reasonable to expect coaches always to produce effective coaching performance? There may be a number of contributory factors, for and against:

- The duration of the coaching process allows time for reflection, adaptation and change.
- Goals are generally adopted that are on the optimistic limit of the range likely, and orientated to competition outcomes. Performance achievement in the lower range of possibilities does not imply ineffectiveness, but it does suggest that there is a challenge to achieving goals and that effectiveness cannot be assumed.
- Presumably there is an element of diligence, application and decision making involved in coaching practice (in areas such as goal setting, programme design, competition management and programme management) and the contextual element of this makes this problematical. This is another way of saying that coaches may not apply themselves equally diligently on all occasions.
- Coaches recognise the constraints within which they operate (Cross 1995b) and are able to articulate these. It is likely that coaches are effective because they adapt to the constraints.

5 *Is it easier to be effective in specific sports?* This is also a very interesting question. There is no doubt that the sophistication and scale of some sports (the so-called 'minor' sports) have less intensive competition and attract a smaller proportion of able athletes because of the smaller reward environment. It could be argued therefore that success is easier to achieve. A further argument is that effectiveness may be more difficult to achieve in sports with a tradition of intensive commitment and keen competition, recruitment and technical development. Team sports present challenges to effectiveness because of the multiple goals, very diverse performance components, individualisation and additional organisational complexities. However, these very difficulties may reduce expectations of effective practice.

ALTERNATIVE APPROACHES TO EFFECTIVENESS

The terms 'coaching effectiveness' and 'effective coaching' have lacked conceptual clarity. The most common approaches to measuring effectiveness have been to infer effective practice either from competence in one or more of the components of the coaching process, from goal achievement or from athlete success. A useful differentiation is between effectiveness as an individual's capacity and effective coaching performance, which is bounded by a particular time and process. This section identifies a number of further approaches, which complement those mentioned above:

- process competence
- coaching method
- input constraints
- value added
- data-led goal setting
- success
- strategic effectiveness.

Process Competence

The basic unit of the competence-based education and training movement is the vocational 'competency'; that is, a tightly defined ability to perform a task (Fletcher 1992). However, the application of this approach to professions has widened the conceptual debate and the notion of a broader competence has developed (Hodkinson 1995; Bridges 1996). Chappell and Hager (1994) argue that there is a specialised body of knowledge underpinning a profession but that 'application of specialist knowledge and cognitive skills within practice-based contexts . . . leads to competent performance' (1994: 13). This integrated or holistic model of competence stresses the 'complex structuring of attributes needed for intelligent performance in specific situations [which] incorporates the idea of professional judgement' (Hager and Gonczi 1996: 249).

For this purpose, therefore, generic groups of skills in specific occupational contexts have to be identified (demonstrating the value of the conceptual framework). There is a process orientation to this approach – the capacity of the coach, measured by performance *in situ*, to carry out sub-processes of the coaching process forms the basis of the judgement of effectiveness.

Figure 14.2 elaborates on a starting point for the identification of sub-processes by using the levels of functional roles within the coaching process. These sub-processes have been discussed a number of times throughout the book. The competences and sub-processes identified in Figure 14.2 could form the basis of an approach based on professional

Role 'level' descriptor	Competence	Sub-processes (examples)
Direct intervention	Training management	Programme design; session management; organisation; administration; managing exercise loadings; implementing drills/exercises.
	Competition management	Competition preparation; contest management; selection; recording
Intervention support	Planning	Training programme; competition programme; individual programmes
	Recording	Maintaining database; communication
	Personnel management	Managing support team
	Athlete support	Counselling; development programme; goal setting; adherence management
Constraints management	Human resources	Recruitment; 'contracts'; development planning
	Material resources	Facility planning; financial management; equipment management
	Extended role	Organisation liaison; NGB liaison; personal education and development; promotion
Strategic co-ordination	Strategic planning	Goal setting; integrated planning; prioritising; review and audit
	Contingency management	Contingency management; implementing change

Figure 14.2 *Potential coaching process competences*

A BASIS FOR PROFESSIONALISATION

competence to coach education. It is inevitable that those skills considered to be key would figure significantly in the list of competences in Figure 14.2. Planning, monitoring and regulating the coaching process will be central, as will the decision making associated with these process skills.

To some extent, these competences may seem rather too generic, but that is one of the benefits of this approach. Basic principles of good practice are established in each area, including the use of appropriate skills and knowledge. The effectiveness is demonstrated by the use and *application* of these principles, but the application and output are evaluated against the constraints relevant to the process. There are a number of potential advantages to this approach:

- The dynamic nature of the coaching process is captured in the element of adaptation.
- It is possible to balance the weighting of sub-processes across sports.
- This approach acknowledges that effectiveness goes beyond observable measures.
- It may be possible to evaluate the impact of sub-processes on the performance. This would contribute greatly to the issue of the coach's contribution to performance.

Coaching Method

The issue is whether one 'method' of coaching is better than any other, although, of course, many different methods could be effective! However, it has to be established, first, that 'method' exists. Certainly, it is used in the literature: Cross (1999: 51) says, 'It is almost certain that there is no one 'best' method of coaching'. Although the term is used somewhat imprecisely, method should not be thought of as a 'style' issue but as a more general set of practice recipes that the coach applies to the varying circumstances at hand. It is this element of application that provides some potential for evaluating effectiveness.

Accepting that there will be different sets of recipes for practice, the question is whether (1) these conform to established principles of good practice, and (2) whether the coach has applied the recipes appropriately. If so, this will obviate the dangers of lack of individualisation and 'fitting the performers to the method'. In the sense that effective coaches have demonstrated their effectiveness over time, it is likely that they will have developed a professional practice that is both efficient and effective. This was described earlier in the development of the conceptual framework as *routinised and recipe-based*. Method, then, is a set of preferred routines and recipes that have been 'proved to work' in varying circumstances.

 Critical Concept

In the sense that effective coaches have demonstrated their effectiveness over time, it is likely that they will have developed a professional practice that is both efficient and effective. Method, then, is a set of preferred routines and recipes that have been 'proved to work' in varying circumstances.

There is no general evidence that any 'holistic method' is best, but this raises the issue of best for achieving which goals, for whom, and in which circumstances. It seems likely that some recipes can be shown to be effective (particularly in sport-specific contexts), and that the competence approach described above can be incorporated into evaluation of 'method'. The effectiveness measure is the adaptability of the coach's practice and this has some potential for further development.

Input Constraints

It has become obvious that one of the key issues is the coach's ability to operate within the constraints that apply to a particular coaching programme. There is a general view that success is dependent on constraints (including athlete ability) but that effectiveness, including appropriate goal setting, need not be. Judgements of effectiveness cannot be constraint-free if adaptation and application are two of the principles employed. Coaching performance has to be understood within boundaries of time, place and situation. Nevertheless, taking constraints into account when evaluating practice is a difficult task.

The argument can be better understood if the coaching process is considered as an input–treatment–output system. The output (performance) is dependent on the treatment (the intervention of the coach), which is determined by the inputs available for the process (Lyle 1997b). If the treatment stage is thought of as the active implementation of the coaching process, there is an obvious need to acknowledge and appreciate the resources and other inputs available. Effective coaching is the appropriate adaptation of the coaching process to these circumstances.

The apparent simplicity of this approach masks the difficulties involved:

1   balancing the impact of the various constraints;
2   evaluating the ability/potential of the athletes concerned;
3   the coach's capacity for effective practice is one of the constraints;
4   lack of knowledge of how constraints impact on coaching; and
5   the dynamic nature of the environment.

Although it makes sense to include this element of effective behaviour as a criterion of effectiveness, much work needs to be done to make this a practical proposition, and it may be that it is a more useful evaluation tool for evaluating success. A greater number of analytical case studies and the establishing of expectations of progression in varying circumstances would help this process.

The following list of constraints has been developed from an article that examined the possibility of comparing coaching practices (Lyle 1993). It is by no means exhaustive but it is intended to demonstrate the range of environmental constraints. The emphasis is on environmental constraints rather than qualitative judgements about the athletes or the coaching team.

A BASIS FOR PROFESSIONALISATION

Access to sports medicine services
Administration requirements
Athlete life-style support
Availability of managerial support
Athlete commitment and adherence to the
    programme
Club/squad structures
Coaches Association and peer support
Coaching team scale and quality
Comparative international ranking of the
    sport
Competition programme intensity
Domestic competition programme
Employer/institutional support

Equipment specifications
Financial resources
NGB support
Overseas competition and training
    programme
Recruitment and development strategy
Reward environment
Scale of the training programme
Sports science programme
Team sport organisation and player
    availability
Technical resources
Training facility access

Question Box

One of the lessons to be learned from the list of constraints is the degree to which contributory factors may well be beyond the control of the coach. How does this impact on accountability, or measures of success?

Value Added

The notion of value added as a measure of effectiveness is based on the premise that the coach's contribution can be conceptualised as the difference between the athlete/team's current status and their eventual goal achievement. In other words, incremental improvement in goal attainment is attributed to the coach's intervention. Coaching performance would be measured by improvement, and in performance sport that would normally be a comparative measure of the athlete's performance in competition. Value added might apply equally well to measures of effectiveness or success.

Effectiveness could be conceptualised as 'progress within the limits of acceptable improvement' (see Figure 14.3). Exceptional progress (under or over) would lead to a re-evaluation of goals. Although not yet a practical proposition, the value-added concept is closer to an outcome-related measure and has potential for measuring coach accountability.

Again there is an apparent simplicity to the idea but a multitude of problems in implementation:

■   The improvement ought to be evaluated against athlete potential, goal expectations or established norms (incremental improvements established through longitudinal studies, accounting for maturation).

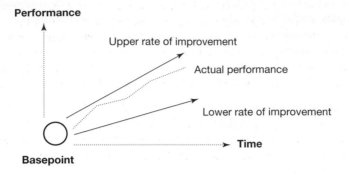

Figure 14.3 *Simplistic representation of the evaluation of value added*

- The athlete performance itself needs to be susceptible to measurement. Although component improvement can be used, performance in interactive team sports is difficult to measure.
- Either it is accepted that the coach is responsible for facilitating the coaching process in its entirety or other confounding factors would have to be acknowledged: major impacts by training intensity changes or the availability of equipment.
- This approach would not remove the need to take constraints into account.
- One simple measure of performance is unlikely to be helpful for process monitoring purposes and several calculations might be needed for performance components. Coach accountability would be likely to be evaluated on comparative competition performance.

Once again, this is an approach with some potential but it is far from ready for immediate implementation. This measure of effectiveness might be more appropriate for younger, developing athletes in whom performance improvement increments are sizeable. It may be less appropriate for more mature athletes and in the context of multiple goals.

Data-led Goal Setting

This short section points to the need for data-led goal setting. Although the need for goal setting is understood by coaches, the setting and recording of goals is not always precise (Lyle 1992). The setting of targets and the distinctions between outcomes and outputs is apparently recognised, but coaches still report that they measure progress by results (Lyle 1992; Cross 1995a, 1995b). This is significant in the light of the emphasis placed on goal achievement in a number of potential effectiveness measures.

In the context of performance sport, goals will usually be athlete performance-related, but some key questions would prove difficult for many coaches to answer:

1   Is there sufficient use of match statistics and statistical analysis to demonstrate improvement in team sport performance components?
2   Are performance targets, in training and competition, based on component statistics?
3   Have sports established incremental improvement norms for various groups of performers, particularly age-groupers and developing athletes?

A BASIS FOR PROFESSIONALISATION

4   Have sports established incremental improvement norms for performance compo-
     nents? (What percentage improvement can be expected in one year?)
5   Is there sufficient understanding of the relative contributions of hereditary factors
     (physical, psychological) and environmental factors to performance?
6   Has there been any attempt to quantify the contribution of the coach's contest
     management to the performance of a team/athlete? How is this contribution assessed?

The coach's ability to answer such questions has suffered from the absence of coaching
process-related research, particularly in performance sport. The coach will therefore resort
to experience and idiosyncratic mental models of performance and improvement. These
may be effective implementation tools but they will not assist more public and auditable
effectiveness measures.

Question Box

Coaching practice is centred on ambitious outcomes and realistic intermediate targets.
These are amended as the planning period progresses. The 'moving' nature of the goals
is contributed to by not being data-based. Is this an accurate analysis?

Success

This section acknowledges that in a practical and realistic sense effectiveness cannot be
entirely divorced from results or success. Goals are often outcome-based, albeit accompanied by output performance goals related to outcome aspirations. In a sense, they are
achievement motivations rather than expectation thresholds. Also, it was noted earlier
that success could be argued to imply at least some measure of effectiveness. There are
two further considerations:

1   Anecdotal evidence from professional sport and the North American literature
     suggests that selection for coaching positions is based on proven results/success. Cross
     (1999) cites the example of appointments to swimming teams of coaches associated
     with the successful performers.
2   The professionalisation of the occupation of sports coaching has not reached a
     point at which levels/stages/competences have been established for career positions.
     There is a vacuum in establishing mechanisms for marking career progression through
     expertise. This vacuum is filled, therefore, by observable measures of success.

It is perhaps true to say that subjective evaluations of coaching success by association
with successful athletes/teams will attempt to apply some criteria – such as success
over time, the constraints applying, evidence of consistency and so on. The substitution
of success for effectiveness is perhaps not an over-concern for results but the absence of
alternatives. There needs to be a much more sophisticated understanding of the relationship between athlete success and coaching practice to inform the debate about
effectiveness.

Strategic effectiveness

This section introduces some ideas that are related more to strategic progress as a measure of effectiveness. The basic notion is that measures of effectiveness have to be evaluated against longer-term objectives not only for the coach and athlete, but also for the organisations within which the individuals operate.

Cost-effectiveness

The coaching process will involve a calculable amount of resources – time, finance, organisational 'space', places in squads and so forth. It would be (at least theoretically) possible to make a judgement about whether the results obtained match the resources expended. This is the basis of the accountability built in to National Lottery funding in the UK. Although not a direct measure of coaching effectiveness, cost-effectiveness highlights the context within which evaluations of coach-related achievement may be carried out. In an interesting paper, Dawson et al. (2000) used player transfer values to estimate the effectiveness of soccer managers/coaches. However, success and effectiveness were confused, and the nature of the coaching input was problematical.

Effect-size

This is a concept used in statistical comparisons of experimental results and is very similar, in principle, to cost-effectiveness. A judgement is made as to whether the improvement obtained is 'worth the effort'. It is unlikely that this could be a statistical judgement, but for mature athletes there may come a point at which a decision is made that the improvements in performance (and the outcome consequences) do not justify continued involvement in the programme. (In the initial stages this may result only in a re-balancing of component emphasis – less physical, more tactical.)

Organisational strategy

The coaching contract may be part of an organisational programme – club or Governing Body, for example. These organisations will have strategic, long-term objectives, which are, of course, subject to change. Organisations will make decisions about whether their resources are being expended in ways that lead to achieving their objectives. Again, this is not a direct measure of coaching effectiveness, but the results may be measured against organisational objectives (preparation of teams for championships, development objectives) rather than individual goals.

COMMENTARY

This chapter has served two purposes: first, to increase an awareness and understanding of effectiveness in coaching and, second, to demonstrate the importance of conceptual clarity in understanding such issues. Unfortunately, the practical realisation of potential effectiveness mechanisms has not matched their theoretical potential.

The definition offered by Lyle (1998c) remains pertinent, but converting this to a usable indicator of professional performance is far from solved:

Effective coaching performance is a measure of output over input and can only be understood in relation to external factors: for example, material context, goals and performer capabilities. Like successful coaching performance, it is bounded by time and circumstances. The effective coach is one whose capacity for effective coaching performance has been demonstrated over time and circumstance.

(1998c: 172)

A number of additional factors continue to cloud the issue. The time-span over which effectiveness can be demonstrated is unusually long. The realisation of output or outcome goals may take a number of years – even short-term component gains are not immediate. The implications from this are that (1) the judgement of effectiveness is not immediate; (2) there is opportunity to amend goals through process monitoring; and (3) time allows for expectations to be accommodated to the unfolding achievement. Second, the distinction between capacity and performance is very important for the analysis of coaching performance. Measuring the coach's capacity by sub-processes or generic delivery methods does mean that effective coaching performance can be assumed. A minimum 'competence' to fulfil the coaching role is not sufficient guidance for the analysis of coaching practice.

The emphasis in this chapter has been on coaching effectiveness being measured by athlete attainment, whether by results or intermediate targets and goals. One further process competence which has received relatively little attention is the coach's contest management. In this situation, the coach's performance may directly influence the outcome of the contest (the image here is of the basketball or volleyball coach whose contest manipulations have a very direct bearing on the flow of the contest).

The conceptual framework has made much of the dynamic, complex nature of the coaching process, with multiple goals and a contested arena. Perhaps the key factor, therefore, in coaching effectiveness must involve *adaptation* of generic process competences and *application* of principles of good practice/sub-discipline knowledge to goal attainment in the context of environmental conditions. The components approach is valuable for establishing good practice. Unfortunately, the failure to demonstrate that these components are causal in terms of output limits their use in effectiveness studies.

The difficulty in resolving the problems of measurement means that the achievement of results in performance sport is an undeniably important evaluation mechanism. This is not merely filling the vacuum created by these practical difficulties but also constitutes recognition that performance outcomes are the goal for many in performance sport. The academic advisers on goal setting remind us that outcome measures are poor motivators because they are extrinsic and uncontrollable. Nevertheless, the coach's accountability and the need for outcome moderation in planning may force the coach to mitigate the disadvantages through realism, contingency and contextualisation.

SUMMARY

This chapter will have familiarised you with the following:

- the importance of the measurement of effectiveness to the business of sports coaching;
- the range of confounding variables that problematise the concept and its potential realisation and implementation;
- definitions of 'effective' and 'effectiveness', and distinctions between 'successful', 'effective', 'competent' and 'expert' practice;
- the difficulties in adopting a 'goal-realisation' approach;
- effectiveness as performance and effectiveness as a capacity;
- a summary of the coaching effectiveness literature, stressing the sub-components research approach and the good practice prescription approach;
- responses to a number of key conceptual questions;
- detailed exploration of a number of alternative approaches: process competences, coaching method, input constraints, value added, data-led goal setting, success and strategic effectiveness.

PROJECTS

There is an enormous range of potential projects because of the number of possible measures of effective practice. There are also some difficulties, one of which is the period of time over which effectiveness would be evaluated. Safe projects could repeat some of the research papers, for example, asking performers for their opinions on effectiveness or comparing a coach's practice in two contexts. The examples given are more challenging:

- Carry out a Delphi technique (constant refinement by experts) procedure to identify the components of professional competence (Figure 14. 2) and compare these to National Occupational Standards.
- Interview two or three coaches in depth. Focus on internal and environmental constraints and try to explore the distinctions between capacity and performance, using the coaches' experiences.
- Engage with a team/squad over a 'season'. Chart goal-setting amendments by periodic exercises to identify goals. Establish any changes in goals and try to relate these to progress in targets and outcomes.
- Select one of the sub-processes of the coaching process and establish criteria for describing practice. Identify six coaches and record the coaches' practice in that component (questionnaire or observation). Try to match the coaches' behaviour to a matrix of environmental factors.

Reading

A review of literature can be found in Douge and Hastie (1993). A comprehensive treatment of the concepts and issues is contained in Cross (1999). Eraut (1994) is a useful source for concepts related to expertise and professional development.

CHAPTER FIFTEEN

▼ **COACH EDUCATION AND COACHING PRACTICE**

■ Introduction 274
■ Education and Training 275
■ Historical Development 277
■ Conceptual Lessons 279
■ Coach Learning and Coaching Practice 281
■ Principles of Coach Education and Training 282
■ Delivery Issues 285
■ Reflective Practice 288
■ Summary 289
■ Projects and Reading 290

INTRODUCTION

The purpose of this chapter is to examine the potential impact of the conceptual framework on coach education. It is less about the nuts and bolts of coach education programmes and more about how the principles on which coach education and training are based need to be informed by a conceptual understanding of the coaching process. Three issues related to the professionalisation of sports coaching are particularly influenced by a developed appreciation of the coaching process: evaluation/effectiveness, education and research. It is no coincidence that these form the substance of the final three chapters of the book.

Most chapters have begun with a rationale that has included a need for greater conceptual clarity in order to inform education and training. The overall argument is a simple one: coach education should be based on a clear set of intentions about what the trainees/ learners are expected to achieve. Any prescription for education and training will be centred on producing effective practice, and to establish this requires that the analytical framework be developed throughout the book. A judicious blend of models *for* sports coaching (to provide a template for education) and models *of* coaching (to understand the implementation of the template) is required by coach educators.

A number of examples will serve as reminders of the elements of the conceptual framework that are likely to have an impact on coach education: the process nature of coaching, the need for procedural and propositional knowledge, the distinction between participation in performance coaching, decision making and cognitive models as mechanisms for professional practice, and the regulation of activity through thresholds and contingency planning. This is not a 'how to' chapter on coach education and training: the purpose is to provide a critical conceptual analysis of coach education.

EDUCATION AND TRAINING

Education and training (in the context of a specialised field such as sports coaching) serve the function of preparing individuals for occupational practice. However, the range of purposes stretches from specialist technical skills to personal development and social-isation into the field of practice. The socialisation element also includes values and ethical practice. There are, therefore, a number of both formal and informal processes that characterise this preparation. These can be summarised as follows:

1   teaching and learning of specialised knowledge, values and understanding that underpin the activity;
2   training and practice in the skills-based implementation of practice;
3   initiation/induction into the social and professional mores of the occupation.

The importance of education and training cannot be overstated. For any occupation, the quality of future practice is a central concern and, to some extent, shapes the development and success of the profession. In an earlier chapter, issues of professional status rested on the nature of formal qualifications and the extent to which these were regulated. Educational programmes serve as quality assurance mechanisms by regulating recruitment and by standardising delivery and expectations. The accreditation and 'kitemarking' of educational courses, and the licensing of practitioners through these courses, is an indicator of professional development. The consultation document 'The Development of Coaching in the United Kingdom' (UK Sports Council 1999) perceived there to be changes in the environment for sports coaching in demand, opportunity and expectations. In response to this, the document notes the implications for coach education:

> They have brought increased pressure on . . . coaches to become trained and qualified. The coach education and training that has been available has therefore had to move towards a position where it serves the needs of employment and the responsibility (legal, service standards, safety) that goes with that position.
>
> (1999: 3)

Certification, therefore, is important to a profession. Individuals progress through structured and standardised levels of award that are related to occupational requirements. (Certification of coaches is not universal, however. In a regional survey (Centre for Leisure Research 1992), 27 per cent of practising coaches did not have NGB awards.) For the most part, certification acts as a gatekeeper to the profession and ensures, therefore, that the competence of the practitioner can be assured. Indeed, the absence of certification in recruitment to some professional sports, and the consequent lack of quality assurance, is a difficult issue for the sports coaching profession. However, education and training depends on a mix of formal and informal provision, and understanding how learning and preparation is taking place is important in analysing practice. Provision of coach education will have a range of activities from award courses and programmes of seminars, workshops and conferences to publications, visiting and mentor coaches, and a variety of structured forms of experience.

It is important to acknowledge that these more informal aspects of provision are not merely intended to be opportunities for enhancing the formal certification process. These activities both complement the formal programme and constitute an essential element of the coaches' education and training. Experience plays a central role in the implementation, initiation and induction processes described earlier. The preparation of the practitioner cannot be left to experience alone. Even without formal training provision, novices have a structured initiation into an occupation (Lave and Wenger 1991). Education accelerates the learning that takes place from experience and helps to differentiate between good and bad experience (although learning takes place from both). Experience may be rather narrowly focused and may not, of itself, provide the necessary preparation for adaptation and mobility within the occupation.

 Critical Concept

Education accelerates the learning that takes place from experience and helps to differentiate between good and bad experience (although learning takes place from both). Experience may be rather narrowly focused and may not, of itself, provide the necessary preparation for adaptation and mobility within an occupation.

The operationalisation of educational provision provides an enormous range of implementation issues: content, assessment, training of educators, the delivery system, levels of award, genericism versus specialisation, training 'on the job' versus courses, and so on. One particular issue is the distinction between education and training. Dearden (1984) suggests that training is narrower, more structured and more directly related to vocations. Anything with 'educational value' will contribute to the development of knowledge and understanding; examples might be: enhanced personal skills, a capacity for critical analysis and reflection, decision making and problem solving, appreciation of values and ethics, and flexibility/adaptability. Obviously, educational outcomes are to be valued, particularly for future practice and the development of individual capacities, but there must also be a balance between vocational skills training sufficient to fulfil the role functions and vocational/professional education.

 Question Box

There is no doubt that, traditionally, coach education has emphasised the training and technical elements. Has the absence of an 'educational' element been a contributory factor to the slow development of the profession?

A BASIS FOR PROFESSIONALISATION

HISTORICAL DEVELOPMENT

Coaching award programmes have been a significant part of National Governing Body (NGB) interests since their inception in the pre- and post-war period. These early structures were designed largely as teaching awards and as recruitment mechanisms. However, by the seventies and eighties, the great majority of NGBs had fairly comprehensive programmes, albeit (as this section will demonstrate) with some significant limitations. The demands of the awards were minimalistic in comparison to the career-guaranteed higher education training characteristic of Eastern-bloc and North American 'systems'. Campbell (1993) and Sutcliffe (1995) describe coach education programmes around the world. However, such accounts are symptomatic of the attention given to structures and content, rather than critical accounts of preparation for practice.

In the late 1970s and early 1980s, attention became focused on the delivery system in the UK in response to the acknowledged diversity in provision and the development of national systems in Canada and Australia. These systems had accredited levels of award across sports and a core of 'common theory' modules. This was the catalyst for the establishment by the National Coaching Foundation of a wide range of modules and materials at introductory, key course and advanced levels to support sport-specific NGB award schemes.

 Question Box

It might be argued that specific sports are merely the context for a generic coaching capacity and that, therefore, the focus should be on the common education and training elements. Is this too simplistic an argument?

The next substantial step forward in the UK was the inclusion of sport-related occupations in the National Vocational Qualifications (NVQ) framework. Very considerable energy and finance was expended on establishing coaching competences for the five levels of accreditation and on realigning NGB awards to the framework. The incorporation of the NVQ/National Occupational Standards approach into coach education has been a limited success. There have been some valuable innovations to previous practice but the undoubted benefits of the system were somewhat mitigated by not building on existing practice, the additional costs and time involved, the increased demands on what had essentially been certification of a voluntary leisure activity, and it being a significant change to what had been a previously minimalistic approach.

The consultation exercise on sports coaching (UK Sports Council 1999) notes that there is an opportunity to incorporate national standards for coaching, teaching and instruction within the government's national framework for qualifications. Assessing the competence and effectiveness of coaches in the workplace is lauded, although it has to be said that this overall approach (now part of the aims in the UK Strategy for Coaching) is a repetition of that advocated and implemented with very modest success throughout the 1990s.

In the context of this chapter, it is interesting that the whole NVQ movement focused attention onto assessment criteria and delivery structures rather than on how these competencies could be developed in coaches. The advent of National Lottery funding and an increased number of performance coaches have focused recent attention onto the needs of 'high performance coaches'. This may have the effect of reversing the balance of outcomes of coach education programmes in the UK over the past twenty years. Although 'minor' sports have been assisted by award programmes, the impact has very largely been at participation levels and performance coaching practice has not been significantly influenced by developments in coach education.

The perceived shortcomings in coach education were confirmed by the publication in 1991 of *Coaching Matters* (Coaching Review Panel 1991). This built upon work carried out for earlier documents (BANC/NCF 1987; Scottish Sports Council 1988). Figure 15.1 identifies the deficiencies in coach education and training highlighted by the Review Panel. These findings were confirmed in the English Sports Council's (1997) study, which affirmed that coach education was adequate at participation and club levels but was less adequate for working with elite performers.

System feature	Evaluation	Comment
Content	Too focused on sport-specific 'skills and tactics'	The greatest amount of time in award programmes was taken up by sport-specific skills and tactical knowledge. There was insufficient attention to medicine, analysis, psychology, planning, etc.
Content	Too focused on sport-specific 'skills and tactics'	Coach education has not paid attention to education in values and ethics, and the social role of the coach has not been emphasised.
Scale of requirements	Minimalistic	In comparison to (time and scope) demands in other person-related occupations and national systems in many other countries, the overall training demands were comparatively light.
Evaluation	Input-related	More recent changes have emphasised the place of mentor-related logbooks and 'supervised' practice. However, to date there has been limited assessment of behaviour or practice *in situ*.
Regulation	Unlicensed	Neither a licence nor membership of a professional body is required to practise as a coach. Some insurance and Local Authority employment regulations have required only a minimum qualification.
Quality assurance	Lack of rigour	There is variability in assessment, no requirement for continuous monitoring, and tutor training and selection are given less attention than is desirable. The dilemma between coaches who educate or educators who know about coaching is unresolved.

Figure 15.1 *Summary of findings of Coaching Review Panel (1991) on coach education*

A BASIS FOR PROFESSIONALISATION

The changes to coach education in the 1990s have brought welcome improvements to mentoring, structured experience and tutor training. Changes to the structuring of the NCF (sportscoach UK) coach education support programme into introductory, coach, and performance coach workshops, are a welcome recognition of the performance coach role. sportscoach UK, working with the United Kingdom Sports Institute, also offers a High Performance Coaching Programme to give substance to a continuing professional development programme.

To finish this section on historical development, there follow a few summary comments about research into coach education and the literature available. As the previous chapter has shown, there is considerable difficulty in demonstrating improved competence in performance sport; the general capacity to interact with and 'teach' young children may be much easier to demonstrate. Most of the writing on coach education is prescriptive in nature, although, as Abraham and Collins (1998) point out, very little of this is based on empirical research. Those authors criticise coach education for an unrefined experiential approach, an insubstantial base for critically appraising procedural knowledge, and the absence of a breadth-first approach. They support reflection by coaches as a mark of the expert. The literature is also characterised by content analyses and descriptive critiques of national systems. There is no work in which the output of coach education is evaluated in the context of coaching practice.

Gould *et al.* (1990) surveyed elite coaches in North America. The coaches' responses to being asked to identify the most important factors in preparing elite coaches gave significant support for additional challenging experience and mentoring programmes, in addition to more specialised knowledge. Haslam (1990) is one example of the limited research endeavours. However, this paper focused solely on the appropriateness of the content of the 'theoretical component'. Douge *et al.* (1994) also questioned the link between education courses and effective practice.

CONCEPTUAL LESSONS

An important distinction is that between coach education systems (the structures, levels and delivery issues) and coach learning (the processes, content and mechanisms through which the coach's behaviour comes to be changed). The latter is subsumed by the former, but there is a danger that it is given less attention. A good exemplar is the design, initiation and development of the NVQ and National Standards approach to coach education in the UK. The structures and delivery system, and the basic elements and their associated competencies, have been identified but the individual's means of enhancing their capacities are no further forward. This over-states the case, since there have been advances in the use of supervised, experienced mentors and logbooks, as elements of good practice have infiltrated the system. Nevertheless, the principle of questioning macro-level decisions put into practice without evidence of micro-level implementation is sound.

The potential benefits of education over the extended trial and error and imitation characteristic of unstructured experience have already been noted. The trainee or novice receives the benefit of the wisdom of expert practitioners as their experience is distilled and packaged into coach education. However, this assumes that coach education is based on the practice of experts. Perhaps just as important is the emancipatory and developmental aspect of education. Structured education should provide an opportunity for developing capacities that will enable the coach to move beyond existing practice, to innovate, to experiment, to adapt, to reflect, and to build underpinning knowledge and skills for the requirements of 'higher levels' of coaching. Expressed in the language of the chapter on effectiveness, coaches need to develop a capacity for competent and effective (future) practice, and not merely to polish their existing practice.

 Critical Concept

Structured education should provide an opportunity for developing capacities that will enable the coach to move beyond existing practice, to innovate, to experiment, to adapt, to reflect, and to build underpinning knowledge and skills for the requirements of 'higher levels' of coaching. Coaches need to develop a capacity for competent and effective (future) practice, and not merely to polish their existing practice.

The capabilities of the coach have to be matched against the requirements of practice. Put another way, it is not sufficient for coach education and training to produce generic capabilities; there should be a complementarity between the skills and knowledge being developed and the roles that the coaches will fulfil. This has been one of the issues in harmonising levels of award across sports and across countries. What does club coach, senior coach, and so on, imply? Numbering levels 1 – 5 achieves nothing if not related to a meaningful role in practice. Harmonisation is essential for professionalisation but it and the systems it represents must be based on a sound conceptual understanding of sports coaching, the coaching role and the coaching process. The harmonisation of levels is made more difficult by making the assumption that participation and performance coaching are on a continuum and the skills and knowledge requirements necessarily build from one to the other. A simpler and more accurate conceptualisation of performance coaching is required.

One issue that has been given very little attention (perhaps because of its sensitivity) is that of the educational 'level' of coach education. A number of factors combine to suggest that performance sports coaching should be a practice that requires a significant level of developed intellect.

- Much of the professional's competence is clearly cognitive.
- Surveys (see Chapter 11) show that the majority of coaches in the surveys have experienced higher education.
- The sub-discipline knowledge on which principles of practice are based require an understanding at an advanced level.
- Coach education materials have been successfully incorporated in undergraduate degrees in the UK.
- Such harmonisation and moderation as have been attempted (Campbell 1993) have placed 'advanced'/performance coaching awards at undergraduate degree level or above. (Much of this has been theoretical speculation, however.)

A BASIS FOR PROFESSIONALISATION

Nevertheless, this is a tricky conceptual issue. Anecdotal evidence suggests that the performance coaching role can be fulfilled without recourse to the kind of developed intellectual activity required for analysis and synthesis of knowledge. Coaches can work from common-sense, experiential recipes and prescriptions without testing these from first principles. Because practice is cognitive and the knowledge base and skills are tacit, practice may not be reflective of the adjustment to the complexity and dynamism of the coaching process that is assumed throughout the book. Raising issues such as these points to the importance of research into coaching practice and reinforces many of the (as yet unanswered) questions about the coach's contribution to athlete performance, the difference between success and effectiveness, and, very importantly, the extent to which coaching process competences are actually assessed during education and training.

COACH LEARNING AND COACHING PRACTICE

Coaching Matters (Coaching Review Panel 1991) and Campbell (1993) suggest that coach education should consist of six elements:

1	sports-specific knowledge	techniques, tactics, strategies
2	ethics and philosophy	adoption of values and code of behaviour/practice
3	performance-related knowledge	principles of training, fitness, nutrition, mental skills, movement analysis
4	management/vocational skills	planning, managing time, managing people
5	teaching/coaching methodology	communication skills, organisation and presentation
6	practical coaching experience	

(Coaching Review Panel 1991: 33)

There is little to dispute in this list. The question for this section is whether there is anything about coaching practice to suggest that this or any other conceptualisation of coach education would be the most appropriate. How should the coach learning process be structured?

There is no need at this point to repeat the substance of previous chapters. In addition to the specificity of the sports coaching process and the sport within which they operate, coaches require a particular configuration of skills and knowledge to cope with a complex and multivariable process, with multiple goals and a very dynamic environment. Coaches exhibit process-related skills of planning, monitoring and regulating. At the same time, coaching is an interpersonal activity and much of the day-to-day activity of the coach is characterised by a variety of face-to-face encounters. The outcomes of much of performance coaching is in the public domain and there are accountability, ethical and moral dilemmas to be resolved.

The breadth of the coaching role is demonstrated by the generic coaching competences identified in the previous chapter: training programme delivery and management, competition management, strategic planning, personnel management, athlete support, human resource management, organisation and administration, material resource management, extended role fulfilment, and contingency management. When focusing more on the operationalisation of the coach's role, the place of recipe planning, contingency planning, threshold regulation, mental models of performance and strategic co-ordination of progress and goal attainment were identified. Coaches also have social and organisational responsibilities and personal development to consider.

The purpose of the previous two paragraphs is to provide a catalyst for a discussion of the basis on which coach education should be structured and fashioned. The substance is very similar to the results of a needs-analysis by Mayes (2001). She concludes that coaches need to gain experience at the higher levels; to be mentored by a more experienced coach; to learn from others overseas; to balance personal and professional priorities; and to obtain cutting-edge technical information. The inference to be taken from that passage is that the requirements outlined therein do not form the basis of current coach education. The issue is not the subdivision into the categories of educational experiences outlined above, but the nature of the coach learning experience that characterises it. A review of these requirements provides the following principles for coach education and training: role-related competences; usable competences; cognitive organisation; process management skills; capacity for performance; progression; interpersonal skills; sport specificity; management; practice/experience based; and research-based education and training.

PRINCIPLES OF COACH EDUCATION AND TRAINING

Role-related Competences

The competences identified for coaches need to be role-related and this requires a sound appreciation of the coaching process. The range of role-related competences was illustrated above – among them, competition management, strategic planning and programme delivery. A key factor here is the requirement not to focus solely on direct intervention, although, even in this set of competences, the appropriate performance sport intervention management role has to be recognised.

Usable Competences

One of the terms to emerge from the discussion of coaching effectiveness was 'application': because of the dynamics of the coaching process, the coach must be able to apply the principles of good practice and other sub-discipline knowledge. In other words, the coach must be able to translate knowledge into effective behaviour. This has two elements. First, the presentation of knowledge needs to acknowledge the distinctions between procedural and propositional knowledge (Abraham and Collins 1998), and second, the integration of theory and practice should not be left to the coach. All education programmes struggle with the need to integrate theory and practice, but innovative ways of developing these links must be found. At the same time, there must be sufficient underpinning sub-disciplinary knowledge to allow coaches to apply theoretical principles to novel situations and to analyse the prescriptions of others.

Cognitive Organisation

The role of the coach is sufficiently well understood for the significance of cognitive processes to the coach's day-to-day activities to be appreciated. An absolutely vital part of the coach's skills are the decision-making and modelling skills that have been given considerable attention throughout the book. Decision making is a capacity that changes as the coach moves from novice to expert: the deliberative problem-solving skills using recipes and routines are very different from the non-deliberative contest management skills of some sports coaches and the crisis management decision making required to cope with the dynamics of the coaching process. The use of mental models to 'manage' and regulate progress and the use of threshold values to minimise detailed regulation is insufficiently understood but needs to be acknowledged. An example of the emphasis on cognitive skills is the nature of the relationship between mentor and coach. The real benefit to the trainee coach is not the principles on which decisions are based (albeit they are very useful), but how these are translated into decisions. This is required to assist the trainee to make the next difficult decision.

Process Management Skills

These have been emphasised throughout the book but it is worth emphasising their importance. Performance sports coaching is a process, and the educated, effective and expert coach must be able to manage the process. This requires skills of planning, monitoring, regulating and evaluating. As described above, these process skills can be most effective when integrated into role-related competences. Note, however, that many of the process skills require the cognitive organisation outlined in the previous chapter. A balance has to be struck between learning the professional shortcuts used by the experts and building this competence on a foundation of deliberative knowledge and analysis. Despite the many advantages, one of the potential dangers of moving too directly from performer to coach is that of acquiring some of the professional practice without the foundation to adapt, apply and contextualise as necessary.

Capacity for Performance

Once again, this principle overlaps with some already identified. The chapter on effectiveness clearly established that the effective coach was one who had the capacity for effective performance. The education and training process should create that capacity for performance. The capacity will be created best by:

- focusing on process-related skills;
- ensuring the development of theory into practice;
- emphasising the contextualisation and adaptation of knowledge and principles;
- pursuing an element of individualisation within the programme. (Clearly, there has to be a degree of standardisation of delivery and assessment. However, minimum competency can be extended by an education programme designed to fit the needs of individual performance coaches.)

Progression

There is an assumption that education programmes will have a progressive and cumulative effect. However, what is it that is becoming more advanced? It is not simply more technical knowledge (although that is vital). Lessons have to be learned from novice–expert differences. The coach's competences have to be improved by dealing with more challenging problems, applying more advanced knowledge, dealing with more difficult 'cases', building more complex solutions – prescriptions, scenarios, schemata, scripts – increasing interpersonal skills, presenting more challenging contest management patterns. At the same time, the coach's learning and experience have been building through coaching practice; the more advanced levels of coach education will adapt and apply that knowledge and experience.

There is no clarity at all at present on the stages or levels of professional development through which the coach will progress. These have to integrate novice–expert levels, role descriptors within coaching practice, and skills and knowledge expectations at each level.

Interpersonal Skills

Coaching is an interpersonal activity and the implications of good/bad relationships can be felt in athlete satisfaction, motivation, dealing with problem solving, athlete support and development, and the interpersonal climate that characterises day-to-day coaching activity. It is also key in the coach's adherence to a code of ethics. Although the early stages of certification include some simplistic relationship principles, coach education programmes have not been characterised by attention to this aspect of practice. Nor can recruitment gateways have been said to sift on the basis of suitability for a positive disposition towards interpersonal skills. This could be thought to be surprising given the intensity of relationships in performance sport, but, more realistically, it reinforces the lack of sophistication of some aspects of current provision. Although this element of coaching competence and effectiveness has been left to in-role socialisation and personal dispositions, future education and training ought to accord it a much higher priority.

Sport-specificity

The earlier chapter dealing with the sport-specific nature of the implementation of the coaching process identified a number of factors that suggest that coach education programmes will be distinctive and sport-specific. The individual power sports dominated by technique and training and the interactive team sports will shape the coach education requirements of their sport differently. One very important element of the coach's role is 'match coaching' (in some sports) and a more general contest-management role in others. Match coaching has not been given sufficient attention in coach education, and appears to be left to 'experience' and trial and error for coaches to establish good practice.

Management

A cursory review of the suggested competences in coaching process will show that many of them are characterised as 'management' functions. This has a number of implications.

First, there may be some potential for teaching basic management principles (while acknowledging the above plea for role-related competences). Second, there is sufficient genericism for the role of the coach to be portrayed as that of a manager – particularly in the more complex context of high-level performance sport. The management element of the coaching role demonstrates why there has been an entrepreneurial transition into 'management education' by using the principles of coaching and team building (see, for example, Whitmore 1992; Carling and Heller 1995; Owen 1996; Lyle 1997a; Whitaker 1999).

Education Based on Practice and Experience

This may seem an obvious suggestion when coach education now generally requires a period of supervised experience involving a mentor, the completion of log books, a period of experience before moving to the next level of award, and the inclusion of exemplar sessions and practice-based teaching.

However, these have been fairly recent developments for most sports. Two issues are important: (1) the role of the mentor is very important, and (2) the value to the trainee coach of transiting to coaching from a performance sport background becomes obvious. Most writers in the field (for instance, Gould *et al.* 1990; UK Sports Council 1999) advocate coaching apprenticeship schemes and these may in time be built into the structure of coach education and training for performance sport.

Research-based Education and Training

It is hardly novel to suggest that education should be based on research. However, there has been very little research into coach education and, indeed, into some aspects of coaching practice. It should be made very clear to trainee coaches that the prescriptions and principles of good practice to which they are exposed have been derived from research on expert coaches. Part of the education process should be to make the coaches aware of the research that has been conducted. Clearly, and given that the principle is not contentious, the exhortation is for more research into coaching practice and coach education.

DELIVERY ISSUES

The chapter continues by expanding on a number of the issues concerned with the delivery of coach education and training. These contain recommendations for good practice. The first of these involves the recognition that a good deal of coach education has been based on sport-specific technical knowledge – largely about such matters as techniques, tactics, training and equipment. The recommendation is that this knowledge should be achieved by in-service workshops, seminars and other more informal means. This is a move away from 'courses', which are more redolent of participation awards. In much of performance sport, the participants already have considerable technical knowledge and this could (and should) be updated on a regular and individualised basis. Coach education beyond the novice performance coach should be based on the 'how' questions and not on the 'what' questions!

Mentoring is one of the features of coach education that would now also be found in most other forms of professional education. Mentoring in teaching is a good and relevant example (Tomlinson 1995; Mawer 1996). The coaches in Salmela's (1995) study supported a variety of mentoring schemes aimed at enhancing the formal programme (see also Bloom *et al.* 1998). The issue, therefore, is not that it should be part of the delivery system but how coach learning can be further enhanced by its practice.

The most relevant distinction is that between the mentor's supervisory and monitoring role and the master–apprentice role. It is a structured approach to this function that is required. The trainee coach must have available a number of procedures for interrogating the master's practice – stimulated recall, question and answer, critical analysis of practice, simulated examples and joint reflection. This is, of course, in addition to the 'situated learning' that occurs from interaction and observation. Through this experience the trainee coach (who may be quite experienced) is building the mental models required for professional practice. Of course, the mentor must be trained to allow the trainee 'space' to build individualised models, and to recognise the importance of adaptation, application and contextualisation of the mentor's own practice. Schempp (1998) comments on preventing imitation by mentees by having informed and trained mentors. He also recognises the need to develop individual 'how to' models that incorporate application and contextualisation.

This is a reminder that coach education tutors must also be trained to deliver coach education for performance sport. It can be assumed that some teaching skills are required, but the role of the tutor may be more appropriately conceived as that of facilitator. Key to this is a capacity to analyse performance, simulate practice, employ supporting knowledge products and demonstrate application. It seems unlikely that this role (unlike the specialist delivery of technical sub-discipline knowledge) could be achieved by other than an individual with considerable coaching experience and a very sound appreciation of the coaching process.

Reference has already been made to the need to situate the trainee's learning in the practical experience of coaching in an appropriate and supportive context. The element of practical experience in education and training has a number of purposes and each of these indicates the need for a supportive environment:

- Practice allows an element of trial and error, and of the 'practice of changed behaviour'. This needs a supportive environment.
- Changed behaviour needs time and reinforcement to take effect. This cannot be done without practice.
- A practicum also allows for an element of assessment and monitoring to take place.
- The delivery aspect of coaching requires attention and practice. However, many of the process elements of coaching (planning, monitoring and regulating) can only appropriately be enacted over a period of time.
- Decision making often requires an appreciation of the context within which the decision must be taken – an understanding of the contributory factors. This can best be achieved using experiential practice.
- The practice element creates a real-life context in which adaptation, resolution of ethical issues and problem solving are required.

- It is important that the trainee coach has some responsibility and accountability for the results of the experiential period. This again needs a supportive environment.
- Socialisation into the role of the coach and an appreciation of the organisational management issues can best be appreciated through experience.

Given these demands, the most appropriate solution would be a practicum in the coach's own situation, and preferably working with a more experienced mentor from within that organisation. This is one of the reasons that assistant coach positions are important in performance sport.

Learning can also be enhanced by specifically designed teaching methods and products. Perhaps the most important of these products are those that engage the trainee coach actively, with realistic exemplars that are designed to illustrate particular principles. Obvious examples are (1) detailed case studies for planning and interpersonal skills, (2) interactive video scenarios for decision making, and (3) problem-solving exercises. Delivery by e-learning should facilitate new products.

Further support for apprenticeship schemes for the transition of elite athletes into coaching is given by the British Olympic Association Athletes' Commission (British Olympic Association 1996). Interestingly, it speaks of 'fast-tracking' elite performers through the certification system. This is a desirable option but there are a number of conceptual issues. In practice, the early stages of certification are not normally focused on performance sport in any case. In addition, elite athletes normally have technical knowledge well beyond that required at such levels. National Governing Bodies (NGBs) need to work on amending the performer's mental models of performance to those of a coach. Similarly, NGBs have to ensure that process skills and operational shortcuts are based on a foundation of knowledge and principles. The fast-tracking would be most appropriate for those athletes who have engaged, in a structured fashion, in apprenticeship, trainee or 'assistant' positions, and have been engaged significantly in the management of their own programmes.

The competence-based education and training movement was referred to in the previous chapter on coaching effectiveness. The impact of the inclusion of coach education into a 'national standards' approach in the UK has been felt most acutely at the 'system' level of delivery. However, it has been noted that several innovations and consolidations of practice have benefited learning. The collection of evidence, identification of competencies, identification of learning profiles, training of tutors and experiential periods of practice have been beneficial. In addition, the more holistic approach to assessing national standards has matched more appropriately the generic competences thought to be suitable for judgement-based occupations such as sports coaching. For example, national occupational standards for Level 3 are centred on the following units (SPRITO 1998): analysing information and identifying goals; planning a programme to achieve goals; managing and evaluating a programme to achieve goals; dealing with accidents and emergencies; establishing and maintaining relationships which support the coaching process; and coaching sessions to enable participants to achieve seasonal goals. These should be compared with the competences suggested in the previous chapter.

Certification programmes normally involve some form of formal assessment. The traditional demonstration of knowledge and delivery skills has been supplemented in more recent times by evidence of successful practice. On the basis of the arguments presented above, the assessment of the trainee coach has a number of dilemmas to overcome (capacity versus performance, competence versus effectiveness, meaningful criteria for levels of expertise) and some good practice to incorporate (application of knowledge, problem solving, peer evidence of effectiveness, evidence of reflective analysis).

REFLECTIVE PRACTICE

Education and training may be subject to 'movements' or trends, and one current trend in sports coaching is reflective practice (RP) (Ghaye 2001; NCF 2001). To reflect on one's practice in order to improve it may seem like a fairly common and unsurprising approach, and indeed it is. However, RP is a learned skill, and a structured approach to the process of reflection can be integrated into the learning experience. The intention is that education and training should move beyond simply 'having experience' and this partially explains why RP is popular in occupations such as teaching and nursing, with a significant element of practical agency-based experience in their training programmes.

Reflective practice is particularly relevant in situations such as sports coaching, in which practice is complex, applied and contextualised, and in which learning therefore requires a degree of introspection. RP allows this introspection, most significantly into professional practice that is characterised, as sports coaching is, by tacit knowledge, cognitive professional shortcuts (recipes, routines, mental models), and non-deliberative and contingent decision making. In order to learn from experience, it is necessary to generate an understanding and appreciation of practice for subsequent analysis. The various elements of practice can then be examined against established principles and goals, and behaviour either reinforced or amended. De Marco *et al.* (1997) is an example of self-assessment and assisted reflection. Whilst RP may be useful for monitoring and evaluating procedures such as analysis of planning decisions, it is perhaps most beneficial in 'behavioural role activity'. In sports coaching, examples of this might be interpersonal relationship interaction between athlete and coach, directing drills/exercises, or competition management behaviour by a coach during a match.

Reflective practice is best described as an overall approach to professional practice. Although it is very useful in the early stages of education and training, it should become part of day-to-day activity. There is an element of being 'critical' (that is, questioning) about RP, but it is important to note that reflection also focuses on positive features of practice and on achievements. RP involves a structured approach and makes use of procedures such as journals/diaries, stimulated recall, debriefings, reflective conversations and analysis of critical incidents. The 'analysis' of questioning must also be structured. Ghaye and Lillyman (2000) suggest a series of 'frames' through which events can be re-evaluated:

- *Role framing* Was the role exercised appropriately? How might it have been done differently?
- *Temporal framing* Was the sequence of events appropriate? Were any of the decisions made too soon or too late? Why?
- *Problem framing* What was the problem? Was it identified appropriately? Did everyone involved perceive the problem in the same way?

- *Value framing*   Were any value-positions evident during the experiential events? Were there any value conflicts?
- *Parallel process framing*   Could the outcomes have been different? Construct an alternative sequence of events and behaviours with a different outcome.

Reflective practice may, therefore, have particular relevance for sports coaching, given the emphasis, described earlier in the chapter, on practical experience as a key part of the trainee coach's education and training. RP may prove to be a very valuable mechanism for ensuring that this practical experience enhances coaches' learning and contributes to monitoring and assessment. Nevertheless, the purpose of the chapter is to bring a critical perspective to education and training and there are a number of conceptual caveats to be addressed:

1   The RP procedures must be complemented by an understanding of the cognitive activity that coaching practice represents.
2   The RP is not a 'process for its own sake', and the trainee coach must, therefore, have knowledge of principles of good practice and prescriptions in order to inform the analysis and evaluate solutions.
3   RP would appear to be a particularly useful procedure for mentor and trainees to use together. However, the shared reflection process depends on a shared vocabulary and understanding of the coaching process in addition to developed and developing schemata and scripts for performance sport.
4   Reflection on emotion-laden activity is acknowledged to be difficult. The win/lose, contested nature of sport activity is often tinged with emotion, of coach and athletes, and this will bring additional challenges.
5   Participation coaching is episodic in nature. RP may be valuable for analysing the coach's behaviour in such circumstances. Nevertheless, the performance coach has a more strategic, metacognitive overview of a complex, dynamic and longer-term process. Reflecting on either isolated incidents within the 'bigger picture' or reflecting on more extended processes will also bring particular challenges.
6   Reflection is part of a broader learning process and ought, therefore, to be integrated into its other stages. In other words, RP should not be solely a summative activity. This has been described as pre-flecting (anticipation, goal setting, scenario building), in-flecting – Schon's (1983) reflection-in-action – and re-flecting.

What is clear is that a sound understanding of the coaching process is required for successful reflection on coaching experiences.

SUMMARY

This chapter will have familiarised you with the following:

- the nature of education and training and their importance for sports coaching;
- major developments in coach education and perceived shortcomings in current provision;

- the relationship between coach education and a number of conceptual issues: experience, role-specificity, intellectual focus and participation/performance coaching differences;
- the structure and delivery of coach education in relation to appropriate learning opportunities;
- principles for coach education and training;
- a range of delivery issues, including non-course delivery, mentoring, experiential study, fast-tracking, and competence-based education and training;
- an insight into reflective practice and some relevant conceptual concerns.

PROJECTS

- Select six coaches. Chart all of their education and training courses/workshops and so on in relation to changes in their coaching roles. Try to compare their perceptions of role-demand with the nature of the courses and workshops attended.
- Work with one coach in a longitudinal study. Carry out a needs analysis and agree criteria for improved practice. Monitor changes in practice and the coach's diary of events. Report on your analysis of the nature of learning.
- Identify criteria for assessing competence in one or more aspect of the coaching process. Investigate coaches' degree of competence at three levels of coaching practice (six coaches in each). Relate this to role-demands and stages in professional development.
- Select a case-study sport with which to work. Collate information on its coach education programme (including content analyses and interviews) and analyse using the eleven principles of coach education and training.
- Identify a mentor and mentee with whom to work. Ask each of them to maintain a diary and engage in a joint reflection exercise with each of them. Attempt to establish some principles of good practice.

Reading

An historical and comparative account of coach education can be found in Campbell (1993), and a critical analysis of coach education content and structure in Abraham and Collins (1998). Recent thinking is evident in the UK Sports Council's (1999) consultation paper and the UK Sport (2001) strategy for coaching. Details of developments are reported in the Sports Coach UK's (NCF) FHS magazine. Ghaye and Lillyman (2000) provide an insight into reflective practice.

CHAPTER SIXTEEN

▼ **SETTING A RESEARCH AGENDA**

■ Introduction   291
■ The Research Process   292
■ The Coaching Process and Research Issues   294
■ An Expert System   298
■ Suggestions for a Research Agenda   299
■ Implications for the Researcher in Coaching Studies   302
■ Summary   304

INTRODUCTION

The research policy community in sport has undervalued research into coaches and coaching, with the result that the place of coaching studies in the academic world has been compromised. Earlier chapters have demonstrated that the weight of research studies and the level of conceptual and theoretical development have had relatively little impact on education or professional development, and appear marginalised in the research community. The purpose of this chapter, therefore, is to advocate an emergent and developed interest in research into sports coaching and to demonstrate that the building blocks of a research agenda are in place. The ideas are distilled from experience of researching into sports coaching, writing and speaking about coaching, working in coach education, being a coach and having a particular academic interest in developing conceptual frameworks. This is aggregated into a personal perspective on the coaching process and on research into sports coaching. It is not a review of literature, nor a summing up of existing research. It is a set of ideas – intended to be coherent – about a research agenda for sports coaching.

A research agenda should address the following questions:

■ Why do research on coaching?
■ How should it be done?
■ Which issues should be addressed?
■ Where and on whom should it be done?
■ Which are the major constraints?

- How can the field be conceptualised? and
- What is the history of research development in this area?

The chapter provides some insights into each of these questions and is structured into three parts: the research process; the nature of the coaching process; and three sets of assertions from which to demonstrate the generation of research questions.

THE RESEARCH PROCESS

Generally, research is targeted at the resolution of problematic issues which are often contemporary, the improvement of current practice, or the testing of theoretical propositions, or occasionally the genuine exploration of innovative ideas. In addition, research problems in a particular field may have more specific purposes: the need to apply theoretical understandings into demanding and untested contexts; to stop occasionally and review and synthesise the received wisdom in an area; and the need to base education and training on a rigorously achieved understanding of professional practice. The sports coaching context has presented a challenge to the researcher in relation to each of these purposes.

Previous chapters have demonstrated that sports coaching is a contested activity, has a high level of uncertainty of practice and outcome, is significantly under-theorised, is apparently intuitive in its professional practice, has a high level of complexity and even uniqueness, and is extremely widely varied in its scale, form and practice. There is not as yet a consensual conceptual framework which recognises and embraces the scale, scope and complexity of this practice, nor is there a consensual body of knowledge that has informed policy and practice. An understandable reaction might be that its attractions to the researcher are not immediately obvious.

 Critical Concept

There is not as yet a consensual conceptual framework which recognises and embraces the scale, scope and complexity of this practice, nor is there a consensual body of knowledge that has informed policy and practice.

There are three sets of arguments to support coaching research. First, it has already been argued that a ready store of conceptual frameworks or mature theories, within which to locate coaching research, does not exist. The lack of attention to the coaching process would seem to fly in the face of a consensual recognition, perhaps tacit at times, of its importance (and this was the motive for the book). Although some individual, often mature, athletes are self-coached, experience tells us that the coaching role is considered to be essential. This probably somewhat understates the weight given, rather belatedly in the UK, to the role of the expert coach in producing competitive excellence on the world stage.

Second, there is what might be termed a common-sense argument. The coach, rather than the performer, is most often the 'end-user' of knowledge. Perhaps research proposals should have an 'end-user certificate' attached to them. Despite the variety in coaching roles, some elements of the coaching process are normally the prerogative of the coach: programme planning, control of training sessions, interpersonal relationships and competition management (including strategy and tactics). These elements suggest that the coach will always have the strongest influence on performance preparation and should be the focus of applied research.

 Question Box

Should research using public funds always have an 'end-user' certificate? Other than for 'pure' research, should the findings/implications be targeted at a specific element of the coaching process?

Third, there is an argument based on a classification or typology of research forms. Figure 16.1 suggests, not that sport performance research be replaced with coaching research, but that research into coaching is complementary (perhaps essential) if the full picture is to be achieved. Perhaps it would be better to say that performance sport research is incomplete without much greater attention to sports coaching research. It is certainly incomplete if implementation in a naturalistic coaching setting has not been taken into account.

There comes a time when performance components (for example, strength training or technique) are applied in the context of other components and environmental circumstances. What really happens to hard-won scientific knowledge at the implementation stage? Can it be applied, does it work in practice, does it have an impact? There is no question about the centrality of fundamental or applied research on sport performance,

| Research Model | | Balance of research focus | | | Scientist |
(a)	(b)	Performance ⟵⟶		Coaching	
Basic research	Fundamental research	Performance components		(The coach)	Fundamental scientist
Applied research	Ecologically valid research	Applied performance components	Training theory	The coach	Applied scientist
Application research	Applied research		Integrated training programmes	The coaching process	Contextual scientist
Implementation research				The coaching process	Contextual scientist

Figure 16.1 A research typology related to the coaching process

just that there are also other questions to ask. The Fundamental Scientist asks, 'What makes performance better?' The Applied Scientist asks, 'How can performance be made better?' The Contextual Scientist asks, 'In which circumstances can performance be made better?' or 'What will improve (or sustain) the performance of that performer at that time and in those circumstances?' The last question, for example, is remarkably similar to the question that all coaches constantly have in their minds! These questions apply whether the focus is on biochemistry, physiology, psychology, coach behaviour or strategy.

Not all of the entries in Figure 16.1 have been attended to by the research community on a satisfactorily equal basis. If it is caricatured, rather simplistically, as an issue of performance versus coaching, lessons might be learned from a similar model of enquiry into the balance of research between learning and teaching. School performance, league tables, multiple social deprivation and parental expectations and so on is a similarly difficult context within which to apply and implement learning theories.

There can be little doubt that the research policy community has focused on athlete performance, although perhaps less so on athletes performing. The research policy community (that is, university sports science departments, the Sports Councils, the NCF, BOA and BASES in the UK) has treated sports coaching with benign neglect. It seems very unlikely that in the goal of improving sports performance, the coach, the coach's behaviour, and the coach's intervention programme and impact can have been purposefully treated as unproblematic variables. The research community needs to address an holistic set of questions: how has this research influenced coaching practice?, how sure are you that the performer is receiving the benefit of the application of new knowledge?, has it made a difference to performance outcomes? The answers to these questions depend on an increased attention to the coach and the coaching process.

 Critical Concept

It seems very difficult to believe that in the goal of improving sports performance, the coach, the coach's behaviour, and the coach's intervention programme and impact can have been purposefully treated as unproblematic variables.

The benefits of interdisciplinary and cross-disciplinary research are incontrovertible, given the complexity of both performance and the coaching process. Some issues, such as overtraining, that undoubtedly benefit from a multidisciplinary approach, would further benefit from being investigated as coaching process issues.

THE COACHING PROCESS AND RESEARCH ISSUES

A key element in this advocacy of coaching research is to rehearse some previous insights into sports coaching and the coaching process. This is necessary because it is these assumptions about the coaching process that will shape very significantly the research

A BASIS FOR PROFESSIONALISATION

agenda and point up the difficulties of research design. These ideas were discussed in some length in earlier chapters and are summarised rather than elaborated.

As a starting point, it may be instructive to reinforce the central purpose of coaching. Coaching is about improving or sustaining performance towards identified goals, through a structured intervention programme, and delivering within constraints of time, place and resource. This suggests that the outcomes of coaching are measurable – but not easily. The phrase 'reducing the unpredictability of performance' is a useful one to describe the coaching role. Whatever the definition, the contextual nature of both the performance and the intervention programme present problems of using simple outcome measures of athlete performance as a mark of coaching performance. The most immediate issue, therefore, is that simplistic assessment of athlete performance is a poor measure of the quality of the coaching process.

 Critical Concept

Coaching is about improving or sustaining performance towards identified goals, through a structured intervention programme, and delivering within constraints of time, place and resource.

Furthermore, it should also be noted that this is to be accomplished within a contested terrain. Improvement is not only constrained by the limitations of the performer (and the coach), leaving aside the issue of how much value added is acceptable, but by the deliberate and purposeful intentions of other competitors and coaches. Much of sport involves relative achievement; this makes it difficult to attain and difficult to measure. The issue here is not that the performance of the player or athlete cannot be assessed, whether in output or outcome measures, but that ascribing improvement or success within such a complex process is fraught with difficulty.

The coaching process was shown to have a number of important characteristics. The passage that follows identifies six of these characteristics and their attendant research implications.

1   *Coaching is a process*   It is serial; it has interdependent and interrelated elements and stages; it has sub-processes and stages designed to contribute to an overall goal; and it is incremental and accumulative in its effect.

    Research issue: It is difficult to carry out research into processes. Controlling the input variables is very demanding and the confounding environmental variables are difficult to control and almost impossible to replicate. The key elements of processes are planning, monitoring and regulating. Of themselves these are not difficult to address, but they are longitudinal in nature and not informed by rigorously evaluated exemplars of good practice to the extent that would be beneficial.

2   *There is a deep-seated genericism and commonality about the process but it is characterised by apparent uniqueness and variety*   The process varies in scale and in

the extent of the control exercised over the variables that influence performance. The process varies by the intensity of the involvement (duration, frequency, continuity, stability), by the coach's role in competition, by the degree of responsibility exercised by the athlete, by the contribution of other individuals to the implementation of the process, and by the requirement/constraints/resources of the organisation within which the coach operates.

Research issue: It is difficult to effect research designs from which generalisations might be drawn.

3   *Performance and participation coaching*   This distinction was described in an earlier chapter, but deserves more attention because it is at the root of much of the irrelevant research carried out under the banner of coaching. Participation coaching is characterised by being less intensive, often not about competition goals, usually not systematic, more about immediate satisfactions, and not all of the performance elements are attended to. It is largely 'episodic' in nature. Performance coaching has competition goals, longer-term horizons, significant athlete commitment and an attempted control of contributory variables – hence life-style management as a current buzzword. Performance coaching is 'processual'.

The implications of this distinction are really quite important and a failure to appreciate the implications bedevils the literature.

■   The skills and knowledge requirement are different. One emphasises instructional, pedagogic and motivational skills: the other planning, monitoring, decision-making and management skills.
■   The two forms of coaching are not on a continuum. Understanding this would greatly assist coach education and recruitment. The participation coach is not necessarily a beginner performance coach.
■   Without going into details, which would be unfair, in an often-cited piece of research from the USA, the implications for coaching were derived from four 'coaches' teaching a 'give-and-go' in basketball to young children. In another, otherwise admirable, piece of research on gender issues in coaching, there was clearly some significant doubt about the intensity of involvement of the subjects in the coaching process. In addition, larger-scale surveys of coaches have not distinguished in their summaries the findings as they apply to participation and performance coaches.

Research issue: The subjects and contexts used in research must match the intended goals. All of the research is valuable, but researchers must make clear the context within which they are operating and their assumptions about coaching.

4   *Coaching is an essentially cognitive activity*, although there are craft elements to it related to interpersonal behaviour, managing the training environment, managing the competition environment and some specific sports expertise. This has come to be recognised by writers in the field (Salmela 1995; Lyle 1996; Abraham and Collins 1998; Saury and Durand 1998; Lyle 1999a). A good deal of coach activity can be described as decision making – some of it deliberative and some non-deliberative. The nature of this will range from the construction of training schedules and tactical plans to crisis management of interpersonal tensions and outcome-related problems. Much of the

cognitive activity may seem to be intuitive but this form of professional short-cut needs to be understood and investigated rather than ignored and denigrated. It has been said that the distinguishing feature of professionals is their discretionary judgements. Decision making is a mark of the professional and perhaps the benchmark of the expert.

Research issue: The coach's overt behaviour is more visible, more accessible and more easily measured. There is a danger of researching what can be researched, rather than what needs to be researched. Coaching behaviour is emphasised but coaching practice is sadly under-researched. To understand this better, it is valuable to conceive of coaching practice in four parts: direct intervention (directing the training session, counselling, match coaching); intervention support (planning, monitoring and so on); external constraints management (handling, among other things, the resources, facilities, equipment, finance); and strategic co-ordination (metacognitive management of variables). This is complicated by the fact that these roles are not necessarily all handled by one person. In summary, investigating coaching practice is not easily captured by behavioural analysis.

5 *Coaching is about human beings* It is not merely a technical exercise. It almost goes without saying that coaching is a form of interpersonal activity and this brings with it issues of power relationships, ethical behaviours, personal aspirations, emotional highs and lows, and compatibilities. There is also a factor called 'performer variability', which recognises that performers do not always produce their best performances on each occasion (and are not expected to), but it does provide a significant source of difficulty for monitoring and regulating progress.

Research issue: Research into this aspect of the coaching process is complicated by a complex matrix of personal characteristics, individualisation/uniqueness, specificity of context, coaching philosophies, and a dearth of solid evidence on the relationships between these factors and performance.

6 *The coach is a manager* There are two levels to this statement. The coach can be conceived of as a manager of the coaching process or as a part of a larger system. A simple input–treatment–output model would help to identify key parts of the coaching process, from talent identification and recruitment, to programme management. However, the interesting questions are process ones. What does the coach do when the outputs are not being achieved – re-set goals, recruit new performers, modify the intensity of the programme, modify the quality of the programme, ascribe it to injury, illness, among other things?

Research issue: There would be some value in using systems analysis to examine performance coaching, particularly when teams of coaches and support personnel are involved. There is tremendous potential in soft systems analysis (Dyer 1993; Checkland 1999) as a mechanism for understanding messy and untidy processes such as coaching. A body of knowledge that identifies critical paths or models for different coaching contexts would be very valuable. What balance might be appropriate between talent identification and technique development, between match coaching and physical conditioning, between psychological preparation and appropriate tactics? The coach is dealing with these questions all of the time, and with different profiles for each performer. This reinforces the integration element of the coach's role.

AN EXPERT SYSTEM

The 'systems' allusion can be used to point up further research opportunities. Figure 16.2 represents the coaching process as an 'expert system', having three components. In relation to this expert system, consider the following questions as a research agenda (and a commentary on the current status of the research):

1   Which of these factors is the limiting factor to achieving improved sport performance? Where has research effort been focused to date?
2   Which are the limiting factors within the delivery stage – craft, failure to individualise, failure to monitor quality in training loadings, failure to manage competition? Which key skills characterise our expert coaches?
3   Real expert systems become idiot proof, computerised, use default values we know will work – what we might describe as systematic, or even 'scientific'. However, the coaching process is messy, complex, contested and interpersonal – almost beyond control! It is hardly surprising that performance coaches have to find professional strategies to cope with these situations. Where is this to be found in the research on coaching?

This resume of the coaching process may be accurate but may not adequately describe what might be termed the *essence of coaching*. This can be summed up in the following way. The coach's role is to prioritise and integrate into action the enormous quantities of data available. This may often result in tangible schedules, strategies or training loadings. However, it will also describe a capacity or expertise, which only becomes evident in non-deliberative behaviour, contingency planning, crisis management and problem solving. Much of this may appear intuitive. Research into sports coaching has barely scratched the surface of understanding how the coach translates knowledge and information into coaching practice. John Salmela's (1995) conclusion, that sports coaches use a

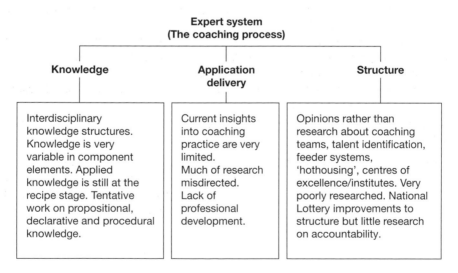

Figure 16.2 *Simplified model of the coaching process as an expert system*

'metacognitive' form of knowledge which they are able to verbalise but which academics have not successfully disaggregated, is an appropriate signpost.

SUGGESTIONS FOR A RESEARCH AGENDA

Example 1

How can coaching practice be best described and analysed? The following description of how coaches operate is summarised from earlier chapters. These are presented as a research agenda on coaching practice. *Each of these statements should be interpreted as a tentative hypothesis.*

Performance coaches:

- operate within an umbrella of detailed planning, but implement this with a high degree of contingency;
- implement more systematic workloads in target sports and less systematic workloads in more cyclical sports;
- play a central role in directing intervention, constantly balancing priorities between performance components and relatively imprecise workload management;
- make extensive use of mental models of day-to-day expectations about athlete performance in both training and competition;
- develop sport-specific, personal cognitive matrices, which are derived from experience and facilitate decision making;
- exercise what appears to be intuitive decision making but which is simply an efficient mechanism for reducing decision options;
- supplement subjective data gathering by objective testing and monitoring at selected times in the programme;
- use contingency planning as a normal and expected part of coaching practice – there is a constant fine-tuning of schedules and major adjustments to accommodate injury, illness and recruitment changes;
- operate a system of crisis thresholds – that is, they recognise and deal with problems only when they reach a threshold of under-achievement or threaten longer-term goals (which takes into account fluctuations in performance);
- coaches have a bank of stored and retrievable coping strategies to deal with common short- and long-term problems;
- integrate the contributions of a team of professionals on a complementary and substitutional basis.

Not only do these assertions suggest many research questions, particularly when considered in a sport-specific context, but they also raise similar questions about coach education. Coaches are users of knowledge and scientists have attempted to provide this knowledge. Coach education to date has singularly failed to provide the bridge to practice.

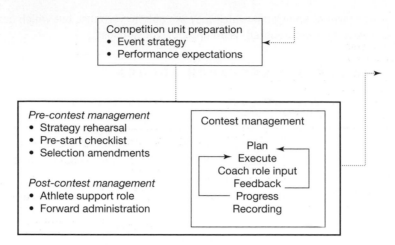

Source: Adapted and refined from Lyle (1999a)

Figure 16.3 *Simplified coaching process, competition phase*

Example 2

Models of the coaching process are required to stimulate theory building and support research. This was elaborated at length in Chapter 5. One method has been to use Weber's approach of constructing an ideal model (Albrow 1990) and then use it to investigate discrepancies from practice in a variety of situations. One of the difficulties in constructing models is to balance the genericism of the process (which aids simplicity) with the inclusion of sufficient degrees of freedom to make it understandable and relevant.

Figures 16.3 and 16.4 reproduce diagrams from Chapter 6. The first is a section abstracted from the ideal model. The second is a version based on experience and a series of research studies. This is only exploratory at the moment, and should be treated as an exemplar. The purpose is to demonstrate that, gradually amending an ideal model by incorporating research findings can be a valuable way of developing theories and research questions. It would also be a very valuable exercise to pool research findings in this way in order to refine models as they emerge.

Figure 16.3 is an abstraction from the ideal model that deals with the coach's competition management behaviour.

Figure 16.4 suggests that the coach's practice is more complicated than first presented and highlights the role of the emergent strategy and the need to identify the threshold criteria and values that influence decision making. The difference between the models is both a reflection of research and an agenda for further research.

Example 3

This exemplar is derived from a research study into the non-deliberative decision making of volleyball coaches (Lyle 1998b, 1999c). The interest was developed from a personal

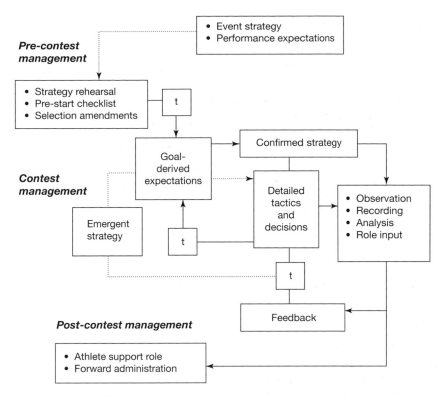

Source: Adapted and interpreted from Lyle (1998b)

Figure 16.4 *Refined model of the competition phase*

experience as a volleyball coach and a curiosity about how coaches coped with the need for speedy decision making during the game itself. The focus of the study was on how coaches made decisions during competitive matches. Expert coaches were videotaped during games and a stimulated recall method was used to generate verbal accounts of six incidents in each match. Subsequent analysis of the accounts used models of decision making culled from the literature.

The objective here is to use some of the implications from this research to illustrate how further questions are generated and to demonstrate that naturalistic, field-based studies are possible.

When making non-deliberative decisions, performance coaches appeared to exhibit the following characteristics:

■ Coaches have to deal with the dilemma of either acting very quickly, but with lack of certainty, or delaying and being ineffective (but sure that the problem is identified correctly). The coach will therefore have coping mechanisms to reduce lack of certainty. One of these is a loss-minimisation heuristic. Coaches choose options based on conservatism – begin diagnosis early, don't get panicked into action, and try not to reduce options too much.

- It is very difficult to 'decompose' the messages from a game sport. Even expert coaches will have some margin for error in their interpretation and diagnosis. Some coaches might use personal heuristics (the last mistake, the performance of the best players, etc.) or attempt to portray the illusion of control through analysis and deliberation.
- Schemata or scripts for solving problems are accessed via 'trip markers'. Although these may be idiosyncratic, it is important to identify these (perhaps) sport-specific triggers.
- Coaches work very much with mental models. The coach creates an individual match script based on information and enabling conditions (weather, player fitness, 'form'). This model then provides a synoptic overview of the anticipated progress of the game, which is monitored constantly, and action is taken when a threshold (of some kind) is breached. Action depends on the strength of the stimulus and the options available.
- Coaches appear to use 'anticipatory reflection' to be prepared for contingencies. In other words, they model potential variations with the likely solutions available (perhaps tacit and pre-programmed), and again tempered by the resources available.
- Crucially there is an opposition coach who is deliberately obscuring information, and any actions will be countered by changing the 'problem space' (not a common phrase in coach education). It is clear from this that match coaching is a skilled business.
- The researcher might construct a 'process trace' such as the following in order to frame the volleyball coach's dilemma:

I understand the problem at the moment, but how serious is it in relation to problems that might arise later? Is the problem likely to impact significantly on the target performance? The solution is obvious but will it work if I do it now? If I make changes, will this restrict my freedom and flexibility to make more important changes later on? If I don't change now, will this problem continue to grow and become insurmountable? Do I have any other strategic/ developmental plans in mind, which might supersede my interpretation of the current situation?
(Lyle 1999c: 224)

It is easy to see why the coach needs a decision-making model with shortcuts.

Great differences exist between expert and novice coaches in what is described above and this adds to the researcher's agenda. Experts can narrow the choices and predict better because they have better informed models – they have developed far more potential scripts based on their previous experience. Their greater predictive ability means that they need fewer potential solutions. Intuitive illusion is maintained because the coach has already 'factored in' the solutions. Many of the action decisions will become routine – another characteristic of the expert!

A BASIS FOR PROFESSIONALISATION

IMPLICATIONS FOR THE RESEARCHER IN COACHING STUDIES

From what has been argued thus far, there are a number of implications for the researcher. Coaching practice can only be understood and appreciated when there is an understanding of the conceptual framework that constitutes the coaching process. This provides immediate insights into the shortcomings of a good deal of so-called coaching research, and reinforces the need for conceptual clarity. Our vocabulary for communicating about the coaching process is as yet somewhat underdeveloped. Given much of what has been said, systematic observation studies have a limited value but, having said that, we are a good way from being replete with descriptive accounts of practice. Attempts to measure coaching effectiveness have not been successful. Researchers have resorted to athlete satisfaction measures and few, if any, studies have come to grips with the issue of 'value-added' as a concept. Despite maligning 'successful-ness' studies, it would not be a bad starting point to establish what our successful coaches actually do!

Because coaching research is still immature, there is a need to access and investigate the practice of our expert coaches. This is not easy because of issues of access, esoteric myth, role confusion, and so on. One tried and trusted means of investigating expert capacities is to study how they deal with problems or difficult cases. This is a potentially very valuable research avenue.

The research community must begin to ask the important, albeit difficult, questions. For example, the autocratic/democratic behaviour theme has satiated the field but told us – what? There is a more important list of issues, some of which have already been hinted at:

1   Meaningful forms of replication and reduction are very difficult because of the complexity of the process. More naturalistic, field-based studies are required. Of course this brings with it significant challenges for research design and data collection.
2   How do performance coaches become involved in performance coaching? Are coach education courses really recruitment mechanisms? What place is there for opportunism and chance? What sort of individuals become coaches? We know the answers to very few of these questions because previous survey samples have been insufficiently focused.
3   How are values transmitted between coach and performer? Performance sport is the shop window for role models. What perceptions about sport are being perpetuated by coaches?
4   There may be some interesting issues about coaching style. However, the significant impact is the effect on the coach's capacity and intentions to deliver, monitor and regulate the process – not on measures of athlete satisfaction. This is a not-too-thinly veiled criticism of many studies.
5   There are some really key questions related to implementation or application research. How can we investigate the efficacy of planning decisions? How should processes be amended to account for illness, injury and weather? How accurate and individualised are workload measurements?
6   Far greater attention is required to be paid to the coach's cognitive processes – mental models, thresholds, action triggers, for example. Performance-enhancement research

cannot be complete without attention to the coach's application, integration and delivery of knowledge. Coaching practice is a largely cognitive activity and the processes that attend this are seriously under-researched.

The complexity of the coaching process makes it difficult for the researcher. However, investigating how the coach copes with this complexity provides a most exciting challenge for the research community. The difficulties involved should not prevent researchers from attempting to control some of the variables in naturalistic research through inventive design, using more action-research based on attempts to improve cognitive processes over time, recognising the value of ethnographic enquiry and case studies, attempting to unravel the coach's cognitive processes – in particular, the professional shortcuts employed – and appreciating the potential of systems analysis for an alternative approach to studying the coaching process.

There are a number of reasons why coaching research should become more widespread. A desire to enhance the coach education of our aspiring performance coaches should be sufficient reason for the research policy community to expand its interest in coaches and the coaching process. A more pragmatic reason is that much more funding is being invested in coaches and coaching. There are legitimate doubts that the knowledge exists on which to base accountability – other than in purely results terms. A more scholarly reason is that the research cycle is not being completed without attention to the application and implementation stages. Answering the 'how' questions about coaching practice will require recourse to supporting disciplines. However, in time, sufficient weight of evidence will be generated to create a coaching-specific family of theories.

SUMMARY

This chapter will have familiarised you with the following:

- the purpose of research and the status of research in sports coaching;
- a research typology that emphasises application and implementation, and an emphasis on the coaching process;
- six characteristics of the coaching process and their attendant research implications;
- sports coaching represented as an expert system and its capacity to generate research questions about the coaching process;
- three examples of generating a research agenda: hypotheses created from a description of coaching practice; an example of comparing ideal and research-derived models to identify important issues; an example of the research questions from a naturalistic study into coaches' decision making;
- a summary of the important questions to be addressed by the research community.

A BASIS FOR PROFESSIONALISATION

CHAPTER SEVENTEEN

▼ **SPRINGBOARD TO THE FUTURE**

A Short Essay on Developments in Sports Coaching

There is a danger that the attempt to present coherent content in each chapter has led to a degree of fragmentation in the message as a whole. The analysis of each topic area in depth and the supporting of these topics with sufficient specialist content has been designed to provide an appropriate academic understanding of sports coaching. However, the coverage has been fairly broad and the reader has been invited (even required) to build on that understanding, chapter by chapter. The purpose of this final chapter, therefore, is to provide a postscript that brings some coherence to the themes running through the book and to situate this within a personal interpretation of the issues that will shape the future of sports coaching. The ideas presented are unashamedly intended to stimulate debate.

The strategy for the development of coaching in the UK that has finally emerged in 2001 is very welcome indeed (UK Sport 2001). However, this sends out mixed messages. The positive message is that sports coaching is being taken seriously, that the priorities have been recognised, and that a co-ordinated approach is signalled. However, there is also a sense of *déjà vu*. The aims and objectives of the strategy are largely those that were recognised ten to fifteen years ago – ones towards which I thought we were already working. Indeed, some of the targets in the strategy are some way distant. We can assume that genuine endeavours have been undertaken to improve coach education, status and professionalisation. The only conclusion that can be drawn is that factors have been conspiring against us and the constraints have been too serious to overcome. The strategy will only succeed if these constraints are removed and the environment for development changes. This short essay deals with some of the issues that will influence the professionalisation of sports coaching and the extent to which these are underpinned by an adequate intellectual and academic argument.

I will begin with two of the statements in the consultation document sent out by the UK Sports Council (1999). The first says that 'an integrated structure of qualifications and training based on national standards, linked to the government's structure of mainstream qualifications, education and training and funding (the National Qualifications Framework)' should be part of the vision (1999: 4). This is a laudable aspiration but it raises enormous questions about the readiness of coach education, as it leaves the twentieth century, to fulfil such ambition. This is particularly so if it is intended that the higher levels of qualifications should be included. The second proposal mentioned is to 'integrate sport science and sport medicine into coach education' (1999: 4). This may be a matter of semantics, but the issue is whether the performance coach is to act as a specialist sport scientist and paramedic. I would hope not – there is enough in the coach's specialist role to be going on with. However, if the intention is to enable the performance coach to direct the endeavours of the specialist and to interrogate the findings, then the intention is entirely appropriate. I have begun with these two examples merely to be able to say that the underlying issues were dealt with at some length in the previous sixteen chapters. I will not reopen the debates, but I do suggest that many of our good intentions must be supported by an appropriate analysis of the coaching process and coaching practice. Central to this is the understanding that can only be achieved by recourse to the conceptual framework that underpins sports coaching.

The second health warning is that the essay may sound a little negative in its analysis. This is not pessimism about the future but, rather, a result of the high ambitions and expectations for the business of coaching that come from a conviction about its importance. The development of the profession has already shown itself to be a very difficult proposition and I do not anticipate that this will become any easier in the UK in the short term. The theme for the essay is how a change in our concept of what is central to the enterprise of performance coaching, and how changes in research and coach education are needed to advance professionalisation. There is a danger that a preoccupation with the structural elements of becoming a profession (an association, code of ethics, conditions of service and so on) has blinded us to the debate about what it is that coaches profess to provide, and what implications this has for education. One consideration is that the drawbridge needs to be pulled up around a more focused role definition.

There are a number of positives in the environment. The National Lottery has greatly increased funding to sport and this has provided a much more comprehensive sport development programme and a more obvious commitment to performance sport outcomes. Undoubtedly, more high-profile coaching posts have been created. However, I believe that the implications are far wider. National Lottery funding has increased the scale of performance sport, has made it more visible, and has increased greatly the resources to support the programmes. Also, the increased attention to outcomes has attached greater importance to accountability. I believe that ultimately this will lead to the role of the coach being examined more closely, to the benefit of the profession. A second positive has been the reversal of the traditional non-coach emphasis in some sports – witness the changes in the profile of coaches in rugby union and cricket. Nevertheless, some professional sport (perhaps most of it) is stubbornly resistant to the notion of qualifications-led employment and its contribution to the development of a profession for sport coaches is decidedly mixed.

Having praised cricket and rugby for becoming much more coach-orientated, it is also necessary to note the high proportion of overseas coaches in employment. Generally, there has been an influx of performance coaches, programme directors and systems managers from overseas. The strategy is clear and the rationale can be defended. Immediate gains are anticipated from investing in proven success at the highest levels. However, it is necessary to highlight a couple of potential dangers. The first is that these coaches (not just overseas) have normally been successful rather than effective (although it is anticipated that they will be both). The debate earlier in the book has pointed out the dangers of assuming that a capacity for effective practice has been developed or that it can be transferred and applied to new situations. My point is not to question in any way the abilities of any of these coaches but to point out that our capacity for engaging in evaluation is still limited. A second danger, and a very serious one, is that we rely on the good practice of these expert coaches without questioning how it was developed. We need to critique and analyse that practice in order to inform our own development programmes.

There has been a clear purpose to the book; that is, to demonstrate that increased attention to the conceptual framework surrounding sports coaching is necessary to appreciate fully the coaching process and associated elements: coaching practice, coach education, professional development, coaching effectiveness and coaching research. Each of these is a problematical area of coaching studies. The conceptual framework has not yet become established and the book is a contribution to this endeavour. In particular, there are serious shortcomings in research associated with coaching. To be specific, there is too much of a participation emphasis, too many observational studies and too many leadership/style issues. Put bluntly, very little of this research has told us much about what coaches do and how they operate. It would be inappropriate merely to reiterate the early chapters of the book but there is a need to emphasise some of the key factors. These are based on a belief that performance coaching is more important, more influential, more cerebral, more difficult, more cognitive, more professional and more humane than it and its proponents are given credit for.

Performance coaching practice can be more immediately appreciated if six factors are taken into account; (1) the difference between participation and performance coaching; (2) the four levels of role descriptor (direct intervention, intervention support, constraints management and strategic co-ordination); (3) the primacy of decision making and other forms of cognitive organisation; (4) the process nature of coaching and its attendant sub-processes; (5) the role of the coach and the relationship to support personnel; and (6) boundary characteristics and their impact on goal attainment. Each of these factors has implications for professionalisation, whether in terms of boundary maintenance or defining the nature of coaching expertise. The message being transmitted throughout the book is that there is a good deal of work still required to incorporate this thinking into education and training, and to influence policy 'movers and shakers'.

A model for coaching was presented in Chapter 6. This was a fairly complex model with attendant assumptions and pointers to operationalisation. Why do it? Because our level of understanding and conceptual/theoretical development should allow us to do so! It was made clear that this is not a prescription for practice: it is a tool to help analyse practice. I am making no attempt to praise the model. It will have served its purpose if energetic students and practitioners amend/improve/discard for a better model. What it can do is help to delineate a research agenda. The chapter on coaching practice was important, largely because there have been so few attempts to examine practice that are not sport-specific. Admittedly, there were some inductions and leaps of faith when working from limited evidence (plus a liberal sprinkling of personal experience) but this task needed to be attempted. Again, if this leads to more informed analysis and a growing aggregation of evidence on the practice of performance coaches, it will have served its purpose.

Sport-specificity has proved to be a genuine dilemma. Professional development may depend to some extent on a genericism with which to tie the profession together and yet there are very obvious sport-specific differences. It seems likely that in the interests of professionalisation there should be a reduced emphasis on technical proficiency. The process elements of the job – regulation, planning and management (the strategic co-ordination of variables) – need to be emphasised. Coaching cannot become a profession until we decide on (and defend) that which makes us different, that which makes us professional. Technical knowledge can be assumed: we need to build on the co-ordinating, managing, planning, decision-taking role, with appropriate levels of delivery expertise.

The issue of the coach's interpersonal role may be more controversial. This is not a result of any doubt over its centrality to the coaching process, but more to do with what is considered important about it. For example, there is equally no doubt that the inter-personal dimension of coaching activity lends itself to abuse of power and to harassment of a variety of types. For this reason, education, dissemination of good practice, vigilance and awareness must be given a higher priority. However, a good deal of energy is expended on another aspect of interpersonal behaviour: leadership style. This may be a favourite research focus, but it is far from clear that the majority of performance athletes find it a live issue. Coaches are not unthinking autocrats. The level of direction and control is more likely to be proportional to that which is commensurate with the athlete's maturity and knowledge, and the demands of the sport. For many athletes, and in particular those in team sports, coaches exercise a directional style that is entrusted to them by the athletes themselves. This, of course, does not mean that coaches do not have the welfare of (in particular) young people at heart. What it does mean is that the relationship cannot be measured by simplistic models of leadership style and that coaching studies have not investigated interpersonal relationships sufficiently well to be able to describe these with confidence.

It will be in the interests of coaching to emphasise the interpersonal dimension: to be perceived as a 'people profession'. However, this is also one of the weakest parts of existing provision and practice. Not only is the education and training of this element almost non-existent, it is not part of coach recruitment. A more salient point is that there is also no evidence of any impact of coaching style in performance sport. The questions that should form the basis of our concerns are these. Is the 'style/method' appropriate to the circumstances and the athletes? Does it allow for effective delivery of the intervention programme? Does it allow learning/development appropriate to the goals of the coaching process?

A good deal of emphasis was placed on the social context within which sports coaching takes place. Just as with the issues of style and professionalisation, it is important that attention is not drawn to the superficial aspects of the problem. This can be illustrated with a couple of examples. There is a significant problem for coaching with a number of ethical issues, such as drugs in sport and harassment. Whilst these specific problems need to be tackled 'head on', there are contributory factors that are common to many of the issues. The lack of professionalisation means that coaching is characterised by volunteerism, lack of accountability, isolation, secrecy, absence of boundary controls and a complete absence of models of expected and acceptable professional practice. It is in this climate of unregulated and unmonitored practice that more specific inappropriate practice related to individual predispositions finds room to flourish. In the case of the lack of women coaches, there is no doubt that there is discrimination, both purposeful and structural. However, one of the underlying factors is the lack of scale of women's performance sport from which most performance coaches will originate. This does not excuse the discrimination and territoriality of male coaches and officials, but it does suggest that recruitment of women coaches will be unsuccessful if policies such as anticipating transition from participation coaching are followed. Recruitment policies need to be tailored to the causes rather than the symptoms.

When subjected to analysis and scrutiny, it becomes clear that the 'profession' does not fare well in terms of its social image. In addition to the perception that coach education is a luxury for some sports, coaching is evidently male-dominated, shows no signs of an ethnicity balance and has an almost complete disregard for disability sport. The emphasis given to a code of conduct is understandable (and, indeed, welcome), but we are at present unable to demonstrate that this impacts on practitioners. Ethical practice forms part of the rhetoric of sports coaching but is not an enforceable indicator of professional practice. It is also in the context of professional standards that the failure to establish criteria of effectiveness is important. This really is an intractable problem, and it is easy to understand why success is used as the most accessible measure. Many potential solutions were examined but there was no evident practical realisation of how any of these ideas might be translated into a working measure. There is no doubt that the conceptual analysis will have brought much greater clarity but in this case I fear that this has merely highlighted the depth of the problem.

Coach education and professionalisation are in something of a chicken-and-egg situation. Coach education has not been substantial enough to support professional status, but traditionally the rewards available have not been sufficient to merit and attract individuals to a lengthy education process. This suggests that the way forward will not be achieved solely by identifying improved versions of coach education (although this is welcome and necessary). One significant concern is that the structures and delivery mechanisms of coach education are being improved without having satisfactorily identified the essence of professional expertise. The question has been raised several times: what is it that coaches do that others cannot do? Leaving aside the technical ammunition required for the task, we need a clear definition of the expertise that performance sport coaches exhibit at various stages of their professional development. This book was a contribution to that task and the message that is intended to come across is that the coach is a manager of a performance system. This is a higher-order task requiring considerable specialist technical knowledge, management and delivery of an intervention programme, co-ordination of a wide range of environmental influences, goal-directed manipulation of a very wide range of contributory performance variables, and operationalised in the context of a largely interpersonal activity with attendant social, emotional, psychological and developmental factors. In order to achieve this, the coach requires developed capacities in delivery, interpersonal and process skills and knowledge. In addition to craft skills, much of professional expertise relies on cognitive organisation developed over time and experience but as yet not sufficiently well understood.

It has been acknowledged that the approach adopted for describing competences and assessing them at the early levels of national occupational standards is inappropriate for performance coaches. We need to learn from other occupational groups that have created holistic professional competences that embrace the occupational role. These can be developed over the range of levels of professional competence. This is not the same as moving from level three to level four, or from four to five. Such structures are not sufficiently sensitive to occupations to embrace the development of a competence through novice, competent and expert status (and remember that in setting out minimum levels of 'competence' they do not attempt to do so). The resolution and accommodation of occupational standards, expertise, occupational roles and professional competences is far from resolved.

Perhaps the most disappointing feature of the book is the number of occasions on which it has been necessary to say that there is little research to support the content. The lack of attention to performance sports coaching by the research community has been both frustrating and surprising. At the same time, it is also understandable. Research into sport performance components is more manageable, closer to traditional research paradigms in implementation, and more 'acceptable' in academic circles by being closer to 'pure' science research. What is disappointing is that research funding has largely originated from non-academic sources but has been channelled in this direction without any apparent critical appraisal. Research into coaching practice is marginalised. There is very little implementation research and even less naturalistic research. The tendency has been to ask questions that can be answered rather than questions that will illuminate practice or influence practice. In addition, this research has predominantly been North American and certainly not directed to performance sport.

Where does this leave us? The portents are certainly positive, even if the realisation of the professionalisation of sports coaching is as yet some way off. There are a number of positive features of the environment: the intent to professionalise, much improved coach education, improved career opportunities, the diffusion of coaching studies into higher education (perhaps leading to increased attention to research), greatly improved Continuing Professional Development (CPD) programmes for coaches, increased resources, and more focused attention to performance sport. However, the scale and quality of the change is not yet sufficient to bring about the goal of professionalisation in the short to medium term. There are more paid posts in sports coaching but the scale of this is not significant enough at this stage to reverse the traditional ascribed occupational status. There are now more Higher Education courses in coaching studies, but the translation into performance coaching practice will take some time and this is still not the traditional route into coaching. The differentiation of coaching roles into participation and performance contexts is very necessary but it does, of course, greatly diminish the number of practitioners.

Key to professionalisation is to identify coaches' expertise. Analysis of coaching practice, coach education and research into coaching are required to support this endeavour. At the centre of this is the need to have a vocabulary and a set of conceptual tools with which to describe, analyse and understand coaching practice. This book is a contribution to the conceptual framework that helps us to understand the coaching process. The diffusion of that understanding into the process of professionalisation will accelerate the achievement of that goal. The athlete is the centre of performance sport and the coach is the facilitator of the athlete's aspirations. Performance systems are said to be 'athlete-centred'. Of course they are: how could they be anything else! However, it might be more appropriate to describe them as 'coaching process-centred'. The coaching process embraces both athlete and coach and provides for a variety of collaborative models. It is also the best descriptor of the purposeful engagement of the athlete, coach and many other contributors to achieving appropriate goals in performance sport. Sports coaching concepts provide a window through which to understand and appreciate coaching practice and should be an essential element of coaching studies.

STUDY QUESTIONS

CHAPTER 1 HISTORICAL AND DEVELOPMENTAL CONTEXT

1 To what extent can the failure to develop coaching at a national level be explained by the autonomy of National Governing Bodies?
2 To what extent has the amateur ethic constrained the professionalisation of sports coaching?
3 Has the low status of sports coaches been influenced significantly by the 'generalist' sport teaching contribution of the PE teacher?
4 What impact has the absence of a strong professional body had on the profile and professionalisation of sports coaching?

CHAPTER 2 DEVELOPING A CONCEPTUAL FRAMEWORK

1 Does this set of conceptual 'posers' adequately represent the full range of questions necessary for a complete analysis of coaching practice? If not, what would be added?
2 A large number of questions have been raised in the preceding paragraphs. Aggregate these questions and attempt to answer them for one sport. Are some of the questions more important than others for understanding coaching practice?
3 Is it unreasonable to expect meta-theory development in a field so diverse as coaching – compare to a theory of teaching! However, this should not preclude the conceptual clarity necessary to analyse practice; should it?

CHAPTER 3 THE COACHING PROCESS

1 The search for commonality and genericism takes place in the context of considerable sport-specific differences and the unusual situation of coaches competing with one another. Is there sufficient commonality in the role to justify the search?
2 Does the ambiguity between the roles of mentor and coach raise the possibility that the term 'a sport mentor' is a better term for the holistic role of the coach, perhaps leaving the coaching role to performance enhancement?
3 The failure to acknowledge sports coaching as a process is perhaps the most limiting aspect of coaching research. However, is the purposeful aggregation of a series of coaching interventions sometimes challenged by practice in team sports?

4   There is no doubt that the boundary criteria are important. Are they more important as concepts or is quantification necessary?
5   The diversity of skills required by the coach is considerable. This suggests that coach education should be 'skills-based'. Are some skills more important than others at each stage of professional development?
6   Participation and performance coaching are not on a coaching process continuum – they are distinctive processes. On the other hand, the performers can generally be placed on a performance continuum. Is level of sport performance a better conceptualisation for coaching forms?

CHAPTER 4 THE ROLE OF THE COACH

1   Role-related terminology can be applied to all complex occupational activities. Nevertheless, the role of the coach is problematical. Is it a matter of historical development, lack of occupational development or simply the vast array of situations within which athletes wish to improve their performances that causes the confusion?
2   There is a complex relationship between function, level of developed expertise and occupational position. Is this evident in coach education?

CHAPTER 5 MODELLING THE COACHING PROCESS

1   Models are generic representations. They are not 'used' by coaches but are available for analysis purposes. Nevertheless, this raises the question of whether the principles embedded in the model are (1) used in coach education, and (2) sufficiently understood by coaches to be used for evaluation purposes.

CHAPTER 6 A PROPOSED MODEL FOR COACHING

1   These assumptions can be divided into those that are sociocultural, about performance, about the nature of the process and about effective practice. Are the assumptions internally consistent? Do they reflect performance sport?
2   Is evidence of the generation, storage and use of information/data a valuable way of determining whether or not the coach operates in a systematic fashion?
3   Is a threshold level of knowledge required before becoming a performance coach? Is the novice performance coach already a sport specialist?

CHAPTER 7 COACHING PRACTICE

1   There is no doubt about the need for specificity of design and delivery, and yet there is clearly a generic coaching process and 'process skills' element. How does coach education deal with this?
2   The use of the words 'control' or 'manipulation' are intended to be directed to the range of performance variables but are often interpreted as a negative feature of interpersonal behaviour. How could this confusion be better explained?
3   Systematic behaviour is perceived not to be a feature of all coaching practice – even successful practice! Does this imply that recognising coaching practice is difficult or that successful athletes are not necessarily the product of effective coaches?

4   There is no doubt that planning, of all sorts, is important. Given the likelihood of contingency and partially fulfilled schedules, the most important record to be kept is that of 'work done', not 'work planned'. Would this be a change in coaching practice?

5   Intuition has been used as a convenient 'hook' for the absence of an explanation of coaching practice. Is it surprising, therefore, that status, education and expertise in coaching are problematical?

6   Remember that this description is dealing with coaches' decision making that is non-deliberative, that is, with little or no time to reflect. How do you react to it? Does it have immediate face validity?

7   It is worth noting that speedy decision making is required not just in competition but in directing training exercises and resolving problem situations as they arise. Once again, how is this integrated into coach education?

CHAPTER 8 A QUESTION OF STYLE AND PHILOSOPHY

1   If we accept that heredity sets the limits of achievement but coaching practice determines the level of achievement within these limits, the interpersonal dimension may be impacting on the small increments of performance that determine success. Is this too strong a statement?

2   Sport performance 'on the day' is subject to some variability. It seems quite likely that interpersonal factors will impact at this stage. Is sufficient attention paid to the management of competition and the coach's role in it?

3   Why is style important? The categories above may describe individuals rather than the totality of coaching practice. However, is style to be left to personal whim or are some approaches more effective, more appropriate and more successful than others? Where is the evidence? If it's too important to be left to chance, how have selection, recruitment and education dealt with this?

4   The capacity to assimilate leadership options may be best achieved through social learning. This has implications for the selection of coach mentors and for senior coaches more generally. This assumes adaptable leadership behaviours. Are they adaptable and have we considered this as a part of the formal training of coaches?

5   It is not unusual for coaches to express statements about how behaviour and practice 'should be'. Is it possible to 'borrow' a philosophy from others or from education, or must it come from experience? Can a non-coach have a coaching philosophy?

CHAPTER 9 A HUMANISTIC APPROACH TO COACHING

1   The balance between athlete welfare and competition success is rarely discussed in print. Is it possible that National Lottery funding and enhanced life-style management have encouraged athletes to accept the traditional disincentives of elite sport participation?

2   We have an intuitive sense that the majority of individuals are not harmed by their sport experience – even given the excesses of youth and elite sport. However, positive personal growth goes beyond this. Is this a matter for individuals or is a cultural shift required?

3   Adopting humanistic practice may well be an issue of security for coaches. Just as athletes become increasingly able to cope with responsibility, this will also happen to coaches. Is this an approach to be adopted by novice performance coaches?
4   Humanistic principles are appropriate but perhaps provide an underlying philosophy for practice. It is not reasonable to expect a completely humanistic approach (is it?). Perhaps behaviour should be measured by these standards, or do you think that they should act as a warning light?

CHAPTER 10 COACHING AND SOCIAL CONTEXT

1   There would be little argument that coach education has neglected the social component. Would it not be true to say, however, that this is only one of a number of missing pieces of the jigsaw?
2   The sub-cultural features of performance sport may be very important, both as determinants of social cohesion and as markers for 'acceptable' coaching behaviours. Do coaches build walls around their areas of expertise and security?
3   The Coach of the Year awards are an entirely appropriate part of the promotion of the 'profession'. However, does this merely reinforce the emphasis on achieved status?
4   Which model should sports coaching use as an exemplar? The instructor might be best thought of as a client patronage practitioner, whereas the teacher/coach is often funded by the state. Is the performance coach more of a manager?

CHAPTER 11 MOTIVATIONS AND RECRUITMENT IN SPORTS COACHING

1   The employment of overseas coaches in prominent positions is justified in terms of the experience required to deal with the elite athlete. However, there is a balance of advantages and disadvantages. How would you interpret the balance of individual quality and catalytic impact versus an absence of role models, perception of 'glass ceiling', lack of development emphasis on UK coaches, and absence of long-term planning?
2   In a sport with which you are familiar, what is the recruitment policy (if there is one)? Is it assumed that coaches will migrate from participation coaching? Is the coach education programme used as a recruitment mechanism? How is it advertised?

CHAPTER 12 WHERE ARE ALL THE WOMEN COACHES?

1   Although perhaps not resolvable in this chapter, an interesting policy question over which to ruminate is whether women coaches must inevitably be a reflection of the situation in sport more generally or whether they can act as a catalyst for change. Which needs to come first?
2   One interpretation of the data in Figure 12.1, and a possible strategic option, is that the focus for increased numbers of women in leadership positions should be in forms of coaching other than performance sport. However, would that (a) reinforce the male stereotype, and (b) reduce the availability of role models?

3   Although it might be argued that the coach's mental models depend to some extent on performance experience in some sports, the interpretation of coaching as a largely cognitive exercise should render it gender neutral. Do you agree?

4   The transition into coaching for women is a good illustration of the failure to appreciate the lessons to be learned from conceptual analysis. Many commentators talk of the reduction in women coaches as the performance level of the athlete increases. However, this fails to account for the fact that there is little transition from participation to performance sport, for either athletes or coaches. In other words, the explanation has to lie solely in performance sport, not in the transition, which is difficult and generally unlikely in any case! Does this help to focus research?

CHAPTER 13 COACHING AND ETHICAL PRACTICE

1   It might be argued that athlete welfare issues should take precedence over matters of regulation. However, if asked to create a list of concerns, which would coaches identify as most pressing? An interesting research question.

2   The acceptance of elite sport sub-cultural excesses of behaviour may be part of their appeal to spectators. Limits are understood and excesses punished. In other words, the actors accept a different set of assumptions. Is this amoral?

CHAPTER 14 EFFECTIVE COACHING AND THE EFFECTIVE COACH

1   It may be easier to identify the ineffective coach. If competence is assumed, must effectiveness be assumed? How would you disprove this? Consider this option as you read the chapter.

2   Despite what has been said, the effectiveness/goal achievement argument is attractive. The proviso is that the goals are appropriate. However, is there a tendency to think in terms of outcome goals when making this judgement?

3   One of the problems in using goals is that they are dynamic and constantly adjusted. They are achieved over an extended period, and accommodation is made to the emerging circumstances (including results) applying to the athletes. There is a tendency, therefore, always to achieve goals! How can this be resolved for research?

4   One of the lessons to be learned from the list of constraints is the degree to which contributory factors may well be beyond the control of the coach. How does this impact on accountability, or measures of success?

5   Coaching practice is centred on ambitious outcomes and realistic intermediate targets. These are amended as the planning period progresses. The 'moving' nature of the goals is contributed to by not being data-based. Is this an accurate analysis?

CHAPTER 15 COACH EDUCATION AND COACHING PRACTICE

1   There is no doubt that, traditionally, coach education has emphasised the training and technical elements. Has the absence of an 'educational' element been a contributory factor to the slow development of the profession?

2   It might be argued that specific sports are merely the context for a generic coaching capacity and that, therefore, the focus should be on the common education and training elements. Is this too simplistic an argument?

CHAPTER 16 SETTING A RESEARCH AGENDA

1   Should research using public funds always have an 'end-user' certificate? Other than for 'pure' research, should the findings/implications be targeted at a specific element of the coaching process?

▼ USEFUL WEBSITES

The following list of websites is by no means exhaustive. You will be able to use any search engine to discover a very wide range of sites dealing with specific sports and also with the use of the coaching analogy for personal and executive development. These examples illustrate the sources available to support studies in coaching. In particular, there is valuable information on current initiatives in coach education, professionalisation issues, and sports science research linked to coaching practice.

1 http: //www.sportscoachuk.org/

   Sports Coach UK. This is an important site for keeping up to date with coaching educa-tion and development initiatives in the UK. There are links to CoachXL and Co@achIT, which support performance coaches. There is also a link to High Performance Coaching services for coaches of elite athletes but this requires a password.

2 http: //www.sportengland.org/

   SportEngland. Very useful for sport development initiatives and, in particular, activities involving participation coaching.

3 http: //www.sportscotland.org/

   SportScotland. Use this site to link to coaching services and examples of national initiatives to develop coach education and services to coaches.

4 http: //www.uksport.gov.uk/

   UK Sport. A very valuable site for keeping up to date with developments in elite sport. There are details of the World Class Coaching Programme and the ACE UK athlete support initiative.

5 http: //www.rohan.sdsu.edu/dept/coachsci/index.htm

   Coaching Science Abstracts. This website is maintained by Professor Brent Rushall. The research and comment papers are grouped thematically and deal with issues such as imagery, over-training and 'coaching factors'.

6 http: //www.sportsci.org/

   Sportscience. The site is focused on sports science research with a good coverage of disciplines related to sport performance. Much of the material is coaching-related.

7   http: //physed.otago.ac.nz/sosol/home.htm

Sociology of Sport Online. This is an online journal that has had a significant number of coaching-related articles.

8   http: //www.education.ed.ac.uk/cis/index/html

Coaches' Information Service. This is the website of the International Society of Biomechanics in Sport. Not all of the research articles are biomechanics-related.

9   http: //www.bases.org.uk

British Association for Sport and Exercise Science. Although there is as yet no specialisation in sports coaching, this site is useful for keeping up to date with performance research.

10   http: //www.coach.ca
     http: //www.ausport.gov.au/acc/

These are the websites of the *Coaching Association of Canada* and the *Australian Coaching Council*. These are very valuable comparators for information on coach education and services to coaches.

11   http: //www.chre.vt.edu/~/cys/

Coaching Youth Sports. This site is North American in orientation but a good exemplar of participation coaching issues and practice.

12   http: //www.brianmac.demon.co.uk/

Sports Coach. Orientated towards track and field athletics. Nevertheless, a good example of attention given to coaching practice.

▼ REFERENCES

Abraham, A. and Collins, D. (1998) 'Examining and Extending Research in Coach Development', *Quest*, 50: 55–79.

Acosta, R. V. and Carpenter, L. J. (1994) 'The Status of Women in Intercollegiate Athletics', in S. Birrell and C. L. Cole (eds) *Women, Sport and Culture*, Champaign, IL: Human Kinetics.

Albrow, M. (1990) *Max Weber's Construction of Social Theory*. London: St Martin's Press.

Anthony, D. (1980) *A Strategy for British Sport*. London: C. Hurst & Co.

Arnold, P. (1997) *Sport, Ethics and Education*. London: Cassell.

Ball, D. W. and Loy, J. W. (1975) *Sport and Social Order: Contributions to the Sociology of Sport*. Reading, MA: Addison-Wesley.

Balyi, I. (1998a) 'Long-term Planning of Athlete Development', *FHS*, 1(September): 8–11.

—— (1998b) 'The Training to Compete Phase', *FHS*, 2 (December): 8–13.

BANC/NCF (1987) *The Development of Coaching in Britain: A Consultation Document*. BANC/NCF.

Barber, H. (1998) 'Examining Gender Differences in Sources and Levels of Perceived Competence in Interscholastic Coaches', *The Sport Psychologist*, 12: 237–52.

Barber, H. and Eckrich, J. (1998) 'Methods and Criteria Employed in the Evaluation of Intercollegiate Coaches', *Journal of Sport Management*, 12: 301–22.

Barry, T. (1994) 'How to Be a Good Coach', *Management Development Review*, 7(4): 24–6.

Bartlett, C. A. and Ghoshal, S. (1995) 'Changing the Role of Top Management: Beyond Systems to People', *Harvard Business Review*, May–June, 132–43.

Beckett, D. (1996) 'Critical Judgement and Professional Practice', *Educational Theory*, 46(2), 135–49.

Beech, N. and Brockbank, A. (1999) 'Power, Knowledge and Psychosocial Dynamics in Mentoring', *Management Learning*, 30(1): 7–25.

Beloff, M. J., Kerr, T. and Demetriou, M. (1999) *Sports Law*. Oxford: Hart Publishers.

Berliner, D. C. (1994) 'Expertise: The Wonder of Exemplary Performances', in J. Mangieri and C. Black (eds) *Creating Powerful Thinking in Teachers and Students: Diverse Perspectives* (pp. 141–86). Fort Worth, TX: Harcourt Brace.

Black, S. J. and Weiss, M. R. (1992) 'The Relationship among Perceived Coaching Behaviours, Perceptions of Ability, and Motivation in Competitive Age Group Swimmers', *Journal of Sport and Exercise Psychology*, 14: 309–25.

Bloom, G. A., Durand-Bush, N. and Salmela, J. H. (1997) 'Pre and Post Competition Routines of Expert Coaches of Team Sports', *The Sport Psychologist*, 11: 127–41.

Bloom, G. A., Schinke, R. J. and Salmela, J. H. (1997) 'The Development of Communication Skills by Elite Basketball Coaches', *Coaching and Sport Science Journal*, 2(3): 3–10.

Bloom, G. A., Durand-Bush, N., Schinke, R. and Salmela, J. H. (1998) 'The Importance of Mentoring in the Development of Coaches and Athletes', *International Journal of Sport Psychology*, 29(3): 267–81.

Bloom, G. A., Crumpton, R. and Anderson, J. E. (1999) 'A Systematic Observation Study of the Teaching Behaviours of an Expert Basketball Coach', *The Sport Psychologist*, 13: 157–70.

Bompa, T. O. (1999) *Periodisation: Theory and Methodology of Training* (4th edn). Champaign, IL: Human Kinetics.

Boreham, N. C. (1994) 'The Dangerous Practice of Thinking', *Medical Education*, 28: 172–9.

Borrie, A. (1998) 'Coaching: Art or Science?' *Insight*, 1(1): 5.

Botterill, C. (1978) 'Psychology of Coaching', *Coaching Review*, 1(4).

Brackenridge, C. H. (1997) ''He Owned Me Basically . . .' Women's Experience of Sexual Abuse in Sport', *International Review for the Sociology of Sport*, 32(2): 115–30.

—— (2001) *Spoilsports: Understanding and Preventing Sexual Exploitation in Sport*. London: Routledge.

Breife, S. (1981) 'Goal Setting in Humanistic Coaching', *Momentum*, 6(2): 1–7.

Bridges, D. (1996) 'Competence-based Education and Training: Progress or Villainy?', *Journal of Philosophy of Education*, 30(3): 361–76.

British Olympic Association (1996) *Athletes' Commission Report 1996*. London: BOA.

Brockbank, A. and Beech, N. (1999) 'Guiding Blight', *People Management*, 6 May: 52–4.

Brohm, J. M. (1978) *Sport: A Prison of Measured Time*. London: Ink Links.

Burke, K., Peterson, D. and Nix, C. (1995) 'The Effects of the Coaches' Use of Humour on Female Volleyball Players' Evaluation of their Coaches', *Journal of Sport Behavior*, 18(2): 83–9.

Burrage, M. (1994) 'Routine and Discrete Relationships: Professional Accreditation and the State in Britain', in T. Becher (ed.) *Governments and Professional Education*. Buckingham: SRHE and Open University Press.

Cahill, B. R. and Pearl, A. J. (eds) (1993) *Intensive Participation in Children's Sport*. Champaign, IL: Human Kinetics.

Cain, G. (1980) 'Coaching – an Art or Science', *Athletics Coach*, September, 10–14.

Campbell, S. (1993) 'Coaching Education around the World', *Sports Science Review*, 2(2): 62–74.

Capel, S. (1997) *Learning to Teach Physical Education in the Secondary School*. London: Routledge.

Carling, W. and Heller, R. (1995) *The Way to Win: Strategies for Success in Business and Sport*. London: Little, Brown & Co.

Cashmore, E. (2000) *Making Sense of Sports* (3rd edn). London: Routledge.

Centre for Leisure Research (1992) 'A Study of Sports Coaching in Grampian Region', Unpublished report to the Scottish Sports Council.

—— (1994a) 'A Study of Sports Coaching in Tayside Region', Unpublished report to the Scottish Sports Council.

—— (1994b) 'A Study of Sports Coaching in Borders Region', Unpublished report to the Scottish Sports Council.

Chappell, C. and Hager, P. (1994) 'Values and Competency Standards', *Journal of Further and Higher Education*, 18(3): 12–23.

Chase, M. A., Feltz, D. L. and Lirgg, C. D. (1997) 'Do Coaches' Efficacy Expectations for their Teams Predict Team Performance?', *The Sport Psychologist*, 11: 8–23.

Checkland, P. B. (1999) *Soft Systems Methodology: A 30-year Retrospective*. Chichester: John Wiley & Sons.

Chelladurai, P. and Saleh, S. D. (1980) 'Dimensions of Leadership Behavior in Sports: Development of a Leadership Scale', *Journal of Sport Psychology*, 2: 34–45.

Chelladurai, P. (1984) 'Discrepancy between Preferences and Perceptions of Leadership Behavior and Satisfaction of Athletes in Varying Sports', *Journal of Sport Psychology*, 2(2): 14–29.

Chelladurai, P. and Arnott, M. (1985) 'Decision Styles in Coaching: Preferences of Basketball Players', *Research Quarterly for Exercise and Sport*, 56: 15–24.

Chelladurai, P., Haggerty, T. R. and Baxter, P.R. (1989) 'Decision Style Choices of University Basketball Coaches and Players', *Journal of Sport and Exercise Psychology*, 11: 201–15.

Chelladurai, P. and Kuga, D. J. (1996) 'Teaching and Coaching: Group and Task Differences', *Quest*, 48(4): 470–85.

Chi, M., Glaser, R. and Farr, M. (eds) (1988) *The Nature of Expertise*. Hillsdale, NJ: Lawrence Erlbaum Associates.

Clarke, G. and Humberstone, B. (eds) (1997) *Researching Women and Sport*. Basingstoke: Macmillan.

Claxton, D. and Lacy, A. C. (1986) 'A Comparison of Practice Field Behaviours between Winning High School Football Coaches and Tennis Coaches', *Journal of Applied Research in Coaching and Athletics*, 1(3): 188–200.

Claxton, D. (1988) 'A Systematic Observation of More or Less Successful High School Coaches', *Journal of Teaching in Physical Education*, 9: 294–306.

Claxton, G. (1998) 'Knowing without Knowing Why', *The Psychologist*, 11(5): 217–20.

Coaching Review Panel (1991) *Coaching Matters: A Review of Coaching and Coach Education in the UK*. London: Sports Council.

Coakley, J. and Dunning, E. (eds) (2000) *Handbook of Sports Studies*. London: Sage.

—— (ed.) (2001) *Sport in Society: Issues and Controversies* (7th edn). Boston: McGraw Hill.

Coe, P. (1985) 'Should Parents Coach their own Children?', *Coaching Focus*, 2(Autumn): 10–12.

Coghlan, J. (with I.M. Webb) (1990) *Sport and British Politics since 1960*. London: Falmer Press.

Cohen, M. S., Freeman, J. T. and Wolf, S. (1996) 'Metarecognition in Time Stressed Decision Making: Recognising, Critiquing and Correcting', *Human Factors*, 38(2): 206–19.

COMPASS (1999) *COMPASS 1999: Sports Participation in Europe*. London: UK Sports Council.

Conway, C. (1998) *Strategies for Mentoring*. Chichester: Wiley.

Cooke, G. (1996) 'The Power of Partnership: Sport, Coaching and Physical Education', *Supercoach*, 2(Summer): 10–11.

Côte, J., Salmela, J. H., Trudel, P., Baria, A. and Russell, S. (1995a) 'The Coaching Model: A Grounded Assessment of Expert Gymnastic Coaches' Knowledge', *Journal of Sport and Exercise Psychology*, 17(1): 1–17.

Côte, J., Salmela, J. H. and Russell, S. (1995b) 'The Knowledge of High-performance Gymnastic Coaches: Competition and Training Considerations', *The Sport Psychologist*, 9: 76–95.

Crisfield, P. and Houlston, D. (1993) *Planning Your Programme*. Leeds: National Coaching Foundation.

Crisfield, P., Cabral, P. and Carpenter, F. (1996) *The Successful Coach: Guidelines for Coaching Practice*. Leeds: National Coaching Foundation.

Cross, N. (1990) 'Terry Denison – An Insight into a Coaching Philosophy', *The Swimming Times*, 67(4): 17–19.

—— (1991) 'Arguments in Favour of a Humanistic Coaching Process', *The Swimming Times*, 68(11): 17–18.

—— (1995a) 'Coaching Effectiveness in Hockey: A Scottish Perspective', *Scottish Journal of Physical Education*, 23(1): 27–39.

—— (1995b) 'Coaching Effectiveness and the Coaching Process', *Swimming Times*, 72(3): 23–5.

—— (1999) 'Coaching Effectiveness', in N. Cross and J. Lyle (eds) *The Coaching Process: Principles and Practice for Sport* (pp. 47–64). Oxford: Butterworth-Heinemann.

Cross, N. and Lyle, J. (eds) (1999a) *The Coaching Process: Principles and Practice for Sport*. Oxford: Butterworth-Heinemann.

—— (1999b) 'Overtraining and the Coaching Process', in N. Cross and J. Lyle (eds) *The Coaching Process: Principles and Practice for Sport* (pp. 192–209). Oxford: Butterworth-Heinemann.

Crotty, M. (1998) *The Foundations of Social Research: Meaning and Perception in the Research Process*. London: Sage.

SPORTS COACHING CONCEPTS

Cusdin, N. (1996) 'The Professionalisation of Coaching', *NIIC News*, 12: 6–7.

Custers, E. J., Boshuizen, H. P. and Schmidt, H. G. (1996) 'The Influence of Medical Expertise, Case Typicality, and Illness Script Component on Case Processing and Disease Probability Estimates', *Memory and Cognition*, 24(3): 384–99.

d'Arripe-Longueville, F., Fournier, J. F. and Dubois, A. (1998) 'The Perceived Effectiveness of Interactions between Expert French Judo Coaches and Elite Female Athletes', *The Sport Psychologist*, 12: 317–32.

Danziger, R. C. (1982) 'Coaching Humanistically: An Alternative Approach', *Physical Educator*, 39(1): 121–5.

Dawson, P., Dobson, S. and Gerrard, B. (2000) 'Estimating Coaching Efficiency in Professional Team Sports: Evidence from English Association Football', *Scottish Journal of Political Economy*, 47(4): 399–421.

De Knop, P., Engstrom, L. M., Skirstad, B. and Weiss, M. R. (1996) *Worldwide Trends in Youth Sport*. Champaign, IL: Human Kinetics.

De Marco, G., Mancini, V. and West, D. (1997) 'Reflections on Change: A Quantitative and Qualitative Analysis of a Baseball Coach's Behavior', *Journal of Sport Behavior*, 20(2): 135–63.

Dearden, R. F. (1984) *Theory and Practice in Education*. London: Routledge.

Department for Culture Media and Sport/Department for Education and Employment (2001) 'A Sporting Future for All: The Government's Plan for Sport'. London: DCMS.

Dick, F. W. (1977) 'Coaching – An Artful Science', *Momentum*, 2(3): 1–3.

—— (1997a) *Sports Training Principles* (3rd edn). London: A. & C. Black.

—— (1997b) 'Shifting the Coach's Focus: Redefining the Role of the Elite Coach', *Coaching Focus*, 35(Summer): 8–10.

Dodds, P. (1994) 'Cognitive and Behavioural Components of Expertise in Teaching Physical Education', *Quest*, 46, 153–63.

Donnelly, P. (ed.) (2000a) *Youth Sport in Canada: Problems and Resolutions*. Harlow: Pearson Education.

—— (2000b) 'Interpretive Approaches to the Sociology of Sport', in J. Coakley and E. Dunning (eds) *Handbook of Sports Studies* (pp. 77–91). London: Sage.

Donovan, M. (1997) 'Role Overload and Role Conflict – Teacher or Coach?' *British Journal of Physical Education*, 28(2): 17–20.

Dooley, D. (1995) *Social Research Methods* (3rd edn). London: Prentice-Hall International.

Douge, B. (1987) 'Coaching Qualities of Successful Coaches', *Sports Coach*, 10(4): 31–5.

Douge, B. and Hastie, P. (1993) 'Coach Effectiveness', *Sports Science Review*, 2(2): 14–29.

Douge, B., Alexander, K., David, P. and Kidman, L. (1994) *Evaluation of the National Coach Accreditation Scheme*. Australian Coaching Council.

Downie, R. S. (1990) 'Professions and Professionalism', *Journal of Philosophy of Education*, 24(2): 147–59.

Drewe, S. B. (2000a) 'An Examination of the Relationship between Coaching and Teaching', *Quest*, 52: 79–88.

—— (2000b) 'Coaches, Ethics and Autonomy', *Sport, Education and Society*, 5(2): 147–62.

Dubin, L. (1990) *Commission of Inquiry into the Use of Drugs and Banned Practices Intended to Increase Athletic Performance*. Ottawa: Ministry of Supplies and Services.

Duke, A. and Corlett, J. (1992) 'Factors Affecting University Women's Basketball Coaches' Timeout Decisions', *Canadian Journal of Sport Sciences*, 17(4): 333–7.

Dunning, E. G., Maguire, J. A. and Pearton, R. E. (eds) (1993) *The Sports Process: A Comparative and Developmental Approach*. Champaign IL: Human Kinetics.

Dwyer, J. and Fisher, D. (1990) 'Wrestlers' Perceptions of Coaches' Leadership as Predictors of Satisfaction with Leadership', *Journal of Perceptual Motor Skills*, 71: 17–20.

Dyer, G. (1993) 'Am I Using a Systems Approach?' *Journal of Systematic Practice and Action Research*, 6(4): 407–19.

Dyson, G. H. G. (1980) 'Forty Years on: Some Thoughts on Coaching and Development', *Athletics Coach*, 14(2): 18–22.

Easen, P. and Wilcockson, J. (1996) 'Intuition and Rational Decision Making in Professional Thinking: a False Dichotomy?', *Journal of Advanced Nursing*, 24: 667–73.

English Sports Council (1997) *Survey of Coaches 1993*. London: ESC.

—— (1998) *The Development of Sporting Talent 1997*. London: ESC.

Eraut, M. (1994) *Developing Professional Knowledge and Competence*. London: Falmer Press.

Evans, J. S. B. T. (1989) 'Problem Solving, Reasoning and Decision Making', in A. Baddely and N. O. Bernsen (eds) *Cognitive Psychology: Research Directions in Cognitive Science: European Perspectives* (pp. 85–102). Hove, East Sussex: Lawrence Erlbaum Associates.

Evans, J. (1990) 'Ability, Position and Privilege in School Physical Education', in D. Kirk and R. Tinning (eds) *Physical Education, Curriculum and Culture: Critical Issues in the Contemporary Crisis* (pp. 139–68). Basingstoke: Falmer Press.

Fairs, J. (1987) 'The Coaching Process: the Essence of Coaching', *Sports Coach*, 11(1): 17–20.

Fasting, K. and Pfister, G. (2000) 'Female and Male Coaches in the Eyes of Female Elite Soccer Players', *European Physical Education Review*, 6(1): 91–108.

Felgate, D. (1997) 'Finding the Limits', *Supercoach*, 2: 11.

Figone, A. (1994) 'Teacher Coach Role Conflict – its Impact on Students and Student-athletes', *Physical Educator*, 51(1): 129–34.

Fletcher, S. (1992) *Competence-based Assessment Techniques*. London: Kogan Page.

Flin, R., Salas, E., Strub, M. and Martin, L. (1997) *Decision Making under Stress: Emerging Themes and Applications*. Aldershot: Ashgate.

Flint, F. and Weiss, M. (1992) 'Returning Injured Athletes to Competition: A Role and Ethical Dilemma', *Canadian Journal of Sport Sciences*, 17(1): 34–40.

Francis, C. (with J. Coplon) (1990) *Speed Trap: Inside the Biggest Scandal in Olympic History*. London: Grafton Books.

Franks, I., Sinclair, G. D., Thomson, W. and Goodman, D. (1986) 'Analysis of the Coaching Process', *Science Periodical on Research and Technology in Sport*, January.

Fry, J. P. (2000) 'Coaching a Kingdom of Ends', *Journal of the Philosophy of Sport*, 27: 51–62.

Fry, R. W., Morton, A. R. and Keast, D. (1991) 'Overtraining in Athletes', *Sports Medicine*, 12(1): 32–65.

Fuoss, D. E. and Troppmann, R. J. (1981) *Effective Coaching: A Psychological Approach*. New York: John Wiley & Sons.

Gardiner, S., Felix, A., James, M., Welch, R. and O'Leary, J. (1998) *Sports Law*. London: Cavendish Pub.

Gardiner, S. (1999) 'Coaching and the Law of the Land', *FHS*, 6(December): 6–8.

Gervis, M. and Brierley, J. (1999) *Effective Coaching for Children: Understanding the Sports Process*. Marlborough: Crowood Press.

Ghaye, T. and Lillyman, S. (2000) *Reflection: Principles and Practice for Healthcare Professionals*. Salisbury: Quay Books, Mark Allen Pub.

Ghaye, T. (2001) 'Reflection: Principles and Practice for Better Coaching . . . Better Sport', *FHS*, 10: 9–11.

Glaser, R. and Chi, M. (1988) 'Overview', in M. Chi, R. Glaser and M. Farr (eds) *The Nature of Expertise*. Hillsdale, NJ: Lawrence Erlbaum Associates.

Gordon, S. (1988) 'Decision Styles and Coaching Effectiveness in University Soccer', *Canadian Journal of Sport Sciences*, 13: 55–65.

Gould, D., Giannini, J., Krane, V. and Hodge, K. (1990) 'Educational Needs of Elite US National Team, Pan-American and Olympic Coaches', *Journal of Teaching in Physical Education*, 9(4): 332–44.

Gowan, G. and Thompson, W. (1986) 'The Canadian Approach to Training of Coaches: Matching the Paradigm', *Coach Education: Preparation for a Profession*. Proceedings of the VIIIth Commonwealth & International Conference on Sport, Physical Education, Dance, Recreation and Health, Glasgow. London: E&FN Spon.

Grayson, E. (2000) *Sport and the Law* (3rd edn). London: Butterworths.

Gruneau, R. (1993) 'The Critique of Sport in Modernity: Theorising Power Culture and the Politics of the Body', in E. G. Dunning, J. A. Maguire and R. E. Pearton (eds) *The Sports Process: A Comparative and Developmental Approach*. Champaign, IL: Human Kinetics.

Hager, P. and Gonczi, A. (1996) 'Professions and Competencies', in R. Edwards, A. Hanson and P. Raggatt (eds) *Boundaries of Adult Learning* (pp. 246–60). London: Routledge.

Hall, A., Slack, T., Smith, G. and Whitson, D. (1991) *Sport in Canadian Society*. Toronto: McClelland & Stewart.

Hamilton, M. (2000) 'Coaching Men and Women – The Same?' *FHS*, 9(October): 9–12.

Hammond, K. R., Hamm, R. M., Grassia, J. and Pearson, T. (1993) 'Direct Comparison of the Efficacy of Intuitive and Analytical Cognition in Expert Judgement', in W. M. Goldstein and R. M. Hogarth (eds) *Research on Judgement and Decision Making: Currents, Connections and Controversies* (pp. 144–80). Cambridge: Cambridge University Press.

Haney, C. J., Long, B. C. and Howell-Jones, G. (1998) 'Coaching as a Profession: Ethical Concerns', *Journal of Applied Sport Psychology*, 10: 240–50.

Hardin, B. (1999) 'Expertise in Teaching and Coaching: a Qualitative Study of Physical Educators and Athletic Coaches', *Sociology of Sport On-Line*. 2(1). Available: http://www.physed.otago.ac.nz/sosol/v2i1/v2i1a2.htm

Hardy, C. and Howard, C. (1995) 'The Realities of Coaching Swimming: A Systematic Observation Study', *Swimming Times*, 72(2): 25–8.

Hargreaves, J. (1986) *Sport, Power and Culture*. Oxford: Polity Press.

—— (1994) *Sporting Females: Critical Issues in the History and Sociology of Women's Sport*. London: Routledge.

Hart, B. A., Hasbrook, C. A. and Mathes, S. A. (1986) 'An Examination of the Reduction in the Number of Female Interscholastic Coaches', *Research Quarterly for Exercise and Sport*, 57(1): 68–77.

Hartley, H. J. (1998) 'Hard Men – Soft on Sport?' *Sport and the Law Journal*, 6(2): 37–58.

Hasbrook, C. A., Hart, B. A., Mathes, S. A. and True, S. (1990) 'Sex Bias and the Validity of Believed Differences between Male and Female Interscholastic Athletic Coaches,' *Research Quarterly for Exercise and Sport*, 61(3): 259–67.

Haslam, I. R. (1990) 'Expert Assessment of the National Coaching Certification Programme (NCCP) Theory Component', *Canadian Journal of Sport Sciences*, 15(3): 201–12.

Hemery, D. (1991) *Sporting Excellence: What Makes a Champion?*. London: Collins Willow.

Hendry, L. B. (1972) 'The Coaching Stereotype', in H. T. A. Whiting (ed.) *Readings in Sports Psychology* (pp. 34–54). London: Henry Kimpton Pub.

Hoberman, J. (1992) *Mortal Engines: The Science of Performance and the Dehumanisation of Sport*. New York: The Free Press.

Hodkinson, P. (1995) 'Professionalism and Competence', in P. Hodkinson and M. Issitt (eds) *The Challenge of Competence: Professionalism through Vocational Education and Training* (pp. 58–69). London: Cassell.

Hoffman, R. R., Shadbolt, N. R., Burton, A. M. and Klein, G. (1995) 'Eliciting Knowledge from Experts: A Methodological Analysis', *Organisational Behaviour and Human Decision Processes*, 62(2): 129–58.

Hogg, J. M. (1995) *Mental Skills for Swim Coaches*. Edmonton, Al: Sport Excel Pub.

Holt, R. and Mangan, T. (2000) *Sport in Britain 1945–2000*. Oxford: Blackwell.

Horne, J., Tomlinson, A. and Whannel, G. (1999) *Understanding Sport: An Introduction to the Sociological and Cultural Analysis of Sport*. London: E&FN Spon.

Houlihan, B. (1999) *Dying to Win: Doping in Sport and the Development of Anti-doping Policy*. Strasbourg: Council of Europe.

Howe, B. (1990) 'Coaching Effectiveness', *New Zealand Journal of Health, Physical Education and Recreation*, 23(3): 4–7.

Hugman, R. (1991) *Power in Caring Professions*. London: Macmillan.

Hyland, T. (1994) *Competence, Education and NVQs: Dissenting Perspectives*. London: Cassell.

Hylton, K. and Totten, M. (2001) 'Developing "Sport for All?": Addressing Inequality in Sport', in K. Hylton, P. Bramham, D. Jackson and M. Nesti (eds) *Sports Development: Policy, Process and Practice* (pp. 37–65). London: Routledge.

IAAF (1999) 'Code of Ethics', *New Studies in Athletics*, 14(23): 39–40.

Jarvie, G. (1990) 'The Sociological Imagination', in F. Kew (ed.) *Social Scientific Perspectives in Sport*. Leeds: BASS/NCF.

Jarvie, G. and Maguire, J. (1994) *Sport and Leisure in Social Thought*. London: Routledge.

Jinks, M. (1979) *Training*. Poole: Blandford.

Jones, D. F., Housner, L. D. and Kornspan, A. S. (1995) 'A Comparative Analysis of Expert and Novice Basketball Coaches' Practice Planning', *Annual of Applied Research in Coaching and Athletics*, 10: 201–26.

—— (1997) 'Interactive Decision Making and Behaviour of Experienced and Inexperienced Basketball Coaches during Practice', *Journal of Teaching in Physical Education*, 16: 454–68.

Jones, L., Reid, D. and Bevins, S. (1997a) 'Teachers' Perceptions of Mentoring in a Collaborative Model of Initial Teacher Training', *Journal of Education for Teaching*, 23(3): 253–61.

Jones, R., Potrac, P. and Ramalli, K. (1999) 'Where Sport Meets Physical Education: A Systematic Observation of Role Conflict', *International Journal of Physical Education*, 36(1): 7–14.

Jones, R. L. (2000) 'Towards a Sociology of Coaching', in J. L. Jones and K. M. Armour (eds) *Sociology of Sport: Theory and Practice* (pp. 33–43). Harlow: Pearson Educational.

Kelly, B. C., Eklund, R. and Ritter-Taylor, M. (1999) 'Stress and Burnout among Collegiate Tennis Coaches', *Journal of Sport and Exercise Psychology*, 21(2): 113–30.

Kew, F. (1997) *Sport: Social Problems and Issues*. Oxford: Butterworth-Heinemann.

Klein, G. A. (1998) *Sources of Power: How People Make Decisions*. Cambridge, MA: MIT.

Knoppers, A. (1987) 'Gender and the Coaching Profession', *Quest*, 39: 9–22.

—— (1988) 'Men Working: Coaching as a Male Dominated and Sex Segregated Occupation', *Arena Review*, 12(2): 69–80.

—— (1992) 'Explaining Male Dominance and Sex Segregation in Coaching: Three Approaches', *Quest*, 44(2): 210–27.

Kuklinski, B. (1990) 'Sports Leadership – an Overview', *New Zealand Journal of Health, Physical Education and Recreation*, 23(3): 15–18.

Lacy, A. C. and Darst, P. (1985) 'Systematic Observation of Behaviours of Winning High School Football Coaches', *Journal of Teaching in Physical Education*, 4: 256–70.

Lacy, A. C. and Goldston, D. (1990) 'Behaviour Analysis of Male and Female Coaches in High School Basketball', *Journal of Sport Behavior*, 13(1): 29–39.

Laughlin, N. and Laughlin, S. (1994) 'The Relationship between the Similarity in Perception of Teacher/Coach Leader Behaviour and Evaluations of their Effectiveness', *International Journal of Sport Psychology*, 25(4): 396–410.

Lave, J. and Wenger, E. (1991) *Situated Learning: Legitimate Peripheral Participation*. Cambridge: Cambridge University Press.

Ledington, P. W. J. and Wootton, K. (1986) 'The Management and Operation of Coaching Systems: A Systems Approach', *Coaching Education: Preparation for a Profession*. Proceedings of the VIIIth Commonwealth & International Conference on Sport, Physical Education, Dance, Recreation and Health, Glasgow. London: E&FN Spon.

LeDrew, J. E. and Zimmerman, C. (1994) 'Moving towards an Acceptance of Females in Coaching', *The Physical Educator*, 51(1): 6–14.

Lenskyj, H. (1992) 'Sexual Harassment: Female Athletes' Experiences and Coaches' Responsibilities', *Science Periodical on Research and Technology in Sport*, 12(6).

Lipshitz, R. and Bar-Ilan, O. (1996) 'How Problems are Solved: Reconsidering the Phase Theorem', *Organisational Behaviour and Human Decision Processes*, 65(1): 48–60.

Lipshitz, R. and Strauss, O. (1997) 'Coping with Uncertainty: A Naturalistic Decision Making Analysis', *Organisational Behaviour and Human Decision Processes*, 69(2): 149–63.

Liukkonen, J., Laakso, L. and Telama, R. (1996) 'Educational Perspectives of Youth Sport Coaches: Analysis of Observed Coaching Behaviours', *International Journal of Sport Psychology*, 27: 439–53.

Lombardo, B. J. (1987) *The Humanistic Coach: From Theory to Practice*. Springfield, IL: Charles Thomas Pub.

—— (1999) 'Coaching in the 21st Century: Issues, Concerns and Solutions', *Sociology of Sport On-Line*, 2(1). Available: http: //www.physed.otago.ac.nz/sosol/v2i1/v2i1a4.htm

Loy, J. W., McPherson, B. and Kenyon, G. (1978) *Sport and Social Systems*. Reading, MA: Addison-Wesley.

Lukes, S. (1974) *Power: A Radical View*. London and Basingstoke: Macmillan.

Lyle, J. (1984a) 'Towards a Concept of Coaching', *Scottish Journal of Physical Education*, 12(1): 27–31.

—— (1984b) 'Sports Medicine and the Coach', *Sports Coach*, 7(4): 39–46.

—— (1986) 'Coach Education: Preparation for a Profession', *Coach Education: Preparation for a Profession*. Proceedings of the VIIIth Commonwealth and International Conference on Sport, PE , Dance, Recreation and Health, Glasgow. London: E&FN Spon.

—— (1991) 'The Development of an Ideal-type Model of the Coaching Process and an Exploratory Investigation into the Appropriateness of the Model for Coaches in Three Sports', Unpublished MSc thesis: Stirling, University of Stirling.

—— (1992) 'Systematic Coaching Behaviour: An Investigation into the Coaching Process and the Implications of the Findings for Coach Education', in T. Williams, L. Almond and A. Sparkes (eds) *Sport and Physical Activity* (pp. 463–69). London: E&FN Spon.

—— (1993) 'Towards a Comparative Study of the Coaching Process', *Journal of Comparative Physical Education and Sport*, 15(2): 14–23.

—— (1996) 'A Conceptual Appreciation of the Sports Coaching Process', *Scottish Centre Research Papers in Sport, Leisure and Society*, 1(1): 15–37.

Lyle, J., Allison, M. and Taylor, J. (1997) *Factors Influencing the Motivations of Sports Coaches. Research Report No. 49*. Edinburgh: Scottish Sports Council.

—— (1997a) 'Management Training and the Sports Coaching Analogy: A Content Analysis of Six Management Training Products', *5th Congress of the European Association for Sport Management*. Glasgow, Scotland: E.A.S.M.

—— (1997b) 'Managing Excellence in Sports Performance', *Career Development International*, 2(7): 314–23.

—— (1998a) 'Coaching Effectiveness and the Teaching Paradigm', *Active Living through Quality Physical Education*. 8th European Congress of ICHPER.SD, St Mary's University College, Twickenham.

—— (1998b) 'Decision Making by Expert Coaches: An Investigation into Apparently Intuitive Practice', Unpublished Ed.D thesis, University of Newcastle, Newcastle upon Tyne.

—— (1998c) 'The Coaching Process', *NCFB2001*. Leeds: National Coaching Foundation.

—— (1999a) 'The Coaching Process: An Overview', in N. Cross and J. Lyle (eds) *The Coaching Process: Principles and Practice for Sport* (pp. 3–24). Oxford: Butterworth-Heinemann.

—— (1999b) 'Coaching Philosophy and Coaching Behaviour', in N. Cross and J. Lyle (eds) *The Coaching Process: Principles and Practice for Sport* (pp. 25–46). Oxford: Butterworth-Heinemann.

—— (1999c) 'Coaches' Decision Making', in N. Cross and J. Lyle (eds) *The Coaching Process: Principles and Practice for Sport* (pp. 210–32). Oxford: Butterworth-Heinemann.

—— (1999d) 'Coaching and the Management of Performance Systems', in N. Cross and J. Lyle (eds) *The Coaching Process: Principles and Practice for Sport* (pp. 233–54). Oxford: Butterworth-Heinemann.

McIntosh, P. C. (1968) *Physical Education in England since 1800*. London: Bell.

Maclean, J. and Chelladurai, P. (1995) 'Dimensions of Coaching Performance: Development of a Scale', *Journal of Sport Management*, 9(2): 194–207.

Maclean, J. and Zakrajsek, D. (1996) 'Factors Considered Important for Evaluating Canadian University Athletics Coaches', *Journal of Sport Management*, 10: 463–4.

McNab, T. (1990) 'Chariots of Fire into the Twenty-first Century', *Coaching Focus*, 13(Spring): 2–5.

McNamee, M. (1999) 'Celebrating Trust: Virtues and Rules in the Ethical Conduct of Sports Coaches', in M. McNamee and J. Parry (eds) *Ethics and Sport* (pp. 148–68). London: E&FN Spon.

McNamee, M. and Parry, J. (eds) (1999) *Ethics and Sport*. London: E&FN Spon.

Maguire, J. (1999) *Global Sport: Identities, Societies, Civilisations*. Cambridge: Polity Press.

Martens, R. (1997) *Successful Coaching* (3rd edn). Champaign, IL: Leisure Press.

Mason, T. (ed.) (1989) *Sport in Britain: A Social History*. Cambridge: Cambridge University Press.

Mawer, M. (ed.) (1996) *Mentoring in Physical Education: Issues and Insights*. London: Falmer Press.

Mayes, R. (2001) 'Reflecting on the Future Needs of UK's Top Coaches', *FHS*, 10: 17.

Maynard, T. and Furlong, J. (1995) 'Learning to Teach and Models of Mentoring', in T. Kerry and A. Shelton Mayes (eds) *Issues in Mentoring* (pp. 69–85). London: Routledge in association with OUP.

Middlehurst, R. (1995) 'Professionals, Professionalism and Higher Education for Tomorrow's World', Paper presented at the Higher Education in a Learning Society, St Edmund Hall, Oxford.

Midwinter, E. (1986) *Fair Game: Myth and Reality in Sport*. London: George Allen & Unwin.

Miles, A. (2001) 'Supporting Coach Education – Towards Reflective Practice', *FHS*, 10: 15–16.

Millard, L. (1996) 'Differences in Coaching Behaviours of Male and Female High School Soccer Coaches', *Journal of Sport Behavior*, 19(1): 19–31.

Miller, A. W. (1992) 'Systematic Observation Behaviour: Similarities of Various Youth Sport Soccer Coaches', *Physical Educator*, 49(3): 136–43.

Moore, C. (1997) *Sports Law and Litigation*. Birmingham: CLT Professional Pub.

Morgan, W. J. and Meier, K. V. (eds) (1995) *Philosophic Inquiry in Sport*. Champaign, IL: Human Kinetics.

Morrow, R. A. (with D. D. Brown) (1994) *Critical Theory and Methodology*. London: Sage.

Mosston, M. and Ashworth, S. (1990) *The Spectrum of Teaching Styles: From Command to Discovery*. New York: Longman.

Mumford, A. (1993) *How Managers Can Develop Managers*. Aldershot: Gower.

Murdoch, E. (1990) 'Physical Education and Sport: The Interface', in N. Armstrong (ed.) *New Directions in Physical Education* (Vol. 1). Leeds: Human Kinetics.

National Coaching Foundation (NCF) (1996) *Code of Ethics and Conduct for Sports Coaches*. Leeds: National Coaching Foundation.

NCF/NSPCC (1998) *Protecting Children: A Guide for Sportspersons* (2nd edn). Leeds: National Coaching Foundation.

NCF (2001) 'Reflective Practice', *FHS*. 10(January).

Nielsen, J. T. (2001) 'The Forbidden Zone: Intimacy, Sexual Relations and Misconduct in the Relationship Between Coaches and Athletes. *International Review for the Sociology of Sport*, 36(1): 165–82.

Office for National Statistics (2000) *Standard Occupational Classification*. London: The Stationery Office.

Orlick, T. and Botterill, C. (1975) *Every Kid Can Win*. Chicago: Nelson-Hall.

Orlick, T. (1990) *In Pursuit of Excellence*. Champaign, IL: Leisure Press.

Otter, S. (1994) *Higher Level NVQs/SVQs – Their Possible Implications for Higher Education*: Occasional Paper Series, No. 1, Employment Department.

Owen, H. (1996) *Creating Top Flight Teams*. London: Kogan Page.

Parkhouse, B. L. and Williams, J. M. (1986) 'Differential Effects of Sex and Status on Evaluation of Coaching Ability', *Research Quarterly for Exercise and Sport*, 57: 53–9.

Pastore, D. L. (1991) 'Male and Female Coaches of Women's Athletic Teams: Reasons for Entering and Leaving the Profession', *Journal of Sport Management*, 5: 128–43.

Pastore, D. L. and Meacci, W. G. (1994) 'Employment Process for NCAA Female Coaches', *Journal of Sport Management*, 8(2): 115–28.

Patel, M. (1999) 'Where are Britain's Black Coaches?' *FHS*, 5(September): 15–16.

Patriksson, G. and Eriksson, S. (1990) 'Young Athletes' Perceptions of their Coaches', *International Journal of Physical Education*, 27(4): 9–14.

Pegg, M. (1999) *The Art of Mentoring*. Chalford: Management Books 2000 Ltd.

Philpott, L. and Sheppard, L. (1992) 'Managing for Improved Performance', in M. Armstrong (ed.) *Strategies for Human Resource Management: A Total Business Approach* (pp. 98–115). London: Kogan Page.

Pickup, D. (1996) *Not Another Messiah: An Account of the Sports Council 1988–93*. Edinburgh: The Pentland Press.

Pieron, M. and Carreiro da Costa, F. (1996) 'Seeking Expert Teachers in Physical Education and Sport', *European Journal of Physical Education*, 1(1): 5–18.

Polley, M. (1998) *Moving the Goalposts: A History of Sport and Society since 1945*. London: Routledge.

Potrac, P., Jones, R. L. and Armour, K. (1997) 'A Comparison of the Early and Mid Season Coaching Behaviours of Top Level English Soccer Coaches', Paper presented at the AIESEP '97 (International Association of Physical Education in Higher Education) World Conference, Singapore.

Potrac, P. and Jones, R. L. (1999) 'The Invisible Ingredient in Coaching Knowledge: A Case for Recognising and Researching the Social Component', *Sociology of Sport On-Line*, 2(1). Available: http: //www.physed.otago.ac.nz/sosol/v2i1/v2i1a5.htm

Potrac, P., Brewer, C., Jones, R., Armour, K. and Hoff, J. (2000) 'Towards an Holistic Understanding of the Coaching Process', *Quest*, 52: 186–99.

Pyke, F. (ed.) (1980) *Towards Better Coaching*. Australian Publishing Service.

Pyke, F. S. and Woodman, L. R. (1986) 'The Education of Sports Coaches and Sport Administrators in Australia', in *Coaching Education: Preparation for a Profession*. Proceedings of the VIIIth Commonwealth and International Conference on Sport, Physical Education, Dance, Recreation and Health. Glasgow (pp. 29–38). London: E&FN Spon.

Rail, G. (ed.) (1998) *Sport and Postmodern Times*. Albany: State University of New York Press.

Randel, J. M., Pugh, H. L. and Reed, S. K. (1996) 'Differences in Expert and Novice Situation Awareness in Naturalistic Decision Making', *International Journal of Human Computer Studies*, 45: 579–97.

Reid, D. and Jones, L. (1997) 'Partnership in Teacher Training: Mentors' Constructs of their Role', *Educational Studies*, 23(2): 263–76.

Rennick, T. (2000) 'Coaching', in R. Cox, G. Jarvie and W. Vamplew (eds) *Encyclopedia of British Sport* (pp. 69–71). Oxford: ABC-CLIO.

Rogers, C. (1961) *On Becoming a Person*. Boston: Houghton Mifflin.

Sabock, R. J. (1979) *The Coach*. Philadelphia: W. B. Saunders.

Sage, G. H. (1978) 'Humanistic Psychology and Coaching', in W. F. Straub (ed.) *Sport Psychology: An Analysis of Athlete Behavior* (pp. 148–61). Ithaca, NY: Mouvement Pubs.

Salmela, J. H. (1995) 'Learning from the Development of Expert Coaches', *Coaching and Sport Science Journal*, 2(2): 3–13.

Salminen, S. and Liukkonen, J. (1996) 'Coach–athlete Relationship and Coaching Behaviour in Training Sessions', *International Journal of Sport Psychology*, 27: 59–67.

Saury, J. and Durand, M. (1995) 'Study of Practical Knowledge in Expert Sailing Coaches: From the Analysis of the Coach–athlete Relationship to an Approach to Coaching as Collective Work', *Sport*, 151, 25–39.

—— (1998) 'Practical Knowledge in Expert Coaches: On-site Study of Coaching in Sailing', *Research Quarterly for Exercise and Sport*, 69(3): 254–66.

Scanlan, T. K., Carpenter, P. J., Schmidt, G. W., Simons, J. P. and Keeler, B. (1993) 'An Introduction to the Sport Commitment Model', *Journal of Sport and Exercise Psychology*, 15: 1–15.

Schembri, G. (1998) 'Copy at your Peril', *Supercoach*, 2: 6–7.

Schempp, P. G. (1997) 'Developing Expertise in Teaching and Coaching', *Journal of Physical Education, Recreation and Dance*, 68(2): 29.

—— (1998) 'The Dynamics of Human Diversity in Sport Pedagogy Scholarship', *Sociology of Sport On-Line*, 1(1). Available: http: //www.physed.otago.ac.nz/sosol/vlil/vl1la8.htm

Schmolinsky, G. (ed.) (1978) *Track and Field: Athletics in the GDR (East Germany)*. Berlin: Sportverlag.

Schon, D. A. (1983) *The Reflective Practitioner: How Professionals Think in Action*. New York: Basic Books.

Scottish Sports Council (1988) *National Strategy for Coach Education and Coaching Development in Scotland*. Edinburgh: Scottish Sports Council.

Scraton, S. and Watson, B. (eds) (2000) *Sport, Leisure Identities and Gendered Spaces*. Leisure Studies Association.

Seagrave, J. and Ciancio, C. A. (1990) 'An Observational Study of a Successful Pop Warner Football Coach', *Journal of Teaching in Physical Education*, 9: 294–306.

Sherman, C., Crassini, B., Maschette, W. and Sands, R. (1997) 'Instructional Sport Psychology: A Reconceptualisation of Sports Coaching as Sport Instruction', *International Journal of Sport Psychology*, 28(2): 103–25.

Siedentop, D. and Eldar, E. (1989) 'Expertise, Experience and Effectiveness', *Journal of Teaching in Physical Education*, 8: 254–60.

Sik, G. (1996) *I Think I'll Manage*. London: Headline.

Slack, T. (1997) *Understanding Sport Organisations: The Application of Organisational Theory*. Champaign, IL: Human Kinetics.

Slainte Ltd (1993) 'A Study of Sports Coaching in Highland Region', Unpublished report to the Scottish Sports Council.

Sloman, S. A. (1996) 'The Empirical Case for Two Systems of Reasoning', *Psychological Review*, 119(1): 3–22.

Smoll, F. L. and Smith, R. E. (1996) *Children and Youth in Sport: A Biopsychosocial Perspective*. Madison, WI: Brown & Benchmark.

Solomon, G. B., Striegel, D. A., Eliot, J. F., Heon, S. N., Maas, J. L. and Wadya, V. K. (1996)

'The Self-fulfilling Prophecy in College Basketball: Implications for Effective Coaching', *Journal of Applied Sport Psychology*, 8, 44–59.

Sports Council (1993) *Women and Sport: Policy and Frameworks for Action*. London: Sports Council.

—— (1994) 'TOYA and Coaching', Unpublished Report to the Sports Council.

Sports Council/NCF (1993) *Sport Science Support Programme* (Progress Report 1993): NCF/ Sports Council.

SPRITO (1998) *A Guide to the S/NVQs at Level Three*. London: SPRITO.

Staurowsky, E. (1990) 'Women Coaching Male Athletes', in M. A. Messner and D. F. Sabo (eds) *Sport, Men and the Gender Order: Critical Feminist Perspectives* (pp. 163–70). Champaign, IL: Human Kinetics.

Sutcliffe, P. (1995) *Comparative Coaching Studies*. Leeds: National Coaching Foundation.

Swift, A. (2001) 'Politics vs Philosophy', *Prospect*, 66: 40–4.

Tamura, K., Davey, C. and Haslam, L. (1993) *A Four Country Study of the Training for Sports Coaching in Australia, Canada, the United Kingdom and Japan*. Osaka: Osaka University of Health and Sports Science.

Terry, P. C. (1984) 'The Coaching Preferences of Elite Athletes Competing at Universiade '83', *Canadian Journal of Applied Sport Science*, 9: 201–8.

Terry, P. C. and Howe, B. (1984) 'Coaching Preferences of Athletes', *Canadian Journal of Applied Sport Science*, 9(4): 188–93.

Theodoraki, E. (1999) 'The Making of the UK Sports Institute', *Managing Leisure*, 4(4): 187–200.

Thorpe, R. (1987) 'Evaluating a Single Session', *Coaching Focus*, 5(Spring): 9–12.

—— (1996) 'Physical Education: Beyond the Curriculum', in N. Armstrong (ed.) *New Directions in Physical Education: Change and Innovation* (pp. 144–56). London: Cassell.

Tichy, N. M. and Charan, R. (1995) 'The CEO as Coach: An Interview with Allied Signal's Lawrence A. Bossidy', *Harvard Business Review*, March–April: 79–80.

Tomlinson, P. (1995) *Understanding Mentoring: Reflective Strategies for School-based Teacher Preparation*. Buckingham: Open University Press.

Tomlinson, A. and Yorganci, I. (1997) 'Male Coach/Female Athlete Relations: Gender and Power Relations in Competitive Sport', *Journal of Sport and Social Issues*, 21(2): 134–55.

Torrington, D. and Weightman, J. (eds) (1994) *Effective Management: People and Organisation* (2nd edn). New York: Prentice-Hall.

Treadwell, P. (1986) 'How Do We Begin to Move Towards a Profession?', *Coaching Focus*, 3(Spring): 9–11.

Trudel, P., Guertin, D., Bernard, D. and Boileau, R. (1991) 'Behaviour of Ice Hockey Coaches', *Canadian Journal of Sport Sciences*, 16(23): 103–9.

Trudel, P., Côte, J. and Bernard, D. (1996) 'Systematic Observation of Youth Ice Hockey Coaches during Games', *Journal of Sport Behavior*, 19(1): 50–66.

Tutko, T. and Richards, J. (1971) *Psychology of Coaching*. Boston: Allyn & Bacon.

UK Sport (2001) *The UK Vision for Coaching: A Strategy into the Twenty-first Century*. London: UK Sport.

UK Sports Council (1999) *The Development of Coaching in the United Kingdom: Consultation Questionnaire*. London: UK Sports Council.

Van der Mars, H., Darst, P. W. and Sariscany, M. J. (1991) 'Practice Behavior of Elite Archers and their Coaches', *Journal of Sport Behaviour*, 14(2): 103–12.

Vangucci, M., Potrac, P. and Jones, R. L. (1998) 'A Systematic Observation of Elite Women's Soccer Coaches', *Journal of Interdisciplinary Research in Physical Education*, 2(1): 1–18.

Veenman, S., DeLaat, H. and Staring, C. (1998) 'Evaluation of a Coaching Programme for Mentors of Beginning Teachers', *Journal of In-service Education*, 24(3).

Verchoshanskij, J. (1999) 'Training Theory – the Skill of Programming the Training Process', *New Studies in Athletics*, 14(4): 45–54.

Vergeer, I. and Hogg, J. M. (1999) 'Coaches' Decision Policies about the Participation of Injured Athletes in Competition', *The Sport Psychologist*, 13: 42–56.

Volkwein, K. A. E., Schnell, F. E., Sherwood, D. and Livezey, A. (1997) 'Sexual Harassment in Sport: Perceptions and Experiences of American Female Student-athletes', *International Review for the Sociology of Sport*, 32(3): 283–95.

Weinberg, R., Reveles, M. and Jackson, A. (1984) 'Attitudes of Male and Female Athletes towards Male and Female Coaches', *Journal of Sport Psychology*, 6, 448–53.

West, A. and Brackenridge, C. (1990) *A Report on the Issues Relating to Women's Lives as Sports Coaches in the United Kingdom 1989/90*. Sheffield: Sheffield City Polytechnic and PAVIC Publications.

West, A., Green, E., Brackenridge, C. and Woodward, D. (1998) 'Leading the Way: An Analysis of Women's Experiences as Sports Coaches', Paper presented at the Work, Employment and Society Conference, University of Cambridge.

Whitaker, D. (1999) *The Spirit of Teams*. Marlborough: Crowood Press.

White, A. and Brackenridge, C. (1985) 'Who Rules Sport? Gender Division in the Power Structures of British Sport from 1960', *International Review for the Sociology of Sport*, 20(1/2): 95–107.

White, A. (1987) 'Women Coaches: Problems and Issues', *Coaching Focus*, 6(Summer): 2–3.

White, A., Maygothling, R. and Carr, C. (1989) *The Dedicated Few: The Social World of Women Coaches in Britain in the 1980s*. West Sussex Institute of Higher Education: Centre for the Study and Promotion of Sport and Recreation for Women and Girls.

Whitehead, N. and Hendry, L.B. (1976) *Teaching Physical Education in England*. London: Lepus Books.

Whitmore, J. (1992) *Coaching for Performance*. London: Nicholas Brealey.

Whitson, D. (1980) 'Coaching as a Human Relationship', *Momentum*, 5(2): 36–43.

Wierzbicki, A. P. (1997) 'On the Role of Intuition in Decision Making and Some Ways of Multi-criteria Aid of Intuition', *Journal of Multi-criteria Decision Analysis*, 6: 65–76.

Wilkerson, M. (1996) 'Explaining the Presence of Men Coaches in Women's Sports: The Uncertainty Hypothesis', *Journal of Sport and Social Issues*, 20(4): 411–26.

Williams, G. (1989) 'Rugby Union', in T. Mason (ed.) *Sport in Britain: A Social History* (pp. 308–43). Cambridge: Cambridge University Press.

Witz, A. (1990) 'Patriarchy and the Labour Market: Occupational Control Strategies and the Medical Division of Labour', in D. Knights and H. Wilmott (eds) *Gender and the Labour Process*. Hants: Grower.

—— (1992) *Profession and Patriarchy*. London: Routledge.

Wolfenden Report (1960) *Sport and the Community*. London: Central Council for Physical Recreation.

Woodman, L. (1993) 'Coaching: A Science, an Art, an Emerging Profession', *Sports Science Review*, 2(2): 1–13.

Zsambok, C. and Klein, G. A. (eds) (1997) *Naturalistic Decision Making*. Hillsdale, NJ: LEA.

▼ INDEX

Abraham, A. 37, 92, 139, 260, 279, 282
academic development 11–12, 17, 280; factors contributing to lack of 29–30
accountability 74, 183, 184, 252, 306
accounts of practice 31
achieved role 61
achieved status 199
Action Sport 15
Active programme 15
Active Schools 23
adaptability 262
agency, structure and 193
Albrow, M. 96, 300
amateur ethic 5–6, 30
analysis of performance 82, 92, 101–2
Anderson, J.E. 126
Anthony, D. 9
anticipatory reflection 138, 302
application research 293–4
applied research 293–4
apprenticeship schemes 217, 287
ascribed role 61
ascribed status 199
Ashworth, S. 163
assessment 287–8
assigned role 61
assistant coaches 71–2, 217, 287
assumed capacity 39
assumptions: building blocks for coaching model 99–106; inappropriate and ethical problems 240; prior assumptions for coaching model 97–9
assumptive reasoning 138
athlete: athlete-coach relationships 211; capabilities 101; empowerment 65, 180–1; interaction of coach, performance and 27–8; performer variability 297; self-coached 65
athletics 6, 8, 111, 112, 123–4
Atkinson, J. 7
attainment 254
Australia 13, 277
Australian Institute of Sport 15
autocratic/authoritarian coaching style 158, 159, 160, 164, 177, 180–1, 185
autonomy 178, 180–1

badminton 224
Ball, D.W. 193
Balyi, I. 128
Bar-Ilan, O. 137
Barber, H. 228, 260
Baria, A. 126
basic research 293–4
Beckett, D. 142, 202
Beech, N. 42
behavioural codes 236–7, 242–4
Bernard, D. 126
Bloom, G.A. 126
Bompa, T.O. 127, 128
Boreham, N.C. 134, 137
Botterill, C. 178
boundaries 155; motivation, recruitment and 217; professionalisation and 202, 204
boundary markers 35, 36, 46–9, 53
Brackenridge, C. 215, 232, 239, 240–1
British Association of National Coaches (BANC) 7, 14
Breife, S. 183
British Institute of Sports Coaches 14, 225
British Olympic Association 14, 16; Athletes' Commission 287
Brockbank, A. 42

Brohm, J.M. 194
'building blocks', model 99–106
Burrage, M. 203
business-like style 160

Campbell, S. 13, 14, 277, 280
Canada 13, 277
capabilities, performer 101
capacity for performance 283
Capel, S. 9
career coaches 12, 31
career rewards 211
career structure 202, 204
case script model 134, 135
catalysts 140
Centre for Leisure Research (CLR) 214, 275
certification 275–6
Champion Coaching Programme 13, 15, 23
Chappell, C. 264
cheating 240, 241
Chelladurai, P. 37, 161, 260
Chi, M. 256
chief coach role 66
Children Act 1989 235, 244
circuit sports 129
Claxton, G. 133
client patronage professions 203
closure, occupational 228
club coaches 70
coach: athlete-coach relationships 211;
    personal characteristics 72, 164;
    relationship between athlete, performance
    and 27–8; role see role
'coach-dominated' sports 12, 146
coach education and training 15–16, 252,
    274–90; beginnings of coach development
    6–8; coach learning and coaching practice
    281–2; competence approach 264, 281–2,
    287–8, 309–10; conceptual framework 26;
    conceptual lessons 279–81; delivery issues
    285–8; and ethical practice 245; historical
    development 13–14, 277–9; motivation,
    recruitment and 212; principles of 282–5;
    professionalisation and 202, 204, 275–6,
    309; reflective practice 288–9; and social
    context 192; strategy documents 16; theory
    development 30; UK Sports Council
    consultation document 275, 277, 305–6;
    use of models 92
Coach of the Year Awards 14

coaching: definition 38–9, 41; as a process
    43–5; in spheres apart from sport 41–3
coaching behaviour 119; see also coaching
    practice
coaching courses 9
coaching expertise see expertise
coaching method 38, 265–6
coaching philosophy 165–72; constructing
    172; guiding principles 167–72
coaching practice 26, 116–47, 307; coach
    education and 281–2; coaches' decision
    making 137–9; condensed description
    142–4; contingency planning 142; decision
    making based on interactive scripts 134–6;
    definition 40; and effectiveness 262;
    ethical concerns 240–1; implementation
    behaviour 131–42; intuitive decision
    making 133–4; knowledge structures
    139–40; mental models 141–2, 286, 302;
    planning the process 125–31, 143; process
    characteristics and 44, 45; research studies
    117, 125, 126; sport-specificity 117,
    144–6; systematic coaching behaviours
    119–24, 246; thresholds and catalysts 140
coaching process 35–58, 310–11; boundaries
    217; boundary markers 46–9, 53;
    components 84, 85; definition 40;
    difficulties in modelling 84–5; model
    see model for coaching; participation
    and performance coaching 52–7; process
    characteristics and coaching practice 44,
    45; process skills 50–2, 73, 231, 283;
    and research issues 294–7; similarities
    with teaching 37
Coaching Review Panel 6, 225, 278, 281
coaching schemes 6–7
coaching style 72, 156–65, 308;
    autocratic/authoritarian 158, 159, 160,
    164, 177, 180–1, 185; and ethical practice
    242, 243, 246
coaching theory 28–30
Coakley, J. 12, 194
codes on conduct 236–7, 242–4
codes of ethics 242–4
Coe, P. 75
Coghlan, J. 7
cognitive models 218
cognitive organisation 283
cognitive skills 144, 283, 296–7
Collins, D. 37, 92, 139, 260, 279, 282

commitment 176, 238
COMPASS 223
compensatory judgements 163
competence: coach education and training 264, 281–2, 287–8, 309–10; and effectiveness 255–6; generic coaching competences 264–5, 281–2; professionalisation, national standards and 309–10; role-related competences 282; usable competences 282
competition: competition management 69, 103, 271, 300, 301; competition programme in coaching model 105; performance sport and importance of success in 176; phase in coaching model 109, 112, 113, 114, 300, 301; planning and the competition cycle 128, 129; and reward 238
complementarity of roles 62; between coaches and support personnel 67–70
complexity 74
components approach 253, 260, 261
conceptual framework 20–34, 307; and application issues 26–7; building 24–8; coaching and theory development 28–30; contemporary sport and conceptual questions 22–4; contribution of literature 31–3; elements of 25; ethical practice issues 241–2; interpersonal relationships and 154, 155; lack of women coaches 229–32; motivations and recruitment 216–19; professional status and 205–6; sport as a concept 33
conceptual models 82
condoning athlete behaviour 240, 241
conduct, codes on 236–7, 242–4
conflict: role conflicts 62, 68–70, 71; value conflicts 71, 165–6
consensual authority 185
constituent parts 39
constraints: input constraints 266–7; models and 91–4
constraints management 64, 66, 244, 264
consultants 67–8
contest management 69, 103, 271, 300, 301
contested activity 242
contexts see organisational contexts, social context
contingency planning 129–30, 142
CONTRACT 74

control box of coaching process 107–10
control of variables 74, 183
Cooke, G. 9
coping strategies 141
core process models 84
core values 167
Corlett, J. 126
cost-effectiveness 270
Côte, J. 80, 89, 126, 139, 141, 164
craft skills 50–1
cricket 7, 8, 306
Crisfield, P. 12, 128
Cross, N. 124, 126, 131, 169, 178, 181, 260, 263, 265, 269
Crumpton, R. 126
Cusdin, N. 4, 5, 194
Custers, E. 140

Danziger, R.C. 184
d'Arripe-Longueville, F. 164, 183
data-led goal setting 268–9
Dawson, P. 270
De Marco, G. 288
De Montfort University 11
Dearden, R.F. 276
decision making 69, 133–9, 296–7; based on interactive scripts 134–6; coaches' decision making behaviour 137–9, 143–4; intuitive 133–4; research and 300–2
declarative knowledge 101, 139
degrees 11
deliberative decision making 137
delivery: coaching process 50–1; issues in coach education 285–8
demand and supply 211
democratic coaching practice 158, 159, 161
development: personal growth and development 178–80, 180–1, 183–4, 237–8; professional 26, 36 (see also coach education and training)
development officers 15, 23
development schemes 10, 15
developmental coaching 53–4, 55
diagnosis and hypothesising 138
diagrams 82
Dick, F. 75
diplomas 11
direct intervention 63, 64, 65–6, 182, 244, 264
directing approach 183–4

discretionary judgements 202, 297
disengagement 218
distance learning qualifications 11, 12
Donnelly, P. 194, 196
Doue, B. 157, 260, 279
Downie, R.S. 202
Drewe, S.B. 37, 240
drugs 235
Dubin, L. 235
Duke, A. 126
Dunfermline College of Physical Education 11
Dunning, E.G. 194
Durand, M. 126, 144, 164
Durand-Bush, N. 126
Dwyer, J. 161
Dyson, G. 6, 7

Easen, P. 133
Eastern Europe 13, 195, 201, 277
easygoing style 160
Eckrich, J. 260
education 276; see also coach educaiton and
    training
effect-size 270
effectiveness 25, 26–7, 231, 251–73, 306–7,
    309; alternative approaches 263–70;
    coaching effectiveness literature 260–2;
    comparison of terms 254–7; competence
    vs 255–6; conceptual issues 262–3;
    effective coaching and the effective coach
    259–60; expert behaviour vs 256–7;
    goal-achievement approach 254, 257–8;
    meaning of 253–60; success and 254–5,
    269
Eliot, J.F. 126
elite athletes: fast-tracking into coaching 287
elite sport 15–16, 23; ethics in 238–9;
    masculine ethos 221; see also performance
    sport
emancipation 280
empathetic coaching style 164
empowerment 65, 180–1, 202
English Sports Council (ESC) 9, 213, 215,
    278
environmental constraints 246
episodic approach 31
episodic planning 130
Eraut, M. 142
essence of coaching 298
essential elements 25, 45

ethical practice 23, 73, 177, 234–48, 308;
    codes of ethics and codes on conduct
    242–4; conceptual framework issues
    241–2; issues 235–9; legal dimension
    236–7, 244–5; problem areas 239–41;
    professional sport 245–6; social image
    of coaching profession 309
European Network of Sport Sciences in
    Higher Education 14
evaluation 25; see also effectiveness
Evans, J. 10
Evans, J.S.B.T. 139
expectations, low 226–7
experience 73; coach education and 276,
    279–80, 285, 286–7; gender, performance
    coaching and 231
expert system 298–9
expertise 25, 131–42, 206, 309;
    coaches' decision making 137–9; coaching
    model 100–1; contingency planning 142;
    decision making based on interactive
    scripts 134–6; vs effectiveness 256–7;
    intuitive decision making 133–4;
    knowledge structures 139–40, 143–4;
    mental models 141–2, 286, 302; research
    and 302, 303; thresholds and catalysts
    140

Fairs, J. 87–9
fast-tracking (for elite athletes) 287
Fasting, K. 161, 221, 224, 226, 227
Felgate, D. 169
feminism 194
figurational sociology 194
Fisher, D. 161
Fletcher, S. 264
flexibility, social 227
frame of reference 39
frames for reflective practice 288–9
Francis, C. 128
Franks, I. 86–7, 130
Fry, J.P. 238
Fry, R.W. 131
functional roles 63–7, 74–5, 146, 297;
    legal dimension and 244; and process
    competences 264; reflective nature of
    functions 65–7; see also under individual
    functional roles
functionalism 193, 194
Furlong, J. 42

Gardiner, S. 244
gender 216; dearth of women coaches
    221–33; differences in coaching practice
    230–1; and participation in sport 223–4
generic coaching competences 264–5, 281–2
genericism vs specificity 25; *see also* sport-
    specificity
gentlemen amateurs 5
Ghaye, T. 288–9
Glaser, R. 256
Gleeson, G. 7
goal achievement 254, 257–8
goal attainment 246
goal model 141–2
goal setting: coaching model 104, 108–9,
    112; data-led 268–9; inappropriate 236
goals: ethical practice and planning 246;
    humanistic approach and 183–4;
    multiplicity of 153; organisational 245
Gonczi, A. 264
'good practice', effectiveness and 253, 260,
    261
Gould, D. 279
government policy 16–17, 22–3, 209;
    beginnings of coach development 6–8;
    from 1980s on 13–16, 17
Gruneau, R. 198
gymnastics 224

Hager, P. 264
Hall, A. 223–4
Hamilton, M. 230
Hammond, K.R. 133
Hargreaves, J. 194, 221
harmonisation of levels 14, 280
Hart, B.A. 227
Hartley, H.J. 235
Hasbrook, C.A. 228
Haslam, I.R. 279
Hastie, P. 157, 260
head coach role 66
Hemery, D. 185
Hendry, L.B. 9
Henley Royal Regatta 5
Heon, S.N. 126
heuristics 137
hierarchies 69
high performance coaches 278
High Performance Coaching Programme
    15–16, 279

higher education 11–12, 17, 280
historical background 3–19; higher education
    and academic development 11–12;
    historical roots 5–8; overseas influences
    12–13; physical education 8–11; recent
    developments 13–16
Hoberman, J. 13
hockey 124
Hodkinson, P. 202
Hoffman, R.R. 140
Hogg, J. 180–1
Holt, R. 6, 7
Horne, J. 192
Houlihan, B. 13, 235
Houlston, D. 128
Housner, L.D. 126
Hugman, R. 202–3
humanistic approach 174–87; adapting
    practice 180–3; basic assumptions 176–8;
    interpersonal relationship and 176, 177,
    182–3; issues 183–6; principles 178–83
Hylton, K. 194

ideal models 82, 96–7, 300; proposed model
    for coaching *see* model for coaching
ideologies 153, 166, 171, 175; *see also*
    humanistic approach
implementation 50–1
implementation research 293–4
improvement, performance 101–2, 262,
    267–8, 295
individualisation 106, 155
individuality 178–9
industry 41–3
influencing outcomes/performance 236, 240
information platform 100
initiation 108, 112
injury 69
input constraints 206–7
institutional career coaches 31
'instruction' coaching model 91
instructors, sports 56
insurance 244
integrated sport development schemes 10, 15
intellectual focus 280
intense style 160
interactive scripts 134–6, 138
interpersonal coaching style 164
interpersonal relationships 151–73, 308;
    coaching and 153–6; coaching styles

156–65; ethical issues 236, 237, 241;
factors impinging on 156; humanistic
approach and 176, 177, 182–3;
motivations and recruitment 217;
philosophies of coaching 165–72;
research issues 297
interpersonal skills 284
intervention support 63–4, 65–6, 182, 244,
264
intuitive decision making 133–4

Jarvie, G. 192, 206–7
Jinks, M. 41
Jones, D.F. 37, 126, 256
Jones, L. 42
Jones, R. 126
Jones, R.L. 192, 194, 195, 196

Kew, F. 194
key factors model 86–7
key features (catalysts) 140
Kinnear, B. 7
Klein, G.A. 133, 136
knowledge: coaching expertise 100–1;
metacognitive knowledge 298–9;
motivations and recruitment 217–18;
professionalisation and knowledge base
202, 203, 204; structures 139–40,
143–4; tacit 117, 132, 140; uniqueness
of coaching role 72–3
Kornspan, A.S. 126
Kuga, D.J. 37
Kuklinski, B. 161

Laakso, L. 126
language/terminology 25, 39
Laughlin, N. 37
Laughlin, S. 37
Lave, J. 41, 164, 217, 276
Leadership Scale for Sport 161
leadership style 156, 161–3; *see also*
coaching style
league sports 129
Ledington, P.W.J. 75, 80
legal dimension 236–7, 244–5
levels of award: harmonisation of 14, 280;
women coaches and level of award 224–5
licence to practise 202, 204
Lillyman, S. 288–9
Lipshitz, R. 137

literature, coaching 31–3
Liukkonen, J. 126, 157
Lombardo, B.J. 176, 178, 179, 193, 195,
197
loss-minimisation heuristic 301
low expectations 226–7
Loy, J.W. 193
Lukes, S. 198
Lyle, J. 9, 24, 31, 37, 43, 66, 120, 123, 126,
131, 134, 135, 136, 140, 143, 159, 165,
167, 169, 170–1, 182, 185, 198, 203,
214, 215, 216, 225–6, 227, 239, 241,
244, 261, 266, 268, 270–1, 300–2

Maas, J.L. 126
Maclean, J. 260
Maguire, J. 192, 194
male dominance 224
management: coach education and 284–5;
coaching in industry and 41–3; process
skills 50–1
manager role 66, 68, 74–5, 297
Mangan, T. 6, 7
Marxian analysis 193–4
Mason, T. 5, 6
Mawer, M. 42
Mayes, R. 282
Maynard, T. 42
MCC 7
McIntosh, P.C. 8
McNab, T. 5, 7
McNamee, M. 243–4
meaning units 170–1
means-ends approach 238
'mental model' coaching model 89–90
mental models 141–2, 286, 302
mentoring 42, 286
metacognitive knowledge 298–9
method, coaching 38, 265–6
Middlehurst, R. 202
Miles, A. 14
Millard, L. 230
Miller, A.W. 126
model for coaching 96–115, 300, 301, 307;
adapting the model 113–14; building
blocks 99–106; control box 107–10;
operationalising the model 107–14;
prior assumptions 97–9; sport-specificity
112–13; thresholds 110–12; visual
representation of 106–7, 108–9

SPORTS COACHING CONCEPTS

modelling/models 25, 79–95; application, constraints and implementation 91–4; evaluation of existing models 85–91; future of model building 92–3; models 'of' and models 'for' 82, 93; problems in model building 84–5; types of models 82; usefulness 80–1

monitoring: coaching practice 123–4; procedures 105

morality 234; *see also* ethical practice

Moray House Institute of Education 11

Morrow, R.A. 28

Mosston, M. 163

motivations 209–20; conceptual issues 216–19; review of evidence 212–16; women coaches 229–30

Mumford, A. 42

Murdoch, E. 9

mystique 29–30

National Association of Sports Coaches 14, 243

national coaches 6–7

National Coaching Centres 13

National Coaching Foundation (NCF) 7, 16, 17; coach education and training 11, 12, 13–14, 277, 279; code of ethics 242–3

National Governing Bodies (NGBs) 5, 7, 8, 23, 210, 277, 287

National Junior Sport Programme 23

National Lottery funding 15, 17, 22, 278, 306

National Occupational Standards 13–14, 22–3, 277, 279, 287, 305

National Vocational Qualifications (NVQs) 13–14, 22–3, 277–8, 279, 305

naturalistic decision making (NDM) 136, 137

naturalistic field-based research studies 300–2, 303

negligence 244

negotiation 74, 164

neo-Marxism 193–4

nice-guy style 160

'no-blame' culture 181

non-deliberative decisions 134–6, 300–2

North American high school/collegiate model 195

objectives model 87–9

occupational classification 39, 200

occupational closure 228

Olympic Games 5; female coaches in UK Olympic squads 225

'open' culture 181

operational models 82

operationalisation 102–3

organisation 74

organisational contexts 48–9, 197–8, 260; coach's role 70–2

organisational goals 245

organisational strategy 270

Orlick, T. 176

Otter, S. 257

overseas coaches 15, 306

Paish, W. 7

parent coaches 214–15

Parkhouse, B.L. 226

part-models 80

participation coaching 3–4, 33, 49, 155, 262; coaching style 158; development officers 15; distinction from performance coaching 52–7; ethical practice 242, 245; functional roles 65–6; gender and 224, 225; motivations and recruitment 216; PE teachers 10; and professional status 205–6; research issues 296; systematic coaching behaviour 121–2

participation in sport 223–4

Pastore, D.L. 227

Patel, M. 240

pattern recognition 137–8

Pegg, M. 42

performance: analysis of 82, 92, 101–2; capacity for 283; coaches' responses to performance deficit 111, 112; coaching style and 157–8; goals 153; improving 101–2, 262, 267–8, 295; primary and secondary components 102; relationship between athlete, coach and 27–8; stable and unstable elements 153

performance coaching 3–4, 33, 49, 152, 155, 307; coach education 280–1, 286; and coaching practice 118; distinction between participation coaching and 52–7; effectiveness 262; ethical practice 242, 245; functional roles and 65–6; government policy 15; humanistic approach and 175, 176–7, 180; motivations and recruitment 216; non-deliberative decision making 300–2; professionalisation and

205–6; research issues 296, 299, 300–2; women and 224–6, 229–30, 231, 232

performance director role 66–7, 68–9

performance experience *see* experience

performance model 141–2

performance sport 306; coach education tutors and coach education for 286; ethics and attitudes 176–7, 238–9; limited scale of 227; national approach 15; women's participation in 223; *see also* elite sport

performer variability 297; *see also* athlete

personal characteristics 72, 164

personal growth and development 178–80, 180–1, 183–4, 237–8

personal meaning 106

Pfister, G. 161, 221, 224, 226, 227

philosophies of coaching *see* coaching philosophy

Philpott, L. 42

physical education 8–11

Pickup, D. 13

planning: coaching practice 125–31, 143; contingency planning 129–30, 142; model for coaching and 103–4; skills 50–1; systematic coaching behaviour 123–4

planning models 82

player coach 70–1

policy *see* government policy

Polley, M. 7

postmodernism 194

Potrac, P. 126, 192, 195, 196

power 198

power-based sports 131

power differentials 156, 236, 237; abuse of 239–40

practical experience *see* experience

practice management 102–3, 182

prediction of outcomes 81

preparation 105, 109, 112

procedural knowledge 101, 139, 140

process competences 264–5, 281–2

process goals 183–4

process trace 302

processes 295; coaching process *see* coaching process

profession, image of 309

professional body 202, 205

professional coaches, early 5

professional club coaches 70

professional development 26, 36; *see also* coach education and training

professional position 39

professional practice 66, 202, 204, 245

professional role 241

professional sport 5, 6, 7, 23; commercial and competition success ethos 176–7; ethical practice 245–6; overseas coaches 15, 306

professionalisation 219, 252; coach education and 202, 204, 275–6, 309; coaches in professional sport 245; issues influencing 305–11; status and 199–200, 201–6; success and effectiveness 269

programme management 103

progression 284; systematic 103

proposed coaching model *see* model for coaching

propositional knowledge 101, 139, 140

public schools 5, 8

purpose 25, 38, 184, 295; and functional role 63–7

qualifications 11–12, 305; NVQs 13–14, 22–3, 277–8, 279, 305

quality control 120–1

Ramalli, K. 126

Randel, J.M. 140

recipe planning 129

recruitment 155, 209–20; conceptual issues 216–19; patterns of 227; populations 218; review of evidence 212–16; transition vs 216–17; and women coaches 227, 229–30

reflective practice (RP) 167, 288–9

regulation 74, 236–7; model for coaching 104, 109, 112; skills 50–1

Reid, D. 42

reinforcing athlete behaviour 240, 241

relationships *see* interpersonal relationships

Rennick, T. 5

replacement role 67–8

replica models 81

representative team/group coaches 15, 49, 56, 71, 225

research 291–304; coach education 279, 285; into coaching practice 117, 125, 126; coaching process and research issues 294–7; conceptual framework 27; emphasis on performance 12, 30; expert

system 298–9; implications 302–4; process 292–4; shortcomings 33, 307, 310; suggestions for research agenda 299–302; typology 293–4; use of models 92
research-based education and training 285
rewards: career rewards 211; performance sport and 238
Richards, R. 159, 160
Rogers, C. 182
role 25, 38, 59–76, 155, 156, 206; and coaching practice 143, 146; concepts 61–2; ethical issues 241; harmonisation of levels 280; organisational impact 70–2; purpose and function 63–7; range of sport leadership roles 35, 36; sport leadership roles and organisational contexts 48–9; uniqueness of coaching role 72–5
role ambiguity 62
role complementarity 62; between coaches and support personnel 67–70
role conflict 62, 68–70, 71
role models 245
role-related competences 282
role-set 62, 67–70
rugby league 6
rugby union 8, 23, 306
Russell, S. 126

Salmela, J.H. 117, 126, 131, 132, 133, 140, 164, 178, 215, 286, 298–9
Salminen, S. 157
Saury, J. 126, 144, 164
Scanlan, T.K. 216
schema model 134, 135
schema script model 134, 135
schemata 139, 140
Schembri, G. 75
Schempp, P.G. 140, 286
Schinke, R.J. 126
Schon, D.A. 289
school sport 5, 23; physical education 8–11; see also youth sport
School Sport Co-ordinators 23
script schema model 134, 135
scripts 140; interactive 134–6, 138
selection 210, 219, 227, 269
self-coached athletes 65
self-control 178–9
self-determination 178–9

self-reflection 167, 288–9
sexual harassment 235, 239, 240–1
Sheppard, L. 42
Sherman, C. 37, 91
simulation model 141–2
situated learning 41, 217, 286
situational analysis 138
skills: coaching process skills 50–2, 73, 231, 283; cognitive skills 144, 283, 296–7; industrial coaching and skill improvement 41–2; interpersonal skills 284; model for coaching 100–1; motivations and recruitment 217–18; and planning 130
Slack, T. 197
Slainte Ltd 214
Smith, H. 7
soccer 6, 8, 66
social context 4, 155, 156, 191–208, 308–9; ethical practice and 241–2; professionalisation 201–6; social issues 195–8; sports coaching and social enquiry 193–5; status 198–206
social flexibility 227
social learning 164
social meaning 106
social role 236
social support 227
social trends 4, 197
socio-economic group 218
Solomon, G.B. 72, 126
specificity see sport-specificity
sport, as a concept 33
sport analyst 68
Sport Commitment Model 216
sport development officers 15, 23
sport development schemes 10, 15
Sport England 17, 23
'sport instruction' coaching model 91
sport medicine 305–6
sport participation 223–4
sport physiologist 68
sport physiotherapist 68
sport psychologist 68
Sport Recreation Industry Training Organisation (SPRITO) 14, 287
sport sociology 193–5
sport-specificity 307–8; coach education 284; coaching practice 117, 144–6; and effectiveness 263; vs genericism 25; model for coaching 112–13; recruitment 218

Sporting Future for All, A 16
sports coach, defining 40
Sports Coach UK (SCUK) 14, 17, 279
Sports Council 214–15, 224, 225
sports instructors 56
sports leadership roles 35; and organizational
    contexts 48–9; *see also* role
sports science/scientists 30, 69, 305–6
Sportsmark accreditation schemes 23
state-mediated professions 203
status 198–206, 275; professionalisation
    199–200, 201–6
Staurowsky, E. 228
strategic co-ordination 64, 66, 74–5, 264
strategic effectiveness 270
strategic planning 108–9, 112
Striegel, D.A. 126
structural-functionalism 193
structure and agency 193
style, coaching *see* coaching style
sub-cultures 196; specificity of practice 195
sub-processes 84, 99–106
success, effectiveness and 254–5, 269
supply and demand 211
support personnel 67–70
support role 67–8
Sutcliffe, P. 6, 277
Swift, A. 251
swimming 6, 8, 17, 111, 112, 123–4
symbolic models 81
systematic (scientific) coaching 13
systematic coaching practice 119–24, 246
systematic development 103
systematic planning 128–9

tacit knowledge 117, 132, 140
Tamura, K. 9, 212–13
target sports 129
targets 74
teaching/teachers 7; coaches trained as
    teachers 9; coaching schemes for 6;
    organisational contexts 49; participation
    coaching and 54, 201; physical education
    8–11; public schools 5; similarities with
    coaching 37
teaching materials 12, 287
team coaches, representative 15, 49, 56, 71,
    225
team sports 30, 48
technical/tactical model 167

technique instruction 56
Telama, R. 126
tennis 6, 224
terminology/language 25, 39
'textbooks' 32
Theodoraki, E. 15
theory development 28–30
Thorpe, R. 10, 262
thresholds 140; model for coaching 110–12
TOPS Programme 15
Torrington, D. 41
Totten, M. 194
traditional professions 203
training 74, 276; coach education and *see*
    coach education and training; industrial
    41–3
training schedules 127, 128
training theory principles 128
Training of Young Athletes project (TOYA)
    214–15
transition: vs recruitment 216–17; women
    coaches 229–30
transition coaches 55
trip markers 302
Trudel, P. 126
truncated coaching process 46–8, 52
trust 185
Tutko, T. 159, 160

UK Sport, *The UK Vision for Coaching* 16,
    305
UK Sports Council 275, 277, 305–6
understanding, analysis and 82, 92
uniqueness of coaching 72–5, 117–18, 295–6
United Kingdom Sports Institute 14, 15, 16,
    279
university team coaches 70
United States (US) 12, 201, 277; North
    American high school/collegiate model 195
usable competences 282

value added 267–8
values 25, 73, 164–5; coaching
    philosophies 165–72; conflicting 71,
    165–6; professionalisation and 202, 205;
    see also ethical practice; ideologies
variability, performer 297
variety 295–6
Veenman, S. 42
Verchoshanskij, J. 142

SPORTS COACHING CONCEPTS

volleyball 111, 112, 123–4, 224, 225–6, 300–2

Wade, A. 7
Wadya, V.K. 126
Weber, M. 96, 300
Weightman, J. 41
Weinberg, R. 226
Wenger, E. 41, 164, 217, 276
West, A. 215, 228, 231
White, A. 215, 222, 232
Whitehead, N. 9
Whitson, D. 179
Wierzbicki, A.P. 134
Wilcockson, J. 133
Wilkerson, M. 231
Williams, G. 6
Williams, J.M. 226
Williams, R. 7

Winterbottom, W. 7
Witz, A. 228
Wolfenden Report 7
women coaches 221–33, 308–9; conceptual issues 229–32; evidence of under-representation 224–6; explanations for under-representation 226–8; women's participation in sport 223–4
Woodman, L. 29, 262
Wootton, K. 75, 80
work ethic 193–4
workload management 146
World Class programmes 15

youth sport 8, 175, 177; *see also* school sport
Youth Sport Trust 25

Zakrajsek, D. 260